RENAISSANCE MAN

—⚭—

THE WORLD OF
Thomas Watson

By the same author

William Alwyn: The Art of Film Music
(The Boydell Press)

RENAISSANCE MAN

—ಐ—

THE WORLD OF
Thomas Watson

IAN JOHNSON

NEW GENERATION PUBLISHING

Published by New Generation Publishing in 2020

Copyright © Ian Johnson 2020

First Edition 2020
Revised 2021

The author asserts the moral right under the Copyright, Designs and Patents Act 1988 to be identified as the author of this work.

All Rights reserved. No part of this publication may be reproduced, stored in a retrieval system or transmitted, in any form or by any means without the prior consent of the author, nor be otherwise circulated in any form of binding or cover other than that which it is published and without a simlar condition being imposed on the subsequent purchaser.

ISBN 978-1-78955-885-2

Typeset in Palatino Linotype

www.newgeneration-publishing.com

New Generation Publishing

For Rosemary,
and for my children and grandchildren,
with love

Contents

List of Plates	viii
Preface	ix
One: Politics and Culture—Players and Patrons	12
Two: Far From My Native Land	48
Three: A Very Learned Man	62
Four: Unsavoury Colleagues?	78
Five: Poetry, Science, Wit and Wisdom	85
Six: William Byrd: "Our Phoenix"	122
Seven: A Brawl in Hog Lane	145
Eight: The Elvetham entertainment	154
Nine: Scandal in the Cornwallis household	167
Ten: "Dearly Loved and Honoured"	185
Appendix A—Was Christopher Marlowe a government spy?	196
Appendix B—Did the Earl of Oxford annotate the Hekatompathia?	199
Appendix C—Elizabethan schools of literature and science	202
Appendix D—The Tears of Fancy: the argument	204
Appendix E—Watson as dramatist. Did he write The Spanish Tragedy?	205
Appendix F—Thomas Watson, dramatist. By Bronson Feldman	218
Thomas Watson: works	252
Notes to chapters	257
Bibliography	309
Index	323

List of Plates

Watson's *Hekatompathia* (1582), Passion LXXXI "into the form of a pillar"	91
Watson's *Hekatompathia*, Passion LXXXI "in conventional manner"	92
A Looking Glasse for Lovers, "My Love is Past"	99
Gabriel Cawood's edition of Watson's *Hekatompathia* (1582), title	102
Gabriel Cawood's edition of Watson's *Hekatompathia*(1582), detail	103
William Shakespeare, *First Folio* (1623), detail	103
The entertainment at Elvetham, plan	155
Cornwallis-Lyson Manuscript, "Anne Cornwaleys, her booke"	161
Two pages from William Covell's *Polimanteia* (1595)	190-1

Preface

SEARCH for Thomas Watson in a modern history and, with a few notable exceptions,[1] you will find little more than a passing nod, perhaps a listing amongst the also-rans, maybe a grudging footnote—or a supporting role in the biography of Christopher Marlowe.

Yet Watson's rich assembly of abilities deserve study. He would undoubtedly have wanted to be remembered as a leading classical scholar of his day, versed in that knowledge of classical Latin antiquity they called the *studia humanitatis*—humanism. More than this, however, he was linguist, poet, playwright, musician, scientist, thinker, a man of intense curiosity. "A very learned man ...", declared a passing observer, "that could tell strange things".

In his day he was famous, and pronounced a sociable companion, a loyal friend and a wit—"witty Tom Watson"—while his actions suggest a joker too, a trait that lured him into slippery ways. No known portrait of him has been unearthed.

He was the epitome of the Renaissance man.

The Renaissance, inspired by the ancient Greeks and Romans, and fashioned in the Italian republics some two hundred years earlier, had crept but slowly to England. Where, suddenly, it blossomed in works of poetry, music, art and theatre. In the twin blessings of the Renaissance and of humanism, Tom Watson luxuriated.

Marlowe, Kyd, Lodge, Nashe, Camden, and a myriad of influential writers and thinkers, printers and publishers—these were his friends and acquaintances, his social milieu. More, as a Catholic in a period of religious division he collaborated on texts of lasting significance with his co-religionist William Byrd, a composer admired in his own age and in ours.

He mingled with a society, too, in which it was easy to dip into a poisonous underbelly of the loathsome, the accursed souls despised even by their contemporaries. But if scraping a livelihood can be painful in the twenty-first century, the sufferings of Elizabethan England demand our charity. Poverty, disease, and criminality were rife. Over all, a dictatorship imposed religious orthodoxy, inflicted military service, and compelled conformity to social station. A literary gentleman like Watson, whose initial inheritance probably ran into the dust, needed assiduity to earn his living. Earnings from the theatre provided something, but wealthy patronage was invaluable—so he associated with nobility, the Walsinghams, the Sidneys, Oxford, and the rest—until at last he found security as a tutor in the Cornwallis household.

I have been indebted to the published researches of the late Albert Chatterley, who regrettably I never met. Chatterley retired from the BBC and made himself an expert on Thomas Watson. The result: an energy showcased in a variety of publications, including the *Oxford Dictionary of National Biography*, and the transcription and editing of *The Italian Madrigals Englished* for Vol 74 of Musica Britannica. His *Amyntas and Phyllis*, translations into modern English from Watson's *Amintae Gaudia* (1592) and *Amyntas* (1585), are notable and beautiful; his introduction and the notes to the same work are valuable and lucid.

The value of Ibrahim Alhiyari's PhD dissertation on Watson's birth and early life, hardly needs stating. As a convenient source of Watson's works I referred principally to Edward Arber's 1870 edition of the *Poems*, but all the extant writings are quickly discovered by browsing online. Especially useful is Professor Dana F Sutton's Philological Museum, a site devoted to humanistic works published under the auspices of The Shakespeare Institute of the University of Birmingham. Here may be found reprints not only of Watson's complete works but those of many other writers of the period. On the same site, Sutton presents his own research and opinions, and these are of immeasurable value.

Thomas Watson's most productive years were spent in London. To study the city in which he lived, married, wrote, schemed, or just walked, my first thought was to reproduce here a map of Elizabethan London. The only choice has to be the Agas Map of around 1561. However, rather than a small, barely readable, reproduction, I now prefer to recommend the website *Map of Early Modern London* (https://mapoflondon.uvic.ca/agas.htm).[2] With this beautiful tool the reader can search locations, zoom and pan, and become immersed in Watson's city.

I have built much on the labours of others, and my indebtedness is evident from the chapter notes and bibliography.

Hopefully a touch of originality pokes through from time to time.

*

Elizabethan spellings have been modernised in the main text, except where the original is essential for comprehension, or where most scholars have retained the Elizabethan style. The original punctuation has usually been retained. The endnotes are not indexed.

A list of Watson's known works will be found on page 252—his other works are lost for ever, or wait to be rediscovered.

*

This edition of 2021, "newly set foorth, overseene, and corrected", is one of the benefits of print on demand, a publishing revolution which would have delighted Thomas Watson and his contemporaries.

One:
Politics and Culture—Players and Patrons

THE Tudor dynasty lasted from 1485 until 1603, little longer than a century. Posterity sees it as the age of the adventurer, the entrepreneur, the lusty risk-taker. Fizzing with confidence and enriched by the annihilation of the great monastic estates, the "new men"—the "gentry"—began to shoulder out the slowly crumbling feudal-rooted aristocracy. Entrepreneurs all, they pioneered a new commercial world, their endeavours mushrooming in Europe, Africa, Asia, Russia, Spanish America—and even North America. The foundation stone of the Royal Exchange was cemented in 1566

But there are two sides to every story, and there is another to this: squeezed by a quadrupling population[1] the regime was wounded at home by restlessness (at best) and dangerous violence (at worst)—aggravated as the Reformation uncoiled into the reign of Elizabeth. Anxieties, internal and international, swirled, intertwined and ensnared the Queen and her ministers: the loyalty of the realm, Spanish rivalry, the Dutch revolt, Catholic alliances, the question of Mary Stuart, the succession to the throne. Double-dealings, dark schemes, secrets and espionage were commonplace.

Elizabeth was crowned on 15 January 1559. The official church was Roman Catholic, re-established in the reign of the Queen's late sister Mary; the coronation service was Catholic with the Latin Mass. Ten days later parliament reopened. When it closed on 8 May, the Mass was legally abolished and a *Book of Common Prayer*—resembling a version hatched in the reign of Edward VI—restored. Again, the link between England and Rome was broken. An Anglican Settlement installed a broad church ruled by bishops, and governed by the crown through parliament. Tradition has it that at the commencement of her reign Elizabeth, fired with a spirit of tolerance, placed national unity above religious contention. She promised, claimed Francis Bacon, to make no "windows into men's souls"; the "promise" was probably a flight of Bacon's retrospective imagination.[2] Yet historians have preferred to believe it, a plan for a *via media* that was doomed amidst swirling passions—too conservative for Puritans, too radical for Roman Catholics.

Many Catholics held true to the old faith, trapped between loyalty to the English government and loyalty to the Papacy. From time to time a few hot-heads hatched plots to establish Mary Stuart, Queen of Scots, as Elizabeth's Catholic successor. They succeeded in one way only—by helping the government to link anti-Catholicism with patriotism, and to identify English Catholics as spies and traitors loyal solely to the Pope and to Spain. Broadly it was untrue, and those who suffered most visibly were the noble and gentle families. Matters worsened in 1570, when the Papal bull *Regnans in Excelsis* deprived Elizabeth of her royal title and absolved her subjects from their allegiance. Government policy hardened; in the crucial year of 1580, proclamations were read out against those who consorted with Jesuits, and, as the year closed, the Earl of Oxford revealed —before the whole court—his involvement in Marianist plots. Harsh Acts followed, and in 1581 the first martyrs were executed at Tyburn, instigated by Lord Burghley, the Secretary of State, and Walsingham, the swarthy Principal Secretary whom Elizabeth called her "Moor".

In the swelter of this hothouse, energised by both Reformation and continental Renaissance, men awakened excitedly to discoveries in science, medicine and cosmography, and to advancements in the humanities— theology, philosophy, architecture and art. Literature and music flowered. And over all was the quickening of the new trades of printing and publishing. Caxton opened the first English press in 1470; by Elizabeth's time the labour of the single scribe straining over a unique manuscript had toppled to the widespread distribution of printed books and papers.

Writers, poets and playwrights found ready customers among those who could afford the latest literary creations. But music, too, was basking in a golden age, and if we seek to understand what powered Thomas Watson, we must browse not only among the bookshops of St Paul's Churchyard but attempt to understand the changing face of English music.

With its roots in a living folk-song tradition,[3] music did not distinguish between social classes—master, mistress, servant, beggarman and thief hummed the same melodies, the schoolboy and his master whistled the same airs, the learned composer echoed the labourer's song. The highest in the land tripped to country-dances enjoyed by the lowest. Observing the Christmas season of 1599-1600, Robert Sidney described how hardly a night passed without Elizabeth delighting "to see the ladies dance the old and new country dances with the taber and pipe!"[4] The traffic was two-way; the humble commoners in turn revelled in the simpler court dances.

From its earliest days the Tudor court had encouraged the practice and enjoyment of music. Niggard he may have been, but Henry VII nevertheless maintained the men and boys of the Chapel Royal choir. In his turn Henry VIII spent generously on the Chapel—as well as on his own secular musicians. He could sing at sight, compose, and play the flute, recorder, virginals and lute.[5] Henry founded Christ Church in Oxford, and Trinity College in Cambridge, and completed there the construction of the Chapel at King's College, just one hundred years since the laying of its foundation stone.

There was a negative side. The closure of monastic and collegiate houses by Henry and his son Edward flung musicians into poverty, and sliced the bond between the church and centuries of musical and religious tradition. Endowments supporting church music withered, and protestant distrust of "Papist" Latin chant and ornamental polyphonic music threatened the church's musical heritage. Some followed "Genevan fashion"—congregational singing, for example; others conceived of no greater joy than to throw the organ on the rubbish heap and banish music altogether, apart from the Psalms. By the time Elizabeth came to the throne, many establishments had given up teaching music and singing, in favour of arithmetic.[6] There were exceptions: Sir Nicholas Bacon, notably, ensured the royal wards had two hours daily of instruction in music; and the Queen herself praised the performances of plays and masques by the boys of the Merchant Taylors' and St Paul's Schools. Richard Mulcaster was head of both schools in turn.[7] He believed in physical education, the right of girls to a liberal education, and in setting exercises in counterpoint and composition to develop his pupils' musical appreciation.[8] Another exception to the prevalent decline in musical education was in the treatment of high-born girls; Chancery proceedings reported two young ladies "brought up in writing, reading, sewing, both white work and black work, and playing of the lute and virginals, as young gentlewomen and maids of their ages are accustomed".[9]

Those inclined to the old religion, and moderate men like John Case, watched the protestant activists with alarm. Philosopher, physician, writer (and author of the first book printed on the new press at Oxford),[10] Case published *In Praise of Music* (1586) in English, and two years later a completely revised academic version of the same work in Latin, *Apologia Musices* (1588).[11] In his younger days, Case had been a chorister at New College School, and was perturbed by the Puritans' threat to music, especially to church music. He defended music as crucial to the whole of society,[12] even (as a writer of books) to delightfully trumpeting the joy of music-making in contrast to the menace of those who favoured books of improvement:

> [W]ithin the airy spirit of the ear (whereby music is immediately brought to the brain) there is a greater sympathy with the mind (and this is a kind of concord), hence a greater delight arises in the mind from the simple hearing of music than from the sight of an image. As for what you add about histories read and heard, I say we take great delight in these if they are understood. But the amount of pleasure reading bestows is proportionate to the spirit consumed by the mental attention required for understanding: then the mind is said both to be delighted and fatigued. For just as there is a sweet savour in learning which makes for pleasure, so there is an effort in learning which engenders tedium and pain. But there is no effort in music, no shadow of pain, since it refreshes rather than shatters the powers of the wit, renders the vital spirits subtler rather than consuming them, sharpens the intellect with its wonderful influence rather than tiring it with study; it instructs and informs the mind, as you fancy. The reason is that it conveys under-standing into the mind's storehouse without any fuss and bother.[13]

Fortunately for Case, the Queen was of a similar mindset and she blocked the total extinction of church music. She loved religious ceremonial and even though neither as generous nor as well-off as her father—she supported the choirs of the Chapel Royal, and those at St Paul's, Westminster Abbey, and St George's, Windsor.[14] It was doubtless her influence that ensured the insertion of a clause under the 1559 Settlement which allowed churches to continue singing "an Hymn or such like song ... in the best sort of melody and music that may be conveniently devised".[15]

Put simply, the Queen loved music. Thomas Tallis and William Byrd were not dissembling in the dedication to their *Cantiones quae ab argumento sacrae vocantur* (1575) when they praised her singing voice and her skill on the lute. There is a portrait of her with a lute, the favoured instrument of the aristocracy,[16] and a famous story tells how Lord Hunsdon and Sir James Melville, Mary Stuart's ambassador, crept into a gallery to overhear her on the virginals. Melville reported that she played "excellently well. But she left off immediately, so soon as she turned her about and saw me" — it was unseemly even for courtiers to show off their talents, let alone the monarch. On this occasion she told Melville that "she used not to play before men, but when she was solitary, to shun melancholy". Nevertheless, Jacob Rathgeb who travelled to England in 1592 in the company of the Duke of Saxe-Weimar claimed they heard the Queen performing on the virginals during a private audience with the French ambassador, who "so far prevailed upon her that she played very sweetly and skillfully on her instrument, the strings of which were gold and silver".[17]

Music resounded around the court, everywhere and at all times. The Pomeranian traveller Lupold von Wedel reported that at Whitehall, "almost in every room there was a musical instrument with gilt-silver ornaments and lined with velvet", and music even accompanied meals. The noise must have been deafening: von Wedel described how at Hampton Court in 1584 eight trumpeters in red livery called the court to dinner, and how afterwards two drummers and a piper "made music according to the English fashion". Another traveller, Paul Hentzner, visited Greenwich in 1598 and commented that as the dinner was carried in, "twelve trumpets and two kettledrums made the hall ring for half an hour together". The diary of a fourth visitor, Thomas Plattner, notes the trumpets and shawms entertaining the guests after dinner at Nonsuch in 1599.[18] A passion for things Italian meant that foreign musicians, especially Italians, were well represented at Elizabeth's court. At the time of her ascension to the throne in 1558 she employed forty-one musicians, singers and instrumentalists of the Queen's Musick in the more important Chapel Royal. Half were foreigners, including five members of the Bassano family. By 1570 there were two more Bassanos, and by then members of the Ferrabosco and—from France—the Lanier families had made their appearances. By the time of her death in 1603, the Queen employed thirty-eight musicians, including six Bassanos, six Laniers, an Irish harpist, and Alfonso Ferrabosco.[19]

Dance was an especial joy for Elizabeth, who nearly every day indulged in it as a form of exercise.[20] Dancing schools were established, and the services of a dancing master were essential for any courtier who craved the Queen's favour. Sir Christopher Hatton and the royal favourite Sir Robert Dudley were especially accomplished. Foreign ambassadors commented on the "dancing English". One diplomat reported in 1599 that "on the day of Epiphany the Queen held a great feast, in which the head of the Church of England and Ireland was to be seen in her old age dancing three or four galliards"[21]—the galliard was a lively dance indeed and needed much energy. In her later years, as foreign and domestic threats dwindled, Elizabeth was able to present a more relaxed face to the world; in contrast, at the beginning of her reign, when she felt less secure, the dances were slower and more stately. In part, the music at court expressed the subconscious of the ruling society.

More manipulatively, music and dance played, and reflected, an important propagandist role. There were no less than some fifty royal residences in the London area, but the chief was the vast, rambling, two-thousand room complex which Henry VIII had named Whitehall Palace, the largest royal palace in Europe which—until it was destroyed by fire in 1698—covered twenty-three acres. Its site was the former London residence of the Archbishop of York, the fallen Cardinal Wolsey. Henry had laid his hands on even more adjacent land and established new gardens and orchards, tennis-courts, a Cockpit and a Tiltyard. The Tiltyard in the open air, and the Great Hall indoors, were settings for extravagant displays of processions, progresses, knightings, betrothals, marriages, dramatic performances, and coronations, usually accompanied by music and dance. Music was an adjunct to court ceremonial, which had an essentially religious element, redirecting towards the court and the "virgin Queen" former Roman Catholic rites associated with the Virgin Mary. Court ceremonies were scheduled for the great feast days of the church—good reason for Elizabeth to resist protestant demands to abolish church ceremony, for even to have reduced it would have reduced the power of the state.[22]

Encouraged to take an interest in music as a sign of breeding and good taste, the great houses followed the court's example, though necessarily more cheaply and modestly. They modelled their ideal education on the northern Italian courtier, and followed the advice of Baldesar Castiglione. Castiglione's *Il Libro del Cortegiano (The Book of the Courtier)* had been published in Italy in 1528, but had to wait until Thomas Hoby's translation of 1561 for an English printing.[23] Its scene was the court at Urbino, passionate about music, and took the form of a dialogue between a group of courtiers concerning the attributes of the ideal courtier and his obligations to his prince, his lady, and to society. Count Ludovico da Canossa led the discussion, declaring himself, "… not satisfied with our Courtier unless he be also a musician, and unless, besides understanding and being able to read music, he can play various instruments."[24]

Music should be the training of the courtier from his earliest days, thought the Count, quoting the very best of authorities,

> "I remember also having heard once that both Plato and Aristotle wish a man who is well constituted to be a musician; and with innumerable reasons they show that music's power over us is very great; and … that music must of necessity be learned from childhood, not so much for the sake of that outward melody which is heard, but because of the power it has to induce a good new habit of mind and an inclination to virtue, rendering the soul more capable of happiness, just as corporal exercise makes the body more robust and that not only is music not harmful to the pursuits of peace and war, but greatly to their advantage."[25]

Nevertheless, Castiglione advises that no commoner should be present at a courtier's performance, and that the courtier should make light of his

1. Politics and Culture—Players and Patrons

musical achievements:

> Therefore, let the courtier turn to music as a pastime, and as though forced [ie. reluctantly], and not in the presence of persons of low birth or where there is a crowd. And although he may know and understand what he does, in this also I would have him dissimulate the care and effort that is required in doing anything well; and let him appear to esteem but little this accomplishment of him, yet by performing it excellently well, make others esteem it highly.[26]

For most of the well-off, music, poetry readings, and dramatic performances (by the owners and guests, or by travelling performers) were important diversions. It was not uncommon for the nobility to support a live-in musician, his duties usually including the tutoring of the younger family members. If this was too expensive, a lutenist could double up as a groom or serving man. If even this was a financial strain, then musicians could be hired for a special feast or event. The families were well-acquainted, even though their estates were widely separated geographically; we look at one of them, the Petre family, in CHAPTER SIX. Most of the greater houses had a London establishment, and, increasingly, numbers of the lesser nobility were acquiring one as well: by 1560 half of the total, and by the 1630s three-quarters of the total.[27] As David C. Price has pointed out,

> ... as the century progressed the network of communications between London and the Court in many spheres of activity was extended to the country at large by informed and well-based amateurs ... as well as by professional participants. In the area of cultural life an especially creative network developed which took its inspiration from the Crown.[28]

Two great houses deserve special attention.

Particularly well-known and important was Wilton House in the countryside near Salisbury.[29] Here it was usual to find Philip Sidney and his sister Mary, two out of Sir Henry Sidney's seven offspring. Sir Henry had risen in rank under the Tudors to become Lord President of the Council in the Marches (the Welsh borders) and Lord Deputy of Ireland. His wife, Mary, was the sister of Guildford Dudley (the husband of Lady Jane Grey), Ambrose Dudley the Earl of Warwick, and Robert Dudley the Earl of Leicester, the Queen's favourite and closest adviser whom she dubbed her "eyes". Mary's favour with the Queen had by no means been harmed by her nursing Elizabeth through a bout of smallpox, a time of crisis and real fears for the Queen's life which had precipitated a revival of the succession question. Elizabeth survived, but Mary herself caught the infection and was so disastrously disfigured that she never again appeared unveiled in public. In turn, she passed it on to her eight-year-old son Philip, who was pock-marked for the rest of his life.

Philip was born in 1554 at Penshurst Place in Kent, and educated at Oxford in the classics, literature and philosophy. Aged eighteen, he set out for Europe to improve and prepare himself for a role in his country's affairs. There he met governments and politicians, writers and thinkers, and witnessed the St Bartholemew's Day Massacre. He returned to England in 1575, and accompanied the Queen on a state progress to his uncle Leicester's estate at Kenilworth, and afterwards to Lichfield. He was young and precocious, but had the misfortune not to win any especial favour from Elizabeth, so that in 1576 he joined his father in Ireland in time to give his full approval to the barbarous treatment of the conquered Irish papists.[29] The following year he returned to the continent, including among his travelling companions his old schoolfellows Fulke Greville and Edward Dyer. Greville had recently resigned a post with Philip's father at the court of the Welsh Marches, and Dyer was Leicester's personal secretary. In Europe, Philip met the Catholic Don Juan of Austria, and renewed his acquaintance with the mild, yet courageous, English Jesuit priest Edmund Campion whom he had known during his university days. He also visited the uncompromisingly protestant William the Silent.

The year after his return to England, he presented the Queen with a short masque entitled *The Lady of May*, which was presented at Leicester's house at Wanstead, East of London by Epping Forest. Under the cover of its classical allusions it presented a clear message to the Queen touching her choice of suitor. The following year, in 1579, Philip grew more reckless, encouraged by Leicester to write an appeal to the Queen urging her to abandon her proposed match with her "little frog" — the ugly, pock-marked, Francis Valois, the Catholic Duc d'Anjou now recently succeeded from the title of Duc d'Alençon. Philip's manuscript *A Letter to Queen Elizabeth* was widely circulated, but not appreciated by the monarch. For offering similar counsel, the Puritan John Stubbs and his publisher had their right hands publicly amputated. There was a difference: Stubbs' propaganda was for the common readership — Philip's was passed between a tiny circle of noblemen. Although Philip seemed not to have suffered for his impertinence, the Queen never appointed him to any position of importance. The historian H R Woudhuysen suspects there may have been other reasons, too: "he was irascible, ambitious, proud, and perhaps unreliable; his religious faith may not have been certain; he behaved and was received as a powerful figure abroad; it may therefore have seemed best to keep his power base at home as narrow as possible."[30]

In the spring of 1580, Philip returned to Wilton where Mary would soon give birth to her first child. Afterwards he stayed on — court life was expensive, and, relatively, Philip was poor. Away from London, and in the freer company of his sister, he devoted himself to literature and drama,[31] and from now on he spent little of his time in the capital.

Mary was seven years younger than Philip. Girls did not attend the universities, but her mother and her aunt Katherine Dudley were well educated, and her father saw to it that she was highly trained at home alongside two younger brothers, and two younger sisters who died while Mary was still young. Two years as a maid-of-honour to the Queen followed, until in 1577 she received the title of Countess of Pembroke on her marriage to the second Earl, Henry Herbert. She was fifteen, he was 43. Mary bore him four children, but she idolised her brother. At Wilton, Mary and Philip Sidney built a "noble librarie" including "a great many Italian books, all their poets; and books of politics and history".[32] Brother and sister employed players and musicians to host lively entertainments at the Pembroke estates of Baynard's Castle in London, at Ludlow in Shropshire,[33] and at the Wiltshire estates of Ramsbury, Ivychurch and especially Wilton. Edmund Spenser portrays Philip as "made for merriment, merrily masquing both in bower and hall"[34] while Mary "led the community in readings or in music".[35]

In the history books Philip has epitomised *il cortegiano*, the "Renaissance man", the archetypal Elizabethan man of many talents. At court this auburn-haired, handsome young courtier seemed marked out for a brilliant career as diplomat, soldier, and national leader. He excelled in chivalry, progresses and entertainments. A Sidney cult was already burgeoning when, in the year after Philip's death, the jurist and Latin dramatist William Gager published his *Exequiae Illustratissimi Equitis D Philippi Sidnaei, Gratissimae Memoriae ac Nomini Impensae* (1587). The cult swelled as Fulke Greville and Mary Herbert edited and published his poems and the prose romance *Arcadia* (1593[36]), and came to full measure with Greville's hagiographical *Dedication to Sir Philip Sidney*, of 1652. Yet Sidney was the man described by Woudhuysen in the terms quoted above, and who in 1578 accused his father's secretary Molyneux of opening his letters, threatening that if Molyneux did so again, "I will thrust my dagger into you". Clearly, about Philip one needs to keep an objective head.

Three years before his self-imposed rustication, Philip had already turned his hand to literature with his *Discourse on Irish Affairs*, a defence of his father's policies in Ireland, and in 1578 his play *The Lady of May* was performed before the Queen at Wanstead. Now, inflamed by patriotism, he determined that English literature would flourish as vigorously in England as in the courts and academies of Renaissance Europe. To achieve that end, he experimented with verse forms inspired by Pierre de Ronsard, Joaquim du Bellay, and the poets of the French La Pléiade group, which itself had been inspired by the Italian Accadamei della Nuova Poesia. Ronsard was a friend of the Earl of Leicester, and there is a strong certainty that Philip was introduced to him during his visit to Paris in 1572.[37]

Sidney laboured long on his pastoral romance *Arcadia*, which he wrote for his sister Mary. He put pen to it first in 1577, but no sooner was it completed in 1580,[38] than he began to revise it all over again for an enlarged second edition. "Your dear self can best witness the manner," he wrote to Mary, "being done in loose sheets of paper, most of it done in your presence, the rest by sheets sent unto you as fast as they were done."[39]

Sidney's poetic works are an easier read than *Arcadia*, and he claims credit for the first English true sonnet cycle *Astrophel and Stella* (1580s, printed 1591), and a rejoinder on the dignity of the poet in his *The Defence of Poesy* (c1579, printed 1595). He was extraordinarily free-handed with his manuscripts. Apart from showing them to his beloved sister, he passed them amongst his wife Frances and his brother Robert, although not (as far as we know) to his parents. He also circulated them to sympathetic courtiers like his trusted friend Sir Henry Brouncker, Sir Henry Lee (a favourite of the Queen, and famous for his tilts, pageants, and masques), the witty Sir John "Ajax" Harington, Sir William Douglas the Earl of Angus, and Sir Edward Dymocke. Perhaps he gave a copy of *Astrophel and Stella* to Lady Penelope Rich. Because he constantly revised and improved his works, especially the *Arcadia*, the opinions of other writers were vital. Amongst them were Henry Constable, protégé of Walsingham, friend of Penelope Rich, and (after Sidney's death) convert to Catholicism; Abraham Fraunce whose college fees at Cambridge were paid by Sidney; Samuel Daniel poet and dramatist; and George Puttenham the probable author of *The Art of English Poesy* (1589). Manuscript copies of Sidney's poems were found among the papers of the gentry of Herefordshire and Shropshire, in the Oxford and Cambridge colleges, and scattered amongst friends of his friends.[40] Thomas Watson was one who saw, or heard about, one of these manuscripts: in his *The First Set of Italian Madrigals Englished* published in 1590 he addresses Sidney as "Astrophel", a term which did not appear in print (and therefore before the eye of the commonality) until 1591 in Sidney's *Astrophel and Stella*.[41] Since Sidney's manuscripts were circulated to the Cornwallis family, in whose house Watson worked in his later years, it is quite probable that he read them there.

Aside from literature, in an age in which the pursuit of knowledge saw no division between the "arts" and "science", the Sidney family took an enthusiastic interest in science and the natural world. At university, Philip had become friendly with Sir Walter Raleigh whose enquiring mind took him beyond poetry to history and exploration. He was friendly, too, with William Camden, the antiquary and historian, and with Richard Hakluyt, associate of explorers, geographer and enthusiast for foreign discovery. The astrologer John Dee taught him chemistry, "that starry science, rival to nature",[42] and Dee was his advisor about other intellectual and philosophical matters including foreign exploration. Philip's friends became Mary's friends, too.

Poetry, however, was the major absorption—with music its sister. Philip defended poetry as the oldest means of learning, and could not resist pointing out that,

> Even among the most barbarous and simple Indians where no writing is, yet have they their Poets, who make and sing songs, which they call *Areytos*, both of their Ancestors' deeds and praises of their Gods ...[43]

The lute ayre, the madrigal and dance, delighted the ear at the Tudor court and many a country house. For the Sidneys, the encouragement of music dated back at least to their father's time. In 1559, during his sojourn in Ireland, Sir Henry had bought a pair of virginals and two lutes, and for two consecutive years the choir of Christ Church in Dublin presented "his honour with songs and new verses". By 1566 he had ordered a set of viols, and in 1569 "a case of new instruments". After 1570 his accounts occasionally refer to payments to visiting "musicians", and he was keen to encourage music in his local church. In 1572 he purchased musicians' liveries for his servants.[44]

His son Philip went so far as to write that a virtue of poetry was "the just praise it hath, by being the only fit speech of Musick (Musick, I say, the most divine striker of the senses)".[45] It therefore comes as a surprise to learn that while Mary could play the lute from at least the age of ten, Philip could neither sing nor play any instrument. Since the ability to perform at music was cultivated at the Elizabethan court Philip's illiteracy in what he called "the well enchanting skill of music",[46] was hateful to him, and he tried to remedy the fault by seeking a tutor during his travels to Venice. At a later date he wrote a letter to his brother bemoaning his inadequacy ("You will not believe what want I find it in these melancholy times"), and encouraged Robert to learn an instrument. Robert took his advice.[47] He became a patron of John Dowland the "Prince of Lutenist-Composers",[48] and was godfather to Dowland's son Robert, who in 1610 dedicated to him *A Musical Banquet*.[49]

Although he could play no instrument, Philip's taste in music was highly developed. He organised concerts at Wilton, and wrote the texts for musical accompaniments. For his Arcadia he wrote the lyrics for one of the first English madrigals. Writing in 1580 to his dear soldier friend Sir Edward Denny, Philip urged him to "remember with your good voice, to sing my songs" while in 1586, on his appointment as governor of Flushing in the Netherlands, he took with him, as servant, the composer Daniel Bacheler.[50] He wrote lyrics for Italian, Spanish and Flemish tunes,[51] and had several of his texts set to music by—amongst others—William Byrd, John Dowland, and Charles Tessier, a French Lutanist living at the English court.[52] Sidney's manuscripts were preserved in important music libraries belonging to collectors such as Edward Bannister in Hampshire, Edward Paston in Norfolk and Robert Dow at Oxford. He also wrote popular songs, ballads and dances, including a piece set to the music of *Greensleeves*.[53]

Although in public they presented a face sympathetic to the theological features of Calvinism, Philip and Mary were open-minded about Catholicism: Byrd, Bannister and Paston were recusants. In his *A New Discourse of a Stale Subject called The Metamorphosis of Ajax* (1596) John Harington, another ally of the Sidneys, portrays as the "excrement" of Elizabethan society men like Thomas Norton and Justice Young, known to be torturers and slanderers of Catholics.[54] The honeyed voice of Edmund Campion also influenced Philip, who had admired his debating and intellectual skills during his Oxford days between 1566 and 1568; when the pair again met in Prague eleven years later Philip is said to "have sighed at having to continue on an Anglican course".[55] In Venice, Philip had other Catholic friends, including Richard Shelley and Edward, third Lord Windsor.[56]

In 1586, seeking glory in the Low Countries and following a skirmish at Zutphen, Sidney's life of 31 years was cut short abruptly and heroically by gangrene following a musket shot in the thigh, through not wearing the proper protective armour (*cuisses*). The nation wept. For Philip to have gone to battle inadequately protected has seemed to historians a gesture of either haste, bravado, comradeship—allegedly in solidarity with his fellow-in-arms Sir William Pelham who wore none—or fashion because of a current vogue to wear light armour only.[57] Perhaps Philip really did act on the impulse of one or a mixture of these motives. There is, however, another possibility.

So far—however sketchily—we have peered mainly at an image bequeathed by his friend Fulke Greville and his sister Mary. This image has been projected for over four centuries—Philip the diplomat, the soldier, the courtier, the protestant martyr. The writer and poet. Yet, as Woudhuysen suggests,

> Sidney probably had few anxieties about the literary worth of his writings, but he may have felt he was destined personally and politically for higher and greater things. "My youth doth waste," he makes Astrophel say, "my knowledge brings forth toyes." Was this really the best he could do with his life, which had promised so much? It was scarcely responsible to devote one's time to writing toys and trifles while the cause of protestant political and religious unity was neglected, the royal succession unsecured, and his family finances in confusion.[58]

Sidney was a pupil of the astrologer and alchemist Dr John Dee. At Sidney's request, Dee had drawn up a sixty-two page zodiacal chart which included two significant predictions: that Sidney would enjoy a glorious career from the age of fifteen until the age of 31; that afterwards he would face possible death from a sword or gunshot injury, from which—if he survived—he would rise to even more breathtaking glories and long life.[59] Is it possible that, just two months before his thirty-second birthday,[60] Sidney, the courtier who "felt he was destined personally and politically for higher and greater things" deliberately placed himself in a dangerous position in the hope, or even the expectation, of fulfilling Dee's prophesy?

The yarn that as he lay injured he bestowed his water bottle to a dying soldier with the words, "Thy necessity is yet greater than mine" was probably a later invention of Fulke Greville.[61] More likely is the story that as he lay dying in the house of widow Gruithuissens at Arnhem in the weeks after the battle, he called for music, "especially that song which himself had entitled 'La Cuisse Rompue'".[62]

In February 1587, four months after Philip's death and just days after Elizabeth signed the warrant for the death of the Catholic Queen of Scots, Philip's body was brought to St Paul's accompanied by 700 mourners who had to force their way through dense crowds of sightseers. It suited the government to stage a funeral of great pomp and circumstance for a protestant martyr and courtier who had met death in battle against Catholic Spain: what better distraction to camouflage the regicide of an anointed Queen? The ceremony was arranged by Sidney's father-in-law Sir Francis Walsingham head of the Elizabethan secret service. His master, Burghley, would have inspired it.

Over 200 eulogies to Philip were composed. They came from throughout Western Europe, several from beyond the English Channel, one from his godfather Philip of Spain, and two even from the King of Scotland. Philip left debts amounting to £6,000, and his sister Mary distraught. It was her fourth family bereavement in little more than a year. First, her little three-year-old daughter Katherine had died on the very day that she gave birth to a second son (Philip Herbert). Then, when she was desperately ill and close to death herself, came news of the deaths of her mother and father. After the passing of her beloved brother Philip, Mary retired from public life.

It took her two years to work through her bereavements. Then, accompanied by over a hundred retainers, she paraded through London and returned to court.[63] She stayed for but a single season, and then went home. She was twenty-seven, and was about to commence her life's work. She wrote her own verse and translations, and actively furthered Philip's reputation through the publication of his writings. *The Countess of Pembroke's Arcadia*, her completion of her beloved Philip's gift to her, "remained the best-loved book in the English language" for a hundred and fifty years.[64] She became a patron of writers, musicians, and scholars.[65]

While, undeniably, the Sidneys were a powerful influence on the literary and musical scene of Elizabethan England, perhaps more weighty was the house of Edward de Vere, seventeenth Earl of Oxford. Born in 1550, he was educated as a child by Edward VI's former Secretary of State, Sir Thomas Smith, "reckoned" according to the seventeenth century historian and biographer John Strype as "the best scholar at [Cambridge] University, not only for rhetoric and the learned languages, but for mathematics, arithmetic, law, natural and moral philosophy".[66] Smith's library was large, comprising at least 400 volumes, mainly in Latin, Greek, Italian, French, Spanish or Hebrew—Sir Thomas was a fluent linguist.

When de Vere succeeded to the earldom at the age of twelve, he became a royal ward under the guardianship of the Queen who placed him into the care of Sir William Cecil. Cecil became the principal administrator of Oxford's estate; he was the most powerful man in England after the royal favourite, Robert Dudley, first Earl of Leicester. If Smith's library seemed huge by the standards of its time, at Cecil House in the Strand, de Vere discovered a truly immense library of at least 1,700 titles and 250 manuscripts. A modern writer has described the house as "England's nearest equivalent to a humanist *salon*... As a meeting place for the learned it had no parallel in early Elizabethan England"[67] It was a financial and prestigious coup for Cecil when in 1571 his daughter Anne married Oxford—there had been a time when she was formally engaged to the poorer and more lowly Philip Sidney. De Vere came to court after service against the Northern Rebellion, and his skill as a jouster, his talent for poetry and literature, music and dance—all admired by his contemporaries—readily brought him to Elizabeth's favour.

However, Oxford's life, like Philip Sidney's, was a troubled one. In 1567, a thrust of his sword killed one of Cecil's servants, perhaps accidentally, perhaps not. Then, in 1572, he defied the Queen by sailing to the continent, an act of dangerous disobedience, although on his return he was restored to favour. Three years later, his urge to travel was satisfied by a 16-month journey across Europe—this time with Elizabeth's approval. He returned tormented by doubts about Anne's fidelity, and subsequently separated from her. More turmoil arose in 1579; on the tennis court at Whitehall he quarrelled with Sidney and called him a "puppy". The cause of the row is unclear; perhaps it concerned the Queen's putative marriage with Anjou, which Oxford supported.[68] Whatever the cause, the Queen upheld de Vere, and reminded Sidney of his inferior social position. For just two years more, Oxford retained the Queen's favour. Then, in 1581, Anne Vavasour gave birth to Oxford's child. Dalliance with Elizabeth's ladies-in-waiting was taboo, and the Earl was sent straight to the Tower. He was banished from court for two years, his release conditional on returning to his wife—and four children were born before Anne de Vere's death in 1588. The Vavasour family were less forgiving, and in 1582 gang warfare between de Vere's followers and those of Vavasour's cousin, Thomas Knyvett, resulted in several casualties. In 1585, de Vere successfully pleaded to serve his Queen in the Netherlands; just two months later he was recalled home. To add to his ignominy his ship was looted by Spanish pirates as he crossed the Channel.

Throughout his life, Oxford was burdened with heavy, and increasing, debts, culminating by 1590 in financial ruin. Salvation came from his sovereign, who allotted him the immense annuity of £250 a quarter for a purpose that can only be conjectured. Perhaps it was for services to espionage, perhaps—as some Oxfordians[69] argue—for his patronage of the arts and the theatre, which may have served a propagandist purpose. By this time, his lifestyle had changed. He retired from the public eye, moved in 1588 to the neighbourhood of Hackney, East of London, and in 1591 married Elizabeth Trentham, another lady-in-waiting. He died in 1604, succeeded by his son Henry, his only child by his second wife.

Edward de Vere had been brought up in a protestant atmosphere. His father John de Vere, the sixteenth Earl of Oxford, a notorious profligate, chose his religion for political convenience. Although his father lacked any depth of faith, Edward's probable tutor, his uncle Arthur Golding, was renowned for his piety and as a translator of Calvin and other reformers— his lively translation of Ovid's *Metamorphoses* (1567) was out of character, an anomaly. Nevertheless, Oxford's education was not limited by this reformist background. The earls of Oxford had maintained acting companies as far back to at least 1492; the sixteenth Earl, Edward's father, (despite, or perhaps because of, his boorish behaviour) sponsored the Earl of Oxford's Men, a troupe of the finest performers. Moreover, Edward's first tutor, Sir Thomas Smith, was a renowned humanist. Oxford's inclinations, therefore, while protestant-tinted, were glossed with humanism.

After their marriage, Anne and Edward lived at the Savoy, opposite Burghley's house on the Strand. Then, early in 1580, de Vere bought a mansion north of the London wall, on Bishopsgate. Built by the goldsmith Jasper Fisher, and known locally as Fisher's Folly, it lay nearly opposite the Bedlam asylum for the insane, and was just a short walk from the first public theatres and the Boar's Head Inn "without Aldgate", another resort of players. Around the same time, the Earl took over the Earl of Warwick's Men, and for several years thereafter references to Oxford's "players", "men" or "boys" appear in the public records, sometimes for the disturbances they created, but more often for their performances in the public theatres in London, the provinces, or at court.[70]

Oxford also wrote poetry and drama, most of which appears to be lost: Francis Meres in his *Palladis Tamia* (1598) thought him "the best for comedy among us". His sponsorship of the Euphuist movement is well-known. Based on the Greek word *euphues,* meaning "elegant and witty", to the modern eye it has come to mean the literature of the show-off, an affectation designed to display both the writer's skill in the use of ornate literary mannerisms, of an exaggerated balance and antithesis,[71] and his grasp of abstruse and classical works, especially Ovid. Yet this opinion is a distortion. At a time when the language was shifting away from mediaeval "old English", the Euphuists were exploring a fresh, flexible and eloquent "new English".[72] They were influenced by literary imports from Italy and France, and—like Sidney's circle—the experiments of Ronsard and the Pléiade group. They were encouraged by their rivalry with the Sidneys, and when in the mid-1580s Euphuism lost its drive and fell out of favour it may have been because the thrill of literary rivalry was sapped by Sidney's death.

Oxford and his Euphuists discovered the name for their circle in two novels by John Lyly. The first was published in 1578, entitled *Euphues, the Anatomy of Wit,* and dedicated to Thomas West, Baron Delaware.[73] It was not, however, what it seemed. While superficially it narrated the travels and loves of an unpleasant self-regarding English Italianate courtier, its silken surface masked a send-up of the Italianate high society of the time, and the fickleness of its women. It is a parody of the courtly book of manners, and the boorish Euphues ("elegant and witty"!) is the antithesis of Castiglione's ideal knight.[74] The work created an outcry, but was an immediate success as much as for the titillation of its plot and the morals of its main character as for its literary style.[75] Lyly and the name Euphues—until then virtually unknown—became fashionable. Two years later, Lyly published his second volume, *Euphues and his England,* which he dedicated to de Vere. By now, the Italianate Earl of Oxford had recruited Lyly as his secretary and bookkeeper, who at this point retracted virtually all the outpourings of the first volume. Gabriel Harvey labelled him the "fiddlestick of Oxford".[76] For at least a decade, Lyly's two prose romances, together with eight or more plays—comedies with classical or mythological backgrounds—made him England's most influential writer, an influence running in a strong, flowing, vein throughout the comedies of William Shakespeare,[77] and much imitated by other writers of the period such as Gosson, Greene, Lodge, and Rich.

Over time a succession of literary associates joined Oxford at Fisher's Folly and his other houses, but especially at Fisher's Folly. Some have been described as servants or secretaries. Perhaps they really were employed as Oxford's secretaries, but "collaborators" or "associates" may be closer titles. Apart from Lyly, other "secretaries" passing through the door of Fisher's Folly included: Thomas Churchyard, Abraham Fleming, Anthony Mundy, Nicholas Hill, Thomas Nashe, Henry Lok[78] — and Thomas Watson. De Vere loved to encourage independent thinkers and he enjoyed their company; in return they brought to his circle: wit, learning, enthusiasm, and a shared passion for theatre, poetry and the arts. "Boring amanuensis" would describe not a single one. To briefly glance at these men, their background, their activities, is to catch a glimpse of the world of Thomas Watson. He knew them, they knew him, they shared a milieu.

Thomas Churchyard, soldier, spy, and writer, had his feet in both the Sidney and Oxford camps. His career spanned a long period—from Henry VIII to James I. He was the son of a farmer, born around 1520 near Shrewsbury, not far from the Pembroke family dominated town of Ludlow which he warmly praised in his *The Worthiness of Wales* (1578). His origins and his military service under Henry Sidney in 1564, 1575 and 1576 may have influenced the epitaphs he composed on the deaths of Henry Herbert, Earl of Pembroke in 1570 and Sir Philip Sidney in 1587. His first employment, however, which lasted for twenty years, was as a page to Oxford's uncle, the poet Henry Howard, Earl of Surrey and his Countess, Frances de Vere. It is possible that from Howard, Churchyard picked up a skill in poetry, such as it was. By 1553 he had published *A Mirror for Man*, and several of his poems appeared later in *Tottel's Miscellany* (1557ff). Most of what is known of Churchyard's life is based on his autobiographical verses with alliterative titles—*Churchyard's Chips* (1575/8) was one. After Howard's execution he became a soldier of fortune in Scotland, Ireland, the Low Countries and France. In the early 1560s he spied for Burghley whilst serving under Prince William of Orange in the Netherlands. Here, as the prince's agent, he placed himself at the head of the protestant insurgents, but managed to so enrage them that he had to flee the country disguised as a priest. We know that by 1567 he had become a retainer to the Earl of Oxford (aged seventeen, and still a minor) because in that year Oxford sent him off to Dillenburg to serve the Prince of Orange yet again. After the passing of a year and many adventures he returned to England, only to become involved in a huge falling out with de Vere, who disowned him.

Nevertheless, in time all was forgiven and Churchyard was received back into Oxford's circle where, until the mid-1570s, he was both servant and spy; Burghley found him useful, too, and employed him in 1570 to spy on Catholic recusants in Bath. More military service followed; he was probably present at the siege of Tergoes in 1572, and followed this up in Ireland under Sir Henry Sidney. He wrote an account of Martin Frobisher's third voyage of 1578 which, in vain, attempted to seek the Northwest Passage, an adventure which lost the Earl of Oxford £3,000. He had influential input into the Queen's progresses of 1564, 1575 and 1578, but in 1579 foolishly botched any hopes of promotion by arousing the Queen's wrath with an ill-considered passage in his *Churchyard's Choice*. Whereupon he found it expedient to flee to Edinburgh—a decision no doubt swayed by his anxiety about some charges pressed by a widow whose husband he had recently killed. From Scotland he appealed successively for financial help; so when, in 1580, he proposed to dedicate his next two works to "the most worthiest (and towards noble man), the Earl of Oxford"[79] one suspects his motive may have sprung as much from desperation as honesty. Hatton and Leicester were also recipients of his attempts to curry favour: the following year he appealed to Sir Christopher Hatton; service with the Earl of Leicester followed in 1585 and he composed an epitaph for the earl in 1591, three years after the earl's death. Even though both Hatton and Leicester had been Oxford's enemies, the Earl took him back as his secretary, and in 1590 found him to be a useful agent in a dispute over rented furnished rooms on St Paul's Hill.[80]

Abraham Fleming, another of Oxford's secretaries, liked to boast that he was a "Londoner borne",[81] which event probably took place around 1552 in Holborn. Eighteen years later, he found himself a sizar at Peterhouse in Cambridge. If London blood flowed in Abraham's veins, his tutor Dr Andrew Perne—like many another in Elizabethan England—was from an East Anglian background, born in the village of East Bilney in Norfolk. Perne's ability to change with the religious weather was notorious: Martin Marprelate scorned him as "Old Andrew Turncoat", and other literary wits are said to have translated *perno* with "I turn, I rat, I change often".

With such a chameleon tutor it would be unsurprising to learn that Fleming acquired a cynicism about the religious movements of his time. That was not the case, however; he firmly believed that the Papists had their places reserved in the "bottomless pit".[82] From Fleming's printed comments, Elizabeth Story Donno deduced a "pronounced religious fervour, a sense of intellectual superiority, and a truculent mode of expression".[83] Certainly, a sense of humour was not at the top of his toolbox.

Although Fleming did not adopt Perne's religious accommodations, he may nevertheless have learned much else from his tutor. Perne's enthusiasms ranged beyond the theological, to medicine, cartography, civil engineering, and a love for the beauty of books[84]—his private library was one of the largest of his day, and is still largely preserved at Peterhouse. Perhaps his bookish devotion rubbed off on Fleming who found employment with at least fifteen London publishers, leaving him little time for academia—his graduation was delayed until as late as 1582, by which time he was some thirty years old. Fleming's inky fingers dipped into many a publishing pie: apart from seven works of his own composition, he compiled, indexed, and translated other people's output into verse, dreamed up addresses to the readers, and corrected and improved the efforts of at least 55 others, and probably anonymously for many more. Although his main employer was Henry Denham, a major printer with four presses, Denham was not the only printer-publisher who found Fleming useful. There was Denham's former master Richard Tottel, whose press was busy running off mainly legal works, though posterity remembers him for possibly the most influential of all Elizabethan poetry anthologies, *Tottel's Miscellany* (1557).[85] Other employers included George Bishop, John Harrison, Ralph Newberie, and Thomas Woodcocke a much respected member of the Stationers' Company and the syndicate responsible for the second edition of Holinshed's *Chronicles* (1587).[86] Fleming's working knowledge of French and Greek was invaluable, and his knowledge of Latin went even deeper. He was the first to translate into English a full Virgilian text, the *Bucoliks* (1589),[87] but nothing daunted him and he happily tackled virtually anything that came his way, from broadsides to folio books.

Few were the literary personalities of the 1570s and 80s that Fleming would not have met, and his laudatory verses headed not only his own works, but those of Barnabe Googe, Arthur Golding, Timothy Kendall, George Whetstone, and Reginald Scot.[88] By 1580, the year in which he dedicated his translation of Niels Hemmingsen's *The Epistle of ... St Paul ... to the Ephesians* to Oxford's wife Anne Cecil, he had been recruited as Oxford's amanuensis.[89] Literary jewels must have strewn his papers and archives. The antiquarian Francis Peck stumbled on some, and in 1732 itemised amidst a long list of documents, "a pleasant conceit of Vere, Earl of Oxford, discontented at the rising of a mean gentleman in the English court, circa 1580". Oxfordians have argued that this may have been Shakespeare's *Twelfth Night*. Peck said he would publish the document in a second edition of his two-volume miscellany *Desiderata curiosa* (1732-5). It was a promise unfulfilled, and with his death in 1744 the "conceit" vanished with the rest of Fleming's manuscripts, including Fleming's account of his own life.[90]

Between 1585 and 1587 Fleming could be found at the Sign of the Star in Aldersgate. Here he acted as general editor of the revised three-volume edition of Raphael Holinshed's two-volume *Chronicles of England, Scotland and Ireland*, first published ten years earlier with a dedication to Sir William Cecil. Like Fleming, Holinshed had a close personal link to the Earl of Oxford. He was a member of Cecil's household, where Anne and Edward de Vere often stayed, had been a juror at the 1567 enquiry which found Oxford innocent of manslaughter, and in an account in the *Chronicles* diverted the blame for a murder on Shooters Hill, near Greenwich, from Oxford to his servant.[91]

When Holinshed died in 1580 the task of supervising the revision of the *Chronicles* fell to Fleming. Fleming made significant improvements in its structure, its marginalia and its indexes, as well as proofreading much of its 3½ million words. More particularly, he brought the account of Elizabeth's reign up to date (to 1586), filled in Holinshed's omissions, and added material by, among others, the historian and antiquarian John Stow. The Privy Council, had censored several passages in the first edition, and now—as was its right—requested several deletions to the new edition, in particular to Fleming's account of the Babington Plot in which he had run away with his protestant enthusiasms. Passages like "these venomous vipers ... hewn in pieces, their tigers hearts burned in the fire" were excised.[92] Nevertheless, Fleming was nothing if not a professional and he almost certainly undertook the revisions himself.[93]

His revised edition of the *Chronicles* is famous as the source for Shakespeare's history plays, the plot of *Macbeth*, and for parts of *King Lear* and *Cymbeline*. In 1588 Fleming was ordained deacon and priest, and later he became chaplain to Charles, Lord Howard of Effingham (Earl of Nottingham after 1596), renowned for his naval and military feats as Lord High Admiral. Howard was acquainted with Oxford, and he was also the patron of the company of actors known after 1576 as Lord Howard's Men and then, from 1585 when he became Admiral, as the Lord Admiral's players. The company premiered most of Marlowe's plays, and later became prominent under Edward Alleyn.[94]

Fleming was curate at St Nicholas' Church in Deptford where he may have assisted the vicar, Thomas Macander, with the burial of Christopher Marlowe in 1592—if, indeed, the body truly belonged to Marlowe. In 1593 Fleming was promoted to rector of St Pancras which lay at the junction of Soper and Needlers Lanes in a small and formerly rich London parish. There, he saw the church continue to fall away into poverty so that ten years later Stow noted in his second edition of *A Survey of London* that the monuments of several important dignitaries were "defaced and gone", and that the broken church bells had been illegally sold at half their value rather putting the parish to the cost of new castings.[95]

Fleming was a good and loyal pastor to his parish through fourteen years and at least two outbreaks of the plague. In 1607, he died at Bottesford, Leicestershire, while visiting the home of his brother Dr Samuel Fleming, the rector there, who some thirty years earlier had been tutor to the poet Sir John Harington. At Bottesford, Abraham's body was honoured with an interment at his brother's church beneath the chancel alongside the costly tombs of Edward Manners and his brother John, third and fourth earls of Rutland. Abraham Fleming's connections with the earls of Rutland are intriguing. Bearing in mind Fleming's work as amanuensis for the Earl of Oxford, it is perhaps significant to note that from the age of fourteen Edward Manners had been brought up with Edward de Vere in the Cecil household. The Manners family held vast estates in Derbyshire and Nottinghamshire, where Edward was involved in disputes with, among others, the Markham family. Edward died in 1587 and his nephew Roger Manners, eleven years old and now the fifth Earl, also became a ward of Cecil, who delegated his education to Francis Bacon. He passed through Corpus Christi, Cambridge, and became a follower of Essex, taking in marriage Essex's stepdaughter Elizabeth Sidney (daughter of Sir Philip). Roger was marginally caught up with Essex's attempted coup of 1600, for which his punishment seems excessive—incarceration in the Tower, later remitted to the enormous fine of £30,000 (although it was reduced, and in fact never paid after James I's accession). He, too, was buried at Bottesford in 1612. How tragic that Fleming's manuscript autobiography, which may have revealed much about his links with this aristocratic family, was lost with the death of Francis Peck in 1744.

Henry Lok (1553?-1608?) was another of the Earl of Oxford's adherents. Lok was the son of a Cheapside mercer, also Henry, and his second wife Anne (née Vaughan). Anne had a literary bent, and she was tough. As a young woman she had been educated by a Mr Cob, proficient in Latin, Greek, and French—and a rigorous protestant. The equally fervent Scottish preacher John Knox lived with Henry and Anne for a few years after 1553. When Mary Tudor ascended to the throne, Knox worried about Anne's spiritual and physical safety under the restored Catholic regime, and encouraged her to join the exiled protestant community in Geneva. Within four days of her arrival there in 1557, her infant daughter had died, leaving her with just her young son Henry and a maid. She passed her time translating some of Calvin's sermons from French into English verse.

With the death of Queen Mary and the ascension of Elizabeth to the throne Anne felt she could safely return to Cheapside, and not long afterwards her translation was published by John Day in a volume entitled *A Meditation of a Penitent Sinner* (1560). It also included a dedication to the protestant Duchess of Suffolk (also exiled) and twenty-six sonnets of Anne's own based on Psalm 51, believed by many scholars to be the first English sonnet sequence.[96] Other literary works followed, her last known being a 1590 translation of *Of the Markes of the Children of God* (1590), a history of protestantism in the Low Countries. Anne Lok continued to work in England to further the protestant cause, serving as a link between Knox, Scotland, and the recently returned protestants from Geneva. After the death of her first husband Henry Lok, she took a second who died soon afterwards, and she settled in Exeter with a third.[97]

As the son of such a mother, Henry evidently had a good role model. According to Anthony à Wood, on leaving Oxford he "was received into the patronage of a noble Maecaenas"—a byword for a wealthy, generous and enlightened patron of the arts,[98] which sounds like the Earl of Oxford. Lok specialised in pious works such as his *Sundry Christian Passions* published in 1593 and reprinted in his *Ecclesiastes* in 1597. Earlier he had contributed a commendatory poem to James VI of Scotland's *Poetical Exercises at Vacant Hours* (1591), a work registered to Richard Field in London but printed in Edinburgh. Pursued by creditors, it was from Scotland in 1591 that he wrote a letter to Burghley complaining that although he had been employed by the Earl of Oxford for "almost twenty years" he was still owed £80 and requested either employment with Burghley or re-employment with Oxford. By early 1598 he was petitioning Cecil for the collectorship of Devon; when that failed he fished for the position of keeper of the Queen's bears and mastiffs, philosophising, 'It is better to be a bear herd than to be baited daily with great exclamations for small debts'. His uncle was Michael Lok the merchant who as governor of the Cathay Company had misled Oxford into investing £3,000 in the failed Frobisher expedition. Henry denied any connection.[99] Six years later he addressed a sonnet to Oxford[100] but this may mean little. It was just one of sixty secular sonnets he addressed to various members of the nobility and important court officials.

Anthony Mundy[101] was Sancho Panza to Edward de Vere's Don Quixote. If it was Fleming's boast that he was a "Londoner borne", Mundy self-styled himself more extravagantly as "a Free-borne Son of this Honourable City", declaring (like John Stow) that London was his "birthplace and breeder".[102] He was born in October 1560 and baptised in St Gregory's by Paul's, the cathedral's parish church built against its south-west wall and ministering to a crowded, often violent, and rapidly burgeoning population.[103] Mundy's father, Christopher, was a freeman of the Stationers' and Drapers' companies, and since St Gregory's parish also encompassed the cathedral churchyard, the centre of the book trade, it followed that he baptised his son there. Anthony's father and mother Jane died before December 1570; Anthony was aged just ten. Little is known of what happened to the boy during the following seven years.

We do know that he was educated by Claudius Hollyband, who remembered Mundy in 1579 as his 'scholler' in a commendatory French verse prefacing one of Mundy's earliest works, *The Mirror of Mutability*. Hollyband, a Huguenot whose true name was Claude de Sainliens, taught French, Italian, Latin, penmanship and arithmetic to the children of prosperous tradesmen.[104] Initially, he kept a school at Lewisham, but from 1573 until 1576 set up in St Paul's Churchyard by Thomas Purfoot's printing house at the Sign of the Lucrece, and later at the Golden Ball,[105] so perhaps young Anthony had not travelled far since his parents' deaths. Hollyband had many works to his name, but was renowned for his *French Schoolmaster* (1573) and *French Littelton* (1576). Both were printed by fellow refugee Thomas Vautrollier and dedicated to Robert Sackville (born in 1561) the young son and heir of Thomas Sackville, Lord Buckhurst.[106] By October 1576 Hollyband was living at Sackville's palatial Buckhurst Place, set amidst 1,500 acres in East Sussex (although he moved twice again within the next two years).[107] Evidently, Hollyband had managed to find employment with an extremely wealthy and powerful arm of the state. Buckhurst's properties were vast, and his career distinguished: diplomat in the Low Countries; present in the Star Chamber at Arundel's interrogation over his connection with the Ridolfi plot; commissioner at the trial of Babington; and proclaimer of the death of Mary Queen of Scots—sure sign of a trusted, steady, hand. In 1598 he succeeded Burghley as Lord Treasurer. There had been a time when Buckhurst had hoped for a marriage between his son Robert with Burghley's younger daughter Elizabeth—a dream dashed by Burghley's ambition for a son-in-law of an even higher rank.

More than this, Sackville was a literary man, most enduringly famous for his Acts 4 and 5 of *Gorbuduc* (1560), later drawn on by Philip Sidney for his *Arcadia* and Shakespeare in his *King Lear*. He was also associated with

Sir Thomas Hoby's English translation of Castiglione's *Book of the Courtier* and the later Latin translation of the same work. This was undertaken by Bartholomew Clerke, then living at Sackville House in Fleet Street. Here Buckhurst also probably encouraged a literary coterie, though smaller than those of Sidney or Oxford. Doubtless, Hollyband was a member. Another member was Thomas Twyne, who was indebted to Buckhurst for his licentiate of the College of Physicians, and who settled at Lewes near to Buckhurst's priory there. Twyne was a skilled astronomer and friend of John Dee. As a friend of Hollyband, he wrote an address to the *French Schoolmaster*: "Tho. Twyne to all the students of the French tongue."

As for Mundy's later education, it seems likely that before he entered his trade he was a boy actor. From information printed by Thomas Alfield's *A True Report of the Death of M. Campion Jesuit and Priest ...* (1582),[108] a Catholic publication hostile to Mundy, we read that "Mundy, who was at first a stage player ... [was] after[wards] an apprentice ..." Is it possible that at one time Mundy was a pupil at St Paul's School? The Children had a long tradition of staging dramas in the churchyard, although in 1576 they found a regular indoor venue nearby at Blackfriars.[109] Some years later, Mundy wrote a play for the Children of St Paul's, *The Rare Triumphs of Love and Fortune* (1582). Or was he a member of Leicester's boys company, as other writers have suggested?[110] Or, more probably, did he take to the stage with the Earl of Sussex's Men, thus offering a connection with Sussex's political ally the Earl of Oxford.[111]

Whatever Mundy's early background, we do know that in 1576, aged sixteen, he was apprenticed to the printer John Allde at his "Long Shop" next to St Mildred's in Poultry.[112] It was a well-equipped and busy shop, producing both books and popular treatises. Mundy was one of several apprentices, and served alongside John's son Edward, as well as John Windet and William Hall. Windet and Hall were to make their own impressions on publishing history. Windet worked for a long time with John Wolfe, came to hold important offices in the Stationers' Company and later succeeded Wolfe as Printer to the City of London. He became associated with some Shakespeare-related works and well-known for his immaculate music printing.[113] The name of Mundy's other work colleague, William Hall, is found alongside those of Hollyband and other dedicators—puffers—of *The Mirror of Mutability*. He is thought by some to be the dedicatee ("Mr W. H. All ...") of Shakespeare's Sonnets (1604). He was murdered in 1614.[114]

The young men's employer, John Allde, had Catholic sympathies. He was jailed in the Wood Street Counter in 1568 for publishing a pamphlet on the Duke of Alva to help out some Belgian stationers living with the Duke of Norfolk. Twelve years later he printed a *Moorning Dittie* on the death of Henry Fitzalan, twelfth Earl of Arundel, promoter of the match between Mary and Norfolk. When Allde died in 1584, his wife Margaret and son Edward ran the business jointly until a few months after Edward's first marriage in 1588, when he started a separate trade at the Gilded Cup in Fore Street, Cripplegate. Some of Shakespeare's Quartos were handled at his press, but in 1597 it was officially broken up for printing a "Popish confession".[115]

During the Autumn and Winter of 1578-9 Mundy journeyed to France and Rome in the company of Thomas Nowell, probably the son of Oxford's former tutor, ostensibly that by absorbing the culture and learning the languages, Nowell's wild oats might be "furrowed in a forreyne ground"[116]. It is nearly certain that his real mission was to spy on the English Catholics, and to this end he enrolled under an alias at the Jesuit English College in Rome. He stayed there for a year and afterwards moved on to Paris and Rheims. By July 1579 he was back in London and by all appearances seems quickly to have resumed a career on the stage. Thomas Alfield noted how

> this scholler new come out of Italy did play extempore, those gentlemen and others which were present, can best give witness of his dexterity, who being wary of his folly, hissed him from his stage. Then being thereby discouraged, he set forth a balet [ballad?] against plays, but yet (O constant youth) he now begins againe to ruffle upon the stage.[117]

As G D George[118] points out, the passage suggests not only Mundy's incompetence as an actor, but the description of his reaction to the hissing implies immaturity. Alfield's further comment, "I omit among other places his behaviour in Barbican with his good mistress, and mother ..." is generally taken to suggest that Mundy was married by this time.

But Mundy's priority was not acting. It looks like his return from the continent marked the start of his employment by the Earl of Oxford. In 1579 Mundy dedicated two works to Oxford and his family, including *The Mirror of Mutability* (printed by Allde) which, like some other works, carried the de Vere arms on the back of the title page.[119] It also included two acrostic poems, one spelling "EDWARD DE VERE EARLE OF OXENFORD" and another spelling out the Earl's motto "VERO NIHIL VERIUS". Another work presented to the Earl was a *History of Galien of France* (1579).[120] Mundy was just eighteen or nineteen years old and, since the original manuscript seems to have been less than perfect, *Galien* was corrected by its publisher Miles Jennings.[121] Those early days may have seen Mundy attempting to secure the patronage of the Sidneys. A work by one "T F Student", thought to be a pseudonym, included verses by Mundy and his friend John Proctor, and carried a dedication dated 26 November 1579 to Sir Henry Sidney, "his singular good Lord".[122] It was a one-off, for not long afterwards Mundy secured the patronage of de Vere. In two works published in 1580 he described himself as "servant to the right honourable the Earl of Oxenford"[123] In his *Discourse on the Late Earthquakes* ... (1580, also published by John Allde), he admitted that he imitated his "friend" John Lyly, then Oxford's secretary. The work was dedicated to two "gentlemen attendant upon the Earl of Oxford", William Waters, and Oxford's physician the literary surgeon George Baker. All this took place in those fertile years before Oxford's apparent "disgrace" at court, the time of his encouragement of the Euphuists, his investment in Frobisher's foreign explorations, and his taking on, in 1580, of the Earl of Warwick's players.

Scholars believe Mundy's novel of Homeric worldly adventure *Zelauto, or The Fountain of Fame* (1580), a work in imitation of Lyly's *Euphues,* may have influenced the plot of *The Merchant of Venice.* Although Shakespeare could have picked from any number of versions of Shylock's story around at the time, the similarities between *The Merchant* and Mundy's work are close, including Portia's famous plea for mercy.[124] From at the latest 1584, but probably earlier, until at least 1602 but probably later, Mundy wrote and plotted a large number of plays (mostly lost), pamphlets and translations.[125] Many were anti-Catholic, for alongside a prolific writing career Mundy achieved considerable success as a spy and recusant hunter. In the Catholic tract entitled *A True Report of the Death and Martyrdome of M Campion Jesuit and Priest ...* he was accused of deceiving John Allde, a charge Mundy refuted by persuading Allde to sign a denial which he then published. Mundy was an important witness at the trial against Edmund Campion, and during this period wrote no less than five anti-Catholic pamphlets including *A Discoverie of Edmund Campion and his Confederates ... whereto is added the execution of Edmund Campion, Raphe Sherwin, and Alexander Brian, executed at Tiborne on the 1 of December ...* (1582).[126] Part of this was read aloud from Campion's scaffold as he awaited his death. Mundy's reward came in 1584 with the grant of the post to a Messenger of Her Majesty's Chamber.

Just as earlier he had courted the Sidneys, Mundy's commitment to the Earl of Oxford also seems occasionally to have wavered — on the surface, at least. In 1580 he dedicated *The Pain of Pleasure* to Lady Douglas Sheffield, who between 1569 and 1578 had been the lover of Robert Dudley, first Earl of Leicester, and by whom she had a son in 1574. But in the year before Mundy's book was published, she married Sir Edward Stafford. Although her affair with Leicester was over, she still pined for him, and on his part Leicester kept her portrait at his Wanstead house until his death. Leicester was not only Elizabeth's favourite, but also Oxford's enemy. Whatever schemes or mind-set lay behind Mundy's dedications is unclear. Since Stafford was an enemy of Leicester too, one must consider that Mundy's dedication did not necessarily reflect support for Dudley's group. Nevertheless, in 1584 he dedicated his *Two godly and learned sermons ...*,[127] to Stafford, and one must also remember that, just possibly, he may once have been a member of Leicester's boys acting company.

He was also an enthusiastic pursuivant of the Marprelate tract writers and printers. By 1591, the Marprelate flurry having passed over, he was taken on as a translator for another enthusiastic Marprelate bloodhound, John Wolfe the printer. Perhaps his acquaintance with his former fellow apprentice and Wolfe employee John Windet helped, while his close relationship with the printing trade also brought him into touch with Thomas East, the master printer associated with the musicians — and shrewd men of business—William Byrd and Thomas Morley.

In the late 1590s Mundy helped Stow to update his second (1603) edition of the *Chronicles of England*, first published in 1580. He took it on again in 1618, and yet again with Humfrey Dyson in 1633 after Stow's death. Just as William Shakespeare consulted Holinshed's *Chronicles*, edited by Oxford's secretary Abraham Fleming, so he also utilised Stow's *Chronicles*, another editorial work of one by the Earl of Oxford's agents.

Information about another of Oxford's secretaries, Nicholas Hill, who probably served around 1592 or 1593, is sparse and unreliable. It relies on two conflicting sources, each built mainly on second-hand tittle-tattle.[128] According to John Aubrey, Hill was

> … a great mathematician, philosopher, traveller and poet. He was so eminent for knowledge that he was a favourite of the great Earl of Oxford who had him accompany him on his travels [as his steward in 1575] which were so splendid and sumptuous that he kept at Florence a greater court than the Great Court.[129]

Since Hill was aged five at this time, Aubrey cannot be correct. Of a small retinue of two gentlemen, five grooms, one payend, a harbinger and a trenchman, the only known named member to have accompanied Oxford from London was a retainer named Nathaniel Baxter.[130]

Hill was born in Fleet Street in London in 1570 and matriculated at St John's Oxford in 1587. He was made a fellow of the college in 1590, a position which he almost immediately forfeited, perhaps because of his conversion to Roman Catholicism.[131] He also spent some time in the service of Henry Percy, the "Wizard Earl" of Northumberland and a leader of the group of associates dubbed in more recent years "The School of Night", which fascinated Hill by its study of the occult, alchemy, astronomy, and literature, and had a reputation for atheism. Hill professed himself a disciple of Giordano Bruno whose ideas apparently still lingered in Oxford after the monk's visit in 1583. It would seem that by the late 1590s Hill was attached to Sir Robert Bassett, a follower of the second Earl of Essex who, it was reported, was turning to Papistry under the evidence of "a lewd fellow Hill".[132] Bassett was not altogether sane; on the Queen's death in 1603, he attempted to occupy Lundy Island and declare himself heir to the throne.[133] Alarmed perhaps by Bassett's project, Hill took to the safety of the continent in 1590 where in 1601 he published a book of natural philosophy, *Philosophia epicurea*. It is likely that grief at the death of his little son Laurence from "pestilential disease" led him to take his own life in Rotterdam at around 1610.[134]

Hill was a follower of Democritus (c460 – c370) who, together with his tutor Leucippus (fl.5th century BC), advanced a theory that the atom was the smallest particle of matter. For holding this opinion Hill was widely scorned. Ben Jonson, for one, wrote of "those atomi ridiculous" to rhyme with "Hill Nicholas".[135] Hill's "atomi" seem less "ridiculous" today, and his theory was acknowledged by William Shakespeare who wrote it into his plays.[136]

Some writers were associated with both the Oxford and Sidney coteries —which suggests not only the writers' need to muster powerful patrons, but also an exaggeration by literary historians of the supposed rivalry between the two groups. Situated in both camps was Thomas Nashe (1567-1601), principally remembered as the founder of the English picaresque novel and the author of a satirical pamphlet entitled *Pierce Penniless his Supplication to the Devil* (1592)—the inspiration for several elements in *Hamlet* including the prince's comment on drunkenness as a Danish vice. Like many another London inhabitant he was born in East Anglia (baptised in November 1567) where his father, of Herefordshire roots, was a minister in Lowestoft and later at West Harling in Suffolk. From 1581 or 1582 he was educated at St John's College, Cambridge as a sizar, and gained a BA in March 1586. Over twenty years earlier St John's had awarded an MA to his patron Edward de Vere. Nashe left Cambridge in about 1588 or 1589, one term short of receiving his MA. He may still have been there when his first work, *The Anatomy of Absurdity* (in John Lyly's euphuistic style) was registered at the Stationers' Hall by the London publisher Thomas Hacket in September 1588.[137] It was during his college days, or shortly after, that he also met Robert Greene, and wrote a preface for Greene's pamphlet *Menaphon* (1589). It took the form of a letter addressed to "The Gentlemen Students of Both Universities" and attacked not only the players (he called them "parasites") but the illiterate dramatists too (with their "swelling bombast of a bragging blank verse"). Thomas Kyd was personally singled out as an upstart without a degree.

Greene's own career commenced with several works imitating Lyly's *Euphues*, two of which inspired parts of *The Winter's Tale* and *Troilus and Cressida*. His technique in his later dramas *James IV* and *Friar Bacon and Friar Bungay* (both c1591) may also have influenced Shakespeare. On the other hand, his private life left much to be desired: he deserted his wife and child to explore the seamier side of London and set up with the sister of a famous thief called "Cutting" Ball who was later hanged at Tyburn. Nevertheless, his protégé Thomas Nashe stayed loyal, and—like others in Oxford's circle—both were recruited by Archbishop Whitgift to reply to the criticisms spewing from the pen of the pseudonymous Puritan Martin Marprelate.

Most studies of Elizabethan literature cite Greene as the author of a deathbed pamphlet *A Groats-worth of Wit* (1592), which contains an attack on an "upstart crow", supposedly Shakespeare the actor. The manuscript, however, is in the handwriting of its printer Henry Chettle, and it was condemned by Nashe in a private letter to Chettle as a "scald trivial lying pamphlet".[138] After Greene's death in 1592 Nashe passionately defended his friend against jibes from the Harvey brothers, Gabriel and Richard, whom he lampooned in his *Pierce Penniless*, Afterwards, he continued the feud in *Strange News* (1593),[139] a reply to Gabriel Harvey's *Four Letters and Certain Sonnets* (1592)[140] which had accused Greene and Nashe of a "villainous" manner of writing called "coneycatching"—as well as accusing Nashe of neglecting his friend, and bitterly mocking him as the "Ape of Euphues" (in other words, of the Earl of Oxford).[141] Nashe flung a final attack at Harvey in 1598 in his pamphlet *Have With you to Saffron-Walden or Gabriel Harvey's Hunt Is up*.[142]

C S Lewis compared Nashe's brilliantly forceful, volatile, satirical attacks on Harvey with the colloquial, Rabelaisian, wit of Sir John Falstaff.[143] Nashe certainly (and Shakespeare, probably) was inspired by the Italian writer and satirist Pietro Aretino (1492-1556)—said to have died of suffocation from "laughing too much". *Pierce Penniless* concludes with Nashe's promise to write to Aretino's host by my carrier, and I hope he'll repair his whip, and use it against our English Peacocks, that painting themselves with church spoils, like mighty men's sepulchres, have nothing but Atheism, schism, hypocrisy, & vainglory, like rotten bones lie lurking among them.[144]

Yet Nashe's *Christ's Tears over Jerusalem* (1593), a religious lamentation published in the year after Greene's death was far different in tone. Its anguished sermon by Jesus, its grisly description of the destruction of Jerusalem, and its plea that London repent to evade the fate of the Biblical city were accompanied by Nashe (the minister's son)'s plea for the pardon of his enemies, including "Master Dr Harvey" (a gesture deleted in the second edition of 1594). This work was followed by *The Terrors of the Night* (1594) a meditation on the black arts, and in the same year *The Tragedy of Dido Queen of Carthage* was published as by "Christopher Marlowe and [in a smaller typeface] Thomas Nash[e], Gent." *The Unfortunate Traveller, or the Life of Jack Wilton* was also published that year, an early work of fiction purporting to be an account of the continental travels of a page to Henry Howard, Earl of Surrey, uncle of the Earl of Oxford. After several (often violent) adventures in which courtly love, sonnets and jousts are all mocked, Surrey and his page arrive in Venice where a courtesan, Tabitha the Temptress, persuades them to accept counterfeit gold. For this crime they are clapped into gaol, from which they are rescued by Pietro Aretino. The first edition of *The Unfortunate Traveller* was dedicated to Henry Wriothesley, third Earl of Southampton, a companion of Robert Devereux the Earl of Essex, and the husband of Sidney's widow Frances Walsingham. It signals Nashe's attachment to the literary coterie at Essex House under Devereux' leadership—the heir to Sidney's circle of earlier years.

In 1597 Nashe joined forces with Ben Jonson to write a now lost satirical comedy *The Isle of Dogs*, performed at the Swan on Bankside by the Earl of Pembroke's Men. "As *Actaeon* was worried by his own hounds commented Francis Meres, "so is *Tom Nashe* of his *Isle of Dogs*".[145] Both the city authorities and the Privy Council exploded with rage, and the play was denounced for containing "lewd matters".[146] The London theatres were closed, Jonson and two other players were gaoled in the Marshalsea, and Nashe fled back to Great Yarmouth from whence he wrote

Nashe's Lenten Stuff (1599) in praise of the local red herring. Although Archbishop Whitgift banned him from ever publishing anything again, his sole drama, *Summer's Last Will and Testament* (named after Henry VIII's jester Will Summer) still managed to find a printer in 1600. It had, however, been performed much earlier, in 1592.[147]

To briefly return to Gabriel Harvey's *Four Letters* of 1592, closer examination reveals that although the work was initially abusive towards Nashe, it quickly transformed into praise. Exhorting Nashe to give up his "grammar-school wit", Harvey pleaded with his rival:

> … be a musician and a poet unto thyself that art both, and a ringleader of both unto others, be a man, be a gentleman, be a philosopher, be a divine, be thy resolute self … Good sweet orator, be a divine poet indeed, and use heavenly eloquence indeed, and employ thy golden talent with amounting usance indeed.[148]

Moreover, Harvey included Nashe among the best writers of his day: "Edmund Spenser, Richard Stanyhurst, Abraham Fraunce, Thomas Watson, Samuel Daniel, Thomas Nashe, and the rest."[149] In the midst of Harvey's list we spot the name of another known secretary of the Earl of Oxford: Thomas Watson.

Two:
"Far from my native land"

> Why is my verse so barren of new pride?
> So far from variation or quick change?
> Why, with the time, do I not glance aside
> To new-found methods and to compounds strange?
> Why write I still all one, ever the same,
> And keep invention in a noted weed,
> That every word doth almost tell my name,
> Showing their birth, and where they did proceed?
> O know, sweet love, I always write of you,
> And you and love are still my argument;
> So all my best is dressing old words new,
> Spending again what is already spent;
> For as the sun is daily new and old,
> So is my love still telling what is told.

IN his Sonnet 76 William Shakespeare explains to his beloved that he needs no fresh verse forms to express his love. Is it possible, however, that beneath its surface the verse hints at more than the poet's emotions? Some Oxfordians have suggested a clue to Edward De Vere's authorship of the Sonnets. Could the seventh line, they ask, be a coded message of the kind the Elizabethans loved? By this theory "every" represents E. Ver, or Vere, which "doth almost tell my name".

On the other hand, an acrostic of the first letters in lines four to nine spells T WATSO[1] — also the kind of coding the Elizabethans loved — spelling Thomas Watson's name, although only, as the verse says, "almost". A better claim than "E. Ver"? Perhaps. Perhaps also too much of a coincidence that it gives point to Thomas Heywood's lines in his *The Hierarchy of the Blessed Angels* of 1635 that

2. "Far from my native land"

"… Tom Watson, though he wrote
 Able to make Apollo's self to dote
 Upon his Muse; for all that he could strive,
 Yet never could at his full name arrive."[2]

*The Hierarchy of the Blessed Angels i*s a thick book of 622 pages. On page 205 Heywood lists ten Latin poet-playwrights who were noted imitators or adaptors of other people's works. Each was given a shorter name, or nickname: thus Publius Ovidius Naso was known as *Ovid*, Publius Virgilius as *Virgil*, Marcus Annaeus Lucanus as *Seneca the Younger*, Publius Terentius as *Terence*, and so on. On the next page, Heywood compares these classical writers with fifteen Elizabethan and Jacobean poet-playwrights, identifying each with a *"curtailed"* familiar first name: so Robert Greene is *Rob* Greene, Christopher Marlowe *Kit* Marlowe, and there is *Tom* Kyd, *Jack* Fletcher, *Ben* Jonson, and more. Heywood seems to be saying that not one of these poets of his recent generation could achieve his name in full because he was a collaborator with, or "front man" for, a nobleman. It may not be coincidental that all ten poets had a likely connection with the Earl of Oxford's circle.

So, says Heywood, *Tom* Watson could never achieve his full name of *Thomas*, because, try as he might ("for all that he could strive"), he still owed a debt to another writer. But Heywood by no means denigrates Watson; he piles on praise, saying that, despite this indebtedness, Watson was no empty wordsmith. Watson's "muse", says Heywood, was so *fine*, so *compelling,* that even Apollo "doted" upon it. Thus he links Watson with the sun-god of music, poetry, art, medicine, light and knowledge. Interestingly, several writers of Heywood's day associated Apollo, the patron of the Muses, with the Earl of Oxford.[3] Either way, whether Heywood's comparison is with Phoebus-Apollo or obliquely with Oxford, he is paying Watson—acknowledged in his day as a master of the literary, music and publishing worlds—a very high compliment indeed.

A man of modest means, even to being born in 1562 to a Westminster poulterer—thus the opinions of earlier studies of Thomas Watson.[4] Now, thanks to Ibrahim Alhiyari's research for his thesis at Texas Tech University

University,[5] we know for certain that Watson was wealthy, a member of the gentry. Writers with less common sense than Edward Arber should have been alerted by his conclusion drawn as long ago as 1870 that Watson's "publications tells us, in one way or another, that he was of gentle blood."[6] Watson's own contemporaries referred to him as a gentleman. Further clues are a costly education and the possession of the wherewithal to spend several years on the continent of Europe.[7] As Alhiyari further points out,

> "his lacking interest in the writing for the purpose of earning a living; the aesthetic, self-indulgent, amatory, long poems he wrote, all seem to confirm that he was indeed of privileged ancestry, and of higher economic status".

Thomas was born in, or around, May 1555, in Hart Street in the Parish of St Olave, London, to William and Anne Watson. Possibly Anne was some twenty years younger than her husband, and perhaps they met when they both lived in Shropshire. Certainly the couple were well-off; they mixed in society, and possessed at least two London houses. William was a member of the powerful Company of Drapers, the third in order of precedence of the great livery companies of the City of London. Our picture of William Watson is mainly a blank canvas, but Ibrahim Alhiyari has discovered a court record which enables us to touch in a small detail. The document is damaged and the date obscure, but it was probably in 1549, a few years before the birth of his son Thomas, that William filed a complaint against the mayor of Newcastle, Cuthbert Ellyson. Ellyson, evidently wanting to cut a dash at local civic functions, had ordered an expensive fleece coat from William, a top London clothier. But he failed to pay up. He probably thought he could get away with it—Newcastle was a northern provincial city far from London, and to arrange the transaction William had employed a business agent (one Edward Contworthe). Expensive is the word: at three hundred and fifteen pounds, the price of the coat was breath-taking. The incident exposes not only the magnitude of William Watson's wealth—only the prestigious could charge so much—but the level of society in which he and his family mixed.[8]

As for Anne Watson, an inheritance from her parents Thomas Lee and Elizabeth Rolleston (later Onley) left her a wealthy woman in her own right. She was William's third wife; at the time of their marriage he had a child by his first marriage and three children by his second. Anne, in turn, produced for William six children, four girls and two boys. The elder boy was also named William and the younger (by two years) was Thomas.

Thomas's aunts, his father's sister Elizabeth and sister-in-law Blanche (née Stanney),[9] were well-connected, too. Blanche married and quickly saw off three wealthy husbands in turn, finally to settle down with William Forman, a haberdasher, alderman and former mayor of London.[10]

Thomas Watson was four years old when his father died; just four months later, his mother Anne followed her husband. Left an orphan, Thomas and his elder brother William were packed off to live with their uncle Thomas Lee—their mother's brother—at Clattercote in Oxfordshire. Like the boys' father, Lee was a wealthy draper. His own mother, Elizabeth Onley, had been an immensely rich mover in the upper echelons of Tudor Society with connections to the Cecil family.[11] She married four times, twice to London aldermen.[12] By her second marriage, to Thomas Lee a merchant tailor of London, Elizabeth had given birth to two children Thomas and Anne, Thomas Watson's mother.[13] On their mother's death, Thomas and Anne Lee came into a considerable inheritance.[14] Thomas appears to have been well educated: his will is intelligent and articulate,[15] and he refers to "all my books". He was therefore the ideal guardian and mentor for his nephew, Thomas Watson.

There is nothing in the wills to suggest that either the Watson or Lee families had Catholic sympathies, but some circumstantial evidence is afforded by the warm presence of George Danvers' name in Anne Watson's will. His presence is also conspicuous in Thomas Lee's will where he appears as an executor—it was to Danvers that Thomas left all his books. Danvers may have been at Thomas's bedside on his death; he was certainly present at his sickbed, for when Thomas was too feeble to add two additional bequests to his will Danvers set them down for him. It is true that Danvers' brother John who died in 1569 benefited from the sale of church lands, but that proves little about his religious sympathies as not every Catholic was scrupulous in refraining from self enrichment at the expense of their church. However, it could be significant that in 1589 articles were brought against George Danvers' elder son John[16] and his wife and servant, for recusancy,[17] and by 1596 they had moved away from the family village of Calthorpe in Oxfordshire, to Leicestershire. There is a suggestion that the move was inspired by John's repugnance at the introduction of Puritan practices in the nearby town of Banbury.[18]

Another indication of a Catholic tendency in the Lee family may be suspected, too, by Thomas Lee's choice for his nephew's education. From 1567 Thomas Watson was sent away to Winchester College, rather than to, say, Eton which was also attached to a collegiate church. At Winchester Watson would have received one of the best educations then available in England, but the school was "Catholic haunted",[19] the last of the old established schools to buckle to the changes in religion. Just six years earlier, a riot had broken out when the then headmaster, Thomas Hyde, was imprisoned for resisting the introduction of Anglican practices. The boys took Hyde's side, refused to accept his replacement, the poet Christopher Johnson, and locked themselves in their dormitories. So serious was the situation that Johnson was forced to call in the militia from Portsmouth, and twelve of the pupils fled.

When Watson entered the school, Johnson was still headmaster. Despite appearances of the events of 1561, Johnson was by most accounts a gentle man, "witty and genial",[20] with a wide reputation as a brilliant inspirational educator.[21] He was deeply interested in physic—scientific matters in which Watson later exposed an interest—and became renowned as the best Latin verse writer of the period. He was especially respected for his Latin verse life of William of Wykeham, the fourteenth century founder of the college.[22] It surely must have been a result of Johnson's encouragement that his pupil Thomas Watson grew into the best Latin verse writer of *his* generation.

A nearly exact contemporary of Watson was Henry Garnet, who joined Winchester in the same year and at about the same age. Later, Garnet entered the Jesuit order, and was executed in 1606 for alleged complicity in the Gunpowder Plot.[23] During the boys' time at Winchester, the Warden was Thomas Stempe, a skilled musician in charge of the cathedral choristers. A later contemporary of Garnet, Fr Stanney, who served under him and, presumably, based his information on conversations with his fellow priest, described Johnson and Stempe as "Catholics at heart".[24] Doubtless, both Garnet and Watson were strongly influenced by Stempe. Garnet had a developed appreciation of music and a love for the sung liturgy; in later life he assisted William Byrd's son Thomas to the English College in Valladolid. Watson was to make his mark on the history of music through his collaboration with Byrd and his "Englished" Italian madrigals.

Winchester was regarded as a part of the University of Oxford, and its pupils usually proceeded to New College, though not as a matter of course.[25] Watson certainly moved on to Oxford, but there is no record that he received a degree there.[26] Writing from hearsay many years later, Anthony à Wood criticised Watson for occupying himself "not in logic and philosophy, as he ought to have done, but in the smooth and pleasant studies of poetry and romance, whereby he obtained an honourable name among the students of those faculties".[27] Some writers have suggested that Watson failed to complete his degree because he was eager to travel in Europe. Dana Sutton thinks Watson may have cut short his time in Oxford from fear of the plague. It was rife in Oxford in 1571, and the majority of the students fled to Reading. Perhaps, suggests Sutton, Watson's uncle Thomas Lee packed him off to safety on the continent. Although in fact the plague was also widespread in Europe, the opinion is plausible as Philip Sidney's family also took the same course.[28]

However, there is another possibility. For Catholics, two significant events took place in the winter of 1569 and early 1570. In December, the Northern Rising led by the Catholic earls of Northumberland and Westmorland was defeated; the following February, when news reached Rome, Pope Pius V published his bull *Regnans in Excelsis* excommunicating Elizabeth and absolving her subjects of their allegiance to her. It was a turning point: those who wrote, distributed or possessed Catholic works became traitors. The government swiftly counter-attacked. In October 1570, Robert Horne, the notorious reforming Bishop of Winchester visited Winchester College to promulgate a series of injunctions aimed at sweeping the school of everything Catholic; Johnson and Stempe retired immediately. At Oxford the commissioners for religion had been already hard at work summoning before them all "that smelt of Popery or were Popishly affected, suspending imprisoning or expelling them."[29] It is believed that, already, between 1559 and 1566 New College lost twenty-seven of its fellows and senior members, many of whom moved abroad.[30] Watson's fellow, Henry Garnet, did not enter Oxford because, as he wrote twenty years later, "No one could enter a university unless he was or pretended to be a heretic". In 1570, Henry's elder brother, Richard, was forced to give up his fellowship at Balliol. He later travelled abroad to study for the priesthood (although he afterwards changed his mind and returned to England and marriage).[31] It was around this period, the early 1570s, that Watson entered the University. It is not inconceivable that Watson's career followed a pattern similar to Richard Garnet's. Watson may have given up his degree because of his Catholic leanings.[32]

In the dedication to his *Antigone*, translated from the Greek to Latin, and published (together with a few poems of his own) in London in 1581, Watson claimed he spent seven-and-a-half years travelling on the continent. "I devoted my early years to study," he wrote, "and far from my native land I spent a *lustrum* and a half learning to utter words of diverse sound".[33] The word "lustrum" was coined from the Latin during Watson's time, and means five years. A lustrum and a half, therefore, is over seven years. Since Watson returned to London in 1577, it follows that he probably left Oxford in 1570—the year when reformers were busy in Winchester and Oxford. In 1570, he was aged about fifteen, not particularly young at that time for attendance at one of the two universities, or for a Catholic to travel abroad to the Catholic seminary.

In 1572 his uncle died. Ibrahim Alhiyari suggests[34] that from then on, when Watson was aged sixteen or seventeen, he was financially strong enough to indulge a taste for foreign adventure. Lee had no children, and in his will lavishly bestowed on his wife Mary entire estates, lands and possessions in towns and villages throughout the country, which after her decease were to descend to William and Thomas Watson, and a relative named Richard Lee of Wybunbury in Cheshire.[35] The bequests to William and Thomas included a useful cash sum of £165 each.[36] The bequests were under the control of Lee's widow Mary and three other executors (including George Danvers). These executors respected Lee's wishes and treated William and Thomas honourably.[37] Nevertheless, at that time Thomas and his elder brother William were minors, and could not properly inherit until they came of age.[38] So any financial support Thomas needed for travel after the death of his uncle could have been only with the consent of his executors. Unless …

There is a third, and I believe, convincing possibility. In the autumn of 1570 Francis Walsingham was appointed ambassador to France, a post he held for 28 months. Most of this time he spent in Paris as matchmaker in the marriage negotiations between Elizabeth and the Duke of Anjou, the French King's younger brother. At the same time, he was also deeply involved in a plan for an alliance of the English, French and the German protestant princes to support a revolt against Alva, Philip II's governor general in the Netherlands (a plan ruined by the St Bartholomew's Day Massacre of 1572).

The ambassador also worked hard at gathering information, most of it covert. Working closely with two Italians, Jacomo Manucci and Tomaso Franchiotto,[39] Walsingham was spinning the first shadowy threads in his web of informers, a thick sticky wily mesh which would in time exceed even those of Burghley and Leicester.[40] It has been asserted[41] that in 1572 he made a connection with Thomas Watson.[42] If this is so, then it may mean that after his uncle's death in 1572 Watson received cash from Walsingham, became a small thread in his intelligence network, and perhaps was employed as a messenger. The closer we examine Watson's movements, the more likely this seems, especially as he would also have required a government passport as a *bona fide* traveller to make his journeys to and about the continent.[43] As we will see later, there is little doubt that when he briefly returned to Paris some years later, in 1581, and again contacted Walsingham, he showed him some of his poems[44] and agreed to carry messages. By this time the government's fear of sedition at home and invasion from abroad had intensified to an almost paranoid degree. Into this context of Watson's relationship with Walsingham must also be placed his close friendship with Walsingham's first cousin Thomas, and, later, his notable eulogy on the death of Francis in 1590.[45]

In 1573, Walsingham returned to England, was appointed Principal Secretary, and became a member of the Privy Council. He quickly rose to become Senior Secretary. His notoriety in history is as chief spy master, in charge of foreign affairs, and subordinate only to Burghley and Leicester in the management of Elizabeth's government. In time his plump cobweb of paid spies burgeoned to fifty-three—fifty-three *known* agents, that is. Since much of his work was off the record, there were probably more. He received almost daily reports from Italy, Spain, France, Germany, the Low Countries (and, later, the United Provinces), Turkey—and England. And when the state jibbed at the cost, he dedicated his own considerable wealth to sustaining the structure, eventually bankrupting himself. Even Catholics acted as government spies—the composer Thomas Morley, for example, or perhaps Charles Paget son of William Paget the noted Tudor statesman.[46]

In summary, a plausible suggestion of Watson's funding and motivation for his foreign travels is as follows. In 1570 Watson left Winchester for Oxford, but because of the Catholic persecution there did not stay to obtain a degree, and instead travelled to Europe subsidised by his uncle Thomas Lee. In 1572 Lee died, and Watson's income dried up: as a minor he could not inherit for some four or five years, or until the decease of his aunt Mary Lee (now Corbet). He came into contact with Walsingham, ambassador in Paris, who henceforth subsidised him in return for either carrying letters or perhaps for information about his "fellow" Catholics.

It is entirely possible, also, that at this time Walsingham—who had himself studied at Padua with much distinction—may have provided Watson with a reference to the university. Is it possible, also, that it was on this occasion that Watson first met Philip Sidney? Sidney was in Paris during the summer of 1592, and took refuge in Walsingham's house from the St Bartholomew Day's Massacre during the weekend of the 24th August.

After Walsingham's death in April 1590, Watson published his *Meliboeus Thomae Watsoni, sive Ecloga* ...[47] in honour of Sir Francis, and dedicated to Sir Francis' cousin Thomas. Later that year Watson dedicated an Englished version[48] to Lady Frances Sidney, Philip's widow, and Walsingham's daughter.

Watson's stay of a "lustrum and a half" abroad was a long time. In the fulsome dedication to Philip Howard, Earl of Arundel and Surrey that fronts his *Antigone*, he says that during his stay abroad,

> … I was taking careful note of the tongues and manners of Italy, and of your language and manners, learned France. So far as I was able, I paid worship to the Muses, wherever I went. Justinian, too, was especially dear. But Mars often broke in upon reluctant Pallas, wars were very often obstacles to my study.[49]

Thomas refers to Italy first and France second, therefore it is plausible to deduce that after crossing the Channel he headed first to Italy. He may have studied at one of the Italian universities: in every one of the several Latin works he published on his return to England he described himself as "Thomas Watson *I V studiosus*" — "student in either law (*Iuris Vtriusque*)". The expression "either law", as Eccles makes clear,[50] refers to canon and civil law, not the common law of England. In Watson's day, the most famous schools were Padua and Bologna, although he could have studied at Siena, Ferrara, Pavia, Turin, or Perugia. Most likely, however, it was at the celebrated Padua that Watson furthered his education. The University had been under the rule of wealthy Venice since 1405[51] and popular with foreigners — not only Europeans, but Hebrews, Persians and Arabs as well.[52] As Lucentio declaims in *The Taming of the Shrew*:

> "…since for the great desire I had
> To see fair Padua, nursery of the arts…"[53]

Registration there was optional, and — except for the very rich — tuition was free. Polydore Vergil, who had written the first history of England some forty years earlier, had been educated there, and at Bologna too. More recently, Sir Thomas Smith had trained at Padua during a European tour in 1542,[54] and Sir Francis Walsingham was another alumnus. Walsingham had excelled so well in the law school that in December 1555, at the age of 23, he was elected to the office of Consularius of the English Nation, a role which involved representing the interests of his fellow Englishmen in return for ensuring their good behaviour.[55] In Watson's day, Philip Sidney studied at Padua between 1573 and 1574, and Watson may have met him there, a possibility because of Philip's family relationship with Walsingham. At Padua, too, Watson would have had a good opportunity to become acquainted with Edward de Vere, the Earl of Oxford, with whom he had family connections through his aunt Mary Lee's second marriage into the Corbet family.[56] Oxford left for the continent in February 1575, travelled to Paris, Strasbourg, and probably Milan, and arrived at Venice in May. After May we lose contact with him for a few months, but he was certainly in Venice in October. In November he wrote to Burghley from Padua. He set off again in December, but made a final stopover in Venice for a week or two in late February and early March 1576 before returning to Paris on 21 March. In mid-April he returned to England. Keeping in mind Watson's later association with Oxford, is it unreasonable to suggest that, besides Sidney, he may also have encountered de Vere during the Earl's months in Padua and Venice?

Watson probably visited other cities in Italy, too. If our guess that he was centred on Padua is correct[57] he would more than once have made the twenty-five mile trip to Venice. He may, too, have made the seven-hour journey to Venice by *traghetto*, the horse-drawn ferry along the river Brenta, past the beautiful and luxurious mansions of the Venetian rich, reputedly the most scenic river journey in all Northern Italy.[58]

We do know for certain that by 1576 Watson had left Italy and headed north. His departure may have been prompted by a serious outbreak of the plague in the Venice area (which lasted until 1577).[59] He arrived at the English College at Douai in Flanders. When he arrived, and for how long he stayed, is uncertain, but the date of his departure for Paris is recorded in the college diary: 15 October 1576.[60] The college had been founded as recently as 1569, the first of the University of Douai—itself only eight years old. It was the inspiration of William Allen, later Regius Professor of Divinity at Douai and later still a cardinal, with the aim of enabling English Catholic exiles to continue their studies—a University of Oxford in exile,[61] and particularly remembered for its role as a seminary for the training of English priests. The University had five faculties, of which canon and civil law ranked high—Watson's subjects. By May 1576, the year of Watson's arrival, the college had eighty students; by September the number had risen to 120.[62] Watson continued his studies there, attending the lectures of Richard White, the regius professor of civil and canon law, and known at the college by the Latin name of Vitus. Watson and White had something else in common. Sixteen years Watson's senior, White was also a former pupil of Winchester School. He had gone on to New College, Oxford, and moved to Louvain in 1560 where he delivered two orations *De Circulo Artium et Philosophiae* and *De Eloquentia et Cicerone*, subsequently published in London with an introduction by Christopher Johnson, the headmaster at Winchester in Watson's day, and Watson's assumed mentor. White went on to distinguish himself at the University of Padua before becoming professor at Douai in 1572.[63] So, to spell this out, Watson, the acclaimed Latin verse writer of his period, was educated by the most renowned writer of Latin verse in England before him, Christopher Johnson. Johnson was evidently on familiar terms with White, a leading authority on civil and canon law at the University of Padua. Watson travelled to Europe, to Italy, and himself became a student of civil and canon law—at Padua? Certainly, the presumption that Watson became a student there—perhaps recommended by Johnson?—is strong. Did White's move to Douai encourage Watson to take up studies there too?

The record of Watson's 150 mile trip from Douai to Paris in 1576 is noted as follows: "*15 die D Watsonus Parisios hinc abiit*" ("on the fifteenth day D Watson went from here to Paris"). The letter "D" is short for "dominus", the holder of a Bachelor's degree, showing that by this time Watson had already received a degree—probably from an Italian university, Padua we guess. He may have left for Paris simply to hear a course of lectures,[64] but the date of the diary entry, 15 October 1576, is interesting. Since the surmised meeting between Watson and Walsingham in Paris in 1572, there had been changes. In April 1573, Walsingham had been replaced as resident ambassador by the hard working, conscientious, lawyer Valentine Dale. Three years passed. Then a close and trusted friend of Walsingham took the post. Sir Amias Paulet was commissioned on 26 August 1576, and arrived in Paris on 3 October (with the fifteen-year-old Francis Bacon in his entourage).[65] Could it be that Watson's need to visit Paris on the 15 October, less than a fortnight later, was to confirm, secure and update his undercover commission with the new incumbent, securing with Paulet the brief already established with Walsingham and maintained by Dale?

Having arrived in the city, Watson may have stayed on. Eccles believed that, if Watson were a serious student, he would have wanted to study under the renowned Jacques de Cujas, a teacher with such a high reputation that at his name German scholars doffed their hats.[66] Cujas had been forced into Paris by the religious wars, and from November 1575 held classes at the University there. In early 1577 he departed for Bourges, where he remained until his death.[67]

In May of 1577, Watson also left Paris and returned to Douai. The registers for the month record that *"15 die Mr Tho. Watsonus e Parisiis huc revertitur et post aliquot dies ad nostra communia est admissus"*[68] ("On the 15th Mr Tho. Watson returns from Paris to here, and, after some days, has been admitted to our community") — whether from the October 1576 visit, or a later one, we cannot be certain. The October 1576 date seems probable, however, for in November unpaid Spanish troops mutinied and sacked the city of Antwerp. During three days of horror described as the "Spanish fury", eight thousand people are said to have lost their lives and a third of the city burnt down. The Pacification of Ghent, which followed hastily just days later, united all seventeen provinces, including the Roman Catholics, under the protestant Prince William of Orange against the Spanish army. The Spaniards withdrew from Flanders. Throughout 1577 the Calvinist guilds, adherents of the Prince of Orange, rioted in Brussels, Antwerp, Ghent, and many smaller towns including Douai. It was all very frightening. By the time Watson returned from Paris, enrolment at the college had dropped from some two hundred to forty-two. Then, in July, Don John of Austria with a company of Spanish troops seized Namur and William's troops arrived at Douai. The diary records that "around this time Mr Burn, Watson, Harley, and others studying law, left our community." (*"Circa hoc tempus exeirunt e communibus nostris Mr Burnus,*

Watsonus, Harleus, et alii juris studiosi").[69] On 6 August, a local rioter at the gates demanded, "Were not all the Englishmen's throats cut last night?"[70] so it is hardly surprising to learn that, "on the 7th, at the time of great disturbances, Mr Watson, Mr Robinson, Mr Griffith and some others, left for England."("*Die 7 occasione turbarum ingruentium discesserunt in Angliam Mr Watsonus, Mr Robinsonus, Mr Griffettus at alii nonnulli.*")[71] "Often my studies were obstructed by wars", Watson later reflected. "Still I fled from camps, save those of Phoebus".[72]

By March the following year, Allen himself felt so threatened by Flemish anti-Spanish and anti-English feeling that he uprooted his students and found temporary refuge on the Rue de Venise in Rheims, a town under the protection of the Duke of Guise.[73]

Three:
"A very learned man"

BACK in England, Watson headed for Westminster. By 1579, he was lodged in "a house of one Waller" where he "did now and then lie with one Mr Beale, a preacher, & his acquaintance in Oxford before".[1] William Beale had left the University in 1572. It is interesting to speculate whether he was related to Robert Beale, Sir Francis Walsingham's aide and brother in law (by marriage to Edith St Barbe, the sister of Walsingham's wife). Another of Robert Beale's friends was Sir Thomas Smith, who had been Edward de Vere's childhood tutor. But Beale is a fairly common name, and little is known of either William or Robert Beale's parentage and family—except that Robert was the first son of Robert Beale, a mercer of London, who with his wife Amy[2] had moved from East Anglia (Woodbridge in Suffolk), like so many others of his generation to seek economic improvement in London.

Before setting forth for the continent again, Watson remained in London for some three or four years, during which time he probably associated with colleagues at the Inns of Court. Sutton thinks it likely,[3] and indeed it was quite usual for the Inns to nurture writers, who found them a useful cover and outlet for their literary pursuits. Several members wrote laudatory poems for Watson's early books, although he himself was probably not enrolled since his own legal training was of a different order.

It was during this time that Watson became involved in the case of Anne Burnell.[4] Burnell, a butcher's daughter from East Cheap, worked herself into a pitch of excitement when a Nottinghamshire witch assured her that marks on her body proved she was a child of King Philip of Spain.[5] Her delusion was dangerous—it could suggest she was a daughter of Queen Mary and a claimant to the throne. It took another seven years, however, until 8 August 1587, until she was called before before the Privy Council. Although Mrs Burnell did not betray Watson's identity (she had sworn on oath not to), another deponent, an Elizabeth Bradshaw, identified him as "one Watson, a very learned man late of St Helen's,[6] that could tell strange things" (a reputation to which we will return later). Anne Burnell declared that, since she and her husband Edward occasionally lodged in the same house as Watson and Beale, she had asked Watson as "a gentleman that was said to be very well learned" whether the witch's assertion were true. Watson had played along with the poor woman's delusions, but when he was called in front of the investigators four days later, quickly denied anything incriminating. Ann refused to give up her claim, and in 1592 (two months after Watson's registered death) was tied to a cart and whipped through the streets of the City of London.

In *The Reckoning* Charles Nicholl describes Watson's involvement in the affair as mischievous fun play, "a story of an unscrupulous young man and an unfortunate old woman".[7] Yet, as Nicholl hesitantly hints earlier,[8] it is possible that Watson had a governmental brief to watch Edward Burnell, her husband, a Catholic subversive who had already served time in the Tower. Anne Burnell declared that Watson had told her, "the best Spaniard that ever came in England" — that is, Philip II — "was your father" and that she had marks about her body "that shall appear greater hereafter". When we come to investigate the unsavoury lives of some of Watson's contemporaries, we shall see that it is likely that, rather than indulging in "mischief", he was acting the role of an *agent provocateur*.

The case holds more than passing interest because it sheds a light on Watson's links with both current politics, and also with his literary peers. Anne was examined by James Dalton, at that time "one of the Counsellors of the City",[9] to whom she spoke of "the late trouble of her husband and herself". Eccles thought this "late trouble" and the cause of Anne's "greatly decayed" wits was brought on because her husband was the "Mr Burnell" imprisoned in the Tower as a result of his association with the Babington Plot in September 1586.[10] It is a strong possibility. Edward Burnell was the second son of William Burnell of Winkburn in Nottinghamshire, and had been brought to the Tower some seven years earlier because of his Catholic faith. Moreover, the Burnells were not an insignificant family. Edward's sister Jane was a favourite of the Royal Bedchamber who by her marriage to Robert Markham became related to Anthony Babington—Robert's mother Catherine was Babington's daughter.[11]

Watson's connection with Burnell also exposes his relationship with two fellow writers. Edward Burnell was the stepbrother of the poet and noted translator, Barnabe Googe. The connection is rather complicated. Burnell's own mother, Constance Blundeville, had died in 1562 and the following year his father William had made a second marriage to Ellen Gadbury, the daughter of a London goldsmith. She had been the second wife, and widow, of Robert Goche or Googe,[12] the recorder of Lincoln. She was therefore the stepmother, by separate husbands, of both Edward Burnell and Barnabe Googe.[13] Googe's birth mother, Margaret Mantell, had died soon after his birth, and he was twelve years old at the time of his father's marriage to Ellen. His father died five years later, in 1557. No love was lost between Ellen and her stepson, who came to hate her, referring to her as his "lewd mother-in-law".[14] As late as 1563, when Googe was twenty-three and well past his majority, most of his revenue was still controlled by his stepmother. Even after her death in 1584 there was a painful hiatus before he came fully into his Lincolnshire inheritance.

In 1555, at the age fifteen, Googe matriculated at Christ's College Cambridge, and it is possible that he also had attended the Catholic New College in Oxford—more than a decade before Watson. On his father's death, Googe inherited considerable property in Lincolnshire as well as his grandfather's house in London, and he became a royal ward under the protection of the Master of the Wards, his kinsman Sir William Cecil.[15] In 1559, or 1560, around the age of twenty, Googe became a member of the Staple Inn and the following year he purchased his own wardship and —doubtless through Cecil's influence—travelled to France and Spain in the company of Sir Thomas Challoner, at that time taking up an ambassadorship there. He returned after some eighteen months, and became engaged to Mary Darrell from Scotney on the Kent-Sussex border. The betrothal had Mary's father, Thomas, hopping with rage—with good cause. Darrell had wished to marry off his daughter to the son of a wealthy neighbour, Sampson Lennard. Worse, Darrell was the head of the senior branch of a Catholic family, passionate about his faith, a recusant, whereas Googe—despite his Catholic connections—was a fervent, and vocal, protestant. This cannot be overstated: Darrell's dwelling was not a simple manor; it was a Norman moated manor, almost a castle, conveniently close to the port of Dover, the gateway to England. For many a travelling priest or co-religionist Scotney was a safe refuge from the prying eyes of government spies.[16] As for Googe, he got his way and married Mary Darrell in 1564 despite all her father's attempts to prevent it: pressure from Cecil and Archbishop Parker saw to that. So, the outspoken anti-Catholic married into a Catholic household: evidence that, away from politics, relationships were not necessarily blighted by religious disagreement. Neither does it seem to have taken long for the Googes and the Darrells to establish fairly affable family bonds. In 1566 Googe sold some land in Lincolnshire to Mary's brother George,[17] and later—always a lover of Kent—he moved his family of eight or nine children to Lamberhurst, close by Scotney. The Darrell family must have found him an irritant, though. In 1569, in his dedication to a work written under the pseudonym of Bernard Garter,[18] Googe attempted to convince his Catholic sister-in-laws, Philippa and Frances, of the value of protestant reformist ideas. One wonders how his wife Mary felt about all this: local legend has it that their marriage was a real love match. The legend is probably true: at various times in 1574 and between 1582 and 1585 Barnabe lived and worked in Ireland away from his family; a letter written to Walsingham during the later period shows him fretting over his wife and children's well-being.[19]

It would be incredible if, by the late 1570s, Barnabe Googe and Thomas Watson were not acquainted. There were conspicuous connections. Watson and Googe's stepbrother, Edward Burnell, occasionally shared the same house in St Helen's. Googe and Watson both (it is suspected) haunted the Inns of Court. Moreover, Googe as a former ward and a member of the Cecil circle was no doubt well acquainted with Cecil's son-in-law the Earl of Oxford, another former ward, whose secretary Watson later became. By the time of his meeting with Watson, Googe had a reputation both as a writer and a zealous reforming protestant. His first printed work in 1559 had been a dedicatory poem condemning the "haughty whore" of Rome,[20] and it was soon followed by a major work, an English translation from the Latin of the first three books of Marcellus Palingenius Stellatus's *Zodiacus vitae*.[21] This mighty work had been published in Venice in the early 1530s in twelve volumes, each named after a sign of the zodiac. The Church so disapproved, that in 1549 the authorities exhumed Palingenius' body and burned it. Ten years later his work was placed on the very first edition of the *Index Librorum Prohibitorum*, the Catholic list of banned books. Googe's partial translation did him no harm, therefore, among English protestant reformers. *The Zodiake of Life*, dedicated to Cecil, was first published between 1560 and 1565 and Googe reworked it again and again during his lifetime.[22] His only collection of poems, *Eclogues, Epitaphs, and Sonnets* (1563), written in the Plain or Native Style—clumsy and plodding in comparison with the later Petrarchian manner of the Sidney and Oxford coteries after their experiments with the sonnet form—was also tinctured by his religious views. By the time he met Watson in the late 1570s he had added two anti-Catholic miscellanies, *The Popish Kingdom, or the Reign of Anti-Christ* (1570) and *A New Year's Gift* (1579). He also translated other works, including studies of farming and medicinal herbs, but his *The Zodyake of Life* (which achieved five editions) was the most popular and influential. Adopted as a textbook for use in the grammar schools, its themes and images were absorbed by many writers of the period, and may have influenced Shakespeare. Certainly, a marginal comment in the 1576 edition, "The world a stage play", is a startling pre-echo of the famous line from Act II of *As You Like It*.

Poor deluded Anne Burnell's whipping through the streets of London took place on 13 December 1592. Five days later a ballad about the affair came hot off the press to sell in those same streets.[23] Its publisher, Edward White, was a bookseller active for thirty-five years between 1577 until 1612 under the Sign of the Gun at the "little north door" in St Paul's Churchyard.[24] Although he was principally a printer of ballads—famous for an edition of *Greensleeves* he brought out in 1580—from time to time

White diversified from this lucrative sphere. By 1584 he had acquired the rights to *The Paradise of Dainty Devices*, a poetry collection published first in 1576, and containing some works by the Earl of Oxford. In 1592 and 1594 he sold early editions of *The Spanish Tragedy,* later attributed to Thomas Kyd,[25] and in 1594 he sold, in co-operation with Thomas Millington, another revenge tragedy: the First Quarto of Shakespeare's *Titus Andronicus*.[26] In 1594, too, his name is substituted for a fellow bookseller's in the register of an anonymous play *The moste famous Chronicle Historye of LEIRE king of England and his Three Daughters*. This play was not then published, however, and was registered again in 1605 and printed (under a slightly different title) for a former apprentice of White's; it is thought by some to be the basis of Shakespeare's work.[27] Edward White was married to Sara Lodge, the half-sister of the dramatist Thomas Lodge.

The careers of Thomas Lodge and Thomas Watson interweave. Like Watson's parents, Lodge's father and his father's first wife, originated in Shropshire. As a lad, Thomas senior, Sir Thomas, had moved to London, been apprenticed to a butcher, and succeeded so well as to become master of the Grocers' Company and Lord Mayor of London—though not well enough to avoid bankruptcy in the second and final year of his mayoralty. That was in 1563, when Thomas junior was five years old, the third of the seven surviving children born by Sir Thomas's third wife, Anne. Although Sir Thomas managed to rescue much of his property from the scandal, his sons were plagued by lawsuits for the rest of their lives. As a child Thomas spent time in the Roman Catholic household of Henry Stanley the fourth Earl of Derby.[28] Then, after studying and matriculating under the enlightened discipline of Richard Mulcaster at Merchant Taylors' School and receiving his BA at Trinity College Oxford in 1577, he entered Lincoln's Inn. The year was 1578. He did not practice law, despite a stipulation in his mother's will of 1579 that if he failed as a student his portion was to be divided among his brothers. He stayed there for some years, socialising with the playwrights and writers, who certainly included Thomas Watson—for Watson's sister Maudlin was brought up with Lodge's family.

It came about like this. Maudlin's mother, the wealthy Anne Watson, gave birth to four girls and two boys. In her will she entrusted the upbringing of her two eldest daughters, Elizabeth and Maudlin, to the wealthiest families of London. Elizabeth was placed with Lady Joan Laxton (née Kirkeby, widow of Henry Luddington), the fabulously rich widow of Sir William Laxton, merchant and former Lord Mayor of London. Maudlin, the second daughter, was placed with Lady Anne Lodge—daughter of Lady Laxton by her first husband Henry Luddington, step-daughter of Sir William Laxton, widow of the grocer William Lane, and (of course) wife of Sir Thomas Lodge and mother of Thomas Lodge.[29]

To summarise. Tom Watson's parents were born in Shropshire, as were Tom Lodge's father and his first wife, Lady Laxton: a connection between the Lodges and Watsons (as well as the Luddingtons) may have been forged there. In London the relationship is clear: Thomas Watson stayed in the house of Anne Burnell and became deeply involved in her case. A ballad about Burnell was published by Edward White the husband of Sara Lodge, sister of Thomas Lodge. The Lodge family brought up Maudlin, a sister of Thomas Watson.

Thomas Lodge's first printed work, *An Epitaph to Lady Anne Lodge*, was put to press by his brother-in-law, Edward White (who more convenient?) in 1579, apparently a week before his mother's actual death.[30] Lodge's next published work was refused a license but privately circulated, also in 1579. Only two copies survive, badly printed, and both lacking the title page. Scholars have suggested several titles; *A Defence of Poetry* is the simplest.[31] It was a polemical answer to Stephen Gosson's recently published *School of Abuse containing a pleasant invective against Poets, Pipers, Players, Jesters and such like Caterpillars of the Commonwealth*, a work whose very title spits out its character. Like Lyly before him and Marlowe later, Gosson was a native of Canterbury educated at Cambridge on a scholarship from a fund set up by Archbishop Matthew Parker to aid the most deserving boys from King's School. Unlike those writers, however, he nursed a grudge; having lacked the financial resources to finish his degree, he later griped that he was "pulled from University before I was ripe".[32] Gosson dedicated his work to Philip Sidney, who was less than grateful for the "honour", and who explicitly refuted Gosson's views in his *The Defence of Poesy*. To take his revenge, Gosson found in Lodge an easier target than Sidney, and a series of exchanges between the two followed.

By 1580 a list of recusants living in Paris includes the names "Lodge" and "Loddington". Since Thomas Lodge later abandoned all discretion and became openly Catholic, historians believe that these recusants were Thomas, and perhaps a Luddington cousin from his mother's side.[33] It is certainly possible that Lodge and Watson met up in Paris, because in the early 1580s Watson was in Paris, too. But Lodge, a principled man, later declared himself no friend to any "counterfeit Catholic".[34] Probably, he had no dealings with Walsingham,[35] and perhaps by now he considered Watson a "counterfeit Catholic". Watson was sojourning in the city with his new friend Thomas Walsingham, younger by three years and a second cousin of Sir Francis Walsingham.[36]

Watson briefly recalls this period of his life in his elegy *Meliboeus*, published in 1590 to mark the death of Sir Francis. The poem takes the form of a dialogue between himself (Corydon) and Thomas Walsingham (Tityrus), his "sweet friend" but, significantly, also Sir Francis's cousin. The fancy is derived from the Roman poet Titus Calpurnius, in whose poem *De Laude Pisonis* Tityrus represents Virgil and Calpurnius himself is Corydon. Calpurnius's real-life patron was Meliboeus, the name appropriately given for Sir Francis Walsingham in Watson's poem. At one stage Watson-Corydon prompts Walsingham-Tityrus to recall their time in Paris when

> Thy tunes have often pleas'd mine ear of yore,
> When milk-white swans did flock to hear thee sing,
> Where Seine in Paris makes a double shore,
> Paris thrice blest if she obey her King.[37]

Tityrus may be referring here to Corydon's poetry, but more likely he praises Watson's pleasant singing voice—since Watson himself wrote these verses, the honour lacks something of modesty. It is a reminder of Watson's musical education at Winchester and his later invaluable contribution to the development of the English madrigal.

Thomas Walsingham at this time, 1580, was a messenger on government service, scurrying to and fro across the Channel.[38] When, in late July 1581, his uncle Sir Francis returned to Paris to negotiate yet again the possibility of marriage between Elizabeth and the Duke of Anjou—a decade after his first impossible effort—Thomas was in the entourage. His friend Watson accompanied him. In Burghley's diary and correspondence, there are references to the arrival at the Queen's court back in England of three separate messengers carrying dispatches, one of whom was Thomas Walsingham, and another a "Mr Watson", who arrived on 13 August "bearing letters from Mr Sec. dated 10 August"—this messenger was almost certainly Thomas Watson.[39]

Also, Charles Nicholl draws attention to an anonymous work called *Ulysses upon Ajax*, written in 1596, in which the author recalls "witty Tom Watson's jests" which he "heard in Paris fourteen years ago",[40] in other words 1582. At this time, therefore, the evidence is sufficient for us to be certain that Watson was in Paris in the early 1580s, at the same time as Thomas Walsingham, and in the pay of Sir Francis Walsingham.

Nevertheless, the exact dates of Watson's visits to Paris in 1581 and 1582 are a trifle vague. We believe he was in Paris in 1581 because of the message carried to the court by "Mr Watson" in August that year. However, since Watson undertook some literary enterprises in 1581 it is possible that he remained in London until these were seen to. Then, if the calculation from *Ulysses upon Ajax* is correct, in 1582 he was back in Paris again. When Watson reclined with Thomas Walsingham on the banks of the Seine where the "milk-white swans did flock to hear" him sing, was it the glorious summer of 1581, or was it the glorious summer of 1582?

It is worthwhile pausing here, to consider the wider historical context. It was in December 1580 that the Pope made his announcement, disastrous for Roman Catholics, that God would reward the assassinator of Elizabeth, "that guilty woman who is the cause of so much intriguing to the Catholic faith and loss of so many million souls". The following January, the government ordered the return "of the Queen's Majesty's subjects remaining beyond the seas under the colour of study, and living contrary to the laws of God and the Realm". Therefore, any person studying abroad was in a dangerous position—unless he was in the government's employ, whether openly or secretly.

In the Paris of 1581 Watson and Thomas Walsingham may (or may not) have met up with Sir Francis's secretary Nicholas Faunt. The three were certainly acquainted. Faunt was yet another fortunate from Canterbury educated at Cambridge on an Archbishop Matthew Parker scholarship. He graduated in 1576 aged twenty-two, and within two years was thoroughly enmeshed in Walsingham's web. So much so, that later he took a leading role in the supervision of the English agents. A dedicated Puritan, Faunt was a personal friend of Anthony Bacon, though Anthony's younger brother Francis found him a bore. If he met Watson and Walsingham in Paris in 1581, the meeting would have been brief, for in that year Faunt travelled widely: Germany, Padua, Venice, Pisa and — finally — Geneva. By March the following year Francis Walsingham commanded him to return to London. It is Faunt who is reputed to have helped recruit to the secret service a friend of both Thomas Walsingham and Watson.[41] His name was Christopher Marlowe.[42]

Nevertheless, that Watson, Walsingham and Marlowe were well-acquainted during the 1580s is indisputable. So the question arises: how *was* Marlowe drawn into friendship with Walsingham and Watson? Was Nicholas Faunt, returned to England after February 1582, involved, as some writers have suggested?[43] Or perhaps Marlowe, having made his way from Cambridge to London, became acquainted with Tom Walsingham as they browsed the booksellers in St Paul's Churchyard, as Honey and other writers have fantasised.[44] If one is allowed to indulge in this imaginative game it is more likely that the link was Watson. In 1581 and 1582, quite apart from to-ing and fro-ing between Paris and London, Watson was seeing several of his works through the press, and therefore was also busy about St Paul's Churchyard.

By however way Christopher Marlowe and Thomas Watson met, almost inevitably they would have been drawn together by their common interests. Both were steeped in the classics, both loved music, both had good voices and loved singing. Marlowe was eight or nine years younger than Watson. He was born in 1564 in Canterbury, the son of John Marlowe, a relatively hard-up shoemaker, and his wife Katherine. He was the sole surviving boy of nine offspring with four younger sisters, although another son was born twelve years later. His early education is poorly documented, probably he went to a grammar school; but by 1578 he was granted a scholarship to the King's School (then, of course, called the Queen's School) in Canterbury. Under its headmaster, John Gresshop, the classics were rigidly imposed: at no time, whether at lessons or play, did a pupil speak any language other than Latin or Greek. "Marlowe," wrote Park Honan in his biography,

> came under the spell of the classics. And that changed him. It is hard to grasp the depth, shock, or the initial, naive thrill and sensuousness of *this* change, though to a degree similar effects were felt by other Elizabethan schoolboys. Marlowe was dazzled by the classics. Nothing in his imaginative life was to be the same again, and it may be that no discovery he made, and no love he ever felt, affected his mind and feelings so terribly, so unsettlingly, as the writers of ancient Rome.[45]

One could say the same of Watson.

From King's School Marlowe proceeded on an Archbishop Parker scholarship to Corpus Christi College, Cambridge, and received his BA degree in 1584. His MA degree was awarded in 1587 after some hesitation because of a rumour that he perhaps intended to prepare for ordination as a Roman Catholic priest at the English college at Rheims. The degree was awarded following the written intervention by Burghley and the Privy Council commending him for his "faithful dealing" and "good service" to the Queen. Most writers think this means he had been working for Burghley as a spy. A few years later, in 1592, Marlowe was arrested in the English garrison town of Flushing in the Netherlands for his alleged involvement with the very serious crime of counterfeiting. No charge or imprisonment resulted, and espionage is again suspected.[46] In the meantime, Marlowe's first play, *Dido, Queen of Carthage* (published 1594), was performed between 1587 and 1593 by the Children of the Chapel, among the first English plays in blank verse. His first play performed on the popular stage in London, in 1587, was *Tamburlaine the Great*. Success met every one of his dramas, all written and performed in the late 1580s and early 1590s, but their order is unknown. Their modern titles: *The Jew of Malta*, *Edward the Second*, *The Massacre at Paris* and *Doctor Faustus*. Marlowe also wrote poetry: *Hero and Leander* (c1598), the lyric *The Passionate Shepherd to His Love* (pre-1593), and translations of Ovid's *Amores* (c1580s) and the first book of Lucan's *Pharsalia* (date unknown). In 1599, his translation of Ovid was banned as offensive and copies publicly burned.

Park Honan calls Marlowe "Poet and Spy":[47] his life is shady and his death the subject of a confusion of well-known theories. In late April and early May 1593, with the plague raging in London, the government went on a heresy hunt: seditious libels attacking French and Dutch protestant refugees had been posted in the City. One of these, a placard on the wall of the Dutch churchyard in Broad Street, had allusions in bad iambic pentameter to Marlowe's plays *The Jew of Malta* and *The Massacre at Paris*, and was signed, "Tamburlaine". The Queen was not pleased, and the Privy Council set about searching out the perpetrators. On Saturday 12 May, they examined Marlowe's room-mate Thomas Kyd, and found a few atheistic papers—in fact, extracts from an old theological book shelved in Gresshop's library at King's School. Kyd claimed the sheets had accidentally had been shuffled with his own and belonged to Marlowe. He was taken away and worked over by the sadistic chief interrogator and torturer Richard Topcliffe, after which treatment he described Marlowe as blasphemous, disorderly, holding treasonous opinions, being an irreligious reprobate, and "intemperate and of a cruel heart". The matter was no longer one of the Dutch Church libel, but one of atheism. Through its ongoing undercover investigations the Council was already running scared at the possibility of dangerous links between Roman Catholics and a small gang of atheists led by one Richard, a government spy who the Council feared was intent on assassinating the Queen. In some anonymous writings against Cholmeley, "Remembrances of wordes & matters against Ric: Cholmeley",[48] Marlowe was given a small but specific mention as "able to show more sound reasons for atheism than any divine in England is able to prove divinity". [49]

The evidence of the allusions in the Dutch libel, the "Remembrances", and the papers found in the lodgings Marlowe shared with Kyd, proved an overwhelming combination, and on Friday 18 May a Queen's Messenger was ordered to bring Marlowe—then staying with his friend Thomas Walsingham at Scadbury in Kent—before the Privy Council, who commanded him to make daily attendance on their lordships. Interestingly, Kyd was tortured for holding a few atheistic papers he claimed were not his; Marlowe escaped a similar fate. Perhaps Burghley had intervened. We recall his instruction to the Cambridge authorities to award Marlowe his MA degree; also in CHAPTER SEVEN we shall see that in an incident involving both Watson and Marlowe, Marlowe got off relatively lightly with a mere two weeks in gaol, while poor Tom Watson had to linger on for another six months. It looks as though someone, probably Burghley, was protecting Marlowe.

Twelve days after his presentation before the Privy Council, on Wednesday 30 May, Christopher Marlowe was at the Deptford house of a bailiff's widow named Eleanor Bull. Bull had connections: both she and Lord Burghley were legatees under the will of Blanche Parry the Chief Gentlewoman of the Privy Chamber—once again Burghley's name insinuates itself. Moreover, the widow's property was "within the verge", that is, less than a mile from the court at Greenwich, which meant it fell under the jurisdiction of the Lord High Steward, rather than the local Justice of the Peace. At Deptford, Marlowe had a meeting with three unsavoury characters, Ingram Frizer, Nicholas Skeres and Robert Poley. At this time, Frizer and Skeres were scheming with Thomas Walsingham to swindle a young gentleman named Drew Woodleff out of his inheritance.[50] Poley earns several paragraphs for himself in our next chapter: spy, liar, lecher, murderer—and another employee of Sir Thomas Walsingham. What happened next is brought to light in the report of William Danby, the Coroner of the Queen's Household, discovered in the Public Record Office as comparatively recently as 1925 by Dr Leslie Hotson.[51] According to Danby, the men met about ten o'clock in the morning in a small upper room in the house, which faced the Green beside the royal shipyard. They "dined, walked in the garden of the house until about six in the afternoon, then returned to the room and supped." After supper Marlowe lay down on a bed in the room, while Frizer, Skeres and Poley remained seated on a bench at the table with their backs to the poet. A quarrel arose concerning the payment of the bill, "le recknynge". Then, wrote Danby, Marlowe seized Frizer's dagger and wounded him twice in the head. A struggle ensued and "in defence of his life" Frizer stabbed Marlowe above the right eye. He was killed instantly. The jury of twelve local men concluded that Frizer acted in self-defence, and within a month he was granted a full pardon. Marlowe was reportedly buried in an unmarked grave in the churchyard of St. Nicholas, Deptford, a few hundred yards away.

Since Hotson's publication of the coroner's report, the theories and arguments about Marlowe's death have been endless. Was the coroner's report true, or a cover-up? Was he murdered? If so, at whose instigation? Why? Or was the body somebody else's and the inquest a scheme to publicly demonstrate his death and allow him to escape prosecution, and flee abroad? Here, in a work largely devoted to tracing the life of Thomas Watson, is no place to discuss these and other theories—in any case at this time Watson was already dead by a few months. Yet Watson's death has an odd echo in Marlowe's, as we shall see. And one has to concede that the situation is curious: all four men in the small room were associated with Thomas Walsingham (Watson's friend), three of them known liars and confidence tricksters. There is the association with Burghley, and, moreover, according to statutory law a local county coroner should have accompanied the Coroner of the Queen's Household; theoretically the inquest was null and void. The situation has the appearance of having been staged (perhaps an apposite choice of word?).

During his lifetime, Marlowe was reputedly an atheist. It is possible that he was a government agent who took on that image to work undercover with atheists and those seen as the enemies of the government. The question of Thomas Watson's stance, the extent of *his* employment on government anti-Catholic business, his friendship with the supposed atheist Marlowe, and how all this squares with the depth of his own Catholicism, is ambiguous. His boyhood and education, and his stay at Douai, speak of a Catholic faith. Later, he dedicated works to both Philip Howard, who was to become a prominent Catholic, and to the allegedly sometime Catholic Earl of Oxford whose secretary he became. Later still, he tutored the eldest son of the Catholic Cornwallis household.

However, little can be assumed. It is possible that his stay at Douai was as a government spy, as Kendall in his illuminating *Christopher Marlowe and Richard Baines* believes likely.[52] The theory is reinforced by my own surmise that he may have visited Sir Francis Walsingham in Paris in 1572 and 1576. As for the Earl of Oxford's conversion to Catholicism and Watson's relationship with the Cornwallis family, the circumstances may have been more devious than they appear, a question we shall consider later. Regarding his dedication to Philip Howard in his *Antigone*, the timings are sufficiently close to suggest at least the possibility that Watson and Philip Howard met at Douai in the 1570s. However, even if Watson's dedication to Howard was an acknowledgment to a fellow Catholic it was at best no more than a salute to Howard's antecedents. For at this time Howard was a much lapsed Catholic. True, the godfather after whom he was named was Philip the King of Spain, and his father Thomas Howard had been executed in 1572 following the Catholic Northern Rising. Moreover, in his younger days Philip had been a pupil of the Catholic scholar Gregory Martin, famous for his translation of the *Rheims New Testament* (1582). But when Watson published and dedicated *Antigone* to him at the end of July 1581, Philip Howard, aged twenty-three, was still "an unfaithful husband and a thoughtless spendthrift"[53] noted for attempting to seduce Mercy Harvey, the sister of the three Harvey brothers, Gabriel (writer), Richard (Anglican minister) and John (physician). Evidently, he had still a long journey back to the values of his family religion. It was after his wife Anne's conversion in 1582 or 1583 that Philip began to repent of his transgressions, a repentance said to have climaxed with a mental struggle in the Long Gallery at Arundel Castle in 1584. Then, so profound was his contrition that he attempted voluntary exile, followed by his subsequent capture and a long imprisonment—consummated in 1589 by death in the Tower. This was for the future, however; back in 1581, the year of *Antigone*'s publication, he not only showed no sign of remorse for his sins, but was still relishing the first seventeen months of his inheritance as thirteenth Earl of Arundel. Perhaps it was this fairly recent event that prompted Watson's dedication.[54]

Thus, despite superficial hindsight, Watson's Catholicism in 1581 seems at the very least uncertain. He was certainly not pious, and possibly he was an undercover spy. 1581 was the very year in which he was employed to carry messages for Secretary Walsingham from Paris to London, yet most writers have suggested[55] that as a "yeoman" of St Helen's he was also quizzed by the authorities as one of the "Strangers that go not to church"—a term used for visitors from Europe, mainly refugee Huguenots following the Massacre of 1572. We think those writers mistaken (see CHAPTER FOUR), but even if they are right, it is still possible that Watson was acting out a double bluff. Perhaps, like some of his co-religionists,[56] he preferred to run with the government while at the same time hoping—somehow—for an accommodation of the faith. Nevertheless, as Roy Kendall speculates, Watson's faith may have been weakened by meeting and mixing with the St Bartholomew's Day victims, whether on the continent or at St Helen's.[57] Moreover, his friendship with Marlowe does not appear to have been damaged by *The Massacre at Paris*, an anti-Catholic play which Marlowe may have written as early as 1589, three years before Watson's death.[58]

Four:
Unsavoury colleagues?

CHARLES Nicholl unhesitatingly claims[1]—and in the absence of hard evidence it is hesitatingly speculated here—that by the 1580s Watson seems to have mingled with the underworld of government agents in Paris and London, regions crawling with turncoat Catholics and anti-Catholic skulduggery.

Of these agents Robert Poley was undoubtedly the sleaziest. He was roughly the same age as Watson and had attended Cambridge in 1568 as a lowly sizar at Clare College—in other words, because he lacked inherited wealth he acted as a kind of dogsbody. By birth he was Roman Catholic, and in 1582 married "one Watson's daughter" in a quiet Catholic ceremony near Bow Lane in Bishopsgate, London. The ceremony took place at the house of a tailor and distributor of Catholic literature named Wood, and was conducted by a seminary priest whose identity is unknown. The couple's daughter, Anne, was christened a year after the ceremony.[2] Several writers have speculated that Poley's bride may have been Thomas Watson's sister. Since Thomas had nine siblings, some of whom were half-brothers and sisters, it is not impossible. But Watson is a common name and there is no evidence that "Watson's daughter" was a relative, even though Thomas, the poet and writer, was undoubtedly a resident in the ward in which Poley married, St Helen's, Bishopsgate.

Another doubtful attribution appears in a list of "Names of Strangers that go not to church" surveyed in the parish of St Helen's on 24 June 1581. Here is to be found the name of *"Thos. Watson, yom[an]"*, listed beneath that of one *"Georgius Pooley, yom[an]"*.[3] Scholars have claimed this Thomas Watson as "our" Watson, interrogated because of his Catholic leanings. However, the writer Thomas Watson ought to have been described as a "gentleman" rather than a "yeoman". And a listing on a later page[4] of *"Margerita uxor Thome Watson"*, casts further doubt on the identification since Thomas Watson "gent", is not known to have been married to a "Margaret" at this or any other time. Nevertheless, the juxtaposition of the names Thomas Watson and George Poley is intriguingly coincidental. Perhaps Poley's bride was a daughter or relative of the Thomas Watson listed as a "stranger". Or perhaps not.

Related or not, around 1582 both Poley and Watson were feeding Francis Walsingham with information.

That was the year in which Poley attempted to enter political service. In a letter to Leicester he refers to his "three years past determination" to "do Her Majesty and the State some special service".[5] Success came shortly afterwards when Poley was made "prisoner in the Marshalsea upon Mr Secretary's commandment".[6] The news was less good for his wife. Her frequent visits to the gaol met with Poley's refusal to see her, and he took up with a London cutler's wife, Joan Yeomans, "who had many fine banquets in his chamber".[7] To her he entrusted a chest full of "good gold"; Poley was living well on squalid government handouts as an undercover plant; with forty-seven Catholics in the Marshalsea[8] the prison was a particularly fruitful source of intelligence.

Not everyone was fooled. Fr William Weston observed that Poley "was so obsequious in his manner that he made me recoil as at an unpleasant smell";[9] and Richard Ede, the jailer of the Marshalsea, whose job must have brought him into contact with a good many distasteful characters, advised Joan's husband, William, that Poley "will beguile you of your wife or your life".[10] By 1584 Poley, fresh out of the Marshalsea, moved to the house of Joan Yeomans' widowed mother, who coming upon the pair one day and finding her daughter "sitting upon the said Poley's knees" was so stricken by the sight that she "prayed God to cut her off very quickly". Her prayer was answered the following weekend.[11]

Walsingham never fully trusted Poley. In early 1585, he interrogated him for possessing Catholic seditious libels, which Poley hotly denied. Walsingham did not believe him, "looked out of his window and", reported

Poley later, "grinned like a dog".[12] But he could not break him.

After that, Poley found employment for a while with the spy ring organised by the Earl of Leicester. It was at about this time, too, that he described himself as working as a finance clerk for Sir Philip Sidney—Leicester's nephew and Walsingham's son-in-law. Although Leicester and "Mr Secretary" Walsingham ran separate spy rings, Poley was known to both. When Sidney set off for the Lowlands and fatal injury at the Battle of Zutphen in 1586, Poley stayed behind with Philip's wife Frances. Using his position as Sidney's secretary as a blind, he formed a friendship with Christopher Blount, a Catholic soldier in Leicester's entourage, and through him became acquainted with Thomas Morgan, the Queen of Scots' agent in Paris, himself a double-dealer. Blount and Morgan saw Poley as a convenient ally and spy with government connections. Copies of the letters between Morgan and Mary found their way back to the Privy Council.

Walsingham must have swallowed down his distaste of Poley, for we next hear of the agent as living in "Mr Secretary's" house at Barn Elms near Richmond, and afterwards at "The Gardens", a house in Bishopsgate set up for him by Burghley, the third spy master—for whom Walsingham largely operated. Then he was off to Watson's friend Thomas Walsingham's grandiose estate at Scadbury near Chislehurst in Kent. By this time Thomas Walsingham had been enlisted as some kind of confidential aide to his cousin "Mr Secretary", with Poley acting as go-between. Poley's own letters reveal that he carried correspondence between the cousins; he was at this work in May 1586. That was the very month in which the Catholic lawyer Anthony Babington joined John Ballard for a tankard in the Plough at London's Temple Bar. Ballard, recently returned from France, spoke of rumours of an imminent Catholic invasion of 60,000 troops. It was the ripening of the Babington Plot. Babington, though himself sceptical and unenthusiastic, was delegated to organise a rebellion among English Catholics. Utilising his friendship with Blount and Morgan, Poley weaselled his way into Babington's trust. No matter that many of his fellow Catholics were deeply suspicious of Poley, Babington stayed loyal, unable to believe Poley would betray him: when events forced him to make a bolt for it, Babington's final, pitiable, letter to Poley included the line, "Farewell sweet Robyn, if as I take thee true to me. If not, adieu *omnium bipedum nequissimus* [of all two footed creatures the worst]".[13]

In August, Babington was trapped in a barn near Harrow-on-the-Hill, and with every other single conspirator, Poley included, scooped up and clapped in the Tower. The following month, all, except three, were cruelly and violently hanged, drawn and quartered before several thousand spectators at the Cup Field (nowadays absorbed into Lincoln's Inn Fields).[14] Babington's estate went to Sir Walter Raleigh, who became a landowner for the first time. Trapped by her involvement with the Plot, Mary Queen of Scots was beheaded at Fotheringay Castle the following February. Of the three who escaped, one made a getaway (Edward Windsor) and two were spies arrested to protect their cover (Robert Poley and Bernard Mawde). Poley was released in the autumn of the following year. Few trusted him. Not Walsingham, not the Catholics. Robert Southwell, the poet and Jesuit priest, concluded he was "either an atheist or a heretic, or both", and doubted not the rumour that while sojourning in the Tower Poley had murdered the venerable Catholic Archbishop of Armagh with poisoned cheese.

A month or two after his release, Poley was again working openly for Francis Walsingham, taking as his first commission a journey to Denmark for a fee of £15. He continued to work for "Mr Secretary" until Walsingham's death two years later, in 1590. Thereafter, times were changing: the Earl of Essex set up his own intelligence network, and Walsingham's coterie was temporarily cared for by Sir Thomas Heneage. Nevertheless, Poley remained an important undercover messenger, especially on journeys to the Lowlands, Denmark, and to Scotland.[14] In May 1593 he was one of the four men in "a little room" at Deptford where Christopher Marlowe allegedly died from a stab to the eye.

Whatever the truth of that event, the involvement of Robert Poley comes as no surprise: liar, schemer, murderer, employee of Sir Thomas Walsingham, acquaintance of Watson and Marlowe, and agent for four of Elizabeth's spy masters, Leicester, Burghley, Mr Secretary Walsingham and Heneage.[15] Soon, Heneage passed the keys to a new, fifth, master, Robert Cecil, who had previously met Poley in 1592; "I have spoken to Poley", he remarked then, "and found him no fool".[16] Thus into the hands of Robert Cecil passed the ruthless, squalid, creature whose boast had once been, "I will swear and forswear my self rather then I will accuse myself to do me any harm". After carrying some letters to Paris in September 1601, he seems to have fallen from favour and disappears from the records.[17]

Compared with Poley, Watson's other possible associates of the early 1580s look almost saintly — though ruffians all.

Richard Baines, our first example, graduated in 1576 from Caius College, Cambridge. Caius had strong Catholic links, and by the early 1580s Baines had found his way to the English College in Rheims. There he was ordained in 1581, while all the time spying for Walsingham and plotting against the college, even to calculating the poisoning of the seminary well. But the college authorities were not stupid and kept a vigilant eye on him, finally having him clapped in the city gaol, from which he bought his release with a published public confession.[18] Kendall draws to our attention that Baines' preparation for ordination "exactly corresponds" with Watson and Marlowe's arrival in France between 1581 and 1583,[19] and Nicholl suspects a link with Christopher Marlowe around 1585, not long after Baines' return to England — the timings are right[20] — which means we may therefore suspect a connection with Thomas Watson too. Baines hated Marlowe, possibly because he had been lampooned in *The Jew of Malta* in the scene where Barabas, the villain, boasts of "poisoning wells". When in 1592 Baines and Marlowe were on anti-Catholic business in Holland, Baines turned on Marlowe and tried to have him arrested for "coining". Counterfeiting was a capital crime. The governor, Sir Philip Sidney's brother Robert, shipped the pair back to England, together with a goldsmith named Gifford Gilbert (not to be confused, one supposes, with the spy Gilbert Gifford).

It was Baines who in May 1593 incriminated Thomas Kyd with an offence leading to Kyd's imprisonment and torture. Shortly after, he again tried to incriminate Marlowe in a report accusing him of atheism and heresy, in terms nearly identical to his own recantation a few years earlier—adding that all Christians "ought to endeavour that the mouth of so dangerous a member be stopped". This time he was more successful, setting in motion wheels that carried Marlowe to the shady events in Deptford a month later. There is a suggestion that in 1587 he was appointed rector of Waltham in Lincolnshire as pay-off for his services to the state. It is more likely that he was hung at Tyburn on 6 December 1594 for stealing a cup. He may even have been framed.[21]

There is the curiosity, too, of the knockabout banter in Act 3 Scene 3 of the 1616 Quarto of Marlowe's *Doctor Faustus* concerning Dick the horse-keeper's clownish knavery in stealing a cup, followed up by Mephistopheles' turning him into an ape. "Dick" is a nickname for Richard; part of the counterfeiter's art was to melt down plate for its metal. The dialogue seems to mirror the circumstances of the Tyburn Baines.[22]

Thomas Morgan was another shady character, whom we met earlier. Originating from a Monmouthshire Catholic family, he was employed as secretary to the Archbishop of York until 1568, at which time he transferred to the service of Lord Shrewsbury, Mary Queen of Scots' warder. It is possible that in 1584 Morgan was involved with the publication of *Leicester's Commonwealth*, a serious attack on Robert Dudley, first Earl of Leicester—Poley had a copy, and it was this (with other seditious papers) which landed him into trouble with Walsingham. Dispatched to the Scottish embassy in Paris, Morgan corresponded secretly with Mary, plotted to assassinate Elizabeth, and hand-in-hand with Charles Paget recruited and involved the unfortunate Anthony Babington in their schemes. But Morgan was unaware that his secret code had been broken by a young servant to Walsingham, Thomas Phelippes, and that an embassy mole, Gilbert Gifford, was passing copies of his letters to Walsingham.

When the Babington Plot exploded, Morgan was in Paris, and no doubt thought that being flung first into the Bastille and subsequently into a Flemish prison was a lucky escape compared with the fate of his fellow plotters. He was set free in 1593 and probably died in the Amiens region of France in 1606. We shall encounter Morgan's co-conspirator, the double agent Charles Paget, later. A flavour of the man may be caught from a letter he wrote from the Low Countries in October 1591 to "Mons. Giles Martin, Frenchman, London". It concerned the activities of Thomas Morley, organist and singer (vicar-choral) at St Paul's, and later Gentleman of the Chapel Royal, successive holder of the music printing patent held by Byrd, and the greatest of England's madrigalists. It seems that at this time Morley was also working as a spy for Walsingham:

> There is one Morley that playeth on the organs in Paul's that was with me in my house. He seemed here to be a good Catholic and was reconciled, but notwithstanding suspected his behaviour I intercepted letters that Mr Nowell wrote to him. Whereby I discovered enough to have hanged him. Nevertheless he showing with tears great repentance, and asking on his knees forgiveness, I was content to let him go. I hear since his coming there he hath played the promoter and apprehendeth Catholics.[23]

A draft reply from Walsingham's secretary, Thomas Phelippes, confirms Morley's activity:

> It is true that Morley the singing man employs himself in that kind of service ... and hath brought diverse into danger.[24]

A fascinating verbal picture of Phelippes, a person also quite possibly known to Watson, was drawn by Mary Queen of Scots. Mary described him as short, skinny, pock-marked, short-sighted, and with dark yellow hair on his head". He was a clever mimic who could parrot accents and mannerisms to perfection, a brilliant linguist with command of several languages, and—importantly—a skilled code breaker. After Walsingham's death, the Cecils refused to employ him, and he turned to Essex. Intelligence-gathering obsessed him, and cost him: he funded much of his activities from his own purse, accumulating so much debt that he was flung into gaol. Where he died.

Five:
Poetry, science, wit, and wisdom

AFTER his early exploits on the continent, Watson settled in London and devoted most of the remaining ten years of his life to poetry, literature and the theatre. In 1581 he published two Latin poems and three translations into Latin, including the whole of Petrarch's *Canzoniere,* most of which is now lost.[1] Then, on 31 July 1581, his translation of Sophocles' play *Antigone* was registered at the Stationer's Company by John Wolfe. Dana F Sutton suggests that the play was performed at the Inns of Court before its publication, and also draws attention to the influence of Sidney's *The Defence of Poesy* upon the work.[2] It is probable, too, that Watson composed an eleven-stanza commendatory poem "Even as the fruitful bee", signed T.W., which fronted George Whetstone's *An Heptameron of Civil Discourses* in 1582.[3]

Ten printed works, including five in Latin have survived, although a considerable portion of his opus appears to have been lost,[4] including all his drama. Initially he found employment as a secretary to the Earl of Oxford with whom he shared interests: Europe (especially Italy), languages, literature and the classics—in particular Ovidian poetry.[5] The poet George Peele urged Watson to cherish the connection:

> And shroud thee under shadow of his wings,
> Whose gentle heart, and head with learning fraught
> Shall yield thee gracious favour and defence.[6]

In their essay "Was Thomas Watson Shakespeare's Precursor?"[7] Eric Lewin Altschuler and William Jansen, writing from an Oxfordian viewpoint, bring to light and summarise several curious literary connections between the Earl of Oxford and Thomas Watson. Without making an absolute claim for such a case, Altschuler and Jansen suggest that Watson "may have been

Oxford's primary pseudonym immediately preceding the use 'Shakespeare'". We need not follow that route. Their paper was published before Alhiyari's thesis, quite apart from the additional matter assembled here. They assume that Watson had little education, doubt that he visited the continent, and find a scarcity of information about his early years. We now know that there is no reason to doubt Watson was a well-travelled writer of imagination and immense talent. Which is not to deny that, as Oxford's "secretary", he may have benefited from collaboration and discussion with his employer, or the possibility that he may have loaned his identity to some of Oxford's work—or vice versa.

It is worth quoting Altschuler and Jansen's evaluation of Watson's achievement. "The breadth and depth of Watson's *opus*", they write, "is remarkably Shakespearean … These works established him in his day and today as the greatest modern Latin poet and finest translator of Latin and Greek. His *Hekatompathia* can be seen as the godhead of the English Renaissance." Many of Watson's touches can be sensed in Shakespeare's Sonnets, and Shakespeare adopted Watson's rhyming scheme in preference to the Italian style.

His shining moment arrived in March 1582, with the publication of a major work, the *Hekatompathia*.[8] This, again, was "Emprinted by John Wolfe for Gabriel Cawood in Paul's Churchyard at the Sign of the Holy Ghost". It was dedicated to Oxford, and it was from around this time Watson took up with the earl.

Gabriel Cawood, its bookseller, had taken over the lease at the Sign of the Holy Ghost in 1559 from his father John, formerly Queen Mary's Printer.[9] A year before the publication of *Hekatompathia*, Gabriel had congratulated the Jesuit Edmund Campion on his triumphant conferences with the protestant clergy, for the Cawoods had Catholic sympathies— John Strype nominated him "the Catholic printer". Works sympathetic to Catholicism streamed from his press for twenty-six years, between 1576 and 1602. In 1591, following Robert Southwell's gruesome martyrdom, Cawood took on the priest's poetry, presumably a lucrative publishing initiative since it was reprinted in 1595. Curiously, his sympathies seem to have left him unharmed: for five years he was Master of the Stationers'

Company (1592-7). Among his large catalogue the most popular books were Lyly's *Euphues, the Anatomy of Wit* and *Euphues and his England*, printed by Thomas East, and frequently reprinted. Lyly (like Watson) was a secretary to the Earl of Oxford. Also on Cawood's lists, too, were George Gascoigne and George Peele; they, too, were associated with Oxford.

Although, superficially, Watson's publisher appears a fairly blameless individual, his principal (although not exclusive) printer was a larger-than-life personality of more unscrupulous inclinations. At around the time of the publication of *Hekatompathia*, John Wolfe had become a tiresome irritant to the publishing and printing establishment. In earlier days he had followed his father's trade and entered the Fishmongers' Company, but left the company after 1562 to receive grounding in the printing trade as an apprentice to John Day. He was sufficiently well off to travel abroad, and by 1576 studied and published religious poetry in Florence. Although he was back in London by 1579 and issuing his first English titles, it was not long before he again set sail for the continent.[10] A book published in 1581,[11] purporting to be published in London, has the typographical style of a continental publication.[12] In it Wolfe describes himself as "seruitore de l'illustrissimo Filippo Sidnei", confirming some sort of association with Sidney. Until 1591 a number of his titles were also listed in the catalogues at the Frankfurt Book Fair, so we may assume that he made occasional visits there too.[13] Europe is a large place, but the dates are right for Wolfe and Watson to have—perhaps—crossed paths during their roamings through Europe. That could have been in 1576 or 1577, or in 1581. But not in 1582 when Wolfe was printing the *Hekatompathia*, because for most of that year he was most assuredly in London. In May he was charged by the Queen's Printer Christopher Barker to "leave your Machiavellian devices,[14] and conceit of your foreign wit, which you have gained by gadding from country to country". Barker's outburst was sparked by Wolfe's printing of "other men's copies", that is, the infringement of patents belonging to his fellow printers. Wolfe not only rebuffed Barker's demand, but proceeded to become the leader of a group of self-styled "poor printers" intent on infringing and overthrowing the monopolies of the likes of Barker and Day. Wolfe was imprisoned twice in 1582, but was at large again in early 1583 when members of the Stationers' Company complained to the Privy Council, portraying Wolfe as

> arrogant ("Luther was but one man, and reformed all the world for religion, and I am that one man, that must and will reform the government in this trade"), as contemptuous of Elizabeth ("She is deceived") and her rulings ("it was lawful for all men to print all lawful books what commandment soever her Majestie gave to the contrary"), and, more damagingly, as a dangerous political and social agitator. Wolfe and his confederates incensed the meaner sort of people throughout the City as they went, that it became a common talk in alehouses, taverns and such like places, whereupon dangerous and undutiful speeches of her Majesty's most gracious government.[15]

In 1584 Wolfe involved himself in further violent altercations by infringing Day's patents to print the metrical Psalms. After that, respectability took over. John Day died and his son, in holy orders, assigned his father's rights to Wolfe and four others. Wolfe's change of heart may have been influenced, too, by the loss of an influential protector in Sir Philip Sidney, who died in the autumn of 1586. Importantly, a Star Chamber decree of that year permitted the Stationers' Company to search for and seize secret presses without appealing to the city officers. Now the poacher turned gamekeeper. In April 1587, Wolfe was appointed acting beadle of the Company, and confirmed in the post in July. He became notorious as a prosecutor of illicit printers. Not even his former "confederates" were safe, and the printers of the Presbyterian Marprelate tracts in 1589-91 were in especial danger. A tract of 1588 laments the treatment of Robert Waldegrave, whose

> press and letters were taken away: his press being timber, was sawn and hacked in pieces, the iron work battered and made unserviceable, his letters melted, with cases and other tools defaced (by John Wolfe alias Machiavel,[16] beadle of the Stationers and most

tormenting executioner of Waldegrave's goods), and he himself utterly deprived of ever printing again, having a wife and six small children.[17]

Wolfe was especially favoured by Burghley and his son Robert Cecil. It was to Wolfe that Burghley turned in 1588 to publish *The Pope's bull in Dutch with the answer thereto, to be translated*, to be followed swiftly by a letter written in 1584 to Mendoza the former Spanish ambassador. Other official printing contracts followed, as well as, in 1591, the task of calling in an illegal edition of Sidney's *Astrophel and Stella*.

Wolfe was well acquainted with Gabriel Harvey, who may have assisted him as some kind of publisher's reader.[18] Certainly, he handled three of Harvey's attacks against his enemy Thomas Nashe,[19] and an allusion in another work by John Florio seems to advise that Nashe take to heart the warning, "*A carne di lupo, dente di cane*" — in other words "To a Wolf's flesh apply the tooth of a dog".[20] Lyly pointed a finger at Harvey as "a notable coach companion for Martin",[21] but Harvey's involvement with Marprelate is ambiguous. He seems to have had friends or acquaintances on both sides, and while in his writings he despises Lyly's "alehouse and tinkerly stuff", he rebuts the Martinists in a comparatively cool, level-headed, writing style.[22] Nevertheless, for Wolfe — who was working alongside Nashe's anti-Marprelate, pro-government, circle — to have put Harvey's anti-Nashe pennings under his own imprint seems a curious, even foolhardy, gesture. Perhaps he was swayed by the subject matter: the role of the printing press in the encouragement of learning and good behaviour.[23]

Wolfe's exertions against Marprelate paid off: he acquired the lucrative patent to handle the City's printing orders, and in 1598 was elected to the Stationers' livery. By 1591 he had sold off his presses to John Windet, an associate of Anthony Mundy, and concentrated solely on publishing. His establishment was extremely influential and handled a variety of matter — religious ballads, news sheets, and works by writers and poets, significantly Spenser, Thomas Churchyard and Robert Southwell. In 1592, Wolfe was one of the two publishers[24] who took on Robert Greene's notorious *Groats-worth of Wit*. Moreover, he had an interest in the theatre: in April 1600 the Privy Council banned his construction of a playhouse in Nightingale Lane near East Smithfield. It was a troublesome year for Wolfe: in the summer, he cooled off in gaol for two weeks after publishing John Hayward's *The First Part of the Life and Reign of King Henry IV* over a year earlier—it was madness to chose this time to dedicate to the Earl of Essex a narrative of the deposition and death of Richard II. Hayward was also imprisoned and even its censor, Samuel Harsnett, narrowly escaped gaol. We shall meet John Wolfe again in this narrative: the printer and publisher, with connections to Gabriel Harvey and the Marprelate crisis. By his deeds we have learned something of the man who handled the bulk of Thomas Watson's literary output.

Hekatompathia was first circulated in manuscript, and then licensed to Gabriel Cawood on 31 March 1582 with the title *Watson's Passions, manifesting the true frenzy of love*.[25] It was "a brand-new literary kind: the one-author, printed, uniform love-lyric sequence".[26] and was quickly published soon afterwards with the revised title of *Hekatompathia or Passionate Century of Love*.[27] The changed title represented an alteration to the structure of the volume, perhaps a last-minute change of mind. The title page (reproduced on page 102) reads that the work is

> Divided into two parts: whereof, the first expresseth the Authors sufferance in Love: the latter, his long farewell to Love and all his tyrannie. Composed by *Thomas Watson* Gentleman; and published at the request of certain Gentlemen his very frendes.

Watson tells us the one hundred passions are divided into two parts. Part One comprises Passions I to LXXIX; Part Two, Passions LXXX to C. Passion C is followed by a single page to conclude the work which the commentator describes as an "Epilogue to the whole work, and more like a prayer than a passion". It is in Latin and translated from Petrarch. In Part Two every page is headed "MY LOVE IS PAST" until the completion of the book. Passion LXXX marks the division of the book into two parts. In fact it is not a passion at all, but a prose description of the rather special Passion LXXXI that follows.

5. Poetry, science, wit, and wisdom

LXXXI.

MY LOVE IS PAST.

A Pasquine Piller erected in the despite of Loue.

```
              A   1  At
                  2  last, though
                  3  late, farewell
                  4  olde well a da: A
           m  5  Mirth or mischance strike
           a  6  vp a newe alarM, And   m
              7  Cypria    la    nemica
        r  8  miA  Retire to Cyprus Ile, a
        e  9  t cease thy waRR, Els must thou proue how   r
     E 10  Reason can by charmeS Enforce to flight thy    e
     s 11  blindfolde bratte t thee. So frames it with mee now,  E
     t 12  that I confesS, The life I ledde in Loue deuoyde  s
     I 12  of resT, It was a Hell, where none felte more then I,  t
                                                              I
     n 11  Nor anye with lyke miseries forlorN. Since     n
     s 10  therefore now my woes are wexed lesS, And     s
        a  9  Reason bidds mee leaue olde welladA,    a
           n  8  No longer shall the worlde laughe mee
              7  to scorN; I'le choose a path that    n
           r  6  shall not leade awrie.  Rest   i
                  5  then with mee from your
                  4  blinde Cupids carR.    r
                e. 3  Each   one   of
                       2  you, that
                       1  serue,
                     3  and would be
                   5  freE. H'is dooble thrall  e.
                 7  that liu's as Loue thinks best, whose
               9  hande still Tyrant like to hurte is preste.
```

Huius Columnæ Basis, pro sillabarum numero & linearum proportione est Orchematica.

Watson's *Hekatompathia* (1582), Passion LXXXI.
"Compiled by rule and number into the form of a pillar" and containing "many pretty observations".

LXXXII.

MY LOVE IS PAST.

Expansio Columnæ præcedentis.

A	At last, though late, farewell olde wellada;	A
m	Mirth for mischaunce strike vp a newe alarm;	m
a	And Ciprya la nemica mia	a
r	Retyre to Cyprus Ile and cease thy warr,	r
e	Els must thou proue how Reason can by charme	e
E	Enforce to flight thy blyndfold bratte and thee.	E
s	So frames it with me now, that I confess	s
t	The life I ledde in Loue deuoyd of rest	t
I	It was a hell, where none felt more then I,	I
n	Nor any with like miseries forlorn.	n
s	Since therefore now my woes are wexed less,	s
a	And Reason bids me leaue olde wellada,	a
n	No longer shall the world laugh me to scorn:	n
i	I'le choose a path that shall not leade awri.	i
r	Rest then with me from your blinde Cupids carr	r
e.	Each one of you, that serue and would be free.	e
	* H'is double thrall that liu's as Loue thinks best	
	Whose hand still Tyrant like to hurt is prest.	

τόν τόι τύρα-
νον ἐυσεβεῖν
οὐ ῥᾴδιον.
Sophoc. in
Aia. flagell.

Watson's *Hekatompathia* (1582), Passion LXXXII,
which sets out Passion LXXXI
in the conventional manner.

Watson tells us it was "compiled by rule and number into the form of a pillar", and contains "many pretty observations ... if any man have such idle leisure to look it over, as the Author had, when he framed it." He draws our attention to the "principal" observation which is that on the outside of each pillar are placed the first and last letters of the each line. These letters are identical and read vertically down to spell the Latin legend "*Amare Est Insanire* [To Love is Madness]". To make his meaning clear, Watson sets out the verse all over again in the conventional manner on the following page, as number LXXXII. The Elizabethans were fond of this kind of conceit, and Watson invites the reader to "judge how much art and study the Author has bestowed in the same."

This poem is not the only example of Watson's experiments. Considering the work as a whole, Dana F Sutton has commented on its "integrated nature" and quotes from S K Heniger's Introduction to his photographic reproduction of the work:

> "Actually, this publication represents a collected edition of Watson's miscellaneous verse to that date. It is a scrapbook of experiments: dialogue poems (III, XXII, LVI), an echo poem (XXV), an example of reduplication (XLI), acrostics (LLXXXII), a shape-poem (LXXXI), a list of translated one-line aphorisms (LXXXIX) a quasi-sestina (XCIII), a long poem of Latin hexameters (not numbered, but after XCVIII). Watson undoubtedly reworked many poems to comply with the set metrical form, and he included four Latin poems to make the number an even hundred (VI, XLV, LXVI, XC). Shrewd selection and arrangement produce a piquant modulation of form throughout."[28]
>
> To leave the matter here [continues Sutton] would be to miss the essential point, for the above-quoted words seem to describe a kind of one-man *Tottel's Miscellany*. Heniger failed to appreciate that by giving the cycle a narrative thread and by selecting a single dominant theme—the conflict of passion and reason—our poet has managed to fuse what might otherwise indeed be a mere anthology or scrapbook into an integrated literary performance. Use of this

theme adroitly imposes a satisfactory measure of artistic unity, achieving a whole that is palpably greater than the sum of its parts. Closer analysis could probably demonstrate other thematic leitmotifs running through the cycle. For example, The Author repeatedly compares his beloved to various species of bird, in such a way that the qualities of the bird in question constitute a barometer of his current attitude towards her.[29]

Watson called its eighteen-line love poems "Passions", or sometimes "sonnets"; each addresses an aspect of a lover's suffering, most are in English, some are in Latin, and they originate in translations of the French and Italian sonnet writers—although they are not literal or straightforward renderings into English. Nor, as A E B Coldiron has pointed out,

> ... is the work chiefly substantive translation: it is not as content-based effort to bring a foreign work's theme, matter, or idea more or less intact into English (such as Mary Sidney's Psalms). Instead Watson fragments, decontextualises, and radically recontextualises the bits and pieces he translates—acting as a polyglot *cento* writer, or as a maker of poetic mosaics, smashing up poems and recycling the bits into his own planned varicoloured patterns.[30]

These "patchwork poems" predate in print by some nine years all subsequent true, fourteen-line, sonnets including those by Sir Philip Sidney[31] and were the pioneering spark for the sonnet craze of the 1590s.

Watson's dedication of his book to the Earl of Oxford was a loyal and courageous act at a time when de Vere was disgraced at court. Vere's crimes were cumulative. His refusal at reconciliation with his wife was followed by the scandal of his confession that, with Henry Howard, Charles Arundell and Francis Southwell, he had secretly adhered to Catholicism.[32] Howard and Arundell fought back, flinging mud at Oxford, accusing him of blasphemy, pederasty, homosexuality and other Elizabethan crimes—innuendo which should be treated with caution.[33] As if this profligacy were not enough, one of the Queen's maids of honour,

Anne Vavasour, gave birth in the spring of 1581 to an illegitimate son—de Vere was the father. It was all too much for the Queen who committed Oxford to the Tower for two and a half months and afterwards exiled him from the court.

In what he called a "Protrepticon" to *Hekatompathia*, Watson addresses his "timid book" to the reader,[34] imagining its reception at court. Several of the poems appear to be addressed even to the Queen herself. Watson also tells his book that, should it "cross Sidney's desk, or Dyer's"—noblemen involved in poetic rivalry to Oxford, and highly praised at court for their literary excellence[35]—it should plea that it has "nevertheless been shown to Vere, a man who deserves great things for his virtue and true nobility. Then both of these gentlemen will remove the frowns from their brows and read you [*Hekatompathia*] kindly, both will ignore your blemishes …" It was a comment unlikely to earn Watson favour with Sidney and Dyer. Unless, that is, there was no real enmity between the Sidney and Oxford factions; commentators may have exaggerated the rivalry. The two noblemen were sufficiently non-hostile to joust side by side as "The Knight of the Tree of the Sun" (Oxford) and "The Blue Knight" (Sidney) at a tilt hosted by Philip Howard on Twelfth Night in 1581.[36] It also reveals that, although he dedicated his work to de Vere, Watson's personal affiliations with the Sidneys and the Walsinghams enabled him to maintain links with Sidney's *Aeropagus* movement.[37]

Hekatompathia's preliminaries reveal something of Watson's social milieu at this period. They include contributions from several "puffers", friends or acquaintances lauding—advertising—the work in its opening pages. First, is a stylised, yet friendly, letter from "John Lyly to the Author his friend", and, following the "Protrepticon", five commendatory poems. The first was by "G Bucke". George Bucke, Buck or Buc, was later a Master of the Revels and, like Lyly, at this time a literary protégée of Oxford. Another poem was by "M Roydon". A contemporary of Buc at Thavies Inn,[38] Roydon had a huge reputation in the 1580s as a leading poet and as a friend of important poets including Christopher Marlowe and George Chapman. Chapman called him his "dear and most worthy friend".[39] Nashe described him as the author of "many most absolute comic inventions (made more public by every man's praise than they can be by my speech)".[40] Another colleague of Roydon's was Peter Ferryman who numbered Ben Jonson among his acquaintances, and claimed to be a servant of Sidney and Walsingham. Roydon's *An Elegie; or, Friends Passion for His Astrophill* written for Sidney after his death in 1586 resembles Shakespeare's *The Phoenix and the Turtle*.[41] It is the only substantial work of Roydon's to survive, although he is thought by some to be the possible author of *Willobie his Avisa* (1594).[42] Like Marlowe, Watson, and many another traveller, Roydon became a courier for William Cecil, bringing letters from Prague in 1591.[43] His praise for Watson's *Hekatompathia* is tempered by shadows of "reproof" and "disgrace", which suggest perhaps that Watson's association with Oxford was indeed brave. Grudgingly, Roydon nevertheless concludes on an upward note:

> ... And Industry well cherish'd to his face
> In sunshine walks, in spite of sour Disgrace.
> This favour hath put life into the pen,
> That here presents his first fruit in this kind:
> He hopes acceptance, friendly grant it then;
> Perchance some better work doth stay behind.
> My censure is, which reading you shall see,
> A Pithy, sweet, and cunning poesy.

Other commendations prefacing Watson's work came from the minor poet Thomas Achelley, "C Downhalus" (perhaps, but probably not, Gregory Downhall or Downham, a Cambridge graduate of 1575)[44] and George Peele. And if Roydon's praise was hesitant, the same could not be said of Peele's fulsome praise of a work which he considered was "... [c]ompiled with judgement, order, and with art."

Peele's judgement was correct. Fresh from his years in France, and taking his cue from French poetry collections, especially Ronsard, Watson's work revolutionised English poetry miscellanies. He introduced "structural and architectural relationships often supported with overt commentaries, titling conventions, and other kinds of para-text".[45] Each of his hundred Passions is headed with an erudite prose introduction, an "annotation", which explains the structure of the verse that follows, the rhetorical devices used, and the mythological sources. They show, perhaps, the influence of the Euphues school of Lyly and his patron and colleagues.[46] Spenser had attempted something similar three years earlier with the "Arguments" and "Glosses" by "E K" to his *The Shepheardes Calender*, but Watson's erudition is truly breathtaking. His introductory comments cite, or quote from, some thirty-two mythological and classical references, including Aeneas, Homer, Horace, Lucan, Martial, Ovid, Pliny, Propertius, Seneca, Sophocles, Theocritus, Tibillus, and Virgil. They also acknowledge, or quote from, twenty-five Italian and French Renaissance sources, including Firenzuola, Mantuanus, Petrarch, Ronsard, Serafino, Parabosco, Pontano, Poliziano, Silvius, Polydore Vergil, Xenephon, and Strozza "a noble man of Italy and one of the best poets of all his age".[47]

Several of these sources are Roman dramatic works. The previous year had seen the publication of Watson's translation of Sophocles' *Antigone;* now, in Poem XXX, he returns to the play to query, "what though … Haemon chose to die/to follow his Antigone by death?". He also alludes to another five (possibly six) plays by Sophocles.[48] Inevitable, Watson also draws on Seneca, a dramatist widely studied at the European universities. He imitates him in Passion LI, and Seneca's *Hippolytus* and *Oedipus* are referred to in poems LXXXIV and XXXV respectively.[49] Seneca's tragedies were an important influence on Elizabethan drama, and are regarded as a source for the series of "revenge tragedies" initiated by *The Spanish Tragedy* (?1582-1592). In view of contemporary references to Watson's dramatic works, his expertise as a Latinist of the period may be significant, although none of Watson's dramas are thought to be extant (APPENDIX E). Here, it seems pertinent to quote Bronson Feldman's comment that "it would not surprise us … to find him devoutly emulating Sophocles and Seneca in tragedies of his own".[50]

In his "Protrepticon" to the work, Watson includes the lines: "And if he asks who has enhanced your ["timid" *Hekatompathia*'s] lines with prose, say that the man's name has slipped your mind."[51] Watson's reluctance to reveal the identity of the writer of the prose introductions, which refer objectively to Watson as "the Author", has sometimes puzzled commentators. In his introduction to Watson's works, Edward Arber remarks that the annotations

> are most skilfully written. Who wrote them? Who was the Annotator? May he have been the Earl of Oxford? Was he the friend, whom Watson addresses in No. LXXI as "Deere Titus mine, my ancient friend?" Or was he the author himself, writing in the third person? We cannot say. Whoever he were, he was perfectly informed—certainly by the Poet himself—as to every allusion made, every Author imitated or referred to.[52]

Both Chapman and Lyly have also been suggested as possible annotators, but two writers have suggested that the writer was Watson himself. As evidence, they draw our attention to an undated manuscript in the British Library. Entitled *A Looking Glasse for Lovers*,[53] it contains 78 of Watson's Passions together with their headnotes, the dedication to Oxford and the concluding Epilogue. Eccles[54] believed the document to be in the same hand as two other manuscripts of Watson's works[55] and that all three are holographs. Like Sidney and other Elizabethan writers, Watson circulated his works in manuscript before sending them to the printer, a habit he informs us of in his introduction, "To the friendly Reader" (APPENDIX B). Eccles thought The British Library's *A Looking Glasse for Lovers* was possibly one of these manuscripts. S K Heninger Jr, in his introduction to a photographic reproduction of *Hekatompathia* published in 1964, even suggested it may have been Watson's presentation copy to Oxford,[56] although Sutton rejects this, believing that "the disfigurement of the title page by some pen-testing exercises probably excludes that possibility"—a rash supposition considering the manuscript's long history.[57] Another possibility is that this is a manuscript prepared for the printer. Fascinatingly, both the manuscript and John Wolfe's printed version follow the same style. In the manuscript the annotations are in italic and the English poems are in script; Wolfe's version is in roman and

5. Poetry, science, wit, and wisdom 99

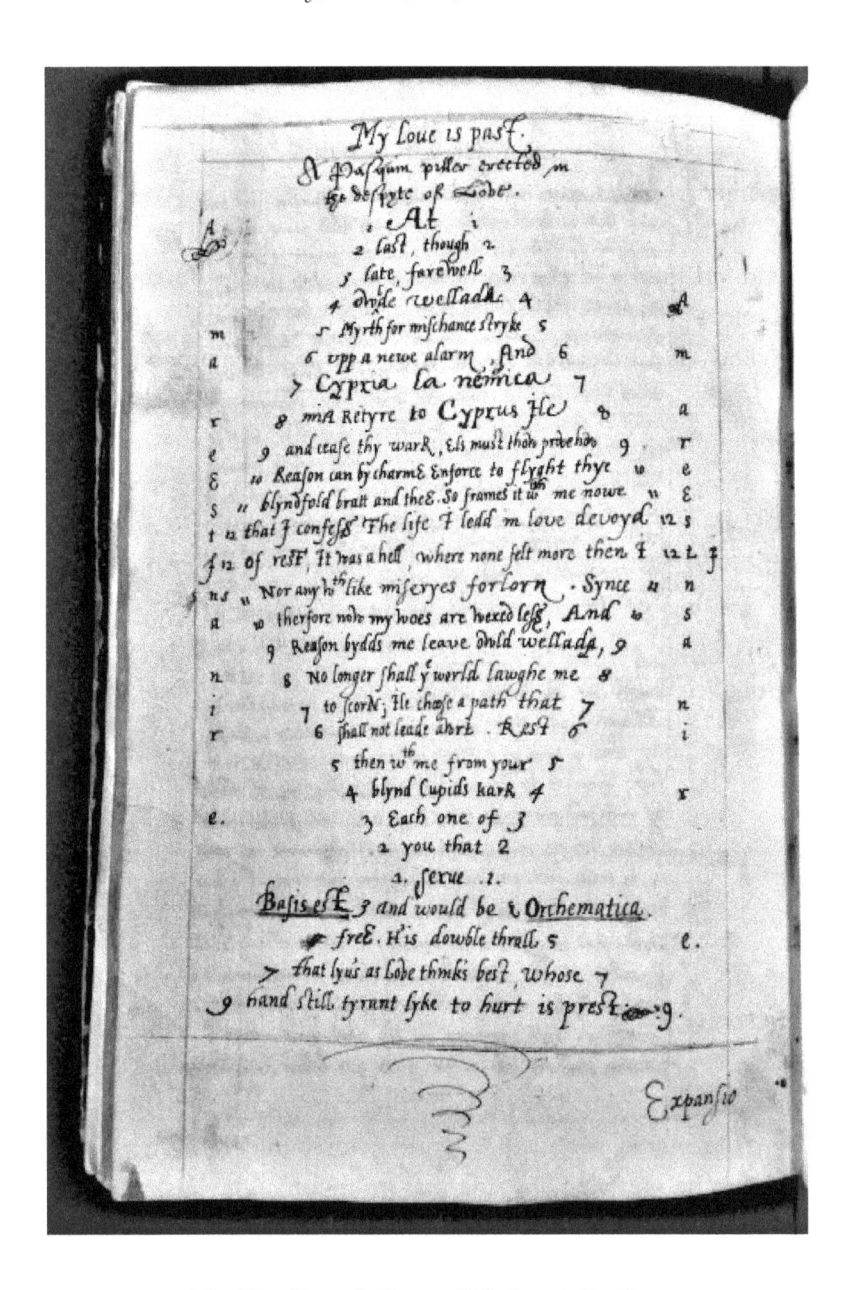

A Looking Glasse for Lovers, "My Love is Past".
A holograph of Watson's Hekatompathia Passion LXXXI?
Or a transcription made in 1633? (See endnote 59).
British Library MS 3277, f.37. Permission gratefully acknowledged.

blackface. The Latin poems are in yet another style, and Wolfe prints these in italic. Also, any space at the bottom of a page in the MS *A Looking Glasse for Lovers* is filled with a decoration, which the printed book apes with ornamental woodcuts.[58] To summarise: according to Arber and Heninger, the manuscript of *A Looking Glasse for Lovers* could be in Watson's own hand, including the headnotes. If that is the case they would seem, therefore, not to be composed by Oxford, Chapman, Lyly, or indeed anybody but Watson himself. Yet, even if the manuscript is a fair copy of *Hekatompathia*—introductory matter, headnotes, and all—prepared for the printer, there still remains a doubt about the authorship of the headnotes.[59]

Dana S Sutton quotes Heninger's pertinent point that Watson, the educated Classicist and European, wrote the prefatory material to educate his reading public: it defers "to the untutored with the expectation of edifying him and conditioning his taste. Watson was self-critic in order to be public arbiter".[60] Sutton elaborates,

> In the *Hekatompathia* [Watson] sets himself up as a didactic *arbiter elegantiae* for his fellow countrymen, a publicist for Europe's most advanced culture, and showed how the most fashionable and up-to-date Continental poetry could be adapted to English purposes.

Sutton reminds us that, besides writing the first English sonnet cycle, Watson was also involved in importing the Italian madrigal to England. Moreover, when we write here of Watson's breath-taking erudition in his introductory comments, with their citations and quotations from mythology and continental works, we should bear in mind that soon enough he will write his manual on the invaluable skill of the training of memory.

A connection between Watson, the Earl of Oxford and William Shakespeare is underlined by a close study of Watson's works, especially of *Hekatompathia*, The title-page of Gabriel Cawood's edition of *Hekatompathia*, the edition of 1582, is decorated with four separate woodcuts ruled around the perimeter and forming a tight frame around the text. The block at the bottom is cut-down from an emblem which is closely similar (the differences are minor) to another repeated four times on separate pages through the *First Folio* of Shakespeare published forty-one years later in 1623. Two figures, right and left, point long arrows inwards to the figure of a "boy" wearing some sort of headdress (or perhaps his head is backed by foliage) sitting cross-legged in the centre. This figure grasps the feet of two long-tailed birds (perhaps peacocks) which face him on each side. However, in the *First Folio* version of the decoration two hares face outwards at the top left and right corners, and two calygreyhounds face inwards at the bottom left and right corners; whereas on the title page of *Hekatompathia* a tiny portion of the bottom edge is lost, the two hares have vanished and the calygreyhounds have been sliced in half. Nevertheless, the head and horns and a front leg of each calygreyhound is visible. It would seem that the bottom block has been neatly trimmed to fit the page, resulting in the loss of the detail revealed in the *Folio*. The work is well executed, except for the giveaway of the small detail of the tip of the greyhound's tail (or is it a piece of foliage?) on the right-hand-side, which has not been expunged.

Those calygreyhounds are interesting. The calygreyhound, to quote J P Brooke-Little a former Clarenceaux King of Arms, is, "a rare monster. It has the head of a wild cat, frond-like horns, tufted body and tail, rather like a lion's, and fore-limbs which end in claws. It was a badge of the Vere family."[61] The calygreyhound was taken up in the arms of the thirteenth, fourteenth, fifteenth and sixteenth Earls of Oxford. Edward de Vere, the seventeenth Earl, ceased using the arms. Perhaps it is unsurprising that a secretary to the Earl should use a woodblock which had associations with him. The *First Folio*, which also used the illustration, was sponsored by the earls of Pembroke and Montgomery, brothers. The wife of the Earl of Montgomery was Susan de Vere, the daughter of the seventeenth Earl of Oxford; so there is a connection. On some inside pages, the *Hekatompathia* also utilises a "green man" device in the shape of a V, or vase, with the face of a man inside. A similar block appeared some eighteen years later in the First Quarto of *Henry the Fourth Part Two* (1600).[62] These curiosities may be of significance, but speculation is difficult.

THE
ἙΚΑΤΟΜΠΑΘΙ'Α
OR
PASSIONATE
Centurie of
Loue,

Diuided into two parts: whereof, the first expresseth the Authors sufferance in Loue: the latter, his long farewell to Loue and all his tyrannie.

Composed by *Thomas Watson* Gentleman; and published at the request of certaine Gentlemen his very frendes.

LONDON
¶Imprinted by Iohn Wolfe for Gabriell Cawood, dwellinge in Paules Churchyard at the Signe of the Holy Ghost.

Title page of
Gabriel Cawood's edition of
Watson's *Hekatompathia or Passionate Centurie of Love* (1582)

5. *Poetry, science, wit, and wisdom* 103

Woodcut, enlarged, at bottom of the title page of
Gabriel Cawood's edition of Watson's *Hekatompathia*(1582).
Printed by John Wolfe for Gabriel Cawood.

Woodblock at top of page A3 of
William Shakespeare's *First Folio* (1623).
Printed by Isaac Jaggard and Edward Blount.
The image is repeated four times in the folio.

Of interest, too, is the curious acrostic found in Shakespeare's Sonnet 76 noted at the beginning of CHAPTER TWO.

In addition, as long ago as 1898, the Danish scholar Georg Brandes quoted the Danish translator of the Sonnets, Adolf Hansen, to draw attention to Shakespeare's Sonnets 46 and 47 which, "on the debate of the eye and the heart, are written in terms borrowed from the twentieth Sonnet in Watson's *The Tears of Fancy*."[63] Moreover, both Hansen and Brandes failed to observe that, as well as Sonnets 46 and 47, Sonnet 19 in *Tears* also elaborates the conceit of a dispute between the eye and the heart. Bearing in mind a doubt as to whether *The Tears of Fancy* should be attributed to Watson (APPENDIX D), it is nevertheless worth quoting all four Sonnets for their resemblances, which are palpable.

> *The Tears of Fancy, Sonnet 19*
> My heart impos'd this penance on mine eyes.
> (Eyes the first causers of my heart's lamenting):
> That they should weep till love and fancy dies,
> Fond love the last cause of my heart's repenting.
> Mine eyes upon my heart inflict this pain,
> (Bold heart that dared to harbour thoughts of love)
> That it should love and purchase fell disdain,
> A grievous penance which my heart doth prove.
> Mine eyes did weep as heart had them imposed,
> My heart did pine as eyes had it constrained:
> Eyes in their tears my paled face disclosed,
> Heart in his sighs did show it was disdained,
> So th'one did weep th'other sighed, both grieved,
> For both must live and love, both unrelieved.

> *The Tears of Fancy, Sonnet 20*
> My heart accused mine eyes and was offended,
> Vowing the cause was in mine eyes aspiring:
> Mine eyes affirmed my heart might well amend it,
> If he at first had banished love's desiring.
> Heart said that love did enter at the eyes,

5. Poetry, science, wit, and wisdom

And from the eyes descended to the heart:
Eyes said that in the heart did sparks arise,
Which kindled flame that wrought the inward smart,
Heart said eyes' tears might soon have quenched that fl[ame,]
Eyes said heart's sighs at first might love exile:
So heart the eyes and eyes the heart did blame,
Whilst both did pine for both the pain did feel.
Heart sighed and bled, eyes wept and gaz'd too much,
Yet must I gaze because I see none such.

Shakespeare, Sonnet 46
My eye and heart are at a mortal war
How to divide the conquest of thy sight.
Mine eye my heart thy picture's sight would bar,
My heart, mine eye the freedom of that right.
My heart doth plead that thou in him dost lie,
A closet never pierced with crystal eyes;
But the defendant doth that plea deny,
And says in him thy fair appearance lies.
To 'cide this title is empanelléd
A quest of thoughts, all tenants to the heart,
And by their verdict is determinèd
The clear eye's moiety and the dear heart's part,
As thus mine eye's due is thy outward part,
And my heart's right thy inward love of heart.

Shakespeare, Sonnet 47
Betwixt mine eye and heart a league is took,
And each doth good turns now unto the other:
When that mine eye is famish'd for a look,
Or heart in love with sighs himself doth smother,
With my love's picture then my eye doth feast,
And to the painted banquet bids my heart;
Another time mine eye is my heart's guest,

And in his thoughts of love doth share a part:
So, either by thy picture or my love,
For thou not farther than my thoughts canst move,
Or, if they sleep, thy picture in my sight
Awakes my heart, to heart's and eyes' delight.

It is worth recording, too, that Shakespeare often borrows formulations, phrases, or figures and words from Watson, his predecessor. Some have been noted, especially by E Pearlman,[64] Eric Lewin Altschuler and William Jansen,[65] and Barboura Flues[66] — it is easy to uncover others by examining the texts. An outstanding (and well-known) example[67] is Shakespeare's Sonnet 130 which parodies Watson's Passion VII of the *Hekatompathia*, though its significance may be little more than Shakespeare's mockery of a well-known sonnet by a rival poet. It was a common practice at this time:

Watson: Hekatompathia VII
Hark you that list to hear what saint I serve:
Her yellow locks exceed the beaten gold;
Her sparkling eyes in heav'n a place deserve;
Her forehead high and fair of comely mould;
Her words are music all of silver sound;
Her wit so sharp as like can scarce be found;
Each eyebrow hangs like Iris in the skies;
Her Eagle's nose is straight of stately frame;
On either cheek a Rose and Lily lies;
Her breath is sweet perfume, or holy flame;
Her lips more red than any Coral stone;
Her neck more white, than aged Swans that moan;
Her breast transparent is, like Crystal rock;
Her fingers long, fit for Apollo's Lute;
Her slipper such as Momus dare not mock;
Her virtues all so great as make me mute:
What other parts she hath I need not say,
Whose face alone is cause of my decay.

Shakespeare: Sonnet 130
My mistress' eyes are nothing like the sun;
Coral is far more red, than her lips red:
If snow be white, why then her breasts are dun;
If hairs be wires, black wires grow on her head.
I have seen roses damasked, red and white,
But no such roses see I in her cheeks;
And in some perfumes is there more delight
Than in the breath that from my mistress reeks.
I love to hear her speak, yet well I know
That music hath a far more pleasing sound:
I grant I never saw a goddess go,
My mistress, when she walks, treads on the ground:
And yet by heaven, I think my love as rare,
As any she belied with false compare.

These sonnets owe much to the Old Testament, to *The Song of Songs*, especially Chapters 4 and 7 in which the Bridegroom likens his Bride to things of beauty. Watson's annotation preceding Passion VII acknowledges a classical inspiration, however, adding that the writer "partly borroweth from some others where they describe the famous Helen of Greece", which calls to mind Christopher Marlowe's description of Helen, a more euphonious and beautiful eulogy than Watson provides for his "saint":

> O, thou are fairer than the evening's air,
> Clad in the beauty of a thousand stars.
> Brighter art thou than flaming Jupiter
> When he appeared to hapless Semele,
> More lovely than the monarch of the sky
> In wanton Arethusa's azured arms;
> And none but thou shalt be my paramour.[68]

By comparing Helen's beauty to "a thousand stars" Watson's friend Marlowe awakens us to another fascinating aspect of *Hekatompathia*, discussed in several papers by Eric Altschuler[69] and William Jansen.[70] The opening lines of Watson's Passion XXXI read as follows:

> Who can recount the virtues of my dear,
> Or say how far her fame hath taken flight,
> That can not tell how many stars appear
> In part of heav'n, which Galaxia hight,
> Or number all the motes in Phoebus rays,
> Or golden sands, whereon Pactolus play ...

Altschuler and Jansen suggest this is probably the oldest description of the "discrete nature of the Milky Way", preceding Galileo's discovery in 1609 by nearly thirty years. The important lines are the third and fourth: in the introductory note to the poem, "Galaxia" is identified as "a white way or milky Circle in the heavens". But Altschuler and Jansen also draw attention to the word "recount" in the first line, indicating the large but discrete number of number of stars and the word "far" in line two which possibly indicates the vast distance of the Milky Way. The great but discrete number of stars involved is indicated by lines five and six.[71]

How did Watson learn about the nature of the Milky Way? The question is perhaps answered by an understanding of the new theories of the universe expounded throughout Europe at this time. In his *De Revolutionibus* of 1543 Nicholas Copernicus had championed the theory of heliocentricism, the concept that the Sun rather than the Earth was at the centre of the planetary system—a heretical notion unpopular with both the Roman Catholic and protestant churches. In England, John Dee encouraged his protégées John Field (c1525-1587) and the brilliant mathematician Thomas Digges (c1546-1595) to explore the question of heliocentricism. When, in 1573 Digges and Dee published separately their discovery of a new star[72] their reports divided theological and political opinion across Europe—the theory of cosmology of the time stressed the unchanging nature of the universe since the moment of creation.[73] When Digges advanced Copernican theory by publishing in 1576 a figure of the heavenly spheres[74] he explicitly stated that the stars, numberless, stretch out to infinity, scattered throughout space: "This orb of stars fixed infinitely up extendeth itself in altitude spherically".[75]

It was a matter about which Copernicus had declined to commit himself.[76] For his part, to escape censorship and persecution, Digges placed his paper as an unobtrusive appendix to a new edition of the popular almanac *A Prognostication Everlasting*. This publication had been initiated by his father, Leonard Digges (c1515-c1559), whose questing mind had enabled him to propose examining the heavens with a unique "perspective trunk", or telescope, based on a convex lens. The device was described by John Dee in 1570 and by Thomas Digges in 1571 when he completed his late father's work, *Pantometria*.[77] It is not known whether Dee and Digges actually owned a telescope—more likely they used cross-staffs, which in Digges' case would have been a six-foot ruler.[78]

Altschuler and Jansen suggest that Watson may have learned of the Milky Way from Digges.[79] It well may be, but in that case, since Digges' work was published in 1576, earlier than Watson's in 1582,[80] they are mistaken to suggest that Watson's was the first "description of the composition of the Milky Way". Digges was first.

It should not surprise us that Watson was aware of Digges' work. The printing history of Digges' *A Prognostication Everlasting* (republished in 1578, 1583, 1585, 1592, 1596, 1605, and 1626) suggests a best-seller with a wide circulation. Moreover, Watson would have known Digges not only by his published work, but also from personal acquaintance. Watson was almost certainly a member of the Dee circle, later dubbed the "School of Night", of which Digges was an important member.

Another point. Prior to its printing in 1582, *Hekatompathia* would probably have been distributed in manuscript (perhaps as *A Looking Glasse for Lovers*). In 1581, while *Hekatompathia* was still in private circulation, Sebastian Verro published in London his *Physicorum Libri X*. "We now refer to the glorious Galaxia, which is also called the Milky Way … ", he wrote, "It is a chaos of minute, brightly shining stars, as if fog or mist, which traverses the sky in oblique path".[81] Verro's publication reinforced Digges research and suggests that the concept of the Milky Way as a collection of discrete stars was familiar to intellectuals in the late 1570s and early 1580s.

Watson even uses the Verro's word "Galaxia" in the *Hekatompathia*. As well as referring to a reflecting mirror, perhaps Watson's "looking glasse" also has a significant astronomical meaning.

However, Altschuler and Jansen may still be right: perhaps Watson did have an inkling of the nature of the Milky Way either before Digges or simultaneously. Watson's knowledge need not have derived solely from Digges. As an authority on the classics, Watson would have known of the work of the Greek philosopher Democritus (c460-c370 BC), known for his formulation of an atomic theory and on the composition of the Milky Way. The Milky Way, wrote Democritus, was the "luminescence due to the coalition of many small stars that shine together because of their closeness to one another".[82] Moreover, assuming Watson had studied at the University of Padua, as we suggest here, he could have picked up, or reinforced, his knowledge of the Milky Way in what was then the world's leading centre for studies in astronomy.[83] Watson's undeniable interest in astronomy extended to his Latin pastoral *Amintae Gaudia* (Epistle 3 and Eclogue 4), seen through the press after his death in 1592 by his friend Christopher Marlowe.[84]

Even amongst the generality, Watson gained a reputation as an intellectual with knowledge of science and the occult. By 1587, when the unfortunate Mrs Burnell was called before the Privy Council, a deponent, one Elizabeth Bradshaw, described him as "a wise man in St Helen's that could tell strange things". As late as 1607 Thomas Dekker still remembered him as "learned".[85]

Burnell's summons was just two years after Watson published his treatise on the art of memory training, *Compendium Memoriam Localis* (undated but thought to be 1585), printed, as usual, by John Wolfe. Interest in the subject was prompted by the presence in England of a quarrelsome, volatile and arrogant ex-Dominican friar, who after serving thirteen years in the order had fled in 1576 charged with heresy—Giordano Bruno. Bruno, Neopolitan philosopher, mathematician, astronomer, heliocentrist, and occultist was noted for his amazing memory and for his belief that magic was involved in the workings of memory. He arrived in England from the Sorbonne in 1583 aged 35, armed with a letter of introduction from the French King, Henri III, to the French ambassador Michel de Castelnau. At Castelnau's house at Salisbury Court near Southwark, Bruno may have enrolled under the name of "Henri Fagot"as a spy for Walsingham, and informed on, amongst others, Throckmorton and Lord Henry Howard — information that ultimately enabled Walsingham to wreck the Babington Plot and manoeuvre the trial of Mary Queen of Scots.[86]

Soon after his arrival Bruno was introduced to the court and the warm approval of the Queen. John Florio, who was employed as interpreter and tutor to Castelnau's daughter, became Bruno's guide and translator during his stay[87] and quite quickly they relocated to Oxford. At the University, Bruno partook in wildly popular and controversial debates with the Aristotelians and Ptolemaists on astronomy, the doctrine of reincarnation and the immortality of the soul. The professors, concluded Bruno, knew more about beer than Greek. His sojourn there ended abruptly when the authorities discovered he had plagiarised the early humanist philosopher Marsilio Ficino. Whereupon he adjourned back to the friendlier *soirées* of London. Here he completed his *De la causa, principio e uno* and, evidently suffering from an attack of paranoia, complained bitterly in its dedication (to Castelnau) of attacks from all sides.[88] To bolster his increasingly tenuous situation, he dedicated two of his works to Philip Sidney and claimed that he was hosted in London by Sidney and Fulke Greville. There is a description in his *La cena de le ceneri* (1584) of dinner with the two friends and other intelligentsia at Greville's lodging in Whitehall on Ash Wednesday, in which Sidney's friend is described as the "*molto nobile et ben creator sig*[*nor*] *Folco Grivello* [the very noble and dignified Sir Fulke Greville]". Nevertheless, we have only Bruno's word for the meeting.[89] Sidney was a follower of the teachings of Peter Ramus, a Huguenot philosopher whose reputation among the colleges at Cambridge was huge, and who had been brutally murdered during the St Bartholomew's Day Massacre. Since Bruno disputed Ramus' logic-based theories, the possibility of Sidney's gracious open-mindedness towards him is worth noting. Sidney's generous outlook on the opinions of others is known; the truth of Bruno's politically motivated assertions is unknown. In the autumn of 1585 the French embassy was attacked by a mob and Castelnau returned to France taking Bruno with him on a road which led fifteen years later to a heretic's stake in Rome.

Although Watson's own *Compendium*,[90] was written in the year of Bruno's arrival it is possible that the two men met in Paris at an earlier date. Watson pays tribute to Bruno's *De Umbris Idearum* (1582) in his dedication, but wisely shuns both Bruno's mystical affiliations and his complicated mnemonic discipline, relying instead upon a simplified, and more pragmatic, local system of memory training.[91] As an authority on the classics, Watson believed his own method originated with Cicero,[92] which suggests that he also disagreed with Ramus (who held Cicero in contempt) and therefore—despite his association with Sidney's group—Sidney too. A copy of the manuscript, entitled *Artificiosae memoriae libellus*, is shelved at the British Library.[93] Watson had intended to dedicate it during a banquet in the Middle Temple Hall to the palatine Adalbert Laski (?1527-1605),[94] a powerful, volatile, yet charming Polish prince, general, and alchemist who had arrived in England at roughly the same time as Bruno. Laski, white beard trailing to his waist, loquacious, and fluent in diverse languages joined the court at Oxford University for four nights of revelry organised by the Earl of Leicester.[95] In contrast, for the feast at the Middle Temple Laski failed to turn up, and when Watson had his work printed he dedicated it instead to the courtier Henry Noell.[96]

Bruno and Laski were welcome diners at Sir Walter Raleigh's magnificent London residence of Durham House, and at Syon House where the "Wizard Earl" of Northumberland, Henry Percy, held court. Here they met members of a covert coterie of free-thinkers whose excited fascination with, and sweeping curiosity about, science, the occult, alchemy, astronomy, astrology, necromancy, and literature, earned them a reputation for atheism. Later the group was assigned the more sinister title of the "School of Night", a title pirated from Berowne's exclamation in Shakespeare's *Love's Labours Lost* which is believed to hold a number of topical allusions—with characterisation and much of its dialogue reminiscent of John Lyly's *Endymion*:[97]

> O paradox! Black is the badge of hell
> The hue of dungeons and the school of night.

5. Poetry, science, wit, and wisdom

It is doubtful, however, whether these men "of the night"—well known to each other and with common interests—composed a formal society. As Mary Ellen Lamb points out, "a group of friends may share an attitude without being a 'school' with a common purpose or programme".[98] Their leading exponents were John Dee, court conjuror and polymath, and his friend Thomas Hariot. Hariot, mathematician, astronomer, philosopher and geographer, was retained by Raleigh in the 1580s as a mathematics tutor. He took advantage of his position to sail with Raleigh's Virginian Expedition in 1585 to study the Indian Algonquian language and beliefs. Later, he served in Henry Percy's principal house at Petworth in Sussex for a generous salary of £100.[99] Marlowe was another member of the "School"; his formula for the depiction of the character of Dr Faustus is a concentrate of Bruno tinctured with Dee[100] and (some say) Raleigh as well.[101] Marlowe was associated with Hariot and Dee, and with Hariot's associate Walter Warner, the one-handed compiler of logarithms, anticipator of William Harvey's[102] theory of the circulation of the blood, and keeper of Percy's huge 2000 volume library.[103] Naturally, Marlowe also knew Raleigh—his poem "Come Live With me and Be My Love" had earned a riposte from Raleigh, and Raleigh was reputed to have been among the group which listened to the atheistic lecture that brought Marlowe down in 1593.[104] It would be surprising if Watson had not joined his friend Marlowe at Raleigh's table at Durham House, or especially—since he dedicated at least two of his works to the Earl—dined with Percy at Syon and Petworth. Present also may have been Matthew Roydon or George Peele whose praises had graced Watson's *Hekatompathia*. Perhaps Roydon's friend George Chapman was there, too.

The heyday of the movement is often placed in the 1590s, but its foundations were laid in the '80s, and it had fallen into disrepute well before the start of the '90s. Its astrological prediction of 1588 as a year of disasters was spectacularly wrong by any standards, especially after the defeat of the Spanish Armada. The fraternity was savaged by both the printing presses and the playhouses. An outbreak of the plague in the early 1590s prompted an attack on Dee as the fomenter of demonic phenomena, and in 1593 he was accused of foretelling Roderigo Lopez's attempted assassination of the Queen.[105] When, in 1592, the Jesuit Robert Persons' pamphlet *An Advertisement written to a Secretary of My L. Treasurer's in England* [106] attacked the group for setting up a "school of atheism", Dee believed that he was the unnamed "conjuror that is master", while Thomas Hariot was a contender for "the certain necromancer-astronomer as teacher". Dee's paranoia was probably misplaced. It is now believed that the pamphlet's real target was Raleigh, ambitious for election to the Privy Council, and enmeshed in a power struggle for the Queen's favour with the Earl of Essex.[107] Person's work was popular, and went through eight editions over two years.

Since the existence of the "School" cannot be proven, and its clandestine membership in any case was fairly informal and fluid, historians have been free to allocate anybody they choose to its fellowship. As an associate, Watson was mixing with an eclectic gathering which, apart from those already named, is believed to have included the poet and alchemist Ferdinando Stanley (Lord Strange, Earl of Derby); Henry Wriothesley (Earl of Southampton); George Carey (later Lord Hunsdon and a patron of Stanley's Earl of Derby's Men);[108] Fulke Greville;[109] Raleigh's aide Laurence Keymis; Richard Field a printer associated with the publication of Shakespeare's poetry; Robert Hues the geographer; Emery Molyneux a globe maker and expert in longitude; the conjurer and astrologer Simon Forman famous for his love potions; Nathaniel Torporly, described as "the Atlantes of the mathematical world";[110] and Michael Drayton, a popular poet thought by some to be the "rival poet" of Shakespeare's Sonnets. Edmund Spenser was also a member during his time in London.

So many leading intellectuals were associated with Dee that it is unsurprising that Sir Philip Sidney's circle was drawn in. Dee had taught Sidney's uncle the Earl of Leicester as a child, and the two remained on friendly terms. It is entirely possible that Leicester's favourite nephew Philip Sidney and Sidney's intimate friend Edward Dyer were also pupils of Dee. He drew up Sidney's astrological chart and taught him chemistry (then known as alchemy) — in other words, cosmography.[111] "Led by God, with Dee as teacher and with Dyer as companion," wrote Dr Thomas Moffet a contemporary biographer of Sidney, and himself a scientist, "he learned chemistry, the starry science, rival to nature."[112] Alchemy seems to have obsessed the whole family. Leicester's learned sister Mary Dudley, Philip's mother, was a devotee who commissioned two works from Dee and on her marriage to Sir Henry Sidney introduced Dee into their household too.[113] Another of Dee's friends was Mr Secretary Walsingham, whose house at Barn Elms was close to Dee's at Mortlake, and whose daughter Frances became Philip Sidney's wife.

Mary Sidney, Philip's beloved sister, was certainly not free from Dee's influence, being also a devotee of chemistry and medicine. Her chemist at Wilton was Adrian Gilbert, the half-brother of Sir Walter Raleigh, seeker of a Northwest Passage to China, and brother of Sir Humphrey Gilbert, a close friend of Dee.[114] Again, there are hints that Sidney may obliquely refer to Dee in his poetry,[115] and Peter J French convincingly argues that Sidney's *Aeropagus* movement was influenced by Dee.[116]

Sidney was also fascinated by Dee's dream of an English empire in the New World and the domination of the northern seas in a search for the unknown. In 1576 Sidney, Dyer and Philip's mother Lady Sidney, had lost £25 each on Martin Frobisher's Cathay Company's ill-fated voyage, ostensibly set up to discover a Northwest Passage, but also with the hope of unearthing fabulous quantities of gold ore.

Undaunted by Frobisher's failure, during the following year Sidney, Dyer and Leicester visited Dee at Mortlake and, fortified by Dee's expert advice, increased their investments to £50. When that expedition in turn failed the year after, Sidney and others nevertheless gambled yet again on Frobisher. Frobisher and his backer, the entrepreneur Michael Lok, depended on Dee for instruction on the mathematics and navigation for their voyages. It was certainly not Dee's fault that neither of his pupils completed his studies with any measure of competency, that navigational data at this time was poor,[117] or that all three voyages, in 1576, 1577 and 1578, ended in financial disaster. Recklessly, Sidney and Dyer had given their bond to Lok, with the result that when the Company fell into receivership in 1579 they were charged to fulfil it, and found themselves mired in financial troubles.

Early in 1583 Walsingham and Dyer, addicted still,[118] again visited Dee to plan yet another voyage of discovery to the West, and in time an expedition set off under Captain John Davis who named a foreland on the northern coast of Canada as Dyer's Cape. So attached was Dyer to Dee that when he had finished acting as Walsingham's emissary to the Northern Provinces in 1588, he journeyed across the continent to join Dee in Bohemia, where the alchemist was experimenting with a magic powder he hoped would turn base metals into gold.[119]

Another glimpse of Dee's attraction for the Sidney circle is perceived on the occasion of Lord Albert Laski's arrival in England in 1583. Sidney, who had met Laski in Venice nine years earlier, took a leading role in showing him around England, perhaps most famously on a trip by the royal barge — accompanied by Sidney, Leicester, Dyer and other gentlemen — heralded on its arrival at Dee's house in Mortlake with a grand fanfare by the Queen's trumpeters. Several days' sojourn followed. Meeting Dee may have been the primary purpose of Laski's visit to England; a highlight of his stay was, reportedly, an introduction to angelic spirits, which Dee arranged. When Laski returned to Poland, John Dee was amongst his company.[120]

Because he was an associate of the Sidneys, there is a strong probability that Watson also had some connection with Dee, a probability strengthened by Watson's association with the Earl of Oxford, another of Dee's affiliates. It is known that Oxford was acquainted with John Dee in the winter of 1570, for as a defence against the attacks against him over 20 years later in 1592, Dee cited in his *A Compendius Rehearsal* "the honourable the Earl of Oxford, his favourable letters, anno 1570" amongst his many gentle and noble patrons. Like many others, Oxford practised and believed in astrology, as noted by the publisher John Soothern in his small book of verses, *Pandora*, dedicated to Oxford in 1584.[121]

Another clue, more circumstantial, to Oxford's acquaintance with Dee is his friendship with Raleigh, a sometime drinking companion; during the time of Oxford's disgrace in 1583, it was Raleigh who put in a good word for him with the Queen.[122] Raleigh had links with Dee: his half-brothers Adrian and Sir Humphrey Gilbert were frequent visitors at Mortlake, and

Sir Humphrey took instruction in navigation from Dee—his publication *A Discourse of a Discovery for a New Passage to Cataia* (1576) was influential in promoting Frobisher's first voyage of discovery. It was published by George Gascoigne, a relative of Gilbert and an acquaintance of Oxford.

The links accumulate. For Frobisher's third voyage Oxford took out a massive £3,000 bond, the single largest investment in the enterprise. His losses were huge, but even so he joined with Dee, Raleigh and Adrian Gilbert, Sir Humphrey's brother, to help plan the expedition of Captain John Davis in 1585. Again, Oxford invested heavily, and lost heavily. It is also worth observing that Dee's journals for 1595, when he was living in Manchester not too distant from the seat of the Derbys, show that he received several visits from the sixth Earl of Derby and the Countess Elizabeth, Oxford's daughter.

However, the "School of Night" was but one of several overlapping and entwined circles of intellectuals and literary professionals of Watson's acquaintance. Another grouping has been dubbed the "University Wits". Like the "School of Night" the title was bestowed in a later age, it seems by the Victorian literary historian and critic George Saintsbury in his *A History of English Literature* (1887).[123] Several of Saintsbury's successors have been so taken with the notion, that it is as if a grouping by that name actually existed.

Interestingly, the term "wit" with its modern meaning was first introduced around the time of Lyly's *Euphues, the Anatomy of Wit* in 1578. Until then, the word *wit* was used in the Old English sense of a predilection to study, to reason, and to engage in intellectual activity. By contrasting *wit* with *wisdom* Lyly hinted at an additional connotation of facetiousness, much like we understand the word today.[124] This double meaning held sway during Elizabethan times, and presumably the epithet "University Wits", with its nineteenth century invention, also has this double meaning.

Saintsbury suggested a small circle headed by Lyly, Marlowe, Greene, Peele, Lodge, Nashe and (probably) Kyd.[125] His short list should certainly have included Watson, even though Watson's dramatic works are now lost.[126] Oddly, Saintsbury undermined his close definition of

"University Wits" by suggesting the inclusion of Kyd, whom he acknowledged probably never attended either university.[127] He also included Greene, a Cambridge scholar, despite Lyly's acknowledgement in *Euphues* of his "very good friends the gentlemen scholars of Oxford".[128]

Saintsbury's suggestion of a limited circle of literary colleagues is reinforced by Thomas Dekker's pamphlet *A Knights Conjuring* (1607), even though it was written much later than the generation of "wits". Dekker's work depicts a laurel grove in which "Poets and Musicians" are gathered. There are three bowers. In the first Spenser is seated with Chaucer, another shows Marlowe, Greene and Peele, joined later by Nashe and Chettle, and,

> [i]n another company sat learned Watson, industrious Kyd, ingenious Atchlow [Thomas Achelley], and (though he had been a player, moulded out their pens) yet because he had been their lover, and a register to the Muses, inimitable Bentley ...

Some more recent literary historians have let their imaginations run riot, pretending that the term "University Wits" was common in Elizabethan days, asserting that the Wits were hard drinking frequenters of the London taverns[129] (where's the evidence?), and expanding completely out of hand the size of the group to around forty poets, playwrights, pamphleteers, and "wits".[130]

Camaraderie certainly existed amongst these writers—they penned commendatory verses for each other's works—but there were also bitter rivalries and jealousies. They were united as playwrights by heroic dramas which sparkled with gusto, action, and strong lines—and they flaunted a similar vigour in their poetry. Often they overdid it and coarsened their lines with bombast. When the drama turned to slapstick, Lyly alone shunned the coarse or infantile.

It was a cultural movement, a drift of young men from university to London, to the theatre and to the court. These were the "gentlemen scholars of both universities" cautioned by Robert Greene in his *A Groatsworth of Wit* against seeking their fortune in the London theatres. Greene had good reason to know, his own seamy reputation notoriously ending abruptly after a "banquet of Rhenish wine and pickled herring" in 1592. Lyly's experience was summed up by his letter to Elizabeth in 1598: "But three legacies I bequeath, Patience to my creditors, Melancholy without measure to my friends, and Beggary without shame to my family."[131]

There were connections, too, which owed nothing to a university education. Kyd, who attended neither of the universities, studied at the Merchant Taylors' School under the headship of Richard Mulcaster and alongside Edmund Spenser and Thomas Lodge. One detects a small network here. Kyd studied with Lodge; Watson's sister was brought up with the Lodge family; Watson was the friend of Marlowe; Kyd and Marlowe lodged together from 1590 or 1591 until 1593. Common interests and acquaintance may have counted for as much as a university education.

Both Watson and Lodge were members of the Earl of Oxford's circle. Indeed, in the opening passages of his *Catharos* (1591), Lodge had the temerity to satirise Oxford's father-in-law Burghley[132]—just as Shakespeare's Polonius also satirised the Queen's chief minister.[133] In fact, of Saintsbury's core group of University Wits—Lyly, Greene, Peele, Lodge, Nashe, Marlowe and Kyd—only Marlowe and Kyd have no recorded association with the Earl of Oxford. Yet, because of their close association with each other and with Thomas Watson, the probability is that they also found their way into Oxford's literary retreat at Fisher's Folly. Feasibly, Saintsbury's "wits" and Oxford's disciples are the selfsame group. Like Watson, they may also have been associated with Mary Sidney and the Earl of Pembroke's group (APPENDIX C).

With the publication of *Hekatompathia* Watson's reputation rose high. In the year of its publication, he also contributed a short Latin dedication to Christopher Ocland's *Eirēnarchia, sive, Elizabetha*, a work ordered by the High Commission to be used in all grammar and free schools. His next three works were in Latin, too. *Compendium Memoriae Localis* and *Amyntas* both appeared in 1585,[134] and both were dedicated to the popular courtier Henry Noell. A friend of Sir Walter Raleigh, a patron of literature and music, and an enthusiastic participator in the Whitehall tilts, Noell was described by Peele as "noble-minded",[135] and by Sir John Harington as "one of the greatest gallants" of the early 1590s.[136]

Watson's *Amyntas* is mostly indebted to the Renaissance eclogue tradition, although it also may have borrowed elements from Torquato Tasso's Italian drama *Aminta*, published as recently as 1573.[137] In Watson's version, an Arcadian shepherd seated on the banks of the Thames laments the death of his wife. His anguish lasts for eleven days, represented by eleven verses, until suicide is the only means of reunion with his lover. His body transforms into an amaranthus plant on which Amor, or Cupid, bestows the power to staunch bleeding.

Two years later, Watson's Latin work was pirated into English by the poet and lawyer Abraham Fraunce, a specialist in translating classical and continental works. Indebted to Philip Sidney's purse for his Cambridge education, Fraunce cosied up to the Wilton House circle and stayed on after his patron's death, dedicating his *The Lamentations of Amyntas for the Death of Phillis* to the Countess of Pembroke in consolation for the loss of her brother. It became his most popular work. Since the translation was made without acknowledgement to Watson, Watson was hardly pleased. In his English version of *Meliboeus* published on the death of Sir Francis Walsingham in 1590, he wrote, "I interpret my self, lest *Melibaeus* in speaking English by another man's labour, should lease my name in his change, as my *Amyntas* did."[138] Fraunce put his work through three editions,[139] but a year after Watson's gripe he published *The Countess of Pembroke's Ivychurch*,[140] in the Second Part of which he at last acknowledged his source: "I have some what altered S. Tasso's Italian, and M. Watson's Latin Amyntas, to make them both one English". In this version Fraunce changed the name of Tasso's "Sylvia" to Watson's "Phillis" and added a conclusion, "The Twelfth Day", to describe Mary Sidney's remembrance of her brother.[141]

Watson's third Latin work during this productive period was his *Helenae Raptus* of 1586, a translation of Coluthus' sixth century Greek narration of the story of Helen and Paris.[142] Marlowe is reputed to have Englished the poem in the following year, but since the attribution was made by a reputed forger,[143] and in any case has since been lost, that trail runs cold. Of Watson's Latin version, only a single copy survives,[144] one of two works he dedicated to Henry Percy, the Duke of Northumberland.

The other is an unpublished manuscript dating from around 1588, and discovered as recently as 1928, entitled *A Learned Dialogue of Bernard Palessy, Concerning Waters and Fountains, both Natural and Artificial*.[145] The manuscript is a translation from the French Huguenot potter and hydraulics engineer Bernard Palissy (c1510-1589) and offers an insight into Watson's scientific interests.[146] At this time, Palissy's discourse on waters and fountains would have been useful to Percy whose enthusiasm for horticulture was reflected by his considerable exertion into improving his gardens at Petworth.[147] Whether Watson volunteered to translate the work or Percy commissioned his translation is of no matter: the significance is that it was the "wise man in St Helen's, that could tell strange things",[148] Dekker's "learned Watson", who made the translation.[149]

Six:
William Byrd: "Our Phoenix"

AFTER his return from the continent in 1579 Watson stayed for a while in Westminster. Close to the Abbey lay Westminster School. Here, the second master was William Camden, four years into his profession and soon to achieve fame as the respected—indeed, esteemed—historian, herald, and author of the renowned survey of the Great Britain and Ireland, *Britannia* (1586)

How Camden met Watson we cannot know, but for Watson it was a beneficial and far-reaching fellowship. Clearly they had interests in common. Both were Oxford men; Camden entered Magdalen in 1566, Watson entered New College some three or four years later. They shared a life-long enthusiasm for music.

Camden contributed a commendatory puff in Latin to Watson's first printed work, *Antigone,* which was nothing short of effusive:

> ... why am I sounding your praises from my meagre store of talent? Thus I am attempting to brighten the sun with smoke ..."[1]

Moreover, both had connections with the Sidney group, which had meetings in Westminster, too. Camden's own friendship with the Areopagus circle originated in his student days, when, as a poor young chorister, he put up at an Oxford hostel for law students, called Broadgates Hall (its status rose in the early seventeenth century when it became Pembroke College). At Broadgates, Camden had the good fortune to attract the notice of Dr Thomas Thornton of Christ Church College. Dr Thornton is remembered on his funerary monument as "a common refuge for young poor scholars of great hopes and parts ...", an accurate description of his endeavour to find more comfortable lodgings for Camden.[2] The epitaph continues by recalling Thornton was "tutor to Sir Philip Sidney when he was of Christ Church",[3] so it is perhaps understandable that Thornton's protégé also became close to Sidney. Watson had connections with the Sidney circle, too: a possible meeting with Sir Philip in Paris or Padua, acquaintance with both Sir Francis and Thomas Walsingham, and, as we shall see, an involvement in the world of the esoteric. To which we can now add his friendship with Camden.

It was not only Camden's connection with the Sidney set which made him important as a contact: Camden was also a close friend of Elizabethan England's greatest composer, William Byrd. "Our Phoenix…" wrote Henry Peacham, "in whom in that kind, I know not whether any man may equal"; while John Baldwin declaimed, "In Europe is none like our English man."[4] For his contemporaries to call him "*Britanniae Musicae Parens*" (the father of British music), was no mean compliment at a time of a great flowering for British music.[5]

Since Byrd's collaboration with Thomas Watson was of benefit to both men, we need to catch a glimpse of the world of William Byrd, the man of music, faith, and business.

His early life is poorly recorded, although it is thought that he was born around 1540, the son of Thomas and Margery Byrd, about whom little else is certain. On reaching his tenth year, it is likely that he followed two elder brothers, Symond and John, into St Paul's Cathedral as a chorister. There he was instructed by "Master Sebastian" Westcote, minor canon, organist, master of the choristers, writer of twenty-nine court plays with accompanying incidental music, and founder of the "Children of St Paul's".

Westcote was a stalwart Catholic: he directed Mary's coronation music in 1553, and the following year prepared the music for High Mass at St Paul's, including di Lasso's motet *Te spectant Reginalde Pole* (published 1556) in the very presence of the composer, then visiting England. On Elizabeth's accession, Westcote refused to subscribe to the Act of Uniformity, and in 1577 his Papistry landed him in gaol. Nevertheless, like Byrd later, he had the support of Elizabeth herself who secured his release, and he began again to present plays for his Queen. His Catholic sympathies almost certainly influenced many of his pupils, including both Byrd and Thomas Morley (another great composer who mixed artistry with business).

In his will made shortly before his death in 1582, Westcote appointed Henry Evans as lessee of the Blackfriars Playhouse, the theatre he had established for fashionable public indoor performances by the Children. Afterwards it was acquired by John Lyly and the Earl of Oxford.

Probably it was the connection between St Paul's and the Chapel Royal that brought Byrd to the notice of the organist there—Thomas Tallis. A warm friendship burgeoned, and it is possible that Tallis took on Byrd as his assistant organist as well as a pupil. In the meantime, Byrd's circle of acquaintances and contacts was broadening to include seasoned composers like John Sheppard and William Mundy.

Byrd's four driving characteristics unfolded: first an immense musical talent, second an unshakeable Catholic faith, third a soaring ambition. The fourth will become apparent. Around 1562, still in his early twenties, his career began to take off with an appointment as organist and master of the choristers at Lincoln Cathedral. Marriage to Julian Birley in 1568 produced a son, Christopher, in the following year. Then, a dispute in 1569 with the Cathedral's Chapter—did his extended playing of the organ offended their Puritan sensibilities?—was a setback to his ambitions, until the offer of a vacancy at the prestigious Chapel Royal early in 1572 must have seemed something of a Godsend. He shifted back to London to be sworn in as a Gentleman and to share the organist's post with his old master and friend Thomas Tallis. He also struck up a friendship with Alfonso Ferrabosco the court's resident Italian musician—and spy.

Although now resident in London, Byrd astutely continued to draw an annual salary from Lincoln for almost another ten years, in return for supplying the cathedral with "songs and divine services well set to music"[6] for the rest of his life. Thus we observe the fourth of Byrd's leading characteristics: not only was he a peerless and ambitious composer and a loyal Catholic, he was also a shrewd man of business.

In 1575, his nose for business led to the joint grant to Byrd and Tallis of a royal licence for the sole right to print music and ruled music manuscript paper, and to import music books from the continent. By now, Tallis was getting on in years: just two years later he described himself as "very aged", implying he was over seventy. His birth date is uncertain, but probably he was born in Kent around 1505. He first appears in the records in 1532 as organist for the small and impoverished Benedictine monastery of Dover Priory. Then, around 1537 or 1538 he joined the choir at St Mary-at-Hill in London's Billingsgate, notable for its choir and its progressive encouragement of music. He did not stay long, however; in the autumn of 1538 he was given a place with the lady chapel choir at the Augustinian abbey of Holy Cross at Waltham in Essex. When, two years later, the abbey was dissolved, the last of the English abbeys to fall, Tallis received as compensation "20s for wages, and 20s for reward". Almost at once, he found fresh, though brief, employment at Canterbury, formerly a Benedictine priory which just a fortnight earlier had been established as a secular establishment under Thomas Cranmer's radical leadership. Perhaps it was Cranmer's influence that, three years later, found for Tallis a prestigious appointment as a Gentleman of the Chapel Royal. The post was secure and permanent, and he held it until his death. By 1577 he could declare that he had "served the Queen and her ancestors almost forty years", and truly he was much valued—and well rewarded—by his royal patrons. Apart from his fee as a Gentleman, he received livery at the funeral of Henry VIII and the coronation of Edward VI, and in 1557 Queen Mary granted him a lucrative 21-year lease on the Manor of Minster-in-Thanet in Kent.

Some writers have suggested that Tallis was a prudent yes-man who amended his religious beliefs to accommodate the changing policies of the monarchs he served. During his lifetime, the Latin of the Catholic liturgy was replaced by English, changed back to Latin, and finally reverted again to English; yet without apparent effort he was able to switch from the austere anthems of Edward's short reign to the elaborate polyphony beloved by Queen Mary. However, the canard that his religious belief blew with the political wind is probably untrue: he is likely to have remained a committed Catholic throughout all four reigns, escaping persecution only because of his highly placed connections. His later works certainly suggest a leaning towards recusancy; for example his *Lamentations of Jeremiah* (composed in 1560 and 1569), a plea for Jerusalem to return to the one true God, widely interpreted as an allegoric call for England to return to the Catholic faith. The times were perilous and probably he shared the faith of his Catholic friend Byrd, another giant of the Tudor musical scene, and similarly managing to evade serious penalties.

The aged Tallis was the doyen of the Chapel Royal by 1575 when he and Byrd were granted their royal patent. To acquire such a wide-ranging licence to print songs or part songs, both church and secular in any language, could have led to conflict with one of the most important printers of the time, John Day, who also owned a patent—to print the standard psalm texts of the established church. However, there was no quarrel. While Day's patent was lucrative, Byrd and Tallis's first—and sole joint—publishing venture, undertaken in the first year of their patent, was a fiasco. This superbly crafted volume of seventeen compositions to honour Elizabeth in the seventeenth year of her reign, appeared under the title *Cantiones quae ab argumento sacrae vocantur*. It included works not only by Tallis and Byrd but also by other influential composers including Sir Ferdinando Richardson and Richard Mulcaster, the educator. The printer, Thomas Vautrollier, a refugee Huguenot, used a set of music type imported from the Nuremberg type-cutter John Petreius. The outlay was staggering: it cost the two composers personally the huge sum of at least 200 marks. Yet sales were poor, and in an appeal to the Queen just two years later they claimed that their "license for the printings of music … hath fallen to our great loss and hindrance".[7]

Their lined manuscript paper was more successful. The Queen's Printer, Christopher Barker, reported to Burghley that he found it "somewhat beneficial". Sadly, he added that "as for the music books, I would not provide necessary furniture to have them". Most likely Byrd and Tallis started too ambitiously and lacked the experience and means to market *Cantiones* efficiently. But the times were also against them. While their manuscript compilations were eagerly received by a small circle of enthusiasts,[8] for the printed volumes there was no sizeable market amongst the largely protestant public.

Their fingers burnt, no further books were published until after Tallis's death a few years later, when Byrd refreshed the licence. The two composers cum businessmen were by no means impoverished, however, for the patent to print lined manuscript paper and import continental printed music was very lucrative. Moreover, it was these two categories that in time fostered the transfusion into England of madrigal works from the continent and boosted the great flowering of English music. It was then that music book publishing took off, and Byrd's patent became a priceless asset.

Tallis died in 1585. Byrd marked his death with what has been described as "surely the greatest consort song ever written, 'Ye Sacred Muses', an unforgettable lament notable for the absolute purity of its text-setting and for the harmonic manipulation of sentiments that is nothing short of uncanny".[9] Long after the music has finished, its poignant last line lingers in the memory: "Tallis is dead and Music dies".

Byrd, the canny businessman, sought patronage wherever he could. His acquaintance with the Sidney group is fairly certain (although not agreed by all historians) and traced by the music historian John Harley through Byrd's family and friends to his association with William Camden, a known disciple of the Sidneys as we have noted.[10] The certainty is reinforced by Byrd's music settings of erotic pieces from Sidney's *Astrophel and Stella* in the mid-1580s, possibly during Sidney's lifetime. In addition, a set of four songs beginning with "Constant Penelope"[11] contains hidden allusions to Sidney's contrition over his treatment of Penelope Rich,[12] and there also seems to be an additional agenda in the publication of moving tributes composed at the time of Sidney's death, "Come to me grief for ever" and "O that most rare breast".[13] In addition, Byrd set texts written by Sidney's close friend Sir Edward Dyer [14] and appears to have been friendly with the Sidneys' Norfolk acquaintance, Edward Paston—to judge by the large quantity of Byrd's manuscripts in Paston's library.

Edward de Vere, the seventeenth Earl of Oxford, also knew Byrd. In 1574 Byrd signed a lease with the Earl for Battyshall Manor in Essex, close to Stondon Massey near Ongar. Many years later, Byrd eventually settled at Battyshall with his second wife, Ellen, not far from some relatives in Ingatestone. At Ingatestone, dwelt the Catholic Petre family, close friends of Byrd.[15] Some of Byrd's musical settings of verses by Oxford have come down to us.[16] Oxford was distantly related to George Puttenham, thought to be the author of *The Art of English Poesy*, who by turn was related by marriage to Sir Edward Dyer (for whom Byrd set texts), the close friend of Sir Philip Sidney—thus another connection.[17] Byrd's collaboration in the late 1580s with Watson—sometime secretary to the Earl of Oxford—is also significant. Years later, in 1605, Byrd dedicated the first volume of his *Gradualia* to de Vere's cousin Henry Howard, the Earl of Northampton; de Vere had died in the previous year, so its timing may have been a matter of circumspection on Byrd's part.

Far more dangerous was the patronage of Thomas, Lord Paget. Paget and Byrd shared two important passions: religion and music. Thomas was the second son of William, Lord Paget, dead since 1563. William had descended from stock so humble that he preferred to keep quiet about it. Although his father had been a Shearman and Sergeant-at-Mace to the Sheriff of London his enemies put it about that he was the son of a catchpole,[18] or (worse) that his father had been a nailer in the Midlands.[19] Since nailing was the least skilled of all the iron trades, it was lowly indeed. Nevertheless, William took a degree at Cambridge, where he was a contemporary of Thomas Wriothesley, first Earl of Southampton. He was, moreover, a Tudor "new man", a role in which his pragmatism, especially in religion, eased him into one of the most powerful positions in the kingdom.

When Thomas Cromwell fell, Paget took over his post as principal adviser to Henry VIII, a package which included a network of spies, as well as the title of Lord Paget of Beaudesert. As the King decayed and his death drew ever near, Paget was constantly at his side, sorting out his will and concluding a deal to become on his death the adviser to Edward Seymour, then Earl of Hertford. When that momentous event occurred, Paget was among the few counsellors—alongside Thomas Cranmer and Thomas Smith—to rally to Seymour, now promoted to Duke of Somerset. Once Somerset was installed as Lord Protector to the nine-year-old Edward VI, Paget navigated skilfully through the murky political waters, though even he could not avoid a short spell in the Tower. Slick manoeuvring, including switching support from Lady Jane Grey to Mary Tudor to a jaw-clenching nicety, resulted in his appointment as her Lord Privy Seal and a member of Philip of Spain's inner council.[20] Thus it was that from the humblest of origins William rose to become one of the kingdom's most powerful rulers. On Elizabeth's accession he gave up public life, and he died in 1563 with a fortune of £3,000 a year, garnered largely from huge estates acquired through the dissolution of the monasteries—at Burton and Beaudesert in Staffordshire and West Drayton in Middlesex. He had eleven children, but all his wealth, to the last groat, passed to his eldest son Henry.

Henry, Lord Paget, enjoyed his inheritance for just five years.[21] When he died shortly after Christmas 1568 he was succeeded by his brother Thomas. Their father's success had depended largely on his ability to yield to the religious wind; his sons had purer consciences and were less pliable. The younger brothers Thomas and Charles were not only committed but also prominent Catholics: before taking up his title, Thomas spent fourteen weeks in gaol for his religion.

After her husband William's death, their mother Anne Lady Paget had continued to live at the manor at West Drayton, which—like the Paget houses in Burton and London—had become a Catholic rallying centre, and continued as such until her own death in 1587.[22] Meanwhile, by about 1570, Thomas had married a rich Catholic widow from Norfolk, Nazareth Southwell. A son was born, but the marriage was unhappy, and by 1578 the couple had parted. The crisis came when the Jesuit priests Edmund Campion and Robert Persons arrived with a large party in England in June 1580; Thomas arranged for Campion to preach on the Feast of St Peter and Paul before a huge gathering at the house of Lord Norris in Smithfield. Both society and government were shocked, and Thomas could not have been surprised when he was called before the Privy Council. His punishment was confinement at the house of the Dean of Windsor, a fervent protestant who had orders to instruct him in Anglican doctrine. The punishment was lenient, which suggests the Privy Council had an ulterior motive: Nazareth had some influence at court, and—perhaps significantly—as soon as Thomas had placed a generous financial settlement on his wife he was released. Nazareth did not live long to enjoy her new personal wealth: the settlement was in December,[23] she died the following year.

Thomas's championship of Campion was no solitary aberration. His recusancy was fervent, and his circle of Catholic friends and servants wide. He retained a Catholic chaplain, and supported a resident liturgical choir at Burton House.[24] That was not all: he cultivated an interest in the arts, rebuilt the house at Beaudesert, owned a huge library, and read Latin,

Italian, French, and quite possibly Greek and Spanish as well.[25]

Thomas's enthusiasm for music was perhaps inevitable. It was inherited from his father, William, who had kept a resident musician, Thomas Tusser. It was Tusser's first position since leaving Cambridge; later he achieved fame as the Suffolk farmer who wrote *A Hundreth Good Pointes of Husbandrie* (1557), a long poem in rhyming couplets recording the country year, and dedicated to his patron. Augmented to *Five Hundred Points of Good Husbandry* in 1573 it became a sixteenth century best seller.

Thomas Paget's love of music was even greater than his father's. His accounts show that he probably owned an organ in his lodgings in London's Charterhouse, while in 1578, he invested in a pair of virginals for his stepdaughter, and paid a tutor to instruct her. For his son he bought an elementary music book. Up in Staffordshire, he twice provided fodder for some Lichfield choristers in 1580, and even paid a piper to entertain and encourage some lucky corn binders labouring in the hot August fields of 1582.

Moreover, he himself was a composer. "And for your songs," commented his friend Edward Somerset, Lord Herbert, in a letter dated 24 June 1573, "sure if they be better than ever I heard they had need to be very good ... but to the judgement I refer to Mr Charles [Thomas's brother]."[26] Even imprisonment could not curb his musical enthusiasm. He continued to compose while he was confined at the Dean of Windsor's house, and had his songs and songbooks sent down from Staffordshire. Meanwhile, Somerset sent him copies of some of his own compositions which William Byrd had cast an eye over and corrected; Somerset and Paget were also familiar with Tallis, Parsons and Whyte.

It was not only Somerset who relied on Paget's musical knowledge. In May 1582, Edward Manners, the third Earl of Rutland, wrote to him to ask "in the behalf of my daughter that it will please to send her some Italian and English ditties to sing".[27] Byrd's known association with Paget may have led Manners to ask him in 1585 to suggest a teacher for his daughter Lady Elizabeth at a salary of £10 a year: (In 1587 a young Thomas Morley—later the noted madrigalist—was appointed tutor of the virginals to a daughter of John Manners, by now Edward's successor as the fourth Earl).

It has been speculated that Byrd may have visited the Pagets as early as his younger days in Lincoln, perhaps to write some music to entertain the family and its friends.[28] There is much stronger evidence that he was communicating with the Pagets by 1573, and there is no question that from 1576 (at the latest) the family was granting him an annuity of £10, which continued even after Thomas fled to Paris in November 1583, never to turn back. When, as a young man, Byrd returned to London from Lincoln, he may have first taken lodgings in London's Clerkenwell district, a known heart of Catholic recusancy. By 1577, however, he had moved to Harlington in Middlesex, a stone's throw from Thomas Paget's Catholic centre at Drayton. There are other clues of an association between Byrd and Thomas Paget: a "Mr Byrd" lunched and dined at Burton for a week in August 1580, arriving just as "Mr Babington", was leaving;[29] and there are letters to suggest that Byrd was a guest of the Pagets in 1581 and 1582. In addition, Byrd taught Thomas's brother Charles the art of composition, and kept in touch even after Charles had sailed for the continent.

To be associated with Thomas Paget, a well-known recusant tainted with conspiracy, was dangerous.[30] Thomas's position was vulnerable. When the Throckmorton Plot was uncovered in 1583, he fled to Paris to join his brother Charles who was an agent for Mary Queen of Scots. A few months later, Byrd was called for examination by the Council—we may suppose because of a certain letter which had fallen into Walsingham's hands. It was dated November 1583, signed "W B", and addressed to Charles Paget in Rouen. William Parry, a government spy and agent-provocateur living in Paris, reported that Byrd was "very honourably treated" and not arrested.[31] Nevertheless he had to pay over a bond for the large sum of £200 and make himself available at his house "within any reasonable warning".[32] A year later, when Philip Howard also took refuge on the continent, Byrd's house was thoroughly searched.[33]

Three years later, the Privy Council got their hands on one of the choristers at Thomas Paget's Burton estate, one Henry Edyall. Edyall vehemently denied both that he was a Papist and the singing of "any dirges in his house", claiming only "songs of Mr Byrd's and Mr Tallis' and no other unlawful song".[34] Paget's estates were seized, and in 1587 he was convicted of conspiracy with the Babington plotters. He died in exile in 1590.[35]

The two faces of his equally Catholic brother Charles Paget are amply exposed in the letter from the Low Countries dated 3rd October 1591, quoted on page 84, which he wrote to a "Mons. Giles Martin, Frenchman, London" betraying the early activities of Thomas Morley, singer organist, protégé of William Byrd, spy for Walsingham—and successor to Byrd as the officially licensed publisher of music, and in time the greatest of England's madrigalists.[36]

Byrd's recusancy was no secret; his name appears in the recusancy returns of October 1586 and April 1592. As well as the Pagets he had other friends among the Catholic nobility—men such as the Lords Herbert, Lumley, Northampton and Petre, who found comfort in mutual support in distressing times. Lord Herbert (Edward Somerset, fourth Earl of Worcester from February 1589) possessed a large collection of music books, including English, Italian, and sacred music. The volumes were kept at his residence in London's Strand where Byrd is known to have lodged. When Byrd's *Liber primus sacrarum cantionum quinque vocum* was published in 1589, Worcester was the dedicatee. The Worcesters had a close relationship with the Petres, affirmed by the marriage of Herbert's daughter to the son of the first Lord Petre. A rather convoluted genealogy[37] reveals that Worcester was in fact distantly related to Byrd, who could also claim a weak connection with the Catholic Vaux family.

The Lumleys was another family with whom Byrd trod dangerously. In 1569, John, First Baron Lumley was imprisoned in the Tower, alongside his father-in-law the Earl of Arundel, on suspicion of treasonable dealings in the Ridolfi Plot. Later John was moved to a house near Staines, and from 1571 to 1573 to the Marshalsea. As time passed, he had some sort of reconciliation with the government: October 1586 saw his joining the judges at the trial of Mary Queen of Scots, and in 1590 he conveyed his inheritance of Nonsuch Palace to the Queen. The following year he entertained her at Lewes. For all his efforts, however, he was unable to rid himself of suspicion; as late as 1594 a letter refers to his harbouring of seminary priests.[38] His collections of pictures and books were renowned; when he died they were purchased by James I, whence in time they became the basis of the British Library. He also owned a considerable collection of musical instruments and supported a large number of singers. To him Byrd dedicated his *Liber secundus sacrarum cantionum* (1591), and it is possible that Lumley allowed Byrd to browse amidst his huge music library, which included several Continental motets.[39] When in 1592 Byrd's son Christopher married Katherine More, a great-grand-daughter of Sir Thomas More (and sister to a seminary priest), William Byrd could claim a family connection to Lumley since both Katherine and the Baron were descended from the Scrope family.[40]

Yet another dangerous recusant acquaintance was Henry Howard, Earl of Northampton. A learned man who had taught civil law at Cambridge, and possessor of what was said to be a sparkling wit, he was also a member of one of the country's most prominent Catholic families, and a cousin of the Earl of Oxford. When, in 1572, his elder brother Thomas, the fourth Duke of Norfolk, was executed for conspiring to marry Mary Queen of Scots, Henry fell under suspicion too. He managed to clear himself, but was little trusted and he retired to Audley End in Essex where he made strenuous efforts to regain Elizabeth's favour. To that end his friendship with his cousin Charles Arundell was unhelpful—together with Edward de Vere, one Francis Southwell, and another cousin, Arundell had spent four years scheming to return the country to Roman Catholicism.[41] At Christmas 1580 de Vere threw himself on his knees before Elizabeth and confessed all. Whether he had sincerely toyed with Catholicism, or whether his confession was the climax of an elaborate undercover scheme to expose his former companions, is not ascertainable, but the latter seems likely. Howard and Arundell were arrested. When Oxford proposed subjecting them to some thirty-four questions, they retaliated by making slanderous defamations against the Earl. With the exposure of the Throckmorton Plot in 1583, Arundell fled to France and Howard was flung into the Fleet Prison. During his lifetime he was arrested and imprisoned five times.

Howard would have been a totally unsafe ally for Byrd. By no means recusant, he often dissociated himself with the Catholic opposition. Moreover, because of his position on the royal commission appointed to pursue Jesuit priests in England he oversaw the trial and sentencing of Fr Henry Garnet, a lifelong friend of Byrd. Howard's return to the favour of government and court was gradual, to the extent that from the mid-1590s he was an ally of the Earl of Essex. His guile, though, was exposed when he managed to disengage himself from the Earl's circle in good time to be uninvolved in the revolt of 1601. Full favour was restored under James I who invited him into his inner circle—where he became known as "his Majesty's earwig".[42] He was reconciled to the Catholic Church on his deathbed.

Howard had a keen, intellectual, interest in music. A letter describes how he was "of late very well disposed to bestow some idle time upon the lute."[43] Early in 1605 Byrd dedicated to Howard his *Gradualia* which has been judged, "the most uncompromising Catholic collection of music published in England for two centuries",[44] Byrd described how Howard "often heard my compositions with pleasure".[45] It was seven months after the death of Howard's enemy, Oxford, and ten months before the Gunpowder Plot.

Byrd's *Gradualia II* of February 1607 was published after the trauma of the Plot and was dedicated to Sir John Petre. It is worth pausing here to snatch a glimpse both of the bond between William Byrd and the Petres, and also something of the affairs of an Elizabethan Catholic family of the lesser nobility with which he mixed.

Sir John Petre's father, Sir William, was the son of a wealthy Devonshire cattle farmer and tanner whose seat close to Dartmoor dated back some two or three hundred years. William had left the West Country to study law at Oxford, and after graduating in 1526 at around the age of twenty, became a doctor of law in 1533. A connection with George Boleyn—the brother of Anne, son of Sir Thomas, and after 1529 the second Viscount Rochford—triggered his steady advancement in government circles where he caught the attention of Thomas Cromwell, who persuaded the King to commission him as his deputy in ecclesiastical matters. Thus, from 1535 until 1540 Petre spent much of his working days travelling, visiting and dissolving religious houses. The best that can be said for him in this unsavoury employment is that he was detested less than his rapacious fellow commissioners.[46] When Barking Abbey was dissolved in December 1539, he acquired its smaller property at "Gynge Abbess" in Essex, pulled down the buildings, and built his seat on the site: Ingatestone Hall.

After Cromwell's fall in 1540, Petre was sworn into the King's Council where he helped with those lesser cases beneath the consideration of the powerful Privy Council. His rise was steady: Deputy Seal of the Duchy of Lancaster; Junior Principal Secretary of State to Sir William Paget; a knighthood; and then King's Principal Secretary—an office he shared with Paget. The post led to automatic promotion to the Privy Council. On Edward's assumption of the throne, Petre became sole Principal Secretary for about a year until Thomas Smith joined him in 1548. He was replaced after the fall of the protector Somerset. On Edward's death, Petre was one of those councillors who switched allegiance from Lady Jane Grey to Mary Tudor. His miscalculation had been potentially disastrous, but no damage came of it. The Queen reappointed him as Secretary to the Privy Council where he became a leading negotiator of her marriage to Philip II. By 1557, Petre had left the secretaryship, but he continued to make himself useful both to Mary and, after her death, to Elizabeth who retained him on the council. He continued to attend until 1567, and he died in 1572.

Sir William's first wife, Gertrude Tyrell of Little Warley, Essex, had died in late 1541 leaving two infant daughters in need of care. Within months, Sir William made a profitable marriage to another Essex woman. Anne Tyrell was the daughter of a former Lord Mayor of London and as the widow of John Tyrell from Heron Hall in East Horndon, Essex, she was distantly related to Petre's first wife. Just four days before Christmas in 1549 she gave birth to William's only surviving son. John thus had three half-sisters and an elder and a younger full sister.

Common interests drew John Petre and William Byrd together: Catholicism and music. John may have inherited his love of music from his father—Sir William certainly encouraged it. He had recreation in mind when he designed the Long Gallery at Ingatestone, roomy enough for exercise, entertainment, and—not the least—music-making. The archives reveal his excitement for music.[47] There was, for example, his impatience over the Christmas period of 1547-8 to get away from the affairs of court and King. As soon as he could—on 3 January—he rode hard and impatiently from Hampton Court to Essex, arriving in time to join his wife and children at breakfast on Twelfth Night. After his ride he relaxed to the entertainment of several Welsh harpists, three minstrels and Gilder the tumbler. Come the following Christmas he made sure to buy fresh wire in London in advance for the virginals, which not long afterwards were moved "from the Court" to his fine house in Aldersgate Street. Another time, in June 1550, we discover his purchase of a viol and a gittern, and during that same summer a lute. He most likely packed off the three instruments to Ingatestone, where amongst his servants was one "John the Frenchman that playeth on the instruments". In all probability John the Frenchman was teaching Petre's daughter Dorothy the lute (another had been recently repaired by an Ingatestone joiner) and entertaining Petre's guests at their meals.

Over the Christmas period of 1551 the beneficent Petre invited Ingatestone townsfolk to dinner and supper in the Great Hall, an invitation which included "poor folks". Moreover, on St Stephen's Day that year "four singers and players" made a trip from the nearby village of Margaretting to join the Petres and their guests. Some records have been lost, so we must leap a few years to 1555 when a servant's son had the honour of becoming a child of the Chapel Royal.[48] In the same year, the virginals are again mentioned in the account books, while in 1562 three pairs are listed in the books at the Aldersgate Street house. In the passing years, repairs are made and new strings and parts ordered. Petre was also interested in the organ; the Ingatestone accounts for 1556 record the repair of an organ by one Gylham, and Sir William bought a new instrument from the same organ builder in 1561.

Significantly, the records also show that he patronised St Paul's boys. In April 1559 they were paid 6s 8d for "singing and Playing before my master" at Aldersgate Street, and again in 1560 for playing at the wedding of his daughter Thomasine. Over the years, the accounts show Sir William employing musicians at both his Aldersgate town house and at Ingatestone for accompanying waits, minstrels, morris dancers, and other musical entertainers.[49]

It is no surprise, therefore, to learn that Sir William was keen to educate his children musically. In May 1556 he employed a resident tutor, Thomas Jeffe, probably to teach the girls; virginals, lute, and viol strings are paid for as well as Jeffe's lodging for three weeks. In 1560, 10s was paid "to Percy for teaching the gentlewomen to play on the virginals" (Mary Percy was the senior housekeeper).[50] Petre's ward, John Talbot, was treated to a "Colen" (Cologne) lute, and for Talbot's marriage to Katherine Petre two years later Currance's school of dancing contributed to the entertainment. Petre's son John had his own viol and, as we have seen, his own virginals as well, and it is clear that he had a pair of virginals from at least the age of ten, for a tutor was sought for him in 1559,[51] and in the same year "Ambrose the smith" was sent for to provide a hinge and a "wrest" for his instrument.[52] Two years later, John was presented with a Cologne lute of his own, and he was enrolled at Currance's too.[53] Song was important and in 1562 the madrigalist Henry Lichfield sent his man over with some music sheets for John.

In 1567, at the age of eighteen the young John went up to Middle Temple—it was not uncommon for rich landowners to attempt to broaden their sons' minds by dispatching them to the Inns of Court. John appears to have had little aptitude for study: among his pleasures he numbered fencing, hawking, and paying Goodwife Hill to take care of his water spaniel.[54] He also spent a great deal of time visiting his friends and relatives. He did, however, show an enthusiasm for music; he started each term by having his lutes brought over from his father's Aldersgate house to the Temple, and he quite frequently paid anything from three to five shillings a dozen for new strings. In 1567 he bought yet more lute music from Lichfield, although afterwards he also patronised a Mr Pietro, probably a court musician, from whom he not only bought a "Book for the lute" for 20s, but a new instrument for 50s.[55]

Since dancing was an essential skill for young noblemen, the ten shillings John spent in April 1568 to renew his classes at Currance's—plus another two to the ushers and musicians—was no doubt a good investment. His was a well-rounded social education, for while he may have forked out two shillings for the wrestlers at Strode, he also found a shilling for the "minstrels at Montacute playing at my chamber window".[56]

He was a romantic. He again enlisted musicians at Ingatestone for "playing at my chamber window on the 18th day" of April 1570. It was the morning after his marriage to Mary, the eldest daughter of Sir Edward Waldegrave. Currance's musicians had ridden over specially for the ceremonies earlier in the month, for which they charged 23s. 4d plus six shillings for the performance beneath the chamber window.[57]

Sir William's last years before his death in 1572 were marred by ill health probably brought on by land scurvy: renal malfunction, dropsy, difficulties with his sight and hearing, and other health problems brought him so much suffering that he was unable to walk and had to be carried in a litter.[58] A year after his father's death, John bought the Thorndon estates near Brentwood with the help of a loan of £1000 from his father's youngest brother, Robert (who, interestingly, was married to another member of the Tyrell family). For the next three hundred years Thorndon became the Petre family's chief residence, although the more clandestine Ingatestone Hall was never relinquished. Petre was now the fourth largest landowner in Essex—only the estates of the Lords Oxford, Darcy and Rich were slightly larger.[59] He was knighted in 1576, sat as an MP for Essex between 1584 and 1587, and was created Baron Petre of Writtle in 1603.

His wife Mary was uncompromisingly Catholic, twice presented for recusancy. She had like-minded friends and relatives throughout Southern England with whom John mixed during the London seasons, an honourable course because it precluded him from public office (and the consequent monetary gain). Nevertheless, these were dangerous days and wisely he kept his head down whenever possible. It could not always have been easy, for his mother—whose will affirmed that she had lived and would die "a true member and in the unity of the Catholic Church"—had retained the priest John Payne as the family chaplain at her less public residence of Ingatestone. Payne was imprisoned and exiled in 1577, but returned to England within the year. One of the Ingatestone servants betrayed him, and he was executed at Chelmsford in 1582 on the trumped-up charge of plotting to assassinate the Queen. Lady Anne died the following year.

Although John Petre turned to Mr Pietro for some of his musical purchases, he kept in friendly touch with the madrigalist Henry Lichfield. John's wife Mary settled a bet with the musician on Sir John's knighthood in 1576—"Delivered to my Lady the 5th day to give to Mr Lichfield, one of the Earl of Oxford's Men, lost to him upon a bargain made with him, when she was a maid, to be paid when she would be a lady, 40s".[60] At some date later than 1586 Lichfield entered the employment of Lady Jane Cheney of Toddington, near Luton, to whom he dedicated his *First Book of Madrigal*s in 1613, judged in more recent times as "smoothly written and pleasant to sing, although none of them are of outstanding elegance".[61] Of John and Mary Petre's six children only three achieved maturity, all sons: William, John and Thomas. Sir John no doubt continued his father's tradition of educating his children musically, and—like his father—the accounts reveal he bought young John a pair of virginals [62] as well as a new organ from Robert Brough in April 1590. It cost £50 and was carted up to Thorndon all the way from St Giles in London.[63]

Sometimes Brough would ride over from London to Thorndon in the company of William Byrd.[64] The warm friendship between John Petre and Byrd may have had its origins in John's father's day. One of the pieces collected in *My Ladye Nevells Booke of Virginal Music* is entitled "The Tennthe Pavian: Mr W Peter" which suggests good terms between Byrd and Sir William, although by the time of the book's presentation in 1591, Sir William had been dead for nearly twenty years. There is also a motet belonging to the early 1570s, "*Petrus beautus*", perhaps engendered by Byrd's friendship with the Petres.[65] Two further indications of an early friendship have been discovered: in 1576, not long after he had gone up to the Middle Temple, there is the curious record that John gave a penny "To Byrd's Boy",[66] although Byrd was living in Lincoln at this time; also, in 1580, Sir John was one of two arbitrators in one of Byrd's several disputes over the manor of Battyshall.[67]

Certainly, by at least 1586, Byrd was a visitor at Thorndon or Ingatestone, usually travelling in the company of one of the Petres' servants dispatched to "fetch Mr Byrd down from London".[68] One of his stays at Ingatestone lasted the fortnight from St Stephen's Day 1589 until 8 January 1590. On this occasion, though, his return to London may have been delayed by a "Great Wind" which wreaked considerable damage to Thorndon on Twelfth Night, though it barely touched Ingatestone.[69] Five violinists had also been brought over from London, and a local blacksmith named Dyer sent in his bill for a "pair of iron brackets to set the double virginals upon in the Great Chamber there". It was settled by Sir John's organist John Bolt, a former music master at the Chapel Royal and the Queen's virginals player.[70] When she was told that Bolt had converted to Catholicism, Elizabeth was so infuriated that she threatened to fling her pantoffle at his head. Bolt didn't give her the chance. He ducked well away from the court—putting up at the Petres at various times between 1586 and 1590.[71] Later he fled the country and became ordained.[72]

Despite his Catholic sympathies, Byrd's association with the Sidneys and with Watson undoubtedly brought him into personal contact with Sir Francis Walsingham. For his part, Mr Secretary, hawk-eyed and ever suspicious, had little reason to trust the musician—as early as 1580 Byrd's name appeared on a surveillance list of those Catholics thought to be in contact with enemies abroad. Harley suggests [73] that Byrd's "Walsingham" ("Have with yow to Walsingame)" which is also collected in *My Ladye Nevells Booke of Virginal Music* of 1591[74] may have been the composer's stratagem to keep the favour of Walsingham. It is a tempting theory, undermined by the fact that this set of variations is based on an old pre-Reformation popular tune about the *town* of Walsingham. As the old verse to the music makes clear, it was (and is still) a popular destiny for Catholic pilgrimage.[75] Nevertheless, whether or not the verses were written to placate Mr Secretary, the investigations into Byrd's activities at the time of the Throckmorton Plot reveal that he had good reason to be cautious.

It is impossible to date the germination of Byrd's Catholic faith. William and his wife Julian were sympathetic during their earlier life in Lincoln, but it is not until November 1577—five years after her move to London—that Julian was named as a recusant. Significantly, the charges were made just months after the family settled in Harlington where they had come under the stern ecclesiastical eye of John Aylmer,[76] Bishop of London since 1576, and formerly Bishop of Lincoln during the Byrds' residence there. He would tolerate nobody whose beliefs—whether Puritan or Papist—differed from his own. If Aylmer had been aware of the Byrds' religious leanings in Lincoln he may have kept a special watch on the family when it moved to London. Following the first indictment against Julian in 1577, there were repeated bills between 1580 and 1591 against her name, and against that of the family servant John Reason— who in 1582 suffered a year in the Clink for his inability to pay a £60 fine for three months' recusancy. As an "obstinate recusant" it was not the last time that Reason would find himself in gaol.[77]

Byrd himself was not named as a recusant during this earlier period.

Perhaps his situation was the not uncommon one of a Catholic wife making a stand for her faith while her husband attended Anglican services as a "church Papist". Moreover, as a composer of music for the established church Byrd may have found it impossible to shun its services. Harley suggests an associated factor may have been Byrd's absences from Harlington to work for the Chapel Royal.[78] Nevertheless, after early 1584 Byrd was bound to his house in Harlington on a surety of £200; when Fr William Weston met him in 1586 he thought Byrd had "sacrificed everything for the faith", including his position at the Chapel Royal.[79] Restriction to Harlington would have drawn attention to his absence from the parish church[80] and henceforth Byrd was repeatedly presented for recusancy, sometimes singly and sometimes in the company of Julian. After 1587 his children were presented too.

Just as religious and political subversion was concealed in Elizabethan literary texts, so musicologists have discovered a similar resistance disguised in the songs of Byrd. Although Byrd composed a significant amount of liturgical music for the state religion, some of his other works signal an alternative agenda. From around 1581 his commitment to Roman Catholicism seems to have hardened, for which an explanation may lie with the arrival of the first Jesuit mission to protestant England on 25 June of the previous year—and the subsequent treatment of the three priests heading it. Edmund Campion was the most famous, described in his younger days as "the flower of Oxford"[81] with a huge reputation as a scholar and writer. His admirers, known as "Campionists" included Sir Philip Sidney. Even the Queen had been impressed by his debating skills when, accompanied by the Earl of Leicester, she visited Oxford in 1566. Just two years later, by now a priest of the Anglican Church, and amidst a crisis of conscience, Campion left for Ireland. There his views stirred up controversy and in 1571, following an alert from the Lord Deputy Sir Henry Sidney, he returned to England, whence he set off for Douai and Rome and in due course was ordained a priest of the Society of Jesus. Time passed. Then, in 1580, English spies alerted the authorities that a mission of zealous Jesuits was to sail from the continent and would soon drop anchor in English waters. Campion came ashore disguised as a jewel merchant, but just four days later, and now transformed into a gentleman, he addressed the large gathering at Smithfield organised by Thomas Paget at Henry Norris's residence. The house was well secured, but it was impossible to prevent news of the mission spreading; the Privy Council was horrified at what it considered to be political and treasonous subversion of the status quo. In July 1581 Campion was captured in Berkshire and taken to London by armed escort, bearing on his hat a paper inscribed "Campion, the Seditious Jesuit", even as braver hearts mixing with bystanders lining the roadside shouted "Judas" at the pursuivant who had arrested him. His name was George Eliot, a defected priest and former servant of Lady Petre, dismissed for embezzlement and attempted rape. Campion's trial in November—following the rack and the extraction of his nails—has passed into history as a judicial mockery. It relied on dubious testimonies by informers, either fearful for their lives or eager for an easy penny. Among them was Anthony Mundy, whose account of Campion's arrest published within a couple of days of his imprisonment[82] was, wrote Eliot in his reply, "as contrary to truth as an egg is contrary to the likeness of an oyster".[83] Together with the two other priests, Campion was publicly hanged, drawn and quartered at Tyburn on the first day of December.

Byrd and Campion were contemporaries: possibly born in the same year and both pupils of St Paul's School. They may have been friends, at the very least they knew each other. Byrd's well-known "Why do I use my paper, ink and pen?" is a covert lament for Edmund Campion and his martyred companions. In it the composer sets to music the first stanza of a poem by a young Catholic barrister, Henry Walpole. It describes how, as Campion's body was being quartered, a drop of blood spurted on to the poet's white doublet. The poem was circulated in manuscript, and a lone attempt to print it in 1582 as part of Thomas Alfield's slim volume *A True Report of the death and Martyrdom of M. Campion Jesuit and Priest & M. Sherwin, and M Bryan, Priests* cost its publisher, Stephen Vallenger, a heavy fine of £100, the pillory, his hand, his ears, and death in prison; its author fled abroad, later converted to Roman Catholicism and was martyred in 1595. It remained unprinted again until 1908.[84] Byrd's setting was included in a large manuscript collection compiled between 1581 and 1588.[85] A Latin motet written around the same time, "*Deus venerunt gentes"* based on Psalm 79 — "they have poured out the blood of your faithful like water around Jerusalem" — seems to be another covert lament for Campion.

In July 1586, Byrd joined his co-religionists for a conference at the house of Richard Bold at Hurleyford, close to Byrd's property at Harlington. It lasted an idyllic ten days.[86] Among the many guests at this happy gathering were three Jesuits: William Weston, Robert Southwell and Henry Garnet. Garnet loved music and the sung liturgy, and sometimes he exercised his fine voice at the daily Masses for which Byrd played the organ and probably wrote the music.[87] It was the start of a lifelong friendship between the two men.

Just five days after the closure of the conference, Weston was arrested outside the London wall at Bishopsgate. He was unlucky. Two agents had been lying in wait, not for him but for Anthony Babington: Walsingham was tightening the net. Before long the bells of the city churches joyfully proclaimed the capture of the principal conspirators. Byrd's own house was searched, and in October and January he was presented for recusancy at the Middlesex Sessions, together with his wife Julian and servant John Reason. Richard Bold, the host of the July conference, was imprisoned, priests were executed, and intense efforts made to arrest Southwell and Garnet. Garnet found refuge at Shoby in Leicestershire where the widowed Eleanor Brooksby, née Vaux, kept house with her unmarried sister Anne;[88] Southwell sought out Lord Henry Vaux at Hackney near London. By early November both Shoby and Hackney were raided, and although the priests escaped, they spent their lives thereafter flitting between safe Catholic houses.

A direct consequence of the Babington plot was the execution of Mary Queen of Scots at Fotheringay. She died in February 1587, by no coincidence the same month as Philip Sidney's ostentatious funeral.[89] Byrd expressed his feelings by seeming to honour her in his lament "In angel's weed", although she is not named in the text which, significantly, was not printed in Byrd's lifetime. It is possible, too, that his two laments for Philip Sidney mask oblique references to the Scottish queen.

Byrd's faith was expressed also in his powerful Latin motets, mainly bound into the later two volumes of his *Cantiones Sacrae* of 1589 and 1591.

About half of these motets are suitable for either protestant or Catholic services; the other half are solely Catholic in sentiment. Several pray for the liberation of "God's people" or for a "congregation", others bleakly lament the passing of the Holy City or Jerusalem, or the captivity of the Jews in Babylon—waiting (like the English Catholics) for freedom. Some texts reflect the last words of Catholic martyrs on the gallows. Byrd published three volumes of these motets, but they were not for public performance: they were for private use in Catholic houses. Long after the Babington Plot, Byrd still mourned the passing in England of his faith. A manuscript which seems to have been written perhaps between 1606 and 1611,[90] "Crowned with flowers and lilies", undisguisedly laments the passing of both Queen Mary and Roman Catholicism with the accession of Queen Elizabeth.

This was after Thomas Watson's day. We must now turn back to his encounter and collaboration with Byrd. To 1585, the year of Tallis's death and the year of Watson's marriage.

Seven:
A brawl in Hog Lane

In Passion XC of his *Hekatompathia* published in 1582 Watson poignantly writes of the death of Petrarch's "beloved" Laura, concluding in his preface, "Under which name also the Author, in this Sonnet, specifieth her, whom he lately loved."[1]

In his paraphrase of Tasso's pastoral *Amyntas* published three years later, Watson relates the tale of a shepherd who, on the banks of the Thames, mourns the death of his companion Phillis. As eleven days pass — each represented by a verse — the shepherd's pain intensifies until finally, to rejoin his love, he kills himself. His corpse metamorphoses into an amaranthus plant. Cupid under the name of Amor grants a gift to the plant: the power to staunch bleeding.

Of course, Watson's translations may simply have been literary exercises, although the introduction to Passion XC implies otherwise. If he did suffer pain from an earlier love, it is to be hoped that the healing power of the amaranthus soothed his anguish. The *Hekatompathia* was written earlier than its publication in 1582; *Amyntas* would have been passed around in manuscript before its publication in 1585. Yet in London on 6 September 1585, Thomas Watson married Anne Swift at St Antholin's Church in Budge Row.[2]

Like many migrants in London, Anne came from Norfolk. She was born in Norwich to Richard and Elizabeth Swift, the second of their ten or more children. Richard was a servant to Thomas Whall, a weaver and freeman of the city who became mayor for a year in 1567; he trusted Anne's father to travel to London on his master's business. There is a deposition on record against a Norwich carrier named Peter Browne; one day in February 1554 he failed to make a registered delivery to Swift who, as Whall's agent, was waiting at the "White Hart without Bishopsgate". Such a tiny glimpse of a sixteenth century working man's dilemma provides a tenuous link between Richard and his daughter,[3] for The White Hart was a popular venue for workers in the nearby Bethlehem Hospital and at the heart of the Norton Folgate district; later, Watson and Anne were to move their home the short distance from St Helen's within the City wall to Norton Folgate.

It was around the time of his marriage that Watson became associated with William Byrd. It is probable that Watson shared his colleague's religious principles, albeit more discreetly. Like many of his time, his heart may have concealed a leaning towards Catholicism, while his caution led him to profess loyalty to the state. Some scholars have discerned Watson's hand in parts of the text of Byrd's two-volume *Psalms, Sonnets & Songs of Sadness and Piety* registered at the Stationers' Hall in the November of 1587 and published the following year.[4] The work was the first fruit of a joint arrangement between Byrd and his "assigne", the printer Thomas East.[5] Fascinatingly, East used the very same type with which, thirteen years earlier, Vautrollier had set the failed *Cantiones* that had cost Byrd and Thomas Tallis so dearly. By now a printer of over twenty years standing, East had built a fine back catalogue which included Lyly's *Euphues* for the publisher Gabriel Cawood. By taking on Byrd's volume, however, East was set on a new course—henceforth, for a further twenty years, he specialised nearly exclusively in English music books.[6]

East, who preferred to spell his name "Este" or "Est", was born around 1540 to a modestly prosperous, gentrified, Cambridgeshire family with its own coat of arms.[7] He had no little pride in his background and impressed the family arms on several of his publications, the more prestigious the more likely. On the arm's crest stood a black horse, which explains why, when (after several moves) East and his family finally settled in Aldersgate Street, his premises became known as "at the Sign of the Dark Horse". Until it was destroyed during heavy bombing in World War II a part of the street was named Black Horse Alley, which was almost certainly the location of Thomas's shop. As we have seen, Aldersgate Street also housed the Petre family's London mansion.

Byrd's arrangement with East was a fresh start for the composer, too. He reactivated his publishing monopoly which had been largely dormant since 1575, and printed music tumbled from his publishing house. By now the combination of musical composition and business acumen had rewarded Byrd with wealth and prestige. He was a public figure with influential (mainly Catholic) patrons and even the Queen's favour. Nevertheless, reputation did not prevent the surveillance of his house at Harlington, and it was at this time that he received a first indictment for recusancy. Here we see a glimmer of Byrd's canniness: he dedicated his *Psalms, Sonnets & Songs* to Sir Christopher Hatton—Hatton the Queen's favourite, newly appointed Lord Chancellor, and with a seat at the recent Babington trial.

Not many months after the publication of *Psalms, Sonnets & Songs*, East's press was busy again with *Musica Transalpina*, edited with English texts by a lay clerk of St Paul's named Nicholas Yonge. At his home in St Michael's, Cornhill, it was the custom for Yonge to be joined by his family and friends for the singing of madrigals—sharing his house for good company and musical entertainment like other well-to-do gentle people and merchants of the time. Like them, too, he felt the need for English translations of the Italian texts.

Yonge had gathered together madrigals by Alfonso Ferrabosco, Luca Marenzio, some French texts, and anthologies of the works of minor Flemish composers published in Antwerp in 1583 and 1585 by Pierre Phalèse. Fifty-seven pieces by at least eighteen different composers found their way into his *Musica Transalpina*, although nineteen had been already published by Ferrabosco the previous year. The idea caught on. Within ten years of Yonge's publication in 1588, four other English madrigal translation works were printed; Yonge's was the most influential, however, and the only one reprinted.

It is likely that Byrd had a hand in its publication, both as the holder of the music patent and by the inclusion of fourteen madrigals by his friend Ferrabosco. The volume also included an English version of Ariosto's "La Verginella" which Byrd had previously published in his own *Psalms, Sonnets & Songs* and which now boasted a bran new second part. Yonge did not translate the madrigals himself, but stated that they were "translated most of them five years ago by a Gentleman for his private delight". The name of the "Gentleman" is a matter of speculation, but Thomas Watson need not be excluded from a list of candidates. A significant publication, in broadside format, came off the press in the following year, 1588: the *Apologia Musices* by John Case, a friend of Byrd and, it would seem, of Watson too.[8] It was a Latin revision of the more informal *In Praise of Music* published in English two years earlier to extol church music in the face of the threat from Puritanism. In it Case had asserted that "the chief end of music is to delight". Watson and Byrd thought Case's *Apologia* too important to let pass and they collaborated on a vocal broadside for six voices entitled *Let Others Praise: A Gratification unto Master John Case for his Learned Book, Lately made in Praise of Music* (1589). It was seven years since Watson had last written in English; after the *Hekatompathia* all his verse had been in Latin. It was a novelty in another way: the composition of poetry designed to be set to music. Although only two parts survive,[9] the co-operation of Byrd and Watson must have been successful since the *Gratification* was followed by a historically important work, *The First Set of Italian Madrigals Englished, not to the sense of the original ditty, but after the affection of the note* (1590).

Ten years earlier, Thomas Watson's fine voice had charmed the ear of Thomas Walsingham on the banks of the Seine. Now, Watson actively involved himself with what—in time—was to be recognised as a glory of English music, he was (and is) the "only well-known literary man associated in any direct way with the English madrigal".[10] He brought to the madrigal not only a lively musical ability, but revealed a talent for free translation far preferable to the earlier slavish literalism of Yonge's *Musica Transalpina*—even though for a master of Italian like Watson literalism would have been easy. As he advised in the title of his work, it was "Englished, not to the sense of the original ditty but after the affection of the note"—and that is what it is: Englished with little relation to the original Italian. Yonge tended towards the old-fashioned. If Watson's hand was in that translation, he had learned much in the years since. Free translation was increasingly the mode, as in Fraunce's version of Watson's *Amyntas* and Watson's of his own *Meliboeus*,[11] and by complementing the flow of notes with the flow of words Watson advanced the form of the madrigal. As Albert Chatterley puts it,

> ... in spite of his understanding and deep regard for the Italian literature which controlled the syllabics of these English verses as much as did the notation and the underlay of the Italian texts he was still prepared to add the odd syllable here and there to improve the literary flow or the sense for the English, or to help the singer. In doing so he also demonstrates that he knows whether a minim, for instance, should be split into two crochets or a dotted crochet and quaver; not only, that is, how to chose the best length note for the emphasis and length of a syllable, but also how not to upset the harmonic movement or the rhythm ...[12]

Watson's volume consists of twenty-three up-to-date works by the great and progressive Marenzio (praised at the start by Watson in a sixteen line Latin poem), three famous works by other Italian composers, and (as a compliment to his new collaborator) "two excellent Madrigals of Master William Byrds, composed after the Italian vein, at the request of the said Thomas Watson". They were the first English madrigals to be claimed as English rather than Italian, and as such were highly significant.[13] Byrd's two madrigals, for four and for six voices, were set to a poem by Watson in praise of Queen Elizabeth. Although the English composer was more at home in the church, his friendship with Ferrabosco would have taught him a great deal about Italian madrigals. Joseph Kerman the musicologist considered the pieces as "indeed Byrd's most Italianate compositions, and show a firm, easy grasp of the madrigal style".[14]

Watson's co-operation with Byrd took place against a backdrop of an increasingly complicated personal life. In December 1588, the Earl of Oxford sold his Bishopsgate residence, Fisher's Folly, to William Cornwallis, the first son of the formerly influential Comptroller of Queen Mary's Household, Sir Thomas Cornwallis. Watson, who had been employed as a secretary to the Earl, stayed on as a tutor to William Cornwallis's son, although by now Watson was married and living in the liberty of Norton Folgate. For Watson a conveniently short stroll southwards from Norton Folgate along Bishopsgate towards the city brought him quickly to his place of work at Fisher's Folly.

There was something else. Between the publication of the *Gratification* and *The First Set of Italian Madrigals Englished* Watson spent six months in Newgate Prison. The affair, which has been often told—it figures large in biographies of Christopher Marlowe—was the result of Watson's involvement in a fencing match.

The match was with William Bradley, the 26 year old son of the well-heeled innkeeper of the Sign of the Bishop on the busy corner of Gray's Inn Road and High Holborn. Bradley was notorious as a belligerent and brawling fellow—in a word, a thug. The back history reads like a modern thriller and starts with Bradley's borrowing fourteen pounds in March 1588 from John Alleyn, or Allen, almost certainly the elder brother of the actor Edward Alleyn. John Alleyn was another prosperous innkeeper and the recent purchaser of four town houses right next door to Fisher's Folly where Watson was employed. He was also the manager of the Admiral's Men with their headquarters at the Curtain Theatre, and he was joint owner with his brother Edward of theatrical paraphernalia—costumes, scripts, musical instruments and the like.[15]

Alleyn's bond with Bradley was due for repayment by 25th August. The date came and passed with no sight of reimbursement, so John Alleyn's solicitor Hugh Swift—a brother of Thomas Watson's wife Anne—threatened Bradley with the Court of Common Pleas. It availed nothing—by the summer of the following year Alleyn was still waiting for Bradley to honour his debt.

Whereupon, in order to seek him out, Swift sallied forth alone and found himself confronted by Bradley's equally unsavoury friend and near neighbour, the churlish George Orrell.[16] Orrell's threats persuaded Swift to petition sureties of the peace against him "in fear of death" (*ob metum mortis*, a legal device).

Next, no doubt trusting to safety in numbers, Swift joined by his brother-in-law Thomas Watson and John Alleyn went to seek out Bradley, found him alone, and threatened him for the repayment of Alleyn's loan. Now it was Bradley's turn to hurry to a justice and, "in fear of death", to petition sureties of the peace. As a result Alleyn, Swift and Watson were summoned to appear at Westminster Hall on 25 November.

Fate intervened. Between two and three o'clock in the afternoon of 18 September 1589, whether by design or chance, Bradley was on the northern city outskirts near Finsbury Fields, at the south-north junction of Norton Folgate (at the northern end of Bishopsgate) and Shoreditch with Hog Lane leading westwards. It was a popular location: from here theatregoers could take a short stroll along the lane before making a right turn into Curtain Road for the Curtain Theatre, or could saunter on a little further to arrive at The Theatre. Christopher Marlowe lived close by, as did Thomas and Anne Watson who by this time had moved to Norton Folgate. Hog Lane still exists, called Worship Street today. Until the mid-1550s or '60s the area had been one "of pleasant fields very commodious for citizens therein to walk, shoot, and otherwise recreate and refresh their dull spirits in the sweet and wholesome air". But by 1589 the district was in the throes of descending into the less desirable scene painted by Stow as "within a few years made a continual building throughout of garden-houses and small cottages; and the fields on either side be turned into garden-plots tenter yards, bowling alleys, and such like".[17]

Duelling at the outskirts of London was so common it had become a problem for the city authorities. On this particular afternoon Watson arrived at this corner of Hog Lane and came "upon the clamour of the bystanders" excited by a fight between William Bradley and Watson's friend Christopher Marlowe. When Watson intervened Marlowe "drew back and ceased to fight", but Bradley cried to Watson "Art thou now come? Then I will have a bout with thee". "And instantly", reads the account of events,

> this William Bradley then and there made an assault upon the aforesaid Thomas Watson and then and there wounded, struck and ill-treated the aforesaid Thomas Watson with a sword and dagger of iron and steel, So that he despaired of his life. By reason of which the said Thomas Watson with his aforesaid sword of iron and steel of a value of iii shillings iiij pence, which he then and there had and held in his right hand did defend himself against the aforesaid William Bradley and fled from the aforesaid William Bradley for the

saving of his life as far as a certain ditch of his life. And the aforesaid William Bradley continuing his aforesaid attack, had then and there closely followed the said Thomas Watson ...

With escape impossible Watson lunged at Bradley and pierced him with "a mortal blow or wound in and upon the right side of the chest ... six inches in depth and one in breadth" from which Bradley "instantly died".[18]

A local tailor and unpaid part-time constable, Stephen Wyld, took Marlowe and Watson before the nearest justice of the peace, Sir Owen Hopton, who lived in Norton Folgate and happened to be the Lieutenant of the Tower of London. Hopton committed them to Finsbury Prison[19] "on suspicion of murder". The next day, styled "yeoman" and "gentleman" respectively, Marlowe and Watson were examined before the inquest at Finsbury conducted by a Middlesex County coroner named Ion Chalkhill backed by a jury of twelve sworn men. It found Watson to have acted in self-defence and "not by felony". The two men were then taken across the town to the grim cells of Newgate. There, according to evidence given in 1593 by Marlowe's enemy Richard Baines, he met a fellow prisoner named John Poole, a counterfeiter and Catholic who later had a profound influence on Marlowe's life.[20] As he was not involved in the actual homicide Marlowe was allowed bail. Two men stood his surety of twenty pounds each; one was Richard Kitchen, an attorney of Clifford's Inn and a man of property in St Bartholemew's, Smithfield.[21] The other was the socially lowly but wealthy Humphrey Rowland from St Botolph's without Aldgate, a "horn-breaker", possibly a maker of lantern horn windows or a preparer of horn for use in horn books, buttons, and suchlike.[22] Rowland was present at the personal request of Lord Burghley. Significantly, Burghley's interference was contrary to the City's ordinances—as the Lord Mayor protested. Marlowe, one suspects, had friends in high places.[23] He was personally bound over for the sum of forty pounds on the undertaking that he would "appear at the next sessions of Newgate" and was released thirteen days later. At the Old Bailey early in December both poets were exonerated. On the bench was Sir Roger Manwood, chief Baron of the Exchequer, a Kentish man who had been a sponsor of Marlowe's

Cambridge scholarship and for whom Marlowe was later to write a Latin epitaph. He was related to the Walsinghams by marriage, and a neighbour of Thomas Walsingham. Also present was William Fleetwood, the Recorder of London, who not long afterwards purchased a copy of *Tamburlaine*.

So all was well with Marlowe. But for his part in the affair Watson languished injured and ill in gaol until the Queen got round to signing a bill of pardon. That took another squalid, wearisome, two months and one week, totalling Watson's imprisonment to some five months.

In his *Christopher Marlowe: Poet and Spy,* the late Park Honan saw the influence of the Privy Council behind the surities appointed for Marlowe and Watson, both potentially useful government agents. In the year of Watson's release, 1590, Sir Francis Walsingham died. Towards the end of his eulogy to Mr Secretary, *Meliboeus sive Ecloga,* Watson praises Christopher Hatton, the Lord Chancellor, and Lord Burghley ("*Cecil*"), Elizabeth's principal minister and the chairman of the Privy Council.[24] Honan suggested that Watson also expresses his gratitude to Thomas Walsingham for intervening on his behalf with his cousin Sir Francis. In his Latin dedication to Thomas Walsingham, Watson writes:

> *Magnus enim (proh fata) diem Franciscus obivit,*
> *Arcadiae nostrae qui Meliboeus erat:*
> *Et mihi subtristes qui (te mediante) procellas*
> *Depulit, hyberno vela ferente Noto.*[25]

Honan translates this passage as

> For, alas the Fates, great Francis has died, he who was the Meliboeus of our Arcady, a man who warded off baleful storms from me when a winter tempest blowing from the south struck my sail, thanks to your intervention.[26]

Eight:
The Elvetham entertainment

BY now Watson was mixing with higher circles. At a time when every writer in London sought a commission, it is probable that he had manoeuvred himself to a position to receive the most envied of all, a royal entertainment.

Elizabeth's elaborate progresses to the estates of her noble subjects were rooted in her flair for propaganda. Always she had some plausible excuse to hold a progress—perhaps to distance herself from an epidemic of the plague, or perhaps to seek relief from the hot summer constrictions of London—but the purposes behind her progresses went much deeper. It was important for the monarch to be *seen* by her subjects, to demonstrate her love for them with public display; it was important, too, to tie the loyal bonds of her nobility tight; and it was important to replace the lost Catholic veneration of the Virgin Mary with a secular royal "virgin".

In August 1591 Elizabeth made her greatest and most splendid progress in several years. Her tour journeyed south, to Farnham, Petworth, Chichester, Titchfield, Portsmouth, and Southampton, and finally via Basing and Odiham to Elvetham in Hampshire for a four-day entertainment. By the time she reached Elvetham it was mid-September. Here, Edward Seymour, Earl of Hertford, was desperate to buy his way back into the Queen's favour, discarded some thirty years since by his clandestine marriage to Katherine, the younger sister of Lady Jane Grey. It was an act of true love which had inflamed the Queen's anger, earning a fine of £15,000 for "seducing a virgin of the blood royal" and imprisonment lasting until the death of Katherine some seven years later. Once, one would have thought, was quite enough, but Seymour stubbornly failed to learn the lesson: his second, supposedly secret, marriage with Frances Howard was again repugnant to the Queen. Now, striving to impress Her Majesty, Seymour hired three hundred workmen

8. *The Elvetham entertainment*   155

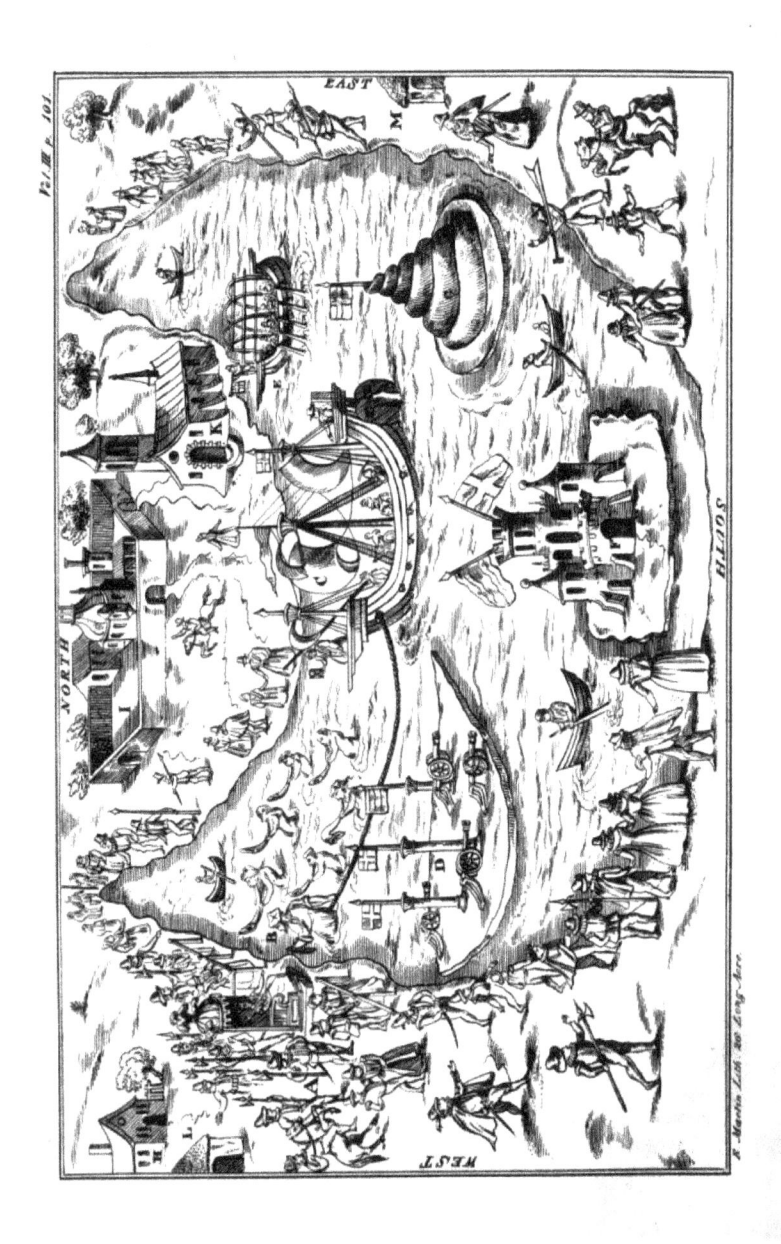

Plan of Elizabeth's entertainment at Elvetham.
From
John Nichols, *The Progresses and Public Processions of Queen Elizabeth* (1823).

to enlarge and beautify his house at Elvetham and to construct twenty-two temporary wooden pavilions on a hillside in the park. These were to house Her Majesty's ample 500-strong Household, and included a great hall with all the necessities—spicery, larder, pantry, wine cellar, chandlery, bakehouse with five voluminous ovens, and much else. The whole was surmounted by a special stateroom covered on the outside with branches, hazelnuts and ivy, while inside heavy tapestries draped the walls, and aromatic rushes and herbs were strewn over the floors. Most impressive of all, a crescent-shaped lake was scooped out of the lawn, with three islands built in its centre: one shaped like a Ship with three trees for masts; another surrounded by willow trees representing a Fort; and the third a "Snail Mount" with green hedges forty feet wide at the base and spiralling twenty feet high. Beside this lake Seymour's builders erected an elaborate canopy of green satin trimmed with silver lace, beneath which the seated Elizabeth would represent a nature goddess presiding over over peace and plenty (a major theme of the entertainment).[1] The canopy was to be "upheld by four worthy knights" (Sir Henry Grey, Sir Walter Hungerford, Sir James Mervyn and Lord George Carey).[2] From her waterside seat Her Majesty could watch the pageants, spectacles, feasting and theatre, and listen to the accompanying musicians floating in gaily painted boats. The Queen planned to stay for four days, entertained throughout with banquets, dances, volleyball, songs, allegorical entertainments, and fireworks.

She was due to arrive at Elvetham in time for supper on Monday 20 September. Close to her arrival time, Seymour rode out with two hundred or more men in train to escort her from nearby Odiham Park to his house at Elvetham. As she approached the house she was met by a Poet dressed in green and wearing a laurel-wreath. Refusing a boy's offer of a cushion, he fell to his knees, declaiming in Latin,

> Now let us use no Cushions, but fair hearts:
> For now we kneel to more than usual Saints.[3]

There followed the poet's 64-line verse panegyric to the Queen commencing with the conceit that

> The *Muses* sung, and wak'd me with these words:
> "Seest thou that *English Nymph*, in face and shape
> Resembling some great *Goddess*, and whose beams
> Do sprinkle heaven with unacquainted light …"[4]

The published account continues,

> While the Poet was pronouncing this oration, six Virgins were behind him, busily removing blocks out of Her Majesty's way; which blocks were supposed to be laid there by the person of *Envy*, whose condition is, to envy at every good thing, but especially to malice the proceedings other three the *Hours*, which by the Poets are fained to be the guardians of heaven gates. They were all attired in gowns of taffeta sarcenet of divers colours, with flowery garlands on their heads, and baskets full of sweet herbs and flowers upon their arms. When the Poet's speech was happily ended, and in a scroll delivered to Her Majesty (for such was her gracious acceptance, that she deigned to receive it with her own hand), then these six Virgins, after performance of their humble reverence to her highness, walked on before her towards the house, strewing the way with flowers, and singing a sweet song of six parts to this ditty, which followeth …[5]

As the song of the virgins concluded, the Queen "alighted from horseback at the hall door" to be welcomed, "most humbly on her knees", by Frances Countess of Hertford and her ladies. The Queen embraced and kissed the Countess, from which we may presume that Frances's transgressions were forgiven. To salute the Queen's arrival, guns were fired from the Fort Isle and the Snail Mount. After supper, a consort of six musicians "so highly pleased [the Queen], that in grace and favour thereof, she gave a new name unto one of their pavanes, made long since by Master Thomas Morley, then Organist of Paul's Church."[6]

On the second day, starting at the lake at around four o'clock, the Seymours staged an important water-show. A study of this show by Harry H Boyle[7] demonstrates that the spectacle was so extremely topical, with "such direct bearing on current developments in this conflict that it could not have been staged with effect or propriety one month before or after it was performed."[8]

The show was in the form of a masque with fighting and battles replacing the customary dancing to represent in allegorical form the current post-Armada rivalry of England and Spain—on the Atlantic trade routes, in the Netherlands and in France. All three arenas were also symbolised by the scenery on the pond facing the Queen. The entertainment included an acknowledgement of the loss in just the previous month of Sir Richard Grenville's galleon *The Revenge* at the Battle of Flores off the Azores, for which many blamed the fleet's commander, Lord Thomas Howard. This misfortune had been taken very much to heart by the Queen and she had scarcely recovered. In addition, the show represented, by allegory, a current vicious enmity which had arisen during the Siege of Graves in the Netherlands between the Earl of Leicester and the great General Sir John ("Black Jack") Norris. The Queen herself had supported Norris and instructed Leicester not to discourage such captains "who had won our nation honour and themselves fame".[9] The show concluded on a positive note—Howard's contribution to the war effort was emphasised, the rivalries of the land and sea commanders ignored, and a resurgence of English sea power foretold. The Queen herself was introduced into the entertainment, presented with a fan-shaped jewel and praised "as the sybil whose power and favour is essential to future success."[10] She announced *The Revenge*'s replacement by *The Bonaventure*, then lying with Howard's fleet off the Azores.

The following morning she was greeted at her casement window by Nicholas Breton's pastoral song "Phillida and Coridon" performed by three musicians who so pleased Her Majesty that she commanded an encore. Dinner was followed by a game of "bord and cord", and after supper fireworks and a torch-lit banquet of some thousand dishes supplied a magnificent climax to her stay.

8. The Elvetham entertainment

The third morning, Thursday, was the morning of the Queen's departure. Before she left, however, a fairy Queen and her maidens danced across the garden to the Queen's window singing a six-part song accompanied by lute, pandora, bass-viol, cittern, treble-viol and flute. The song was composed by Edward Johnson an employee of the recusant Sir Thomas Kytson of Hengrave Hall, and the Queen enjoyed it so much that she asked three-times for the fairies and musicians to repeat it.

Within the hour, the Queen and her entourage were hastening from Elvetham; the rain was torrential. As she passed through the park, characters from the shows stood "on every side wringing their hands, and showing sign of sorrow for her departure". While she beheld this dumb show, "the Poet made her a short Oration", including this plea to his Queen,

> Leaves fall, grass dies, beasts of the wood hang head,
> Birds cease to sing, and every creature wails,
> To see the season alter with this change:
> For how can summer stay, when Sun departs?
> O, either stay, or soon return again,
> For summer's parting is the country's pain.[11]

As Her Majesty passed through the park gate a consort of musicians hidden in a bower revealed themselves and burst into song, "O come again faire Nature's treasure", a ditty which so delighted her that she halted and removed her travelling mask to thank them. Then, at last, she resumed her journey having "openly said to my Lord of Hertford, that the beginning, process, and end of this entertainment was so honourable that she would not forget the same. And many, and most happy may years may his most gracious Majesty continue, to favour and foster him, and all others that do truly love and honour her."[12] For the Earl that was indeed a gratifying reward.

In his paper on the entertainment,[13] Boyle convincingly argues that much of the poetry for the occasion was by Thomas Watson and the writer Nicholas Breton, under the direction of George Buc.

To support his belief that Buc organised the revels, Boyle notes first that, at the time of the entertainment, Lord High Admiral Charles Howard, Lord Effingham, was the supreme commander of both land and sea forces, a sensitive task requiring decisions about constantly changing and complex military situations. To the Howards of Effingham, Buc was intensely loyal; he had served under the self-styled "heroical Howard"[14] in the war against the Spanish Armada, and afterwards honoured the admiral's leadership with a celebration composed in Latin hexameters—for which, on Howard's recommendation, he was rewarded with a parliamentary seat in 1593. Since Howard was the brother of Frances, Countess of Hertford, hostess of the entertainment, it is quite conceivable that he put forward Buc's name as director of the show.[15]

Boyle also draws attention to the possibility that the Howards influenced the political content of the pageant. Lord Charles Howard's cousin, Lord Thomas Howard was the commander of the fleet which had so recently lost *The Revenge* off the Azores. The entertainment acknowledged the tragedy, but was positive about Thomas Howard's contribution, praising him and foretelling a resurgence of English sea power.

Another point made by Boyle is Buc's suitability for organising the Elvetham entertainment; years later, in the early years of James's reign, he is reputed to have written a (now lost) treatise on the art of pageantry and mime. He also had literary abilities and an interest in history: his *History of Richard III* published in 1646, after his death, is famous.[16]

Concerning Nicholas Breton's employment on the show, Boyle suggests a family connection. We do know that Buc was related to Nicholas's sister Anne, but the relationship was remote.[17] Like many Londoners, Nicholas was of East Anglian stock. His mother Elizabeth was from Bury St Edmunds, his father William had moved from Colchester to the parish of St Giles Cripplegate in London, and owned considerable property throughout the City as well as in Essex and Lincolnshire.

He was born in 1554, probably at his father's "capital mansion house" in Red Cross Street, St Giles,[18] and grew up with an elder brother and three sisters. When Nicholas was five his father died, leaving his son considerable property to be maintained by his mother until he was four and twenty. However "the funeral bak'd-meats did coldly furnish forth the marriage tables", for within just two months of her husband's death Elizabeth married Edward Boyes from Kent, who pocketed as large a chunk of the inheritance as he could. Two years later, in 1561, Elizabeth contracted a third, bigamous, marriage to the soldier-poet and dramatist George Gascoigne.[19] This went down badly with Boyes and a resultant affray in 1562 between the two husbands resulted in a Chancery order which forbad Elizabeth contact with either. It was not until 1566 that she gained a divorce from Boyes and legal permission to marry Gascoigne. In the same year the children were awarded their full inheritance rights, and by 1569 their wardship was granted to Gascoigne. Gascoigne was no more trustworthy than Boyes: his personal unpopularity was compounded by a reckless lifestyle—by the time of his death in 1577 his step-children's inheritance was totally squandered.[20]

Little is known of Breton's early life; it is possible that he attended Oriel College, Oxford, and travelled abroad. We do know he was living in Holborn in the year of his step-father's death because his *A Flourish upon Fancy*, a verse miscellany, was published then from "his chamber in Holborn".[21] At this time, Watson was establishing himself in London after his recent long stay on the continent. Probably he knew both Breton and Gascoigne—Gascoigne was related by marriage to the Earl of Oxford for whom Watson acted as secretary.[22] Watson was twenty-two, Breton twenty-three; both suffered from a diminished inheritance, both were at the threshold of a literary career. With his *A Flourish upon Fancy* already on the bookstalls Breton was set to become well-known as a prolific writer of verse and prose. Pastorals, satires, dialogues, religious meditations and the like flowed from his pen, including a book on fishing, *Wit's Trenchmour* (1597). He wrote some of the lyrics for *England's Helicon* (1600) and *The Passionate Shepherd* (1604), and under the pseudonym "Pasquill" contributed a number of satires and burlesques including possibly two Marprelate tracts.[23] Like Watson and other writers, Breton found a patron in Mary Sidney, Countess of Pembroke to whom he dedicated several works on religious themes.[24] One of these, his *The Pilgrimage to Paradise, Joined with the Countess of Pembroke's Love* (1592), compares Mary Sidney to Elizabetta Gonzaga, the Duchess of Urbino in Castiglione's *The Courtier (Il Cortegiano)*. The poem asks her to "build up the walls of Jerusalem" by encouraging piety among her Wiltshire congregations and by providing adequate livings for her clergy.[25] In view of his literary talent and his patron, it is perhaps unsurprising that his song "Phillida and Coridon" should have been included in the Queen's Elvetham entertainment of 1591.

Regarding Watson's contribution to the entertainment there is no doubt about his friendship with Buc, who contributed the first of the five commendatory poems to the front matter of the *Hekatompathia* of 1582:

> The stars, which did at Petrarch's birthday arraign
> Were fixed again at thy nativity...

There is, however, another common denominator between Seymour, Buc, Watson and Breton unremarked by Boyle, or indeed (to the best of my knowledge) anybody else. All four men were familiar with Edward de Vere, the seventeenth Earl of Oxford.

First, let us examine Oxford's relationship with the noble originators of the Elvetham entertainment. For an important clue, we must travel back over seventeen years, to early July 1574, when five hotheads, lusting (so it is said) for continental adventure and military service, crossed the English Channel on a hired ship. They were Edward Yorke,[26] an unknown person called "Cruse",[27] another person, and — importantly — Edward de Vere, Earl of Oxford, and Lord Edward Seymour. Seymour was the younger brother[28] and namesake of Edward Seymour, Earl of Hertford. The venture lacked the royal sanction, and it shook the court. A year earlier de Vere had persuaded his friend Thomas Bedingfield to translate *Cardanus's Comfort*; now Bedingfield was dispatched to Brussels to fetch him home. The young Edward Seymour was left behind and died in Italy a few months later. The Queen forgave Oxford surprisingly quickly, giving rise to Gabriel Harvey's suspicions that the adventure was in fact a cover for one of Cecil's secret spying missions.[29] That apart, from the evidence of this episode it is clear that Oxford was both well-known to, and friendly with, the Earl of Hertford and his family.

Of Oxford's connection with the three contributors to the entertainment

8. The Elvetham entertainment 163

we know, first, that Watson was his secretary. He had headed his *Hekatompathia* with a dedication to the Earl, stating, no less, that "your Honour had willingly vouchsafed the acceptance of this work, and at convenient leisures favourably perused it ..." implying as Alan H Nelson points out "a literary 'circle' with Oxford as patron".[30] Possibly Nicholas Breton was a member of this circle too; at the very least he was known to the Earl. On 3 May, 1591, just a few months before the Elvetham entertainment —the proximity of the date is intriguing—*Brittons Bowre of Delights* was published; it included ten poems which can be fairly certainly attributed to Breton, and, as Breton complained the following year, "many things of other men's mingled with a few of mine"[31] including two, probably three, poems attributed to Oxford.[32]

As for Buc, we have noted that he was an ally of Watson: he was also a member of the Earl's literary circle. He was, moreover, an intense admirer of Oxford. "A magnificent and [a very] learned and religious man ... and so worthy in every way ...", he wrote of Oxford—and much more in a similar vein.[33] Moreover, Charles Howard, to whom Buc owed intense loyalty, was another ally of Oxford—possibly a political ally.[34] Boyle's own surmise about Buc's association with the entertainment, that he organised the revels, is just that—a surmise (albeit well-founded); we can make a different surmise, that perhaps—and no more than "perhaps" is suggested —the event was organised by the Earl of Oxford, or by Buc in collaboration with the Earl. There is a hiatus in the documentation of Oxford's activities from early July to early December in 1591, a period which covers the whole of the entertainment. We have no idea what de Vere was up to at this time —the possibility of his involvement in the event cannot be ruled out.

Of the poetry for the entertainment, how much was composed by Thomas Watson? Albert Chatterley convincingly argues that he wrote a great deal of it.[35] Not the whole event, and not the songs, but Chatterley is convinced that the opening Latin speech and blank-verse sections should be attributed to Watson. To support his case Chatterley presents several arguments.

First, the choice of printer. Before 1591 was out, John Wolfe published two editions of a narration of the *Honourable Entertainment given to the Queens Majesty, in Progress, at Elvetham in Hampshire, by the Right Honourable the Earl of Hertford*. The second edition makes a few corrections to the first and includes the full spoken text, as well as descriptions (including the lyrics) of all the songs and music.[36] John Wolfe was Watson's customary printer.[37]

Another consideration is Watson's contemporary reputation for compositions in English pentameters and Latin hexameters. Chatterley quotes from Thomas Nashe who sizing up the literary scene just two years before Elvetham, wrote:

> ... which makes me think that either the lovers of mediocrity are very many, or that the number of good poets are very small; and in truth (Master Watson excepted, who I mentioned before) I know not almost any of late days that hath showed himself singular in any special Latin poem; whose *Amyntas*, and translated *Antigone*, may march in equipage of honour with any of our ancient poets.[38]

Chatterley also compares a passage from the entertainment with another from the *Amintae Gaudia* (published shortly after Watson's death in 1592):

> Elvetham entertainment, 7:15-17
> *Qui fert ore preces, oculo foecundat olivam;*
> *Officium precibus, pacem designat oliva;*
> *Affectum docet officiis, et pace quietem;*

> Amintae Gaudia, Epistle III, 75-8
> *Hic verbum gerit ore, oculo faecundat olivam;*
> *Verbis officium, pacem designat oliva:*
> *Officio ciet affectum, date pace quietem,*
> *Et beat affectu mentes, et membra quiete.*[39]

Between the two passages, points out Chatterley, "The sentiments are the same, the rhetorical matter identical, and the vocabularies utterly alike, with often verbatim repetition. And Watson's literary integrity and reputation would never have allowed him to stoop to plagiarism"[40]

The lyrics of five songs in the entertainment, however, bear no stylistic resemblance to anything included in Watson's *The First Set of Italian Madrigals Englished* published the previous year, and Chatterley doubts that Watson wrote them. The pressure of preparing the entertainment would have been enough, he suggests, to persuade Watson to hand over their composition to somebody else—in this way any inadequacies in the literary style would be masked by the musical setting.

All of which leads to the attractive suggestion that when the Queen entered the park on her first day at Elvetham and found herself confronted by a poet dressed in green and wearing a laurel-wreath, a poet who fell to his knees and declaimed to her in Latin, that poet was none other than Thomas Watson. Six virgins accompanied the bard and after his address they flowered into melody. The refrain of their verses ("O beauteous Queen of second Troy Accept of our unfeigned joy") resembles in sentiment and metre the words Watson requested Byrd set to music for *The First Set of Italian Madrigals Englished* the previous year ("O beauteous Queen of second Troy take well in worth a simple toy"):

> *The First Set of Italian Madrigals Englished VIII & XXVIII*
> This sweet and merry month of May,
> While Nature wantons in her Prime,
> And Birds do sing and Beasts do play,
> For pleasure of the joyful time:
> I choose the first for holy day,
> And greet Eliza with a Rhyme
> O Beauteous Queen of second Troy,
> Take well in worth a simple toy.
>
> *Elvetham entertainment: The song sung by the Graces and Hours at Her Majesty's first arrival*
> With fragrant flowers we strew the way
> And make this our chief holiday.
> Although this clime were blest of yore,

Yet never was it proud before.
O beauteous Queen of second Troy,
Accept of our unfeigned joy.

Now air is sweeter than the balm,
And *Satyrs* sing about the palm.
Now earth in colours newly dight,
Yields perfect sign of her delight.
O beauteous Queen of second Troy,
Accept of our unfeigned joy.

Now birds record sweet harmony,
And trees do whisper melody.
Now every thing that nature breeds
Doth deck it self in pleasant weeds.
O beauteous Queen of second Troy,
Accept of our unfeigned joy.

Ruff and Wilson, in a contribution to *Past and Present* in 1969, accepted without question that Watson wrote the verse sung to Elizabeth at Elvetham, since the words written for Byrd's madrigals in Watson's *The First Set of Italian Madrigals Englished* "coincide so closely in spirit with his song that was sung by 'six virgins'".[41] It cannot be denied, however, that the song of the virgins is markedly trite in comparison with the lines in the madrigals. Chatterley would agree, suggesting that the poet who wrote this Elvetham lyric "knowing that the song would follow on immediately from the opening address of 'the Poet', had simply decided to make a literary link with Watson by reflecting the two lines from the madrigal book of the previous year."[42]

If it is possible that the Poet who bestowed a welcome to the Queen on her arrival at Elvetham was Watson, then it is similarly possible that the Poet who declaimed the farewell speech on the Queen's departure and which so delighted Her Majesty as she passed through the gates at Elvetham — "For how can summer stay, when Sun departs?"[43] — was Watson too.

Nine:
Scandal in the Cornwallis household

THE argument that precious literary manuscripts should be preserved in the country of their origin did not trouble Henry Clay Folger. The millionaire president of the Standard Oil Company—he was chairman of the board after 1923—had two hobbies: golf (he partnered John D Rockefeller) and amassing Shakespeariana. Whatever his handicap in the first field, he could afford to outbid all competitors in the second. By the time of his retirement his accumulation of books and documents had grown so immense that he set out with his wife Emily to find somewhere suitable to house it. Able to afford nothing but the best, the couple found it on Capitol Hill, and spent nine subsequent years buying and demolishing the properties already there. In 1928, Congress was persuaded to pass a resolution allotting the space for what became known as the Folger Shakespeare Library, and it opened in 1932—too late for Henry, who had been dead for some two years. Today, the library houses the world's largest collection of Shakespeare *First Folio*s and printed works, and is a major repository of rare English documents of all kinds for the period between 1500 and 1750.[1]

Shelved among the vast collections is a tiny nineteen-page quarto leather-bound notebook of verse known as the *Cornwallis-Lysons Manuscript*.[2] After thumbing through several blank pages at its start, one comes upon a smaller sheet on the verso of which is a large self-confident flourish: "Anne Cornwaleys her booke". Perhaps it is the sign of proud possession. On the same page someone has been practising their handwriting or trying out a nib. Facing it, a family tree demonstrates the connection of Anne Cornwallis with "John Vere the Eleventh Earl of Oxford".[3] The pedigree is thought to have been inserted by the other name in the library catalogue, Samuel Lysons, an eighteenth century antiquary and later possessor. Lysons seems to have had pages from the sixteenth

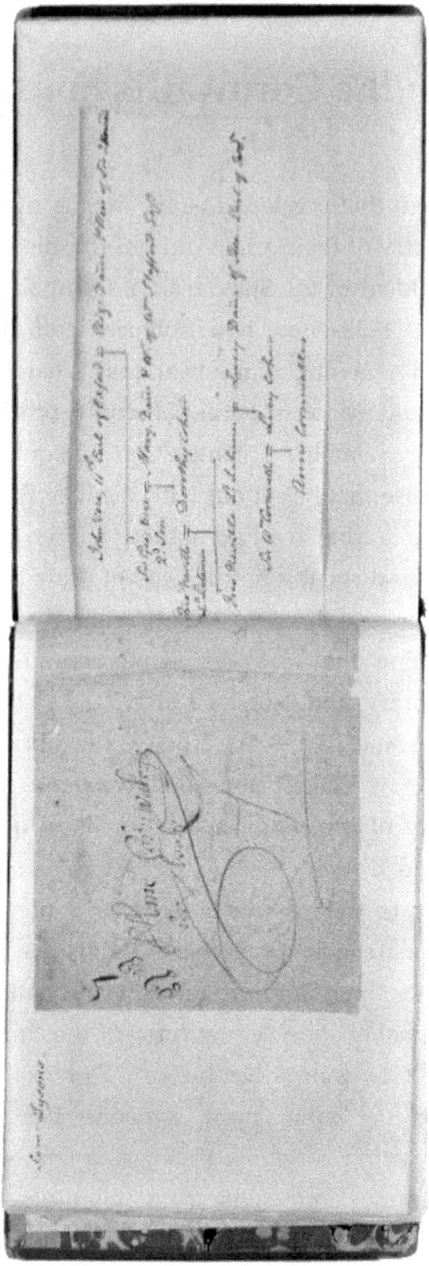

century book bound into a blank album the better to preserve them. Inside are thirty-three poems in secretary hand by a variety of poets, mainly dating from before 1586 (the year of Sir Philip Sidney's death). Some are attributed to: J Bentley,[4] Sir Philip Sidney,[5] Sir Edward Dyer, G M,[6] Anne Vavasour,[7] and Edward de Vere, seventeenth Earl of Oxford. Other poems are unattributed, including the only known extant sixteenth century manuscript copy of a work said to be by William Shakespeare, "When as thine eye hath chose the dame". A much inferior version of the poem was printed in the 1599 anthology known as *The Passionate Pilgrim By W. Shakespeare,*[8] although Anne Cornwallis's version being the better would seem to be the truer original.

The dating of this significant little book is important. After its acquisition by Lysons, it passed, via an auction at Sotheby's on 18 June 1844, through three later hands[9] until it arrived on the desk of James Orchard Halliwell. Halliwell was a collector of Shakespeariana, and a conscientious and respected scholar.[10] In 1852, he confirmed the opinion of the compiler of Sotheby's Sale Catalogue that the poetry was written between 1585 and 1590. Although, "I very much doubt," he wrote, "if any portion of the volume was written so late as 1590".[11] The single difficulty of this dating, which Halliwell apparently failed to notice at that time, is the anonymous verse later credited to "Shakespeare".[12] In the early 1580s William Shakespere was still in Stratford, courting and marrying Anne Hathaway, and fathering her babies. From 1585 until 1592 he disappears

OPPOSITE: *Cornwallis-Lysons Manuscript.*
Pages showing "Anne Cornwaleys her Booke" faced by a family tree.

The pedigree is almost certainly by Samuel Lysons, a former possessor of the book, and is intended to demonstrate Anne Cornwallis' connection with "John Vere the Eleventh Earl of Oxford" (*sic*). Lysons got it wrong: the eleventh Earl was Richard Vere (1385-1417), the John Vere noted on the family tree is the twelfth Earl (1408-61).

(Anne Campbell, Countess of Argyll (1574-1607). *Leaves from a poetical miscellany of Anne Campbell, Countess of Argyll* [manuscript] [London, ca.1600].
Call #: [Hamnet] V.a.89. Used with permission of the Folger Shakespeare Library.)

from history, and it is unbelievable that he could have made himself known to Anne Cornwallis during this period and had his verse copied into her book. The conclusions are limited: if Halliwell's original dating is correct, either the anonymous verse in Anne's manuscript book is not by William Shakespere of Stratford, or the writer called "W Shakespeare" in *The Passionate Pilgrim* of 1599 was somebody other than the actor and businessman from Stratford on Avon. Halliwell's original dating of the manuscript was confirmed in a roundabout way by a more recent writer, William H Bond of the Houghton Library at Harvard, who in 1948 examined the poems copied into the manuscript and concluded that the only exception to the rule that it should be dated to before 1590 is the poem "dubiously", as he put it, "assigned to Shakespeare".[13] In particular, three poems have topical relevance relating only to the late 1580s, including one commencing "The State of France as now it stands ..." which has been dated to 1588.[14] Bond concluded that "on the basis of its identifiable texts ... the manuscript presents a collection of poetry none of which is demonstrably later than 1590 together with three topical poems definitely belonging to the 'eighties." Then, presumably because he could not justify as belonging to this period the anonymous verse assigned to "Shakespeare", he immediately contradicted himself by adding, "Almost inevitably it must be assigned to the period 1590-1600", attempting to rescue the contradiction by adding, "and probably to the earlier rather than the later part of that decade."[15] Between 1588 and 1592 Anne's brother John, the eldest son of the Cornwallis family, was tutored by Thomas Watson. Perhaps—or should we write "probably"?—it was Watson with his literary links to the Oxford and Sidney families who encouraged Anne's collection of verse.

Who were the Cornwallis family? Who was Anne Cornwallis?

The Cornwallises were established in Suffolk in the early 1400s at Brome, a village between Diss and Eye and lying close to the Norfolk border. Over the following two centuries they amassed huge estates in both counties. By the 1580s, the patriarch of the family was Sir Thomas, who died at the ripe age of 86 in 1604. As a younger man, at a date before 1540, he had married Anne, a daughter of Sir John Jerningham of

Somerleyton, a neighbouring Suffolk family so ancient it dated from before the Conquest. The couple had six children; Anne died in 1581, aged 65.

Sir Thomas's life had been active, not to say vivid. In 1549, he volunteered his services to William Parr, the Marquess of Northampton, to take arms against Robert Ket and his rebels. Ket seized him and had him locked in Norwich Castle, where he chafed and squirmed until, in turn, the arrival of Warwick's forces defeated Ket. Like other noblemen of his generation, Cornwallis played his cards carefully. In 1553, as Sheriff of Norfolk and Suffolk he proclaimed for Lady Jane, but when news of Mary's success was carried to him at Ipswich on the very same day, in a rapid (and wily) *volte face* he proclaimed for, and swore allegiance to, Mary. His reward — a seat in the Privy Council, and his wife Anne appointed a lady of the Queen's privy chamber. Mary found Sir Thomas pliant and useful. Amid a good many other duties, he treated with the Scots, calmed Wyatt's rebellion and served at his trial, became comptroller of the Household (in 1557), and was named in Mary's will as one of her six assistant executors. He was treasurer of Calais under Wentworth, until just two months before the port fell to the French in 1558.

When, in December 1553, two hundred horsemen in red and violet accompanied the young Elizabeth from Ashridge in Hertfordshire to London, Sir Thomas was there. When his Catholic colleagues bickered over their plans to remove her from Whitehall to the Tower, he stood against them; though if this was a tactic to secure his position with Elizabeth, he failed. On her succession she removed him from his post — he was, after all, a Roman Catholic. Whereupon, he retired home to Suffolk and spent a great deal of energy and a great deal of money rebuilding Brome Hall. And there he stayed quietly for a number of years until a near disaster in 1569. Thomas Howard, the fourth Duke of Norfolk, a Catholic and, worse, a candidate for the hand of the Queen of Scots, was defeated in the Northern Rising, and fled back to his estates in Norfolk. Cornwallis — who had long been a supporter of Howard, and leased land from him — was arrested and taken in for interrogation, alongside his son-in-law Sir Thomas Kytson. He was held for a year, until he ultimately conformed and protested his loyalty to the throne, though he obstinately read "some Lady psalter or portasse" throughout the service.[16] Suspicion fell on him, too, at the time of the Armada, although he was allowed to remain at the Kytsons' Suffolk home. Sir Thomas was undoubtedly protected by his family connections and lifelong friendship with Burghley. But even Burghley couldn't help when Cornwallis's youngest daughter Mary, unshakeably Catholic, secretly married the Earl of Bath with Kytson's connivance. A trial followed and the marriage was annulled in 1581. Some years later the Earl of Bath remarried, but feelings ran high and Mary obstinately continued to style herself the Countess of Bath until her death in 1623. In 1600, a couple of years after Burghley's death, Sir Thomas was allowed to take his brother William into his home. By now he was an old man and long returned to his recusancy. The gesture was a fine and lenient one on the part of the government, for William was a seminary priest who had seen imprisonment in the Clink.

Although a Roman Catholic, Thomas was canny enough to raise his sons as protestant, William born around 1545 and Charles born some ten years later. Between the brothers there was constant enmity, mainly over succession claims.[17] In a letter to Burghley in 1594, old Sir Thomas describes his elder son as "prodigal", and his younger son as "covetous and too attent[ive] to gain."[18] William was educated at Trinity College Cambridge, and by 1578 had married Lucy Neville, a daughter of John Neville, Lord Latimer, and sister to Dorothy, the wife of Burghley's son Thomas.[19] For reasons not altogether clear, Sir Thomas was by no means pleased with William's marriage. Moreover, he was, he told Burghley, displeased to find his "son and his wife so addicted to live about this City, as I have cause to think the cost done upon my house in the country to be evil bestowed." Why, he wailed, couldn't they "frame their fancies agreeable to my disposition to lead a country life"?[20] It was true: the couple's style of living in London was far from modest. In December 1588 William bought a large and splendid mansion in Bishopsgate looking eastwards over a spread of green space to Spitalfields and beyond.[21] The property had been built by Jasper Fisher, a former goldsmith since fallen into debt, and was known locally as Mount Fisher—or Fisher's Folly. It was, wrote Stow in his *Survey of London*, a "large and beautiful house, with gardens of pleasure, bowling alleys, and such like".[22] Queen Elizabeth had once lodged there.

But the purchase had been a hurried deal with Lucy's cousin, Edward de Vere, seventeenth Earl of Oxford, and kept secret from Sir Thomas (or so he claimed). Oxford had lived there since early 1580 with his wife Anne, Lord Burghley's daughter. On his side too, Burghley was furious when he learned of the sale, and Sir Thomas wrote a panicky letter attempting to mollify Burghley, that he "did dissuade both my son and daughter [-in-law] for dealing with the purchase but when their will and fancy prevailed against my advice, I kept my purse from the loan or gift of any penny towards it."[22]

When Lysons drew up the family tree opposite Anne Cornwallis's signature in her book, he was at pains to demonstrate her kinship with the earls of Oxford, through the marriage of her mother and father, William and Lucy. Lucy's father John Neville, the fourth Baron Latimer, was the son of Dorothy, daughter of Sir George de Vere (the second son of the twelfth Earl of Oxford). Dorothy was also the sister of "Little" John de Vere, fourteenth Earl of Oxford (they were cousins of the thirteenth) who took up his position in 1513 when he was no more than thirteen years old. On his death in 1527 the line returned to the direct descent. In short, Anne's great grandmother, Dorothy de Vere, was second cousin to the sixteenth Earl of Oxford, Edward de Vere's father.

As we have seen, during Oxford's occupancy of Fisher's Folly a coterie of Elizabethan poets, dramatists, and musicians thrived there under his patronage—John Lyly, Anthony Mundy, Thomas Nashe, Robert Greene, George Puttenham and Thomas Watson were but a few of many. Yet William Cornwallis's family had literary pretensions and connections too, and after he acquired the property it continued as a centre for the arts, although less high-flying than in Oxford's day. As an indication of the literary and cultural bent of the Cornwallis family, it is worth noting that on Lucy's death in 1608, nearly thirty years later, William married Jane Meautys, daughter of Hercules Meautys of West Ham in Essex. A son, Frederick, was born in November 1610, although tragically, William died a year and three days after the birth. After a respectable period of mourning, in 1614 the young, and by now very rich, Jane married Nathaniel Bacon by whom she had three more children. She is famous for a remarkable series of letters, revealing much about her life and personality, which she collected between 1613 and 1644.[24] At the very least, therefore, it is unsurprising that, after the Cornwallis family installed themselves at Fisher's Folly, the house retained an ambience which encouraged Anne Cornwallis to compile her manuscript book of contemporary poetry.

Which brings us to the question, who was the Anne Cornwallis who inscribed "Anne Cornwaleys her booke"? Anne was as popular a name at the time of the book's compilation as it is today. Despite any dating qualifications noted earlier in this chapter, we can probably decide that the book was put together at some time in the 1580s; in this period there were at least *four* Anne Cornwallises related to William Cornwallis: a daughter, his mother, his aunt, and both the first and second wives of his younger brother Charles.[25]

To first look at the wives of Charles Cornwallis. Anne, his first wife, was the daughter of Thomas Fincham of Fincham in Norfolk. Because she died in 1584 she can be ignored for our purposes, although—interestingly—around 1579 she gave birth to William Cornwallis, the famous essayist who in 1599 served with Essex in Ireland.[26] Whether his talent derived from his mother or from Charles' second wife, in whose company he would have spent his formative years, depends on your belief in "nature" or "nurture". Perhaps it was a mixture. Charles married his second Anne after June 1585. She was the daughter of Thomas Barrow of Barningham in Suffolk, the widow of Sir Ralph Shelton, the former Sheriff of Norfolk and Suffolk, and she lived until 1617. If we are looking for a literary bent in the owner of "Anne Cornwaleys her booke", then she is certainly a candidate. She was cousin to Sir George Buc, whom we have met in connection with the Elvetham progress in CHAPTER EIGHT, and who was acquainted with Thomas Watson. Buc, an historian, poet and eventually the Master of the Revels was a member of the Earl of Oxford's literary circle as early as 1581-2.[27]

However, owing to intensely bad feelings between William and Charles

Cornwallis it is unlikely that the compiler of the day book was related to the younger brother. Turning to the relatives of William Cornwallis, the purchaser of Fisher's Folly, it is unlikely that the inscription of "Anne Cornwaleys her booke" was written by either his aunt, another Anne (who married a William Halse), or his mother Anne, who died in 1581, too early to have contributed.

In fact, most scholars believe that the book's owner was a daughter of Sir William Cornwallis by his first wife Lucy.[28] Indeed, this argument is strengthened by the short family tree penned opposite the inscription "Anne Cornwaleys her booke" to demonstrate the pedigree of Anne Cornwallis—even though it was almost unquestionably drawn up by Samuel Lysons, the later owner of the manuscript. We have no birth date for Anne, but we know she had two elder sisters, Elizabeth born in 1578, followed by Cornelia whose birth date has also been lost. Since Anne was next, it is most unlikely that she was born before 1580, and almost certainly later if only by a couple of years. According to Richard Mulcaster (*Positions Concerning the Training Up of Children* [1581]) as a high-born female child she would have been educated by a private tutor until she was about thirteen or fourteen years old. In 1588 when Watson took up his position in the house to instruct her brother John she was probably less than eight years old. This is at this time when the *Cornwallis-Lysons Manuscript* is assumed to have been compiled. It is not at all fanciful to suspect that its content was influenced by Watson.

Briefly, to peer into the future. In 1609 Anne married the red-blooded Archibald Campbell, seventh Earl of Argyll, widowed for two years with six daughters to care for, and, worryingly, just one son; in an age of high infant mortality he was desperate for more male heirs to ensure a safe succession. In Anne, he chose well: the Countess presented him with three more sons (and another five daughters).

Since childhood, Argyll had been at the turbulent centre of Scottish politics where infighting, conspiracy and tribal warfare were almost the norm. In 1603, he travelled south to London in the company of his King who was about to take up his new position as King James I of England. Argyll, however, remained unsettled and alternated between the City of

London and the politics and warfare of the North. But not for long. It took just a few years of marriage for his Presbyterian sympathies to wobble, influenced by his unswervingly Roman Catholic wife and the Jesuit priests who were frequent visitors to his house. In 1618 the couple set sail for the continent, putting it about that they were travelling to sample the waters at Spa in the Netherlands. No sooner had Argyll disembarked than he announced his conversion to his wife's faith and enrolled with the Spanish army in Flanders. The following February the King declared him a traitor, a hot-headed decision which he was driven to revoke within three years. Argyll nevertheless remained in the service of Spain until 1627, when, following the accession of Charles I, he returned to London, abandoned his Scottish estates, and settled with Anne in Drury Lane.

During her residence in Europe, Anne collected and published a set of aphorisms from the works of Augustine. As a cultured female of the Cornwallis family with a proven interest in literature, who more likely to have gathered together in her youth the "Cornwallis booke" of poetry?

When in December 1588, William Cornwallis purchased Fisher's Folly from the Earl of Oxford, Thomas Watson stayed on as tutor to William's teenage son John to prepare him for entry to Cambridge.[29] Charles Nicholl catches a glimpse of Watson in the character of Lucentio in Shakespeare's *The Taming of the Shrew*. Lucentio, a student of Padua like Watson (probably), "worms his way into the Minola household as a tutor ... He is presented to his employer as a 'young scholar that hath been long studying at Rheims' and is 'cunning in Greek, Latin and other languages'"[30] There were probably other considerations. Since the Cornwallises had family connections with Oxford and were a leading Catholic family, Watson would have seemed a natural choice because of his secretarial work for Oxford and his own Catholic upbringing and connections. Moreover, he had recently worked alongside the Catholic William Byrd, who was also associated with Oxford (whatever the strength of the latter's faith) — in 1574 the Earl signed a lease with the composer for Battyshall manor close to Stondon Massey in Essex, where Byrd was to settle later on.

There might have been more to this four-way connection between

Cornwallis, Oxford, Watson and Byrd than we can now discern, a web that may make it unnecessary to consider a convincing alternative theory put forward independently by W Ron Hess and Albert Chatterley. This hypothesis pastes a delicious flavour of conspiracy over apparently innocent relationships. Hess suggests that much of Oxford's posturing, his specious leaning towards Catholicism, was cover for espionage operations against the Marianists. Is it possible, asks Hess, that Oxford engineered Watson's connection with the Cornwallis household to keep an eye on this potentially powerful Catholic family at the very time when the elderly patriarch Sir Thomas Cornwallis was under government investigation for recusancy?[31] It may not even be necessary to introduce Oxford into the theory because, as Chatterley recalls, Watson was affiliated to the Walsinghams.[32] On the other hand, mundanely, it may mean little more than that Watson had worked through his inheritance, had a wife to keep, and discovered a regular income as tutor to John Cornwallis. Moreover, William and Lucy had been cleared of Catholic involvement, and, in any case, it was not at Sir Thomas's house that Watson was employed.

There is a good chance that Watson and the Cornwallises knew each other before Thomas moved nearby and became John's tutor at Fisher's Folly in Bishopsgate. He did not live in the house, but simply visited to teach John. When he married Anne Swift in 1585, her brother Thomas had been a servant of William Cornwallis for several years.

William and Lucy Cornwallis had seven children, four daughters and three sons.[33] The eldest, Thomas, had died in infancy in 1572 leaving as heir his brother John who was probably born the following year, and so was about fifteen when Watson took on his education. Two other Cornwallis children are important to our story: the youngest and the eldest of the four daughters. Anne we have already met, no more than eight years old when Watson took up his post, and thought to be the owner of "Anne Cornwallis her booke"; her sister Frances, the eldest daughter, was about thirteen.

Associated with the Cornwallis family at this time was Watson's brother-in-law Thomas Swift. Swift had joined the household through a piece of extraordinary good fortune. When he was about eleven, the

Queen made a seven day visit to Norwich as part of a wider progress to East Anglia. It started on the 16th and concluded on the 22nd of August in 1578, and the weather was horrendous. Persistent and heavy downpours of rain ruined the shows which were so ambitious and had been so elaborately planned that the city fathers had to beg loans of some £400 or £500 to defray their costs.[34] Young Thomas Swift was one of a dozen small boys taking part. It would be pleasant to think he was the boy with an important role on a stage set up in a churchyard—perhaps St Andrews or Blackfriars. Dressed in a long robe of white taffeta with a red and gold turban and a garland of flowers he represented the Commonwealth of the City and so delighted the Queen with his speech that as he flung the garland into the air she exclaimed "This device is fine!"[35] In another pageant later that week the boys were dressed as blonde water nymphs in white silk; all ruined—alas!—by a thunderclap and cloudburst which left them looking—as the entertainments' director Thomas Churchyard recalled—like "drowned rats".[36] The next day Churchyard improvised a fiasco in which seven of the boys disguised as fairies dived through a hedge and recited poetry before an astonished Queen. She applauded anyway. Churchyard himself took on the role of the King of Fairies; his brainwave inspired one of the earliest occasions on which fairies were presented dramatically.

Young Swift's aptitude for acting and music caught Churchyard's eye. By now, the boy's father, Richard, had fallen into deep poverty and Churchyard begged Cornwallis—also in the city for the Queen's visit—to take care of him. As Cornwallis later reported,

> I had him of Churchyard when all the clothes on his back were not worth 2 shillings after given me by his father with tears in his eyes for lack of ability to give him 12 pence.[37]

Elsewhere he noted that Richard,

> delivered me him by these words, "Sir, I give you this boy all saving his soul, but I have nothing to give him", which dying shortly after in

debt, and poverty, I found him apparel and necessaries convenient.[38]

Churchyard (whose biography is briefly summarised in CHAPTER ONE), was a servant of the Earl of Oxford, and he not only directed this East Anglian progress of 1578 but had also supervised the Queen's progress to Bristol four years earlier. Before that he had collaborated with George Gascoigne in 1575 on the greeting for the Queen's arrival at Kenilworth. At the time of the Norwich entertainment he was approaching the age of sixty, after a life—like Gascoigne's—of soldiering and writing.[39]

The connections between Oxford, Cornwallis, Churchyard, Watson—and Swift—are intriguing and lead one to suspect Oxford's hand behind these royal progresses.

Ten years passed since the Norwich progress, and in 1588 William Cornwallis engaged Thomas Watson to teach his son John. By now Thomas Swift had grown into a man of twenty-one and was well established in Cornwallis's household. He felt like one the family. The Cornwallises were enthusiastic patrons of the arts, and music was important to them.[40] It was common practice for a noble family to employ a musician whose duties often included tutoring the younger family members, and perhaps Swift also doubled up as a groom or serving man.[41] But he nursed a grudge. Forgetting that Cornwallis had taken him in as a destitute child, he thought his master miserly, thought himself worthy of better, and in his pride attempted to blackmail his employer and to marry his eldest daughter Frances. His machinations landed him in the highest court in the land, the Star Chamber. They also implicated Thomas Watson.[42]

Perhaps it was in 1589 that Swift confided his feelings to Watson, who —according to Swift's later deposition—helped him hatch a plot of almost unbelievable tomfoolery. For Swift to even consider marrying out of his class was insane, and Watson (like all Englishmen) would have known it. Perhaps he was trying to humour Swift, perhaps he underestimated Swift's determination, perhaps he thought the episode a jape, perhaps he simply failed to appreciate the seriousness of the matter. Perhaps his involvement with the theatre somehow persuaded him that he was constructing a stage plot rather than a real-life one—as Cornwallis declared of him, he "could devise twenty fictions and knaveries in a play which was his daily practice and his living".[43] One recalls his impish behaviour in the Anne Burnell affair, the repercussions of which were still being felt in 1587, eight years after the event, when the Privy Council called him as a witness at Burnell's trial for treason. He had other preoccupations, too. He was busy; several literary endeavours were in hand (including *Italian Madrigals Englished*); and in the autumn of 1589 his prudence might also have been clouded by his duel with William Bradley which had left him severely wounded, followed by five months detention in Newgate Prison.

The plot he hatched with Swift could have been the mainspring of an Elizabethan drama. Frances—thirteen or fourteen years old (although not far off marriageable age) remember, to Swift's twenty-one or -two—had occasionally resorted to borrowing sums of money from Swift "for idle expenses". Swift would now offer to lend her ten gold angels. Ten gold angels was five pounds, a considerable amount, and one ponders how Swift as a humble employee had accumulated such a sum. Perhaps Tom Watson had lent him the money. Little wonder that on this occasion Frances would be asked to sign what appeared to be a debt note, but which was actually, unknown to her, a contract of marriage to Swift. Then the *coup de grace*—Swift would flourish the signed contract in front of Frances's father, William, who would accordingly bribe him to give it over to him.

A bill of debt was drawn up, confirming the sum to be repaid on the day of Frances's marriage. She "did accede to his said offer, accept and take of him the said ten angels of gold", and before witnesses agreed to sign the document. The day came for the signing. The document had been freshly re-drawn by Swift's brother, the lawyer Hugh Swift, and it was laid on the table shortly before morning lessons. Two witnesses were present, Robert Hales and John Camp. Frances arrived, but her younger sisters were not far behind, accompanied by Mistress Hinton, the governess—she would want to know what was going on. All was a flurry, Frances had no time to read the bond which was folded to show only the places for her signature and a seal. Hales signed, Camp made his mark. *Exeunt all*, except Frances. The deed was done.

Some two years passed. Two years in which Watson became apprehensive about Swift's intentions, and anxious to retrieve the bill. How to achieve this? Perhaps by asking Frances to write to Swift persuading him to relinquish it. Her brother John was by now two years at Caius College,[44] but he continued to read with Watson during vacations and he agreed to act as go-between between Watson and Frances. It seems Watson's letter to Frances suggested a hoax to induce Swift to part with his treasured bill. Frances wrote her letter to Swift, but Swift obstinately refused to hand over the bill, even declining Watson's offer to pay him the value of the planned blackmail. Swift had convinced himself that he genuinely loved Frances, now aged fifteen, and he was determined to marry her.

By now he had left the Cornwallis household and held an auspicious appointment in the more influential house of the Earl of Essex. Unfortunately for Swift, Cornwallis had somehow got wind of his treachery and had a word with Essex. The lutenist was dismissed in June 1592. Whereupon, he began to spread it about that Frances loved him deeply and that they were to marry. He also began to activate his blackmail scheme. His first thought was to disclose the bill to old Sir Thomas Cornwallis, but he changed his mind and decided on William's younger brother Charles; finally—we let William take up the story—he "agreed it should be to myself, adding thereto a protestation of knowing of her carnally to shut up my mouth withal, though my heart were never so much in rage." As for Frances, by now in a state of near terror, "she did the most instantly deny all, forswear all, brought reasonable witnesses of the maids and women that were daily conversant to disprove possibility of any truth, that by god of heaven, Sir, had she been the child of a Jew I should have believed her."

As the storm clouds gathered, two leading players departed from the drama. The death of "Thomas Watson, gent" was registered at St Bartholomew the Less in West Smithfield on 26 September 1592. Ten days later, on 6 October, the same register entered the name of Hugh Swift.

Before December, Thomas Swift carried out his resolve and wrote to Sir William to reveal the bill's content. His obsession that he, a humble lutenist, could marry the daughter of a powerful noble house had always been dangerous, the child of a fevered brain. Now, his conduct threatened to bring disgrace on Frances and altogether ruin her chances of matrimony. She had reached marriageable age and her father was seeking a suitor from her own class. Swift, desperately casting around for back up, beseeched Sir Thomas Mounson for his support. But Mounson, a patron of the arts and vaguely an acquaintance of Swift, was hardly likely to help, since he was of similar degree of class to Cornwallis. So the appeal fell through. When Swift next changed his demand for wedlock to an attempt at blackmail in exchange for cancelling the bill, Sir William's rage was aggravated beyond restraint and Swift's ruin inevitable.

Meanwhile, he piled blame on Watson, now deceased and unable to defend himself. In St George's Fields at Windsor, he confided to one Henry Goldingham that "he had never come to that trouble but by ... Watson's means", and in conversation with a Robert Sprignall in St George's Chapel soon afterwards he again blamed the dead writer. Sprignall advised him to confess everything immediately—a suggestion that provoked Robert Hales' reaction: "Godsbody! If he should confess, what should come of me?". As a witness to the document, Hales frantically tried to distance himself from Swift. On Christmas Day 1592 he journeyed with Swift to Essex to see Sir John Petre at Ingateston Hall. It was eleven o'clock at night and the three whispered together in the cold garden—Hales to exonerate himself, and Swift to "'make a preface' for Cornwallis's ears 'to begin his excuses'".[45]

It was to no avail, for Cornwallis had powerful contacts. He was related to both Burghley and the solicitor general Sir Edward Coke who sanctioned placing the case before the Star Chamber. To prevent Swift decamping before the trial he was speedily deposited in the Marshalsea, where he again started making a fuss, this time about the lack of food and bedding. His complaints were untrue: the keeper of the prison reported that Swift fed at the inferior alms basket purposely to justify his complaints about the food, and that "he lieth upon the best feather bed in the prison". His sister

Anne visited the prison and took care of him. Since she was also Watson's widow, Chatterley suspects that "she was naturally confused, being doubly involved. At one point she is reported to have told Swift to stand firm, trying to 'encourage him not to faint or falter for that Hales had promised to stand the contract': this was untrue, for Hales was still busy clearing himself."[46]

With plague sweeping the city, the trial was delayed until 22 June 1594. Its outcome was inevitable. Swift was fined a thousand marks, committed to the Fleet without a date for release, and "set on the pillory in Cheapside with his head through the hole of the same pillory" where he had to declare his offence for four hours, the whole process to be repeated in Westminster. After which he was to go on his knees to confess his offences before the Archbishop of Canterbury who would then "ask the said Mr Cornwallis, his wife and daughter's forgiveness for the horrible wickedness and wrong" that he "right villainously and falsely hath uttered and practised against them". As if that were not enough, a whipping was also on the list of punishments, which Swift was fortunate to escape through a technicality. From the dock he defended himself loquaciously, refusing to admit his guilt, and calling the witnesses "false perjured sycophants". He declared his love for Frances, for whose sake he was "content to endure, with other intolerable wrongs, this disgrace ... with that patience that shall please God to give me."

Frances's reputation was unclouded, and the following year she married Sir Edmond Withipole.[47] It is unlikely that she kept her pledge to repay on her wedding day the ten angels she had borrowed from Swift. A few months after Swift's trial, Cornwallis received the crippling news of the death of his son and sole heir, John. The tragedy occurred as John supervised extensions to old Sir Thomas's house at Brome Hall. A frame holding a block and tackle collapsed, and crushed and killed him.[48] He was buried at Brome on 1 November. Saddened by the death of his son and moved to compassion for his former servant, Cornwallis appealed for Swift's release from the Fleet, "chiefly driven upon an inward motion of Christian charity, which together with time hath qualified my passion ..."[49] For William it had been a momentous year. Not only did it embrace Swift's trial and his son's death, but probably also the award of his knighthood. His emotional stress must have been considerable, so perhaps it is unsurprising that within these twelve months he was himself disgraced following a quarrel at a game of cards with Charles Arundell. The later sale of his house in Highgate at a bargain price to Sir Robert Cecil no doubt stood him in good stead, however, and in 1597 Sir Robert eased him into parliament, where he found places on several committees. His knighthood was of a sufficient degree to give him a place on the reserve list of those honoured to hold the canopy at the state funeral of Elizabeth in 1603.[50] After his wife Lucy died in 1608, a speedy remarriage to Jane Meautys in the same year brought forth the good fortune of a son and heir, Frederick, a year before William's own death in 1611.

Ten:
"Dearly loved and honoured"

THE burials of Watson and Hugh Swift within days of each other in September and October 1592 were, in a sense, convenient. The paranoia of Thomas Swift and the boiling rage of William Cornwallis had threatened to bring ruin on both their heads. They died, it has been suggested, from the bubonic plague, always an imminent and random threat, but particularly infectuous in the capital between the Autumn of 1592 and the spring of 1594. London had the reputation of being the dirtiest city in Europe, and plague exaggerated any existing dangers to health. One of the filthier areas was Bishopsgate, especially at its southern end. Although Thomas and Anne Watson lived at the very north of the street—at Norton Folgate where it joined Shoreditch—they nevertheless needed to pass along the southern stretch to enter and leave the City through the Bishops Gate. Their journey took them past St Botolph's church. Just a few years later[1] Stow described how the church's yard was cut off from the town ditch by a brick wall. However, to the side of the wall was a causeway, or "causeye" as he called it,

> leading to a quadrant, called Petty France, of Frenchmen dwelling there, and to other more regarded their own private gain than the common good of the city; for by means of this causeye raised on the bank, and soilage of houses, with other filfthiness cast into the ditch, the same is now forced to a narrow channel, and almost filled up with unsavoury things, to the danger of impoisoning the whole city.[2]

If the southern end of Bishopsgate was appalling, the northern end, where Thomas and Anne lived, was only a little less unsavoury. North of Bethlehem Hospital, upon the street's side, many houses have been built with alleys backwards, of late time too much pestered with people (a great cause of infection) up to the bars.[3]

It is highly probable that the Watsons themselves lived in one of these houses. In his study of the plague in the period, Paul Slack notes that "the fuel for epidemic disease gradually accumulated here, and so did the carriers of plague"[4] — that is to say, rats.

There was a serious outbreak of bubonic plague in the Low Countries in 1589. It was not the first. These continental epidemics seem to have been carried by sea to London and to England's second largest city, Norwich,[5] where serious plague was endemic between 1589 until 1592. This local epidemic predated London's, which encourages the thought that the many immigrants journeying to and from London and East Anglia could well have transported the plague between the two districts. There were strong connections between the two cities; it is almost a truism that most of the families discussed in this study had East Anglian kinship and relationships — including, for example, Anne Watson and her brothers Hugh and Thomas Swift.[6]

It is possible, therefore, that Watson and Hugh Swift were victims of the plague. Each was buried at the little church of St Bartholomew the Less in West Smithfield and entered in the registers for 26 September[7] and 6 October 1592 respectively. There the matter should rest, were it not that a Hugh Swift has been discovered acting on the Queen's Bench three years later. As Chatterley notes, "If this is the same person then his reported burial — and that of Watson — is called into question."[8] Knowing the character of Watson — apart from helping Tom Swift plot the Bill of Debt we remember the Burnell affair — we might expect him to escape a serious crisis by faking his own death. The parallel with the case of his friend Christopher Marlowe whose death was registered just a few months later on 30 May 1593, is apparent. Notoriously, the circumstances of that playwright's death, the question of its genuineness, and the convenience of his disappearance under the threat of extreme penalties from the government, have been argued and counter-argued for decades.

Moreover, Gabriel Harvey in a marginal note to his copy of Thomas Speght's *Works of Chaucer* published in 1598, commends Dyer's *Amaryllis* and Raleigh's *Cynthia* as "Excellent matter of emulation for Spencer [*sic*], Constable, Fraunce, Watson, Daniel, Warner, Chapman, Sylvester, Shakespeare, & the rest of our flourishing metricians ..." Harvey's notes are neither always seemingly logical nor accurate, but even so his recommendation that Watson, among "our flourishing metricians", should emulate Dyer and Raleigh seems strange, considering the poet was supposedly eight years dead.[9]

That noted, the post history of his works, and the reaction of his former colleagues to the announcement of to his death, suggest that there should be no argument that Thomas Watson truly died in 1592, aged 37.[10]

On 10 November following his death, Watson's *Amintae Gaudia* was published, a lengthy work of ten "letters" and eight eclogues, dedicated in Latin to Lady Mary Herbert, Countess of Pembroke. The dedication, initialled "C M", is presumably by Christopher Marlowe. The book was printed by William Ponsonby, described as "the most important publisher of the Elizabethan period"[11] and the publisher favoured by the Herbert circle since the death of Philip Sidney in 1586. By the time of Watson's death, Ponsonby had already published *Arcadia,* the first three volumes of Spenser's *The Faerie Queene* and his *Complaints, The Teares of the Muses,* and *Daphnaïda.*[12] In time he issued several other works from the Sidney group. That he handled Watson's posthumous works is surely significant. During his lifetime, Watson had employed the printshops or bookshops of John Wolfe, Robert Waldegrave, Henry Marsh, Robert Robinson, and Thomas East—but not Ponsonby. Now, after his death, when he could no longer handle their publication himself, his works were passed to the principal bookseller of the Herbert group.

Both Watson and Marlowe had close connections with the Herberts. Watson's *Meliboeus* in 1590, the Latin eclogue on the death of Elizabeth's intelligence chief Sir Francis Walsingham, was dedicated to Francis's cousin, Thomas Walsingham. It was this same Thomas Walsingham, in this same work, that Watson under the mask of "Corydon", introduced as his "sweet friend", "Tityrus". Later in the same year Watson dedicated his

Englished version of *Meliboeus* to Lady Frances Sidney, daughter of Sir Francis Walsingham and Sir Philip's widow. As for Marlowe, we have evidence that by Spring 1593 he was living at Thomas Walsingham's house at Scadbury in Kent, safely distanced from the London plague.[13]

The passage of another year brought forth one more work attributed to Watson. *The Tears of Fancy or Love Disdained* is an entirely different matter from *Amintae Gaudia*. Its collection of sixty numbered fourteen-line sonnets are unattributed on the title page and a plain "Finis. T.W." follows the final sonnet, a very slightly different version from one written by de Vere in the 1570s to show off his devotion to the Queen.[14] The poetry shows some reliance on the techniques of Daniel and Spenser (prominent members of the Sidney circle),[15] while the evidence suggested for Watson's authorship are the initials T.W. on the final page, as well as an attribution in the *Stationers' Register*. But not all scholars recognise the style as Watson's, and the *Register* entry is a forgery.[16]

The book was published by William Barley and probably printed by John Danter. Like Watson, Danter was unnamed on the title page but his initials can be seen inside a decoration on page one. Unlike Ponsonby's clean reputation, Danter's was notoriously spotted. At the time of his apprenticeship to John Day, between 1582 to 1588, he was caught assisting at a secret press issuing works granted by patent to his master. For this theft he was barred from becoming a master printer and transferred to Robert Robinson. For a reason now obscure, the sentence was remitted after a year and Danter was admitted as a freeman to the Stationers' Company. A short-term business partnership with the printers William Hoskins and Henry Chettle ensued, until in 1591 he set up his own shop, at first near Smithfield then, within a year, close to Holborn Conduit. Around this time he printed a pamphlet known as *Axiochus* (1592)[17] which contains the text of a tournament speech by the Earl of Oxford and is attributed to "Edward" (rather than "Edmund") Spenser. In 1593 Nashe's *Strange News* was licensed to Danter; its dedication to one "Apis Lapis" possibly also referring to the Earl of Oxford. Other works by Nashe followed, including *Terrors of the Night* (1594) dedicated to Elizabeth, the daughter of George Carey, who two years later succeeded as second Baron Hunsdon. As Lord Chamberlain between 1597 and 1603 Hunsdon's role included patronage of the Lord Chamberlain's Men then appearing at The Theatre, and later The Globe. Danter also took on the First Quarto of *Titus Andronicus* (1594) which was sold at St Paul's by Edward White and Thomas Millington.[18] It seems that in 1596 he was living with Thomas Nashe and printed his *Have With You to Saffron Walden* in that same year. Around this time he again fell foul of the Stationers' Company for printing a Roman Catholic devotional work, a Jesus Psalter. As punishment the Company ordered the smashing of a press and some other equipment, and the following spring destroyed two more presses. But Danter bounced back and by the end of the year was collaborating with John Allde on a poorly printed pirated Quarto of *Romeo and Juliet*.[19]

The Tears of Fancy, *Titus Andronicus* and *Axiochus* had short print-runs. Just a single extant copy of each has come to light, and all now reside in the USA. *Axiochus* is preserved with 1,109 other titles in the Carl H Pforzheimer Library at the University of Texas; *Titus Andronicus* was found amongst the books of a Swedish gentleman in 1905, and lodges at the Folger Library in Washington; *The Tears of Fancy* was bought at Sotheby's in 1919 for the Huntington Library in San Marino, California.

Even this brief summary of Danter's career reveals three affinities with Thomas Watson. First, there is the connection with the printer Edward White who, as we have seen, was acquainted with Watson's sister Maudlin. Second, we note the name of Edward de Vere, seventeenth Earl of Oxford, Watson's sometime master. Third, we uncover Thomas Nashe. Nashe was an associate of another secretary to the Earl of Oxford, John Lyly, and connected in some way with Marlowe on the writing of *Dido, Queen of Carthage* (?1593). He was also a participator to the literary coterie now hypothetically known as the "University Wits" of which Watson was another associate. Indeed, the two men appear to have been bosom friends if one may judge by an anecdote related by Nashe of "M. Thomas Watson, the Poet". "A man he was," wrote Nashe,

England to her
deared wit decking admired daughters)
write and let the worlde know that heauens harmonie is no musicke, in respect
of your sweete, and well arte-tuned
strings: that *Italian Ariosto* did but shadowe the meanest part of thy muse, that
Tassos Godfrey is not worthie to make
compare with your truelie eternizing
M. Alablaster. *Elizas* stile: let France-admired *Bellaw*,
Spenser and and courtlike amarous *Rousard* con-
others. fesse that there be of your children, that
in these latter times haue farre surpas-
Lylia clou- sed them. Let diuine *Bartasse* eternally
ped, whose praise worthie for his weeks worke, say
teares are the best thinges were made first: Let o-
making. ther countries (sweet *Cambridge*) enuie,
(yet admire) my *Virgil*, thy petrarch, diuine *Spenser*. And vnlesse I erre, (a thing
All praise easie in such simplicitie) deluded by
worthy. dearlie beloued *Delia*, and fortunatelie
Lucrecia fortunate *Cleopatra*. *Oxford*, thou maist
Sweet Shak- extoll thy courte-deare-verse happie
speare. *Daniell*, whose sweete refined muse, in
Eloquent contracted shape; were sufficient a-
Gaueston. mongst

Two pages from the addendum to William Covell's *Polimanteia* (1595).
In the marginalia to page R3 we read "Wanton Adonis, Watson's heir".

three Daughters.

mongſt men, to gaine pardon of the *Wanton* ſinne to *Roſemond*, pittie to diſtreſſed *Adonis.* *Cleopatra*, and euerliuing praiſe to her *Watſons heyre.* louing *Delia*: Regiſter your childrens *So well graced Anthonie deſer-* petegree in Fames forehead, ſo may *nie deſer-* you fill volumes with *Chauſers* praiſe, *ueth immor-* with *Lydgate*, the Scottiſh Knight, and *tall praiſe from the häd* ſuch like, whoſe vnrefined tongues *of that di-* farre ſhorte of the excellencie of this *uine Lady* age, wrote ſimplie and purelie as the *n ho like Co- rinna conte-* times weare. And when baſe and in- *ding with* iurious trades, the ſworne enemies to *Pindarus was oft vi-* Learnings eternitie (a thing vſuall) *ctorious.* ſhall haue deuoured them, either with *Sir 'Dauid* the fretting cancker worme of mouldie *Lynſay. Matilda ho-* time: with *Arabian* ſpicerie: with eng- *norably ho- nored by ſo* liſh honnie: with outlandiſh butter *ſweet a l oë.* (matters of imployment for the aged *Diana.* dayes of our late authors) yet that then ſuch (if you thinke them worthie) in *Procul hinc,* deſpite of baſe Groſers, (whome I *procul ite profani.* charge vpon paine of learnings curſe, not to handle a leafe of mine) may liue by your meanes, canonized in lear-

R 3   ning

"that I dearly lov'd and honor'd, and for all things have left few his equals in England; he it was that in the company of divers Gentlemen one night at supper at the Nag's Head in Cheape[side], first told me of his [Harvey's] vanity, and those Hexameters made of him,

But o what news of that good Gabriel Harvey,
known to the world for a fool and clapped in the Fleet for a Rhymer.[20]

The single extant copy of *The Tears of Fancy* is almost certainly a printer's proof and is riddled with errors. This adds weight to a theory offered by Albert Chatterley. At the time of its printing, Watson's widow Anne was paying visits to her brother Thomas Swift at the Marshalsea prison while he awaited trial. Chatterley suggests that her husband's death might have placed Anne in financial difficulties and he is "convinced that these sonnets were early work never intended for publication."[21] On the other hand, Professor Dana F Sutton has argued that *The Tears* may not be the work of Watson at all. One must make up one's own mind, but Chatterley has disputed this matter with Sutton and his arguments seem the more convincing. The discussion is briefly set out in APPENDIX D.[22]

We should also consider the somewhat curious appearance of Watson's name in a marginal note to the work *Polimanteia* (1595),[23] a work by William Covell, a clergyman and fellow of Queen's College, Cambridge, armed, as its title page declares, at "the frivolous and foolish conjectures of this age". In a lengthy addendum, "England to her three daughters" (the daughters being the two universities and the Inns of Court), marginalia are set, in type, against the body text. Their meanings are often obscure. In the margin of page R3 are the words "Wanton Adonis. Watson's heir" followed by a lengthy text.[24] The meaning is unclear, but it is evident that here, again, Watson is being upheld as a model.[25]

Watson was, it seems, considered quite a wit. Shortly after the publication of Sir John Harington's scatological satire, *A New Discourse of a Stale Subject called The Metamorphosis of Ajax* in 1596, a response entitled

Ulysses Upon Ajax appeared at the booksellers.[26] Its anonymous writer, "Misodiaboles" ("Devil Hater"), criticised Harington's witticisms, commenting, "Faith, they are trivial, the froth of John [*sic*][27] Watson's jests, I heard them in Paris fourteen years ago: besides what balductum [rubbishy] play is not full of them." "Fourteen years ago"—stale humour indeed. Handily, the writer gives good clues to his identity: time, place, and companion, even though he at first gets the name wrong. It is also noteworthy that after naming Watson his train of thought immediately leads him to the drama.

Misodiaboles has never been positively identified. Bowers and Smith argue that he was the inventor and writer on agricultural subjects, Hugh Plat.[28] Plat, who was knighted in 1605, was a prolific writer whose best-known titles are *The Jewell House of Art and Nature* (1594),[29] *Delights for Ladies* (1602) and *Floraes Paradise Beautified* (1608). Since Harington's *Metamorphosis* attacks Plat (and his colleague James Dalton) for suggesting the operation of a system of patents and monopolies, Bowers and Smith argue that Plat had every reason to reply to Harington. It is an attractive theory but there is no discoverable evidence that Plat ever met Watson. Their ages were roughly the same, but it is unlikely that they met during their university days since Plat graduated at St John's College in Cambridge while Watson's truncated English university education was at Oxford. Nor is there any evidence that Plat encountered Watson in Paris since there is no evidence that he ever travelled there.

Perhaps a weak link between Watson and Plat may be discerned through Watson's service to Cornwallis. Plat was a frequent visitor to the Essex estate of Sir Thomas Heneage at Copt (Copped) Hall.[30] The previous lessee of the hall had been Sir William Cornwallis's father, Sir Thomas, and William and Heneage were acquainted. It was to Heneage that William Cornwallis let off steam over Watson's ability to devise "twenty fictions and knaveries in a play". Strengthening evidence of the link between the families (and therefore acquaintance with Watson) is found in a letter written by John Bourne (1518-75) of Battlehall and Holt in Worcestershire; two years after Bourne was dismissed as Principle Secretary of the Privy

Council in 1558 and lost his place on the Worcester bench, he wrote to his friend Francis Yaxley wishing to be remembered to former colleagues, whom he named—they included Thomas Heneage and Thomas Cornwallis. All in all, therefore, although it is not impossible, it is both unproven and unlikely that Plat and Watson were acquainted in Paris fourteen years earlier.

A more convincing candidate for the title of Misodiaboles is Thomas Lodge, as nominated by Nancy Peters Maude.[31] Lodge fulfils every requirement: his history as as virile pamphleteer, his known family affinity and his friendship with Watson. Moreover, as we have seen, he is listed as a recusant living in Paris fourteen years earlier, in 1580—the exact time of Watson's sojourn in the city with his friend Thomas Walsingham.

If Misodiaboles remembered Watson for his old jokes, it is for his poetic works that Watson is most remembered. In the nineteenth century Edward Arber passionately hoped for his recognition as "our Scholler-Poet [sic] of Love, our English Petrarch".[32]

Among the poets of his own day, Watson's reputation was high, and his works exercised a profound influence on Elizabethan poetry, especially his mythological and pastoral poems: *Amyntas, Helenae Raptus, Meliboeus,* and *Amintae Gaudia*.[33] After his death his friends were lavish in their tributes.[34] They remembered his love-epic of 1585 popularised by Fraunce's translation, and often named him "Amyntas". Barnfield associated him with members of the Herbert coterie, all stricken by Cupid's arrow:

> By thee great *Collin* [Spenser] lost his liberty,
> By thee sweet *Astrophel* [Sidney] forwent his joy;
> By thee *Amyntas* [Watson] wept incessantly
> By thee good *Rowland* [Drayton] liv'd in great annoy.[35]

Despite Watson's low opinion of Gabriel Harvey, Harvey himself praised Watson's "studious endeavours in enriching and polishing his native tongue," and considered him "the equal of Spenser, Stanyhurst,

Fraunce, Daniel, and Nashe".[36] Again, in his *Pierce's Supererogation* (1593) Harvey referred to Watson as "a learned and gallant gentleman, a notable poet".

George Peele, in a prologue to his *Honour of the Garter* (1593), paid tribute

> To Watson, worthy many Epitaphs
> For his sweet Poesy for Amintas' tears
> And joys so well set downe.[37]

Francis Meres, after honourable mention of Watson as a Latinist, treated him as the equal of Petrarch in his collection of miscellaneous essays *Palladis Tamia*, and declared Watson's Latin pastorals *Amyntæ Gaudia* and *Melibœus* to be worthy of comparison with the work of Theocritus, Virgil, Mantuanus, and Sannazarro.[38]

Nashe, we have seen, "dearly lov'd and honor'd" Watson; his praise that Watson "left few his equals in England" could have been no higher.

So, who was Thomas Watson? Mothlike he flits through our pages, known only by his works and his associates: classicist, linguist, poet, dramatist, intellectual, musician, government agent, Catholic, wit, joker, friend of high and low—a loyal friend. Perhaps the last tribute should lie with his contemporary, Richard Barnfield:

> And thou my sweet Amintas vertuous mind,
> Should I forget thy Learning or thy Love;
> Well might I be accounted but unkind,
> Whose pure affection I so oft did prove:
> Might my poor Plaints hard stones to pity move;
> His loss should be lamented of each Creature,
> So great his Name, so gentle was his Nature.
> But sleep his soul in sweet Elysium,
> (The happy Haven of eternal rest:)
> And let me my former matter come.

Appendices

Appendix A

Was Christopher Marlowe a Government Spy?

THE evidence that Christopher Marlowe was a spy rests mainly on a Privy Council certificate of 29 June 1587 stating that "Christopher Morley" had been employed on "matters touching the benefit of his country". What these "matters" are is unstated so one cannot accept unreservedly that they were spying matters, although it is difficult to suggest what else they may have been. The certificate was issued just two or three months before Robert Poley's release from prison following the Babington Plot. Both Poley and Marlowe were well acquainted with Thomas Walsingham who no doubt acted as some sort of spying entrepreneur for his cousin Sir Francis. Nevertheless, it is worth bearing in mind that Marlowe was present at his college without absence for the first eighteen months of his studies, and even thereafter "his patterns of attendance do not appear to be exceptional".[1]

In 1982 William Honey privately published his *The Life, Loves and Achievements of Christopher Marlowe Alias Shakespeare, Volume I*.[2] Regrettably, Honey died before completing the second volume, and his papers were destroyed. The extant first volume is huge (1414 pages in a small typeface) and eccentric, its title enough to inform us that it is beyond a second glance by most academics. Nevertheless, Honey spent a lifetime at his studies and, despite some disputable and odd conclusions, his research was thorough and—if treated with caution—sometimes yields insightful nuggets.

Honey suggested that Marlowe had journeyed to Paris in July 1582. He reached this conclusion by working laboriously through the Quarterly Audit Accounts and Buttery Book of Corpus Christi, Cambridge, contemporary with Marlowe's attendance at the college from December 1580 on a Matthew Parker scholarship.[3] Honey compared his results with the researches of modern historians, notably G C Moore Smith, F S Boas and John Bakeless.[4] He calculated that during Marlowe's five years study at the college he was absent on ten occasions between 1582 until his final year of 1587, that is for nearly 79 weeks out of a possible 328 weeks. In other words, Marlowe was missing for nearly a quarter of his six years and six months at the college.[5] Curiously, Honey missed a trick here, for Marlowe's absences were more glaring than Honey suggested. They commenced only one-and-a-half years after his joining the college; that is, his absences for nearly 79 weeks were concentrated in the final five year period, not the full six-and-a-half years. In that shorter period, therefore, he was absent for roughly one third of the time. On even his figures, Honey thought this "a proportion that points to a distractive influence of considerable power outside the university".[6] Does it? Kuriyama and Downie do not consider his absences exceptional: "consideration of a broader range of evidence points to a less exciting but more likely conclusion: Marlowe spent most of his absence from Cambridge doing the same things that other students were doing."[7]

Marlowe's first period of absence was in the summer of 1582 for six weeks from 15 July until 25 August. It is possible, but cannot be proven, that he was on a mission to France during this period. On 25 July 1582 a letter, written by the Queen, was forwarded by Sir Francis Walsingham to the Duke of Anjou, and Honey argues from evidence in the letter that the bearer was expected to be the trusted Thomas Walsingham. An archived copy is endorsed, "Copy of a letter from the Queen to Monsieur, sent by Mr Walsingham the xxv July, 15811 [i.e.1582], Greenwich." "Mr Walsingham", here, presumably refers to Thomas as his uncle is styled in the accounts as "Mr Secretary Walsingham".[8] Honey argued that the words "sent by" meant the letter was passed to Thomas Walsingham, who pulled out at the last moment and entrusted the message to Marlowe, travelling singly under the pseudonym of "John Lane". This deduction relies on a misinterpretation of the phrase "sent by" which probably means "sent via", and is unconvincing. Honey may—or may not—have been correct about Marlowe's cover name of "Lane" (who knows?), but is it likely that such an important letter would have been entrusted to an untried novice travelling alone? Again, it is possible that Marlowe may have joined Thomas on the journey to Paris, as a government messenger-cum-agent learning the ropes. Most probably, however, at this early date he didn't journey to France at all. This does not invalidate the suggestion that he may have travelled on government service later in his college life.

Appendix B

Did the Earl of Oxford Annotate *Hekatompathia*?

THE suggestion that Oxford was the Annotator of *Hekatompathia* has arisen mainly from Watson's dedication to the Earl.[9] He begins this dedication with a narration of the story of Apelles, the Hellenistic painter regarded as the greatest of antiquity's artists, although his paintings have long since vanished. Watson writes that it was Alexander the Great's admiration for the works of Apelles[10] that led to their being sought by "all the people". In a similar way (writes Watson), because it became well-known that Oxford himself had "at convenient leisures favourably perused" Watson's *Love Passions* [i.e. *Hekatompathia*] Watson has been asked by "many" to publish his poems so that they may see what Oxford had "already perused". Oxford, therefore, is compared with Alexander. Some of these persons, remarks Watson, (either to praise Oxford for his good taste, or to please Watson himself) said that Alexander "would like of no lines, but such as were drawn by a cunning hand, and with the curious pencil of Apelles". But Watson would not himself compare his "Poems with Apelles Portraits for worthiness" (though he would "compare his Honour's person with Alexander's, for excellency"). Out of all this wordiness some writers have therefore drawn the conclusion that the writer of the introductions was most probably Oxford.[11]

However, the matter is sealed by another reference. The introduction to Passion LXVII reads as follows:

> A man singular for his learning, and magistrat of no small account, upon slight survey of this book of passions, either for the liking he had to the Author, or for his own private pleasure, or for some good he conceived of the worke, vouchsafed with his own hand to set down certain posies concerning the same: Amongst which, this was one, Love hath no leaden heels. Whereat the Author glances through-out all this

Sonnet; which he purposely compiled at the press, in remembrance of his worshipful friend, and in honour of his golden posy.[12]

Here, the commentator is stating that the Author "purposely compiled" this Sonnet "at the press" — suggesting that, unlike the other poems, it was written without a customary prior submission by manuscript to the author's friends. It is dedicated to "a man singular for his learning" who, it will be observed, deserves the honorific epithet of "worshipful" and who we can assume is Oxford. One of Oxford's poesies, entitled "Love hath no leaden heels" inspired Watson to write the following verse which depicts Oxford as "Cupid", a "companion with the Wind", light-heartedly flying here and there, and who finally, having spied Watson's heart, swoops like a falcon to force it to tremble. In his biography of Oxford B M Ward posits "posies" as an alternative for "annotations",[13] which is forcing a point: "poesy" is always associated with poetic compositions.

Watson's tribute in Passion LXXI to "Deere Titus mine, my ancient friend?", as quoted by Arber,[14] refers not to Shakespeare's revenge tragedy *Titus Andronicus,* but — as the prologue to the poem makes clear — to Boccaccio's then popular story of Titus and Gisippus in *The Decameron,*[15] written c1351 and first published in English by Thomas Elyot in his *The Boke named the Governour* (*The Book of the Governor*) in 1531.[16] It was a source for Shakespeare's *Two Gentlemen of Verona*, although verbal parallels show that the playwright used Elyot's work rather than the original Italian, even though a full translation into English was not made until 1620.[17] The writer of the prologue to Passion LXXI remarks that the author of the verse (that is, Watson) calls the addressee "by the name of Titus, as if himself [Watson] were Gisippus".[18]

In Boccaccio's story, Titus and Gisippus are inseparable until Gisippus falls in love with a woman. Titus is overcome with jealousy and vows to seduce his friend's fiancée. Learning of this, Gisippus changes places with Titus on the wedding night, thus placing his male friendship above his love for his new wife. The identity of Watson's "Titus" is not revealed. Perhaps it is Oxford as Arber tentatively suggests, or is it more probably

Thomas Walsingham? Speculation is fruitless. The adoption of classical pseudonyms was common practice in Elizabethan poetry.

("Titus" is not to be confused with the "Tityrus" named by Watson for Thomas Walsingham [and himself as "Corydon"] in his later elegy to Sir Francis Walsingham, *Meliboeus*. Nor with "Tityus" in Passion LI of *Hekatompathia;* here "the Author [Watson]" compares the pains of his love with the sufferings of "Tityus" slain for "attempting to dishonest [*sic*] Latona".)

Appendix C

Elizabethan schools of literature and science

RIGHTLY or wrongly, various scholars have "identified" groupings of like-minded Elizabethan intellectuals, or schools. The schools were not exclusive: they overlapped and membership of one did not preclude membership of another. Thomas Watson has been identified as belonging to four of the following schools listed below. Some writers believe that at one time the University Wits and the Oxford circle were the same group. The following lists have been compiled from several sources, and are by no means exhaustive.

THE SCHOOL OF NIGHT is alleged to have included: Bruno, Carey, Chapman, Dee, de Vere, Gascoigne, Hariot, Hues, Marlowe, Molyneux, Peele, Percy, Raleigh, Roydon, Warner, *Watson*, and possibly Churchyard and Spenser.

THE UNIVERSITY WITS are alleged to have been: Robert Beale, Beaumont, Camden, Chapman, Chettle, Daniel, Davies, Day, Dekker, Drayton, Drummond, Fletcher, Florio, Greene, Harvey, Heywood, Jonson, Kyd, Lodge, Lyly, Marlowe, Marston, Massinger, Middleton, Milton, Mundy, Nashe, Peele, Roydon, Spenser, *Watson*, Webster.

THE WILTON HOUSE CIRCLE is alleged to have included: Chapman, Daniel, Drayton, Dyer, Ford, Fraunce, Gilbert brothers, Howell, Kyd, Massinger, Spenser, Peacham, Mary Pembroke, Sidney, *Watson*.

THE OXFORD CIRCLE is alleged to have included: Churchyard, de Vere, Fleming, Hill, Lok, Lyly, Mundy, Nashe, *Watson* and others.

Appendix C

THE ESSEX AND SOUTHAMPTON CIRCLE is alleged to have included: Barnes, Beaumont, Braithwait, Chapman, John Davies of Hereford, Florio, Lok, Markham, Nashe, Sylvester, Wither.

Appendix D

The Tears of Fancy: the argument

Dana F Sutton, Professor Emeritus of the University of California believes that *The Tears of Fancy* should be excluded from the Watson canon. His arguments may be summarised as follows:

1. The collection was included in Edward Arber's *Thomas Watson: Poems* (English Reprints, London, 1870) on the basis of an entry in the *Stationers' Register*. This entry was subsequently exposed as a J Payne Collier forgery,[19] although the initials T.W. on the work are not a forgery.

2. Watson's characteristic artistic thumbprints, as exposed in the *Hekatompathia*, cannot be discovered in *The Tears of Fancy*, apart from some features common to all Petrachan erotic poetry. Moreover, the poetic technique is at variance with his other poetry, especially in the use of feminine endings to the pentameter lines of *The Tears of Fancy*.[20]

Albert Chatterley's counter-argument is comprehensive, and may be précised as follows. The sonnets comprising *The Tears of Fancy* probably represent Watson's early experimental work and were never intended for publication. Since Watson was experimenting with the sonnet form, a difference is to be expected in the course of the ten years which passed between *The Tears of Fancy* and *Hekatompathia*. Moreover, during that time, Watson's technique had matured, he had suffered emotionally and he had become involved with playwrights. The initials T.W. appear nowhere else in the printed matter of the period, apart from an advertisement poem in George Whetstone's *An Heptameron of Civil Discourses* (1582) — initials which could in any case have belonged to the younger Watson.[21]

Appendix E

Watson as dramatist. Did he write *The Spanish Tragedy?*

ALTHOUGH Watson is praised for his verse, he was almost certainly a playwright too.[22] Besides praising Watson in his *Palladis Tamia*, Francis Meres included him as one of "our best for Tragedie" in a list of poets-cum-dramatists.[23] His involvement with the stage is famously revealed by William Cornwallis's often quoted letter to Heneage that Watson "could devise twenty fictions and knaveries in a play which was his daily practyse and his living". A "daily practice" and a "living" add up to a substantial commitment to the theatre.[24]

Also, as we noted in CHAPTER FIVE, Thomas Dekker in his pamphlet *A Knights Conjuring* of 1607 imaginatively proposed Watson seated in a bower with the playwrights Thomas Kyd, Thomas Achelley, and the actor John Bentley. Dekker has no doubt that Watson was a dramatist, for Bentley was "a player, moulded out of their pens".

However, putting aside his translation of Sophocles' *Antigone* into Latin, no English dramas have been credited to Watson, and it is generally acknowledged that—if they existed—they either are drowned deep in an ocean of lost Elizabethan plays or, at best, are nestling among unattributed Elizabethan works.[25]

Based mainly on Watson's assumed friendship with his *Hekatompathia* puffers (Buc, Lyly, "C Downhalus", Peele and Roydon)[26] and his association with Kyd, Achelley and Bentley in Dekker's *A Knights Conjuring*,[27] Arthur Freeman suggests looking for Watson's drama in the repertoire of Queen Elizabeth's Men. The dates to study, he thinks, are between the acting company's formation in 1583 and before the death of Bentley in 1585.[28] By 1582 Watson had put continental travel behind him, and—owing to the illness and subsequent death of the then Lord Chamberlain—it fell to Sir Francis Walsingham in the following Spring to form the Queen's Company. Can one detect, perhaps, a link between Watson's contacts with the

Walsingham family and the acting company? The Queen's Company played in London at the Bull, the Bell, the Bel Sauvage, The Theatre and perhaps the Curtain. It joined the court when it went on tour, and spent time in the provinces during the summer. If Watson did write for the Queen's Company, it also fits well with his probable contribution to the Elvetham entertainment in 1591.[29] Elizabeth's Men performed several plays at court, any of which could have come from Watson's pen since all are lost apart from their titles: *Phyllyda and Corin, Felix and Philiomena, Five Plays in One,* and "an antic play and a comedy".[30]

An apparently spurious attribution to Watson is a tragedy entitled *Thorny Abbey or the London Maid* by T.W. and first printed in the year 1662, the first in a collection of three plays entitled *Gratiae Theatrales*.[31] Halliwell-Phillips drew attention to this early drama in 1880. In his notes to *Macbeth* he commented that its writer "appears to have imitated the scenes describing the murder of Duncan and the slaughter of the attendants".[32] In *The Elizabethan Stage,* E K Chambers noted a paper by E H C Oliphant who, in 1911, suggested that Watson might have been the author.[33] Oliphant also detected borrowings not only from *Macbeth* but also from *The Revenger's Tragedy*, as well as some archaic stage devices and language.[34] More recently, Oliphant's attribution of *Thorny Abbey* to Watson has been firmly rejected.[35]

As I was concluding this book, however, I came across a proposal that Thomas Watson was the author of *The Spanish Tragedy*, and it has seemed to me that this question should be separately addressed. The article was put forward in 1977 by Bronson Feldman[36] in a long-vanished Oxfordian publication *The Bard*, although it will be reprinted in a collection of Dr Feldman's articles in 2020.[37] It is reproduced here in total as APPENDIX F. Feldman's claim was a bold one as virtually all scholars acknowledge that this drama, very popular in Elizabethan times (ten editions by 1633), was the work of Thomas Kyd. Nevertheless, mainstream received opinion did not daunt Feldman; his knowledge was broad and his opinions radical. He was born in 1914, became devoted to the Oxfordian case by the age of eighteen and went on to acquire a PhD in Tudor Drama.

By expressing his Oxfordian beliefs too sturdily and too rashly, however, he was labelled a "trouble maker" and lost his teaching post in English at Philadelphia's Temple University. There followed spells as a curator and archivist until he took up psychiatry in private practice, and later became a tutor in history at the Community College of Philadelphia. He was an admirer of the (disputed, to say the least) revised chronology of Velikovsky, James Joyce, the films of Akira Kurosawa and Charlie Chaplin, the music of Handel, and the "muckraker" journalist and author David Graham Phillips, and made prolific contributions to journals of various persuasions. Two notably successful pioneering works issued from his pen: an attempt to relate psychoanalysis to history,[38] and a biography of Stalin.[39] His short book *Hamlet Himself*[40] in which he lays evidence suggesting Edward de Vere as the author of *Hamlet*, also has admirers. He died in 1982.[41]

Although some of Feldman's biographical knowledge of Watson has necessarily been superseded by more recent research, his proposition that Watson may have written *The Spanish Tragedy* raises fascinating possibilities. Correctly, Feldman emphasises that the sole solid basis of the claim for Kyd's authorship of *The Spanish Tragedy* lies with Thomas Heywood, who attributed the work to Kyd in his *An Apology for Actors* in 1612 (eighteen years after Kyd's death). Heywood, says Feldman, is not "customarily upheld as an accurate historian", yet "his word for the authorship of the *Tragedy* has gone unchallenged for centuries."[42] Although there is also some circumstantial evidence for Kyd's authorship, in the main Feldman's argument that to accept Heywood's attribution is dangerous is indisputable. Moreover, the widespread acceptance of the attribution to Kyd has the semblance of clutching at straws.

Feldman tilted at Kyd's background. Kyd, he rightly said, was a scrivener, employed to copy the stage versions of plays. Feldman went on to claim that Thomas Nashe poked fun at Kyd's ignorance in the preface to Greene's *Menaphon*, while Kyd's editors in Feldman's time also drew attention to blunders in Latin, Italian, and French. The one play believed for certain to have been a work by Kyd is his signed play *Cornelia*. The first edition was dated 1594—Kyd had just emerged from torture, and was suffering agonising poverty. Feldman thought the text showed Kyd's inadequate grasp of French, matched by a poor grounding in classical mythology and history—"the charge of insufficient knowledge of the classics would seem to be enough to damn any candidate for the authorship of *The Spanish Tragedy*".[43]

Against Feldman's assassination of Kyd's skills, however, must be set more recent opinion which no longer seriously considers Nashe's pun in his preface to *Menaphon* as a reference to either Kyd or *The Spanish Tragedy*.[44] Moreover, Feldman fails to mention Dekker's image of the "industrious Kyd" seated in Elysian Fields with Watson, Achelley, and the actor Bentley (above, and CHAPTER FIVE)—although, admittedly, the adjective "industrious", while implying a substantial output does not necessarily suggest literary skill.

Regarding *Cornelia*, both Professors Philip Edwards and Arthur Freeman[45] held an opposite view to Feldman's, seeing a clear connection between *Cornelia* and *The Spanish Tragedy*. Edwards comments:

> [T]here is a peculiarly intimate relation between *The Spanish Tragedy* and Kyd's *Cornelia* (1594), translated from Garnier and the only reasonable way of accounting for the relationship is to say that the same man was responsible for both works. There is no cause for doubting Heywood's attribution.[46]

Feldman actually wrote his study as long ago as 1951. It was unpublished until 1977, and in the meantime Arthur Freeman's authoritative study had appeared in 1967. Feldman felt disinclined, perhaps understandably, to make revisions to his work in the light of Freeman's researches. In a Postscript he excused himself by noting that he deliberately refrained from reading Freeman in order to "provide students with an opportunity of comparison of our two arguments".[47] Had he opened Freeman's book, however, he would have discovered that scriveners were by no means the lowly scribes he had depicted. Freeman points out that the scriveners considered themselves a distinguished guild with a tradition of literacy and high educational standards. John Milton's father was a member of the Company.[48] Moreover, Freeman defends Kyd's seemingly weak knowledge of classical authors:

> It is true Kyd's translation of Tasso is peppered with errors, but no more so than most Elizabethan translations, and one hesitates to hold an author sternly to account for mistakes in a "plaine and unpolished" version "digested thus in haste"...[49]

Kyd's *Cornelia*, added Freeman, "is in the main a faithful translation from Garnier's French,[50] and most of the Latin errors in *The Spanish Tragedy* are probably the fault of the type-setter."

More recently, Lukas Erne,[51] acknowledged that *Cornelia* "may well seem like the odd man out among Kyd's plays", unconsciously adding weight to Feldman's doubts that the author of *The Spanish Tragedy* wrote *Cornelia* and stressing the different character of the two plays—of which *Cornelia* is more a declamation than a dramatic performance. Nevertheless, Erne by no means disparages *Cornelia*:

> On close examination, Kyd's *Cornelia* is really more than a translation. Kyd often paraphrases rather than translates Garnier, unlike the Countess of Pembroke who, in her *Antonie*, translates virtually word by word. Not only is the handling of the original relatively free, but what are arguably the best eighteen lines are entirely Kyd's … He omits a good many lines and adds others. As Roberts and Gaines[52] have shown, *Cornelia* is in some ways an original play: "His amendments constitute a second text, which can be considered independently of Garnier's version, and where the work of the writer can be examined on many planes."[53]

Kyd was educated at Richard Mulcaster's Merchant Taylors' School. "[E]xcellent as that school's curriculum was", Feldman thought an education there to be inadequate as preparation for authorship of *The Spanish Tragedy*, especially as the play of "Soliman and Perseda", set within the final act of the *Tragedy*, was originally intended to embrace French, Latin, Italian, and Greek.[54] One hopes Feldman was sure of his grounds in his opinion of the school. Under the headship of Richard Mulcaster it was one of the most advanced schools of its time and presented plays to the court in both Latin and English. Kyd spent eight years there during which time it is possible that he was chosen as one of these child actors. The school numbered amongst its pupils several respected future poets including Lancelot Andrewes, Edmund Spenser and Thomas Lodge.

Feldman correctly drew attention to Meres' declaration that Watson was among "our best for Tragedie", and Watson's literary accomplishments certainly qualified him as not only a dramatist but also as a candidate for the authorship of *The Spanish Tragedy*. Feldman also demonstrated Watson's deep knowledge of the classics, which included references to Sophocles and Seneca in the *Hekatompathia*—even to imitating Seneca in Passion LI.[55] We might add that during his seven years on the continent Watson would also have experienced the Italian drama and the *commedia dell'arte*.

Feldman examined *The Tragedy of Soliman and Perseda*,[56] an anonymous drama, which he thought Watson might have written in 1579 (and the basis of the play within the play in *The Spanish Tragedy*). It was registered at the Stationers' Company on 20 November 1592, just two months after Watson's death and printed by Edward Allde for the publisher Edward White.[57] Feldman was unaware of Watson's family connection with White through Thomas's half-sister Maudlin.[58] White also published an edition of *The Spanish Tragedy* soon after Watson's death and a month before he registered *Soliman and Perseda*. This single extant copy of Q1[59] was registered by Abel Jeffes on 6 October 1592, just a month after Watson's death (and also printed by Allde).[60] That these works were on sale so soon after Watson's death could be significant, although *The Spanish Tragedy* was performed twenty times at Bankside's Rose Theatre early in 1592 before he died, and three times afterwards in December and January in 1592-3. So perhaps printing the work was simply meeting a public demand.[61]

Nevertheless, it is worth pointing out that Philip Edwards believed that the 1592 edition of the *Tragedy* was printed from an author's manuscript "and a neat manuscript at that".[62] Kyd the scrivener would no doubt have produced a neat manuscript,[63] but we also recall the neat manuscript of *A Looking Glasse for Lovers* in the British Library (page 99), and the possibility should at least be considered that—if *The Spanish Tragedy* were written by Watson—a manuscript of the drama might have been placed in the printers' hands after his death, perhaps by his wife Anne in financial need. The reader will note the words "if", "might," and "perhaps".

To return to *Soliman and Perseda*—and Feldman who drew attention to what is thought to be the prime source for the play, Jacques Yver's *Printemps d'Yver,* an anthology of tales from Italian romances published in 1572 at which time, Feldman noted, Watson was in France (more precisely, we believe, in Paris). Yver's work, however—as Feldman points out [64]—had been translated by Henry Wotton and published in *Courtlie Controuersie of Cupids Cautels* in 1578.[65] Therefore, it is as likely that *Soliman and Perseda* was based on Wotton's translation as on Yver's original work. In the year of Wotton's publication Watson returned to London, which suggested to Feldman that he had written it by 1579. However, neither *The Spanish Tragedy* as a whole nor the version of "Soliman and Perseda" staged in that play are wholly indebted to Yver or Wotton, and show a great degree of originality and fluidity.[66] Feldman suggested that since the dramatic version of *Soliman and Perseda* also expresses much sympathy for the Spanish cavaliers it must date to before the expulsion of the Spanish Ambassador in London, Bernardino de Mendoza, involved up to his neck in the Throckmorton Plot. That was in January 1584, after which time such a show of benevolence towards Spain was simply out of the question.[67] Moreover, added Feldman, "As strange as the praise of Spanish knighthood may have rung in contemporary ears, stranger still must have sounded the dramatist's admiration for the Mahometan prince Soliman, whom he portrayed as the most courteous and kindest of kings." Feldman pointed out that this portrait of Soliman recalls John Lyly's pagan "King Alexander" in his comedy *Campaspe*, composed possibly around 1580.

We know Lyly and Watson were on good terms because of Lyly's friendly letter in *Hekatompathia*, "John Lyly to the Author his friend". A similarity between characters in different plays proves nothing, however.[68]

Elsewhere, Feldman's foundations were even weaker. He noted that on 4th February 1580 a play entitled *The History of the Soldan and the Duke of—* was performed at court by the Earl of Derby's players. If the Clerk of the Revels account had written *"Rhodes"*, thought Feldman, it would have proved that this play was *Soliman and Perseda* as the Sultan appointed Erastus, a character in the play, lord of Rhodes.[69] But the Clerk of the Revels account did not write *"Rhodes"*.

In addition, Feldman points out that the principal argument for assigning *Soliman and Perseda* to Kyd is because its style is thought to be similar to that of *The Spanish Tragedy*, as well as being a full version of the short play within the latter play. This is not good enough, said Feldman, unless we can be absolutely certain that Kyd wrote one or other of the plays.[70] Feldman is right. He could have added that to claim that Kyd wrote *The Spanish Tragedy* because it resembles *Soliman and Perseda* because it resembles *The Spanish Tragedy* is a circular argument. More recently, also, Feldman's argument has been slightly strengthened by opinions that *The Spanish Tragedy*, after all, has little correspondence with *Soliman and Perseda*. Lukas Erne argues that "All things considered, it seems likely that Kyd based the plot of *The Spanish Tragedy* on a narrative source which is and will remain lost."[71]

To return to the major drama, *The Spanish Tragedy*. Its dating will be considered more fully below, but worth considering here is Professor Philip Edwards' argument that it "would be something of a miracle if it were written in the early 1580s", although he finally conceded that "on the basis of what firm evidence we have, the date of the play must remain as between 1582 and 1592", adding, "but one may express a firm preference for a date towards the upper limit".[72] All the dating arguments are inconclusive, and scholars have been unable to agree on one for *The Spanish Tragedy*.[73]

Moreover, Edwards considered the play is "innocent of contemporary allusions".[74] Contrary to Edward's opinion, however, Feldman saw the *Tragedy*'s overall message as a "moral criticism of the 'deadly sin' of pride, particularly the pride of Spain."[75] It showed the "Spanish empire was drunk with tribute and the triumphs of its warriors ... they fail to realise that from this pinnacle there is nowhere to go but down."[76] However, neither the dating arguments nor Feldman's suggestion of benevolence towards the Spanish necessarily point towards Watson. Watson does not show particular favouritism towards Spain in his other works. On those grounds, one could consider Thomas Achelley a candidate for its authorship; a puffer of Watson's *Hekatompathia*, he was also a noted lover of Spain and the Spanish, although little of his work has survived.[77] No one has as yet put forward Achelley as a possible author of *The Spanish Tragedy*.

Feldman considered parallels between Watson's works and *The Spanish Tragedy*, and detected traces of Watson's style at I.iii in a verse-form essayed twice in *Hekatompathia* (Passions XLI and LXIV) which Watson said the Greeks described as "*palilogia* or *anadiplosis*, and of the Latines *Reduplicatio*".[78] Feldman spotted another trick shared by the writers of the two works in the "weaving of phrases from various classic authors into a single lyric." He also saw direct likenesses between Watson's sonnets and the play (I:i 3-6 and 9-10), and compared the verse "O eies! No eies, but fountains fraught with tears" (III:ii) with Watson's song "Mine eies, now eies no more, but seas of teares" printed in *The Phoenix Nest* (1593) and *England's Helicon* (1602). "Not on such parallel, however", wrote Feldman, "do I rely for the conviction that Watson was the creator of Hieronimo".[79]

But Feldman should not have so quickly abandoned textual comparisons, dangerous as they are. There are parallels stronger than those he noted. He did not draw attention to a passage from *Soliman and Perseda* which recalls Passion VII in Watson's *Hekatompathia*, so lovingly mocked by Shakespeare's Sonnet 130, as described in CHAPTER TWO:

> But this kind turtle is for Soliman,
> That her captivity may turn to bliss.

> Fair locks, resembling Phoebus' radiant beams;
> Smooth forehead, like the table of high Jove,
> Small pencilled eyebrows, like two glorious rainbows;
> Quick lamp-like eyes, like heaven's two brightest orbs;
> Lips of pure coral, breathing ambrosia;
> Cheeks, where the rose and lily are in combat;
> Neck, whiter than the snowy Appenines;
> Breasts, like two over-flowing fountains,
> 'Twixt which a vale leads to the Elysian shades,
> Where under covert lies the fount of pleasure
> Which thoughts may guess, but tongue must not profane.
> A sweeter creature nature never made;
> Love never tainted Soliman till now.
> Now, fair virgin, let me hear thee speak.[80]

Moreover, in an appendix to his edition of *The Spanish Tragedy*[81] Philip Edwards detected several verbal resemblances with Watson's *Meliboeus* of 1590. To give a single example here, Edwards compared Watson's "incens'd with sole remorse" with Kyd's "incens'd with just remorse".[82] As well as this instance, Edwards added that, "the ideas and phrases are not in the least uncommon, but the similarity seems more than accidental. If there is a dependence, it seems to be of Kyd on Watson ..."[83] However, Arthur Freeman flatly rejected Edwards' comparisons: "the similarities are both minimal and without indication of precedence".[84]

Most glaring of all, in his own survey of parallels Bronson Feldman ignored, or perhaps forgot, a famous correlative between Thomas Watson's verse and *The Spanish Tragedy*. It arises in the first lines of Passion XLVII of the *Hekatompathia*:

> In time the Bull is brought to wear the yoke;
> In time all haggered Hawkes will stoop the Lures;
> In time small wedge will cleave the sturdiest Oak;
> In time the Marble wears with weakest showers:

> More fierce is my sweet love, more hard withall,
> Then Beast, or Bird, then Tree, or Stony wall.

The parallel between this passage and the following exchange in *The Spanish Tragedy* is certainly too close to be accidental:

> *Lorenzo*: In time the Bull sustains the yoke;
> In time all haggard hawks will stoop to lure;
> In time small wedges will cleave the hardest oak;
> In time the flint is pierc'd with softest shower,
> And she in time will fall from her disdain,
> And rue the sufferance of your friendly pain
> *Balthazar*: No, she is wilder and more hard withal,
> Than beast, or bird, or tree, or stony wall.[85]

The image of the tamed bull also occurs in Shakespeare's *Much Ado About Nothing*:

> *Benedick*: ... I will live a bachelor.
> *Don Pedro*: I shall see thee ere I die, look pale with love.
> *Benedick*: With anger, with sickness, or with hunger, my Lord, not with love ...
> *Dom Pedro*: Well, as time shall try: In time the savage bull doth bear the yoke.[86]

Most modern editions insert inverted commas around Dom Pedro's "In time the savage bull doth bear the yoke", and it is clear from the punctuation of the *First Folio* reproduced here that a quotation is intended. Its use in *Much Ado* suggests that the expression had become a habit of speech, a catch-phrase known to Elizabethan audiences—perhaps "caught" from the popularity of *The Spanish Tragedy*. Shakespeare's use of the term is a useful tool for dating his drama[87] but can be safely ignored in a consideration of a relationship between *Hekatompathia* and *The Spanish Tragedy*.

In that relationship, dating is also important; and here the evidence runs into the sand. *Hekatompathia* was published on 31 March 1582, but no firm date has been established for *The Spanish Tragedy*, which scholars have put between 1582 and 1592, the earliest limits being the yoked bull quotation from *Hekatompathia*[88] and the final the registration of the play at the Stationers' Office in October 1592. Since the play makes no mention of the Spanish Armada, a date before 1588 has sometimes been argued.[89] The two works were, therefore, broadly contemporaneous. It would seem more probable that *The Spanish Tragedy* was the later of the two and therefore quoting from *Hekatompathia*, rather than the other way about. No further conclusions can be drawn.

In the final analysis, the question of Watson's involvement in *The Spanish Tragedy* is non-proven. It is true that the principal basis for Kyd's claim to its authorship lies solely with the unreliable Thomas Heywood in 1612, and that, but for Heywood, Watson (with his known knowledge of the classics and especially of Seneca) would have seemed a candidate for the authorship. But, in the absence of hard evidence, the possibility must be put to one side.

Feldman outlined his theory over twenty pages, employing phrases such as "in my opinion", "could have come from Watson's pen", and "I suspect"—none of which is verifiable. Tempting as the theory at first seems, lack of proof renders it no more than that—a theory. Nevertheless, for daring to make such a radical suggestion and for taking on the academic establishment of the 1950s, Bronson Feldman deserves our admiration.

Before leaving the question altogether, it is worth noting briefly another interesting point of view, put forward by the prolific Professor Levin Ludwig Schücking (1878-1964)[90] and referred to by Professors Samuel Schoenbaum[91] and Philip Edwards.[92] Schücking argued that *The Spanish Tragedy* was a collaboration between both Watson and Kyd. At the least, the friendship of the two authors argues for the possibility. Schoenbaum rejected the theory outright, labelling the study of Watson's attribution a "happy neglect now unfortunately [showing] signs of being remedied" by Schücking. He added that, since no single play of Watson's survives, the matter is incapable of proof or study. Edwards reasons against dual authorship from stylistic analysis:

> Even if Schücking were right, one would have to confess that the blend of the two styles is most effective, and that the ease of movement from the stiffer to the more flexible rhetoric gives the play a range of tone quite beyond, shall we say, *Tamburlaine* on the one hand and *Arden of Feversham* on the other. But this very ease of movement argues for a single authorship; the control of the various levels of formality and informality is too secure for collaboration …
>
> The clinching evidence against the theory of composite authorship is the close weave of the design and unity of effect of the whole play. The design of *The Spanish Tragedy* is most unusual … Those whom one might expect to be heroes, the kings and the viceroys, though they still lead armies and hold the keys of life and death, are in the background in this play: strangely ignorant, impotent and variable creatures. The diagram of *The Spanish Tragedy* is not the heroic diagram of a heavy black line to which all other lines refer, but a web or a net …[93]

More recently, Lukas Erne also found little time for Schücking's arguments, and dismissed them outright concluding, "there is very little ground on which to base this attribution, and it is not surprising that Schücking has not found any supporters."[94]

Appendix F

Thomas Watson, Dramatist. By Bronson Feldman

Published in The Bard, Volume 1, No 4, 1977. Reprinted with permission of the Bronson Feldman estate. A Bronson Feldman collection (provisionally titled Shakespeare, Marlowe, and Other Elizabethans) which includes this article will be published in 2021 or 2022 by Laugwitz Verlag, Buchholz, Germany.

The article is left in its original form, except for the light correction of a few minor typographical errors.

AMONG the mysteries that abound in the world of Tudor drama there are few so tantalising as the question of the place occupied by Thomas Watson (1557?-1592) in the story of that world. The mystery seems to become deeper with each addition to our knowledge of Watson. It was to be expected that research would yield us the picture of a far more complex personality than the singer of sweet sobs whom Edward Arber drew as "our English Petrarch."[1] We have assimilated the fact that Watson had the spirit to produce, beside the *Passionate Centurie of Loue* and *The Tears of Fancy*, sarcasms for Gabriel Harvey, the Cambridge pedant, 'in the company of diuers Gentlemen one night at supper at the Nag's Head in Cheape." [2] Less concilable with the picture of the scholar-lyricist generally conjured up by students of Watson from the days of Anthony à Wood[3] to our own is the revelation of "'the froth of witty Tom Watson's jests" given by the unknown author of *Vlisses vpon Ajax* (1596): "I heard them in *Paris* fourteen years ago; besides what balductum play is not full of them?"[4] It is hard to imagine the poet of the *Passionate Centurie* as a scatalogic wit in the vein of Sir John Harington, the more famous forerunner of Thomas Crapper the sanitary engineer. The discovery of Sir William Cornwallis's remark about the "twenty fictions and knaveryes in a play" which Watson habitually manufactured—"his daily practyse and his living"[5]—does not make it easier.

By the findings of Professor Mark Eccles, published in a volume that might with justice have been titled *Thomas Watson in London* (1934) our information concerning the man who appears to have been Christopher Marlowe's most intimate friend is certainly enriched. We are enriched and simultaneously embarrassed. For the image Professor Eccles evokes of "the wise man" of St. Helen's parish, Bishopsgate, sporting gently with the superstitions of his neighbours about Popery and Spain, mystifies more than all the prior portrayals of Watson. Since the publication of *Christopher Marlowe in London* no researcher has come from the scrutiny of Watson's works and biographic vestiges (in Arber's phrase) "like a diver returning from the deep," with any gem to illuminate these discreet facts. Apparently we are as powerless in 1950 as Arber was in 1870 to ascertain the true position of Watson in "the Story of English Mind."

Starting from the hypothesis that a poor hypothesis is better than none, I have ventured a series of conjectures that may provide future historians of the Tudor stage with the framework for all the facts they collect about Watson. The facts in our possession are now strung with the utmost rigour of logic in the lapidary design I present here.

At the beginning of the sequence is set the testimony of Francis Meres that Watson belonged with Marlowe, Peele, Kyd and Shakespeare among "our best for Tragedie."[6] Since none of his tragedies have survived or rather come down to us under his name, we have to guess what sort of plays they were. It is safe to assume that they were products of a rare erudition, a profound acquaintance with the drama *cothurnata* of Athens, Rome, Italy and France. Our poet first emerged in print with a Latin version of Sophocles' *Antigone* (1581). In his *Hekatompathia or Passionate Centurie of Loue* (1582) allusions occur to five, possibly six, other plays by Sophocles: *Trachiniae* (compare poems xxxviii, xciii), *Electra* (compare lxiii), *Ajax Flagellifer* (lxxxii), *Oedipus Rex* (xxxv), *Oedipus Coloneus* (xciii), perhaps *Philoctetes* (see lxviii). The poet also mentions how "*Haemon* choase to die / To follow his Antigone" (xxx). And of course Watson was familiar with Seneca, to whose *Hippolytus* and *Oedipus* he refers in the poems lxxxiv and xxxv respectively. He imitated the Roman dramatist in one sonnet, li. It would not surprise us, therefore, to find him devoutly emulating Sophocles and Seneca in tragedies of his own.

Anthony à Wood states that Watson came of "gentle" stock. There is no evidence of kinship between him and the Th. Watson who was employed as a stage carpenter at Cambridge University in 1571.[7] More likely, the poet came from the kin of the Watson who served Lord John Lumley, lover of the Muses and plastic arts, as a chaplain, and probably shared the warm loyalty of his Lordship to the old Catholic faith.[8] According to Wood, the poet matriculated at Oxford, where he studied "romance". He left the University without a degree about 1572 in order to pursue the liberal arts in France and Italy, and for reasons less ostensible.

He went to Europe at the time when the Protestants of the Netherlands were winning their first victories against Spain. Watson was a witness of the war. He remembered as late as 1590 how the Iberian,

> a dreadfull Lyon in his pride
> descended downe the *Pyrenaean* mount,
> And roaring through the pastures farre and wide,
> deour'd whole *Belgian* heards of chief account.[9]

Whatever he thought of King Philip as a political power, Watson manifestly felt sympathy for the Spaniard's religious convictions when he travelled on the continent. He dedicated his first book, his translation of *Antigone* to the King's namesake, the Catholic Earl of Arundel. In Latin verses preluding the drama he described how he had long ago dreamed of gaining Lord Philip Howard's patronage (*"dicar tuus esse Poeta"*).[10] For nearly six years, a lustrum and a half, he told the Earl, he journeyed in the realms of Romance outside of Spain. And after a residence in Paris, he entered the college of English Catholics in Douai to study languages and law. He left the school in October 1576, and returned in the following May, overtly absorbed in jurisprudence.

In November 1576 the Spanish army, not far from Douai, horrified both Catholic and protestant Christendom by its rapine in Antwerp. The

English envoy in that metropolis, Dr Thomas Wilson, the friend of Nicholas Udall and author of *The Art of Rhetorique,* employed as a courier this year a certain John Watson, who may have been a kinsman of our dramatist.[11] In July 1577 Don John of Austria and his Spanish legions swooped down on Namur and frightened hosts of Belgian Catholics into alliance with the protestant Prince William of Orange. The latter's soldiers were thus able to march triumphantly through Belgium, and arrived at Douai. Watson quit the town in August, before the protestant troops advanced to drive the English collegians away. "Often my studies were obstructed by wars," he chanted to Arundel. "Still I fled from camps, save those of Phoebus."[12]

Watson returned to England. Perhaps he came home to attend the funeral of Elizabeth, the wife of John Watson, gentleman, who was buried at St Helen's church in Bishopsgate on 5 May, 1578. Her connexion—if any existed—with Queen Elizabeth's agent, John Watson, remains obscure. The poet made his residence in her parish, and won golden opinions for his wisdom there. If Elizabeth Watson was his mother, as I surmise, we can understand why he wanted to make his home by St Helen's Yard. And the allurements of James Burbage's Theatre and the nearby Curtain doubtless helped to keep him in Bishopsgate.

On the fringe of Bishopsgate, in the mansion known as Jasper Fisher's Folly, dwelt the poetic, play-loving Earl of Oxford, to whom Watson later dedicated his *Passionate Centurie,* Lord Edward de Vere had clandestinely become a Catholic and maintained a torrid friendship with the family circle of the Earl of Arundel. Oxford's passion for Romance culture carried him to ludicrous and sometimes dangerous extremes. But in 1578 he basked in the eyelight of Queen Elizabeth, whom even his spiritual divorce from her Lord Treasurer's daughter could not seriously vex. The Earl's ardour for the Italianate gave it wings of wildfire among the scholars and playwrights who clustered round his largesse. He acted as patron for George Baker, the physician whose pastime was translating Spanish rarities, Gabriel Harvey declared in rhapsodic Latin that Oxford once meditated sending him to France and Italy.[13] From the preface to Anthony

Mundy's *Mirrour* and Watson's *Antigone*, using the initials E K. Plausible is the identification of Knight with the E K who enjoyed the friendship of Harvey and Edmund Spenser, and supplied the notes to *The Shepheardes Calender* in 1579.* We know from Harvey's correspondence with Spenser that these scholars and poets were fond of visiting the playhouses, to "laugh their bellies full for pence," or to see popular chivalric novels of the period staged.

It was with a romantic tragedy of chivalry, I imagine, that Thomas Watson began his career as a dramatist. We may behold the ruins of that tragedy, after several companies of players had worked their professional havoc on it, in the anonymous drama called *Soliman and Perseda*, There is no date on the title-page of the extant edition of this play; it was registered by Edward White in November 1592, not long after Watson's death. The prime source of *The Tragedye of Soliman and Perseda*, Jacques Yver's anthology of tales *Printemps d'Iver*, appeared in 1572, the year when Watson is believed to have started his tour of France. The romance itself enjoyed a wide circulation in England when Henry Wotton's version was published, in 1578, in his *Courtlie Controuersie of Cupids Cautels*. In 1578 Watson returned to London, and the next year, in my belief, saw the composition of the original version of *Soliman and Perseda*. It must have been written before the onset of theatrical propaganda against Spain which was signalled by the expulsion of the ambassador Bernardino de Mendoza in January 1584. The play is remarkable for the extraordinary sympathy with Spanish cavaliers that its author displays, while serenely postulating the superiority of English men of war.

Representatives of both nations are shown at a tournament in Rhodes:

> The fiery Spaniard bearing in his face
> The empresse of a noble warriour ...
> And English Archers, hardy men at armes,
> Eclipped Lyons of the Western worlde.[14]

---

*Feldman's text seems corrupt here. IKJ

The Spanish knight thus hailed received his accolade, we are informed, in a battle with German *rutters* on an unnamed field (I, iii). English listeners to the lines, however, might have instantly recalled the "Almain rutters with their horsemen's staves" who were active as mercenaries in the Netherland wars.[15] In the summer of 1579 the rutters (*reitern*) of Prince Hans Casimir of the Palatinate, fighting under the banner of Orange but financed by Lord Burghley's office, had disgraced themselves in encounters with the Spanish troops.[16] The ridiculous knight of the play, Basilisco, contrary to the impression of his nationality we get from his name, is really "a Rutter born in Germanie." He is pictured as a veteran of battles in Belgia, and cheerfully confesses an atrocity he performed there to feed his "Frize-land horse" in a season of drouth. He slaughtered the male children of the region, says he, "That the mothers teares might releeue the pearched earth" (I, iii). "The men died, the women wept, and the grasse grewe." Later playwrights would have made this *miles gloriosus* an Iberian sooner than a German. Some actors apparently made an effort to give the character a stamp of Spain; otherwise it is difficult to explain why Love refers to him as "The fond Bragardo" (I, vi), or why Piston should greet him with a "Basolus manus" (IV, ii). There is no hint of derision however in the scene of the tournament where the knight from Spain exults:

> The golden Fleece is that we cry vpon,
> And Iaques, Iaques, is the Spaniards choice.

As strange as the praise of Spanish knighthood may have rung in contemporary English ears, stranger still must have sounded the dramatist's admiration for the Mahometan prince Soliman, whom he portrayed as the most courteous and kindest of kings. Only in the plays of Watson's dear friend Marlowe do we find an equal critique of Christian monarchy in their time. The portrait of the Sultan Soliman constantly recalls John Lyly's ideal figure of the pagan King Alexander in his first comedy, *Campaspe*, which was possibly composed in 1580. Indeed the moral of Lyly's play could not be defined better than in these noble lines spoken by Soliman (IV, i):

> What should he doe with crowne and Emperie,
> That cannot gouerne priuate fond affections?

How close Lyly stood to Watson at the time when I conceive that *Soliman and Perseda* was first produced may be discerned from the letter of commendation the former wrote for the *Passionate Centurie of Loue*. Lyly perused Watson's love poems before they were sent to the press.

My final fragment of evidence to date the original production of the tragedy is the fact that early in 1580 there existed a play with a title that fits it well. In February the actors of Henry Stanley, Earl of Derby, performed at court *The history of the Soldan and the Duke of* —. The last name was left unfinished by the clerk of the Revels accounts.[17] If he had written *Rhodes* there would have been scarcely an iota of doubt that the "history" was our romance of Soliman and Erastus, whom the Sultan appointed Lord of Rhodes.

Soliman and Perseda is usually claimed for Thomas Kyd, on the ground of its style, so eloquently like the rhetoric of *The Spanish Tragedy*, considered Kyd's masterpiece, and because it seems to be an elaboration of the play within that play. The argument would be formidable if we could be sure that Kyd was in truth the author of *The Spanish Tragedy*. But the glory that Kyd has been crowned with posthumously for the sake of that anonymous drama rests on nothing more substantial than the word of Thomas Heywood, who spoke of Kyd as its creator in his *Apology for Actors* (1612), eighteen years after Kyd's death. Although Heywood is not customarily upheld as an accurate historian, his word on the authorship of the *Tragedy* has gone unchallenged for centuries. I am convinced that he reported the truth as he knew it, the histrionic tradition that Kyd was the writer of the most popular play of the age. But there are writers and writers. In justice we can speak of Kyd's ability as a playwright only on the basis of the single drama issued under his signature, the wretched translation *Cornelia*, printed in 1594.

Thomas Kyd was by trade a scrivener. He might have been employed to copy the stage versions of the anonymous plays which now pass under his name. In view of Thomas Nashe's satiric reference to him in the notorious preface to Robert Greene's *Menaphon* (1589), we are inclined to think that Kyd left his father's trade of *noverint*, and busied himself "with the endeavours of art," trying to make a living as a playwright. Nashe laughed at his ignorance, contending that he could scarcely Latinise his "neck-verse" if he had been sentenced to hang and pleaded for the benefit of clerics. While Kyd's advocates and editors do not go so far as Nashe in criticism of his learning, they candidly exhibit his multitudinous blunders in Latin, Italian and French. The play he signed his own, *Cornelia*, proves he was unable to translate French with any respectable degree of fidelity. "Nor was he sufficiently conversant with classical mythology and history."[18] Yet the charge of insufficient knowledge of the classics would seem to be enough to damn any candidate for the authorship of *The Spanish Tragedy*.

The play of "Soliman and Perseda" introduced in *The Spanish Tragedy* is prologued by Hieronimo with the remark that he wrote it when he was a student in Toledo. Frederick Boas fancied that Kyd may have composed a drama on the subject at some university, but adds, "this is a very doubtful assumption."[19] Kyd's formal education appears to have been confined to Richard Mulcaster's academy for the Merchant Taylors' boys. Excellent as that school's curriculum was, it could not enable a graduate to fulfil the project of Hieronimo's drama. When Edward White, the publisher of *Soliman and Perseda*, issued *The Spanish Tragedy* (likewise without a date), he included a note (IV, iv) saying that the play within the play was originally intended to be recited in French, Latin, Italian and Greek. Hieronimo confirms the statement in alluding to "our sundry languages" (*ibid.*). Such a project would have been a labour after Thomas Watson's own heart. *Aut Watson, aut diabolus!* I am confident he wrote at least the initial version of the *Tragedy*, when memories of his *alma mater* Oxford and the college at Douai were refreshed in his mind, late in 1580, about the time he used to lodge in Westminster with "one Mr. Beale a preacher & his acquaintance in Oxforde before."[20]

Fear and reference for imperial Spain were rife in Westminster in those days. When Watson dwelt there he met a crazy woman who proclaimed herself the child of King Philip; and the poet humoured her fantasy.[21] The Earl of Oxford indulged in dreams of his admission to Spanish aristocracy hardly less mad,[22] but escaped the accusation of craziness under the cloudy reputation of a drunkard. His companions of the cup, Lord Henry Howard, Charles Arundell, and Philip Howard, Earl of Arundel, disdained to conceal their enthusiasm over the victories of Spanish arms, at least in the invasion of Portugal. In April 1580 the French statesman Mauvissière de Castelnau wrote to Queen Elizabeth that his royal mistress Catherine de' Medici favoured a united effort of France and England to prevent Philip's conquest of Portugal. But the Portuguese tragedy had to be enacted to its cruel conclusion at Alcantara without an English interlude. On 26 August the Duke of Alva crushed the arm of the young King of Portugal, Antonio, and the throne of England experienced percussions of rumours about a coming Spanish fleet, and an invasion by united troops of Philip and the Pope.[23]

The Spanish Tragedy displays a consideration of Spain and her autocrat which is not satisfactorily explained by Christian charity. The drama was certainly revised often before Edward White obtained his licence to print it in 1592, one month before he registered his copy of *Soliman and Perseda*. Yet the *Tragedy* is still sultry with the political temperature of the circle of the Earls of Arundel, Oxford, and Derby in the epoch of Alva's victory at Alcantara. The ghost of Andrea as Prologue opens the play with a reference to "the late conflict with Portingale". The carnage is described at length in Act I, scene ii (lines 22-84). Other scholars after J. Schick have recognised the "conflict" in the battle fought on 26 August 1580, but none followed him in taking earnestly the adjective "late" as a clue to the play's chronology. Some are tempted to adopt a suggestion of Ben Jonson's Induction to *Bartholomew Fayre* (1614) and set the date of the *Tragedy* in 1584. That was a year of uncommon butchery by Philip's legions in the Low Countries, and there were not many intellects in England that could have listened with gravity to the nameless King of Spain in the *Tragedy* declaiming, "We pleasure more in kindness than in warres" (I, v). We hear no hint of irony in the King's speech to the defeated Portuguese:

Yet shalt thou know that Spain is honourable ...
Our peace will grow the stronger for these warres. (I, ii)

There is not a word to show that the dramatist was not in sympathy with the conquerors of Portugal. The ruler of that country is depicted as a vassal, a Viceroy, who had betrayed his master of Madrid.

It is curious that the Viceroy confesses his treason in a verse form (I, iii) that Watson toyed with twice in *Hekatompathia* (xli, lxiv), "a somewhat tedious or too much affected continuation of that figure in Rhethorique, whiche of the Grekes is called *palilogia* or *anadiplosis*, of the Latines *Reduplicatio*."[24] Another trick of poetry executed by the poet of the *Tragedy* and the poet of the *Passionate Centurie of Loue* is the weaving of phrases from various classic authors into a single lyric (Act II, Scene iv; Quatorzain lxxxix). More direct echoes of Watson's sonnets have been heard in the second act of *The Spanish Tragedy* (Scene i, 3-6, 9-10). One likeness between the play and one of Watson's poems has apparently gone unobserved. The famous verse "O eies! No eies, but fountaines fraught with teares" (III, ii) reverberates in the line "Mine eies, now eies no more, but seas of teares" from a song by Watson printed in *The Phoenix Nest* (1593) and *Englands Helicon* (1602).[25] Not on such parallel, however, do I rely for the conviction that Watson was the creator of Hieronimo.

The art and content of the drama designate Watson as its prime mover. As I see it, the *Tragedy* was aimed as moral criticism of the "deadly sin"' of pride, particularly the pride of Spain; the play delivers a Sophoclean lesson in *hybris* or, as the Tudor poets quaintly name it, *surquedry*. The dramatist showed the Spanish empire was drunk with tribute and the triumphs of its warriors. He presents Duke Cyprian of Castile extolling his King in the words of the Roman poem of Claudian (I, i): "O much beloved of God, heaven battles for you, and the peoples of the world combined submit on bent knees."[26] In the rapture of the Spaniards over their gilded achievements they fail to realise that from this pinnacle there is nowhere to go but down. And the horrors of the domestic crime and punishment in the play foreshadow the greater horrors of the fall of the house of Spanish royalty.

The moral is driven home by various devices. There is the tragic irony of the King's boast of his power over Portugal (III, xiv):

> As we now are, so sometimes were these,
> Kings and commanders of the westerne Indies.

An explicit rebuke of Iberian arrogance is Hieronimo's "pompous iest" or masque of two legendary English knights who once captured kings of Portugal, followed by Duke John of Gaunt, who took the King of Castile prisoner. The patriotic morality of the poet brought his art to the verge of the naive in this scene of the Conquistadores being entertained by history of their kingdom's disgrace. The King is pleased by the spectacle and solemnly counsels his Portuguese victims to take it as consolation.

> Portingale may daine to beare our yoake,
> When it by little England hath been yoakt.

But the Ambassador points out the actual teaching of the "jest" (I, v):

> Spaine may not insult for her successe,
> Since English warriours likewise conquered Spaine,
> And made them bow their knees to Albion.

The poet's faith in the ability of English soldiers to defeat the terrible Spanish *tercios* blurts through the lips of the Portuguese humbled at the throne of Madrid. Yet his pathos for the fate of Spain never permits the utterance of a single "Philippic" line, such as you get from John Lyly in his *Midas*. For the ethical purpose of *The Spanish Tragedy* the artist deranged history, and punished the insolence of Spain by bereaving its dynasty in the play of the prince, "the whole succeeding hope" (IV, iv). The dramatist may have had in mind the mysterious death of Philip's first heir, Don Carlos, in 1568. In Schiller's tragedy *Don Carlos* the prince's death is likewise treated as if it meant the breakdown of Spain's esperance.

Appendix F 229

In the summer of 1580 English courtiers were more excited by imperial French amours than by Spanish arms. The dynastic heir of France, the Duke of Anjou, courted the Queen to a degree of warmth that kindled Sir Philip Sidney into daring to read where poor John Stubbe had rushed in and lost his right hand. Sidney's antagonism to the French alliance was aggravated by his severest critic, the Earl of Oxford, who was fervidly for it. The Howards and Arundels, devoted as they were to the policy of Spain, imitated King Philip's sport with Catherine de' Medici, and pretended to Elizabeth that they were all "strong advocates of the marriage" with Catholic France.[27] If the author of *The Spanish Tragedy* was Thomas Watson, we should expect to find in the play an allusion to the Anjou affair. Our expectation is fulfilled in these lines, proposing a union of Castile and Portugal by a wedding of their dynastic heirs:

> Aduise thy King to make this marriage vp,
> For strengthening of our late confirmed league;
> I know no better meanes to make vs freends ...
> Yong virgins must be ruled by their freends.
> The Princess amiable and loues her well;
> If she neglect him and forgoe his loue,
> She both will wrong her owne estate and ours.

If Elizabeth ever heard this admonition, she must have been grimly amused by the comment on the government of virgins. Yet she was deeply tempted by the project of the Valois "league", despite its sinister attenant, the Holy League of the Guise ring.

It is hardly conceivable that Her Majesty would have missed her people's favourite play. In my opinion, she heard *The Spanish Tragedy* on 1 January 1581, when, according to the cryptic Revels record, the actors of the Earl of Derby performed for the court *The Storie of* —.[28] The name that perplexed the clerk was, I feel sure, Hieronimo. From the histrionic servants of Derby *The Story of Hieronimo* passed into the property of the actors who served Derby's son, Ferdinando, Lord Strange. These men earned their supreme plaudits with *The Spanish Tragedy*. In *Bartholomew Fayre* Jonson refers to the drama (which he had revised and extended) by the name of *Ieronimo*.

The companion piece of *The Tragedy* known as *The First Part of Ieronimo* seems to have been revived together with it in February 1592, by Lord Strange's company.[29] Few scholars regard *Ieronimo* as worthy of Kyd. In its present form it is certainly not Watson's work. Its posture toward Spain is far less compassionate than the viewpoint of *The Spanish Tragedy*. When its Marshal Ieronimo expresses alacrity to serve his King in the extortion of tribute from Portugal, the heroine, Belimperia, cries (I, ii):

> Trybute? Alas, that Spaine cannot of peace forbeare
> A little coin, the Indies being so neere.

She appeals to her soldier lover,

> O deere *Andrea*, pray, lets haue no wars.
> First let them pay the souldiers that were maimde
> In the last battaile, ere more wretches fall,
> Or walke on stilts to timeless Funerall.

The pacific appeal could have come from Watson's pen (copied for the prompter by Kyd). But whoever wrote the play was no friend of the Howards and Arundels then. It breathes a hot hostility to the Spanish lust for dominion, the majesty which the Earl of Arundel ecstatically lauded, according to a letter Mendoza sent his master in Madrid on 1 March, 1582. One evening, Mendoza reported, the Earl sat at dinner with Sir Francis Drake, who vaunted himself "the man to wage war on Your Majesty. At this Arundel said that a like he could have no sense of shame, to imagine such a thing of the greatest monarch there had been on earth, who was strong enough to make war on all the princes of the world."[30]

By this time, it is true, Watson had taken a stand in opposition to the Earl of Arundel's politics. He had become a close friend of Walsingham,

Marlowe's comrade, the courier and cousin of Sir Francis Walsingham, the Principal Secretary of State, whom the Catholics (and occasionally the Queen) detested as the champion of heretics. It is possible that the dramatist altered his *Hieronimo*, after its premier triumph, into a tragedy in two parts, making it a kind of farewell warning to Lord Philip Howard and his group. One can fancy the poet at work on his study of *surquedry*, murmuring to himself, in Hieronimo's unforgettable phrase on setting the stage for his own little play, "Ile fit you".

At the end of *The First Part of Ieronimo* there is mute testimony of the poet's haste in writing the play. Two Spanish officers named Philippo and Cassimero come on the stage and are left without a word in the extant text. Perhaps they were designed to mimic the King of Spain or his *caballeros* and Duke Casimir or his rutters, whose campaign in the Low Countries had squandered English funds. There appears to be a vicious jibe on the chief of the Dutch forces in the following gloat of Ieronimo, comparing the flesh of his son's adversaries to Sevillian fruit (III, i):

> His sword so fals vpon the Portugales,
> As he would slise them out like Orenges,
> And squeeze their blouds out.

That Watson was capable of the pun, we comprehend from the glimpse of his dirty wit offered in *Vlisses Vpon Ajax*. But I prefer to regard the verse as the handiwork of Tom Kyd, translating Watson's rather academic art into the vulgate, so to speak. One of the few established facts of Kyd's biography is a record of his arrest in 1593 on the suspicion that he was the writer of "lewd and mutinous libels" against the Dutch which were fixed to the wall of their churchyard in London.[31] A gentleman of Watson's attainments would have to be soaked in sack to perpetrate the joke on Orange for the mob of apprentices in the playhouses who hated the industrious Dutch. Watson knew how it felt to be a foreigner. It is likely that he was the Thomas Watson, "'yeoman", who was reported in June 1581 among the "strangers" in St Helen's parish, Bishopsgate, "who did not go to church."[32]

II

DURING Christmas 1580 the fantastic Earl of Oxford exploded the court peace with a scandal that had a decisive effect on Watson's career. Oxford charged Lord Henry Howard, Charles Arundell, and their kinsman Francis Southwell, with conspiracy against the state. He disclosed their political services to Rome, notably the hiding of Jesuits, who entered England at the risk of their necks. Confessing that he had been swayed to fidelity to the Vatican and sheltered "massing priests" himself, the Earl denied that he was ever acquainted with a Papist plot to overthrow Elizabeth until this time. He appealed to the French ambassador, Castelnau, to tell her what he knew about the Howard group's protection of Jesuits. But his sole witness declined to imperil them: "They and their friends," he wrote to Paris, "have always been in favour of the (Anjou) marriage and the French alliance ... The Earl of Oxford," he added, "thus found himself alone in his evidence and accusations. He has lost credit and honour, and has been abandoned by all his friends and all the ladies of the Court." The ambassador wondered if he did not secretly belong to "the Spanish faction."[1]

The Spanish ambassador described the event to Philip, and how he had concealed the "very Catholic" Lord Howard and his companions from violent enemies. They were arrested, but nothing could be proved against them. Lord Harry, testified Mendoza, was profoundly loyal to Philip: "To touch on the greatness of the affection with which he occupies himself in the service of Your Majesty is impossible."[2]

Shortly after, Charles Arundell fled to the continent and occupied himself at Paris with a plot to crown Mary Stuart Queen of England. The Earl of Arundel kept his name clear of conspiracy and treason. He indicated the direction of his heart, however, on 22 January 1581, when he rode as challenger in a tournament against the Earl of Oxford. On the side of Oxford, encountering Sir William Drury, rode none other than Sir Philip Sidney, who had quarrelled with Oxford so cordially more than a twelvemonth before—over possession of a tennis court and the question of the Valois league.³ Arundel went down to defeat in the contest. In March he had the sour satisfaction of watching the victor drop to infamy when Anne Vavasour, a lady of Her Majesty's Bedchamber, and a tender friend of Charles Arundell, gave birth to a boy at court and pointed out Oxford as the father. Elizabeth locked the unlucky Earl in the Tower and he stayed there till June.

In the next month John Wolfe registered Watson's Latin translation of Sophocles, dedicated to the Earl of Arundel. Four allegorical poems entitled *Pompae* accompanied the *Antigone*, also dedicated to the Earl. We do not know what Philip Howard said or did about the offering, or the poet's selection of obedience to the sovereign as the main ethical motive of the Greek play. "*Quam sit malum publico Magistratus edicto non parere, Antigonae exemplum docet.*"⁴

At the time of Oxford's misfortune Watson appears to have been in Paris. The German jurist and poet Stephen Broelmann of Cologne wrote Latin verses for him which were prefixed to the *Antigone*, urging the publication of his work; they were addressed to the French capital. Possibly the jurist was a relative of Elizabeth Broylman, the cutler's widow, "born in Douchland", who lived near Watson's lodging in Westminster.⁵ According to George Peele, the lays of love Watson published in his *Hekatompathia*, and dedicated to Oxford, followed fast his sad *Antigone*.⁶ He probably read them to Thomas Walsingham in Paris, for that gentleman is presented in the poet's elegy on Sir Francis Walsingham complimenting Watson on his songs thus:

> Thy tunes haue often pleas'd mine eare of yore,
> when milk-white swans did flocke to hear thee sing,
> Where Seine in Paris makes a double shore.⁷

What was the poet doing in France? Carrying messages for the Queen's Secretary and spy-master, I suppose. Sir Francis had already employed a scholar-playwright, the late George Gascoigne, as a courier to Paris.⁸

Not long after Oxford emerged from the Tower, he "willinglie voutchsafed the acceptance" of Watson's *Passionate Centurie of Loue*, "and at conuenient leisures fauorablie perused it."[9] Gabriel Cawood licensed the book on 31 March 1582. Cawood was the publisher of Lyly's novels celebrating the courtly philosophy and language dear to the Earl of Oxford, patron of a Latin translation of Castiglione's *Courtier*. In pedestrian Euphuism Lyly wrote a prefatory letter on Watson's sonnets, commending them to the public as genuine love-songs. Lyly and Peele were not the only theatrical men who advertised the *Centurie*. Thomas Acheley and Matthew Roydon, more obscure writers for the stage, also produced commendatory poems for Watson. And so did George Bucke, who eventually became Master of the Revels.

In the happy companionship of these men, perhaps Watson wrote the romantic comedy called the *History of Love and Fortune*, which the Earl of Derby's servants acted for the Queen in December 1582. This is doubtless the play, printed for Edward White in 1589, under the title of *The Rare Triumphs of Love and Fortune*, "wherein are many fine Conceits with great delight."

Sir Edmund Chambers perceived one link between *Love and Fortune* and *Soliman and Perseda*.[10] The subtitle of the tragedy in quarto is "Loues constancy, Fortunes inconstancy, and Deaths Triumphs", which immediately reminds us of the comedy. According to my theory, they were both staged by Derby's men. It is strange that no critic has claimed *Love and Fortune* for Kyd. It has much in common with the dramas credited to him. It commences in Senecan style with a Fury, Tisiphone, broaching debate among the Roman gods. They are set at odds disputing which is the superior goddess, Fortuna or Venus, and these entertain the Olympians with pompous masques of their accomplishments, shows of Troilus and Cressida, Alexander, Pompey, Caesar, Hero and Leander. The rival goddesses are then invited to test their powers on a prince and his love in the nameless land of the play; and so the romance of Hermione (*sic*) and his Fidelia is enacted. We note the same incongruous comparison of a gallant young lover with old blind Oedipus that Watson made in *Hekatompathia*.[11] A light echo of *The Spanish Tragedy* occurs in the scene (III) where Bomelio calls on the Furies Alecto and Tisiphone, and the infernal judge Rhadamanth, to curse his tormentors. Reminiscent of *Vlisses Vpon Ajax* and its smear for "witty Tom Watson" are the excremental humour of the clown Lentulo (IV) and Bomelio's angry obscenity in the same act. The linguistic talent of the anonymous playwright is put to comic use in the passages where Bomelio counterfeits a foreign physician, uttering broken Italian and French. We are poignantly reminded of Watson's friend Marlowe and his *Doctor Faustus* in the scene of prince Hermione's burning of the "vile blasphemous" books of his father, the magician Bomelio. Addressing his gentle auditors, Hermione earnestly exhorts them: "Abhor this study, for it will confound you all."[12] The play concludes with Fortune's prayer, "God save her Majesty that keeps us all in peace," which indicates a date of production prior to January 1584, when the Queen expelled the ambassador of Spain; at any rate, prior to June 1585, when Holland sent twelve deputies to London to make a treaty of war with her. Incidentally, there was a Captain Thomas Watson fighting for the Low Countries at this time.[13]

October 1584 witnessed the movement of the Earl of Leycester for an association of Englishmen to destroy all plotters against the Queen's life.[14] Leycester launched it after the murder of the Prince of Orange had shown how high fanatic assassins could reach. In March 1585 Parliament agreed on a law containing the substance of the association's vow. Perhaps in allusion to this act, the weird compliment to "sacred *Cynthias* friend" was inserted among the speeches of Death in *Soliman and Perseda*:

> For holy fates haue grauen it in their tables
> That *Death* shall die, if he attempts her end,
> Whose life is heauens delight, and *Cynthias* friend.

I suspect that this interpolation came from Kyd, in the precise spirit of his *Verses of Praise and Joy* over the frustration of the Babington intrigue in 1586.[15]

The atmosphere of England in that year was fevered by the arming of regiments to join Leycester's expedition in the Netherlands. Watson apparently was not pleased by the manoeuvres of Mavors in London; he endeavoured to forget the tumults of the military in Lethean melody and Romanesque literature. He dashed off in doggerel "A gratification vnto Mr. John Case, for his learned Booke, lately made in the prayes of Musick," a poem admitting his pacifism, dated 1586.

> Let Eris then delight in warrs,
> Let Enuy barke against the starrs,
> Let Folly sayle which way thee please:
> With him I wish my dayes to spende
> Whose quill hath stood fayre Musicks friend,
> Chief friend to peace, chief port of ease.
> q.^{d} Tho. Watson.[16]

Students of *The Passionate Centurie* will recall the poet's expression of his pleasure in the somnolent lyrics of Luca Marenzio and other Italian tunes.

On 6 September, 1585, Watson married Anne Swift at the church of St Antholin. With her brother and Kit Marlowe he became involved in a tenebrous feud that brought both poets within the shadow of the gallows. In 1586 Watson's paraphrase in Latin of *The Rape of Helen* by Coluthus appeared in modest print. He dedicated it to Henry Percy, the Earl of Northumberland, a man extravagantly fond of books like those the hero of *Love and Fortune* burnt. Marlowe's adaptation of Watson's work in English rime, said to have been made in 1587, is lost. The time when Marlowe entered Northumberland's charming circle is unclear. In the spring of 1587 the Privy Council employed Marlowe "in matters touching the benefitt of his Countrie": matters quite murky. One outcome of his enigmatic activity was the rumour that he had determined to travel "beyond the seas to Reames," where the English fugitives from the Douai college had established their school.[17] Marlowe and Watson had plenty of common interests, including the same adversaries in their art.

The Lord Admiral's men, headed by Edward Alleyn, acted *Tamburlaine the Great* in 1587, and the response of the theatre crowds to Marlowe's colossal muse made Robert Greene virid with envy. He ventured to ape it in *Alphonsus, King of Arragon*, and failed. In the preface to his novel *Perimedes the Blacksmith* (registered on 29 March 1588) he complained that Marlowe and a fellow playwright had insulted him on the stage. "Lately," Greene wrote, "two Gentlemen Poets made two madmen of Rome," *ie* two London comedians, beat his Horatian motto, *Omne tulit punctum*, out of paper bucklers, in a sort of brutal mockery or pun. To this charade on Greene's points they added ridicule—"for that I could not make my verses iet vpon the stage in tragical buskins, euery word filling the mouth like the faburden of Bo-Bell, daring God out of heaven with that Atheist *Tamburlan*, or blaspheming with the mad preest of the sonne."[18] The consensus of scholars holds that "the mad priest of the sun" was the protagonist of a tragedy no longer extant, *The Lyfe and Death of Heliogabilus*, licensed for printing in June 1594. I suggest that Tom Watson was the writer of this tragedy of imperial Rome. His usually tranquil temperament kept him out of the glare of playhouse and tavern publicity, just as Marlowe's perfervid nature thrust him into it. Greene carried on a kind of feud with Marlowe, striving to surpass the popularity of *Doctor Faustus* with his patriotic *Friar Bacon*. If he had recognised a competitor in Watson, he would have waxed fluently clever about him. One nearly regrets that our hero was indeed more a gentleman than a poet.

In the winter of 1587, according to Kyd, he entered the service of the unknown Lord to whom he referred in his pathetic letter to Sir John Puckering of autumn 1592.[19] The opinion prevails that he was already the distinguished creator of *The Spanish Tragedy*, although no contemporary allusions connect them or clarify his repute. We know more about the glory acquired by little Richard Burbage, who seems to have risen to theatrical stardom in the role of Hieronimo. *The Verses of Praise and Joy* by T.K. which the printer registered on 21 September 1586, are destitute of beauty and rudimentary in skill. They mimic verbal tricks used in the *Tragedy*, combining "hope" and "'hap" in one line, and repeating the play's affirmation, "Time is the author both of truth and right." More important is the quest for identification of the nobleman whom Kyd served for nearly six years, at least as a calligrapher, including some kind of collaboration with Christopher Marlowe: "some occasion of or wrytinge in one chamber twoe yeares synce" (in the autumn of 1591 or earlier season).

"My first acquaintance wth this Marlowe," Kyd informed his inquisitor Puckering, "rose vpon his bearing name to serve my Lo: although his L[P] never knewe his service, but in writing for his plaiers, ffor never cold my L. endure his name or sight, when he had heard of his conditions, nor wold indeed the forme of devyne praiers vsed duelie in his L[ps] house, haue quadred wth such reprobates."[20]

Scholars have attempted to find "his Lordship" in the Early of Derby or his son Lord Strange, or the Earl of Sussex, to whose Countess Kyd dedicated his *Cornelia*, But Sussex was Governor of Portsmouth during the period when Kyd and Marlowe wrote for the unnamed patron's players; and there is nothing in Marlowe's life to link him to the house of Derby. Moreover, scholars have been too quick to suppose that "his Lordship's house" must mean his home. And a peculiar presbyopia has steadily steered them away from the singular Elizabethan courtier who was most closely connected with the theatrical world, most intimate with dramatists. We have the authority of Edmund Spenser for singling out Edward de Vere, Earl of Oxford, as the fittest for the role of Marlowe's master and Kyd's Lord. In January 1589 Spenser had the satisfaction of delivering the first cantos of *The Faerie Queene* to the press. He preluded the volume with a series of sonnets to outstanding courtiers, and to "the Earle of Oxenford, Lord high Chamberlayne of England," he appealed for defence of his epic against envious tongues. Spenser appealed to de Vere

> for the love which thou doest beare
> To th' Heliconian imps, and they to thee;
> They unto thee, and thou to them, most deare.

The "Heliconian imps" (the phrase is, I suggest, Oxford's own) were of course poets, and in those days that word signified almost always playwrights. Even Spenser, under the influence of the inn-yard theatres and others of London, ventured to compose nine comedies in the spirit of Ariosto. There is no need to review here the patronage of Oxford for such writers as Lyly, Mundy, and Robert Greene, whose extolments of the Earl are inscribed on dedication pages. It is necessary to call attention to the fact that Oxford maintained a magnificent residence for unknown persons in the mansion that was once the goldsmith Jasper Fisher's Folly, outside Bishopsgate, where the next door was that of messuages belonging to the brothers Edward and John Alleyn.

Tall Ned went from stage training in the Earl of Worcester's company to stardom with Strange's and afterwards the Lord Admiral's men, especially in Marlowe's tragedies.[21] Marlowe resided in Norton Folgate, a short walk from the playhouses of Shoreditch northward and from Oxford's house of luxury and obscure labour southward. The Earl lived in the latter only as a lord of literature; his ordinary residence was in Oxford House by London Stone in Candlewick Street.

The Bishopsgate mansion, in my opinion, served for the office that the Earl held for Elizabeth. On 26 June 1586, the Queen had granted him, under privy seal warrant, one thousand pounds a year from the secret service fund of his father-in-law's Treasury, for work never defined.[22] Whatever the nature of the Earl's employment, he derived little pride from it. He begged Burghley to get him a more honourable post, in a letter his father-in-law did not deem worthy to preserve. The Lord Treasurer, however, kept his reply, dated 15 December 1587: "You seem to infer that the lack of your preferment cometh of me, for that you could never hear of any way prepared for your preferment. My Lord, for a direct answer, I affirm for a truth—and it is to be well proved—that you Lordship mistaketh my power."[23] Colonel B R Ward surmised that the Queen had resolved to engage Oxford's genius in "exploitation of the now famous Elizabethan historical dramas" for purposes of propaganda in the Anglo-Spanish war.[24] Three days before she gave Oxford his secret service payment, the Star Chamber decreed the restriction of all printing in England to the presses of London, Cambridge and Oxford, and the stern supervision of those presses by the Stationers' Company. No similar decree was ever issued for the English theatre, but we know how the London magistrates demonstrated a zeal which academic minds have mistakenly classified as Puritan in religio-political control of the stage companies. Among the measures for this control was the decision to allow only John Charlwood to print the players' announcement bills. The Stationers' Company gave Charlwood this licence on 30 October 1587, less than a month before the Queen summoned her chief warriors to a council to select the tactics of resistance to invaders expected from Spain. Following Colonel Ward, I believe that we have in Oxford's appointment the explanation for the outbreak on the London stages in the summer of 1586 of what might be called "Philippic" plays. On 20 July 1586, Hieronimo Lippomano, the ambassador of Venice to Madrid wrote to his Senate about King Philip's fury against the English theatre:

> But what has enraged him more than all else, and has caused him to show a resentment such as he has never before displayed in all his life, is the account of the maskerades and comedies which the Queen of England orders to be acted at his expense.[25]

To the tempests of patriotism excited by these "maskerades and comedies" were added, perhaps at the instigation of Burghley and Walsingham, plays of propaganda against the captive Queen of Scots: "in divers plays and comedies in public," King James VI learnt from his envoys in the English capital, "they have brought your mother in a rope to the Queen of England in derision, whereof we mind to complain."[26] This report was sent to Scotland in January 1587. It was on 10 January that Philip Henslowe, future father-in-law of Edward Alleyn, turned his mind from the business of a pawnbroker to finish the commercial arrangements for erecting the Rose Theatre. Histrionic enterprise fevered other brains in in England which had never before felt the inspiration of the comic or tragic muses. Even Burghley's son Thomas Cecil experimented with patronage of a troop of players, which left one solitary record of activity at Norwich, also in January 1587.[27]

Among the features of the Earl of Oxford's occupation which made it nastily distasteful to him was the insistence by Burghley that his obscene friends with the inkhorn should be prepared to serve the state as couriers, political reporters, spies. I cannot imagine any other reason for Thomas Watson's intimacy with Thomas Walsingham in Paris. That is what the pilots of the government had in mind when they appointed Anthony Mundy "Messenger of Her Majesty's Chamber". Presumably it was what the Privy Council meant when they informed the Cambridge University dons "that in all his actions" Christopher Marlowe "had behaved him selfe orderlie and discreetly, whereby he had done her majestie good service ... it was not her Majestie's pleasure that anie one employed as he had been in matters touching the benefitt of his Countrie should be defamed by those who are ignorant in the affaires he went about."[28] Remember, Burghley was Chancellor of the University when this message went to Cambridge on 29 June 1587. A letter to Burghley from Utrecht dated 2 October 1587, mentions "Mr Morley" as one of his messengers.[29]

On 6 February, 1588, the Stationers' Register noted the arrival at the press of Thomas Kyd's translation of Torquato Tasso's *Il Padre di Famiglia*, which he called *The Householder's Philosophy*. Admirers of Kyd are compelled to admit, his version is "crowded with blunders, and fully deserves Nashe's sneer in the prefatory epistle to *Menaphon* at the 'home-born mediocritie' of the translator."[30] This sarcasm of Nash, printed in front of Robert Greene's romance *Menaphon*, which the printer registered on 23 August, 1589, merits our microscopy, because it is not only the main excuse for crediting Kyd with the composition of the earliest version of *Hamlet*; it is used to justify his nomination as author of *The Spanish Tragedy*. "It is a common practise now a daies," Nash begins, "amongst a sort of shifting companions, that runne through euery art and thriue by none to leaue the trade of *Nouerint*, whereto they were borne, and busie themselues with the indeuors of art, that could scarcelie latinise their neck-verse if they should haue neede." We recognise that Nashe's barbs here have been aimed at but one man, "Thomas, son of Francis Kidd, Citizen and Writer of the Courte Letter of London," i.e. scribe of legal documents often beginning "*Noverint universi*". "Yet English Seneca read by candlelight," Nash continues, "yeeldes manie good sentences as '*bloud is a beggar*' and so forth: and if you intreate him faire in a frostie morning, he will affoord you whole *Hamlets*, I should say hand-fulls of tragical speeches. But o griefe! *tempus edax rerum*; what's that will last alwaies? The sea exhaled by droppes will in continuance be drie, and Seneca let bloud line by line, and page by page, at length must needes die to our stage." Usually the collegiate cranium accepts the words "English Seneca" as a reference to some British translation of the Roman dramatist, and every known version of his Latin plays in English has been scoured in search of any expression resembling "Blood is a beggar." It seems, however, to me more reasonable to suppose that English Seneca must have been a live poet, not a book, a man who could be approached on a frosty morning with a request for some products of his prolific artistry, a man of some renown for his eloquence in tragedy. The English master of tragic poetry had already surpassed the best rhetoric of Seneca with a play called *Hamlet*. His verses were echoed and emulated by innumerable men of the pen. And Nash comically laments that their constant drawing on the well of his marvels apparently exhausted it. "Which makes his famisht followers to imitate the Kidde in Aesop, who enamored with the Foxes newfangles, forsooke all hopes of life to leape into a new occupation; and these men renowncing all possibilities of credit or estimation, to intermeddle with Italian translations: wherein how poorelie they haue plodded (as those that are neither prouenzall men nor are able to distinguish of Articles) let all indifferent Gentlemen that haue trauailed in that tongue discerne by their twopenie pamphlets: and no meruaile though their home-born mediocritie be such in this matter." At this point there can be no question, who was the target of Nash's laughter, and what had provoked it? "For what can be hoped of those that thrust *Elisium* into hell, and haue not learned, as long as they haue liued in the spheares, the iust measure of the Horizon without an hexameter. Sufficeth them to bodge vp a blanke verse with ifs and ands …"

Professor Boas was able to detect in *The Spanish Tragedy* the influence of

Watson's *Passionate Centurie*, whose Sonnet 47 was clearly adapted for the play (II, i). "Sonnet 21 possibly inspired *Soliman and Perseda*," (IV, i), he observed, But he felt confident that, when Nashe talks about "thrusting Elysium into hell", he had in view *The Spanish Tragedy* (I, i) where the "faire Elizian greene" is pictured as a region beyond Acheron, the dwelling place of Pluto and Proserpina—manifestly not Hell. Nashe's allusion to measuring "the Horizon" with the help of hexameters, Boas took as an attack on the *Tragedy*'s use of Virgil's epic to picture details of the netherworld of death. The picture contains no vision of any horizon. There may, however, be a mockery of the *Tragedy* in the derision of blank verse patched up with ifs and ands. For Act II, scene i presents Lorenzo shouting at Pedringano, "What, Villaine, ifs and ands?" And if that joke of Nashe does attack the *Tragedy*, then it can stand as evidence that he believed Thomas Kyd wrote *Hieronimo*. But he might have been mocking an effort by Kyd to imitate the *Tragedy*.

Toward the end of his preface to *Menaphon* Nashe warns the fellows whom he satirised in it to pray for refreshment of their master's magic. This time he is not called "English Seneca." "Yet let subjects, for all their insolence, dedicate a *de profundis* every morning to the preservation of their *Caesar*, lest their increasing indignities return them ere long their juggling to mediocrity, and they bewail in weeping blanks the wane of their monarchy."

Between the Autumn of 1587, when Kyd went to work for his concealed Lord, and February 1588, when his translation of Tasso was ready for publication, the "Caesar" of blank-verse bards in London underwent a crisis that promised the decline of his kingdom. The only record from the Earl of Oxford in this interval that I am acquainted with is "A view of frank pledge", a document of land economy, in which Oxford granted one Matthew Ellison on 23 September 1587, a portion of waste land in his manor of Hedingham Upland.[31] We know that in this period the Earl manned and armed a ship he named *Edward Bonaventure* in the hope of commanding her crew in a battle with the Armada sailing from Spain. It must have been in connexion with this naval interest that Burghley informed him: "How often I have propounded way to prefer your services. But why these could not take place, I must not particularly set down in writing, lest either I discover the hinderers or offend yourself, in showing the allegations to impeach your Lordship from such preferments."[32] This information is dated 15 December 1587; the Lord Treasurer wrote it with burning remembrance of "my poor daughter's affliction, whom her husband had in the afternoon [of 4 May 1587] so troubled with words of reproach of me to her—as though I had no care of him as I had to please others ... she spent all the evening in dolour and weeping."[33] The poor Countess Anne Cecil de Vere gave birth to her fourth daughter, Susan, on 26 May, but did not live more than a month after the child's first birthday. On 12 September 1587, her little girl Frances was buried near Burghley's rural retreat of Pymmes. We can imagine Oxford's tragic wife—"like Niobe, all tears"—in the weeks that followed the funeral, until 5 June 1588, when she herself died of a fever in the Queen's palace at Greenwich, while her husband apparently hunted for Spanish vessels in the Channel. He had not time for artificial drama; the sufferings of his wife alone would have silenced his muse. Soon after the funeral of his wife in Westminster Abbey, he sold both Oxford Court in Candlewick Street and the house of "Folly" in Bishopsgate. He retained however a residence near his beloved theatres, "a messuage or tenement called the Gate House, with its appurtenances and a garden commonly known as the Great Garden ... situated in the parish of St Bartolph without Aldgate, London."[34]

The story of Tom Watson is almost utterly overwhelmed by darkness all this time. Probably he was the T.W. who supplied verses approving George Whetstone's *Heptameron of Civil Discourses*, which the printer registered on 11 January 1582. That book is said to have inspired Shakespeare to write *Measure for Measure*. On 7 May 1582, the Stationers' Company licensed Christopher Ocland's *Eirenarkia*, which got the privilege of public reading in schools. To its broadcasting Watson contributed a brief Latin applause. Several years later Watson published a little treatise on memory training, *Compendium Memoriae Localis*, dedicated to an obscure gentleman named Henry Noel. In 1585 he dedicated his elegiac *Amyntas* to Henry "Nowell". Humbly Watson warned readers that his work could not be compared with the treatise on memory discipline written by Giordano Bruno, "the mystical and deeply learned *Sigillis* of the Nolan."

In the same year that saw publication of Greene's *Menaphon*, 1589, he also dashed off a trivial pamphlet entitled *Ciceronis Amor*. It carried an advertisement "Ad Lectorem", six lines of Latin, from Watson's pen. The little notice must have made Greene feel that Watson's Catholic generous nature did not share Marlowe's antipathy toward him. So he was glad to include in Nashe's preface to *Menaphon* the two lines about Watson, "whose *Amintas*, and translated *Antigone*, may march in equipage of honour with any of our ancient Poets."

In the summer of 1589 a ruffian William Bradley appealed to law for "security of peace" against the printer Hugo Swift, believed to be a brother of Anne, Watson's wife, John Allen, and Thomas Watson, we know not why. The Sheriff of Middlesex received an order to summon them to Westminster Hall on 25 November. But on 18 September Bradley found himself exchanging sword strokes near the Curtain Theatre with Christopher Marlowe. Watson arrived and interrupted the fray. Bradley turned his weapon on him with hotter zest. Watson drove his blade into his antagonist's chest and killed him. Constable Stephen Wild came to bring Watson, "gentleman", and Marlowe, "yeoman", before Sir Owen Hopton, Lieutenant of the Tower, who lived in Norton Folgate, a few steps from Marlowe's room. From Hopton's house the fighting poets went to Newgate prison. The coroner's jury decided that Watson had slain in self-defence, just as he claimed. On 3 December the two playwrights came before the justices of Old Bailey, including Sir Roger Manwood from Marlowe's home county, Kent. They cleared the younger dramatist of responsibility for Bradley's death, but Watson had to remain behind Newgate bars until 10 February, when he received the Queen's pardon.[35]

Early in April 1590 Sir Francis Walsingham, the expert on espionage, died in torment from his diseases at his home in Seething Lane. Watson composed a Latin elegy addressed to Thomas Walsingham, his patron, but dedicated to Lady Frances Sidney, Sir Philip's widow, the master-spy's daughter. Hardly was the corpse cold when "all his papers and books, both public and private, were seized and carried away," Robert Beale, his brother-in-law declared, "perhaps by those who would be loth to be used so themselves."[36]

Watson diverted his wits from his sorrows by means of favourite music. In 1590 Thomas East printed *Superius. The first sett of Italian madrigalls Englished, not to the sense of the originall dittie, but after the affection of the Noate. By Thomas Watson, Gentleman.* He enriched the book with "two excellent Madrigalls of Master William Byrd, composed after the Italian vaine at the request of the said Thomas Watson." And he added a Latin poem in praise of Luca Marenzio and his sleep tunes. He dedicated *Superius* to Robert Devereux, Earl of Essex, "Noble pupil of Mars, sweet child of the Muses," and thus obliquely told his readers about "the endeavors" of the Earl in literature: "your verses often to be sung to an Aonian lyre."[37] Master Byrd must have been familiar with Watson from the days when they both served the Earl of Oxford, whom Byrd delighted with galliards and marches which were surely performed in plays.

Dated about 1590 is a romantic play in manuscript called *The Dead Man's Fortune*, evidently an actor's copy, for Richard Burbage, Robert Lee, and Darlowe (probably Richard Darloe, player, of St Botolph's parish, Aldgate, where Lee too lived) are named in it. The characters form a medley of Greek and Italian names, including one Laertes, a lover. The play most likely belonged to Lord Strange's servants or the Admiral's, and I suspect it was a frolic of Tom Watson's wit, one of those offshoots William Cornwallis, who employed the poet as a family tutor, remembered when he declared, Watson "could devise twenty fictions and knaveries in a play, which was his daily practice and his living."[38]

1590, according to Tucker Brooke, is the earliest year to which the writing of the anonymous tragedy *Arden of Feversham* can be referred comfortably. The indefatigable Fleay ascribed *Arden* to Kyd on the basis of three parallels with *The Spanish Tragedy*. These did not include the glaring likeness of the villains in *Arden*, Black Will and Shakebag, to Pedringano and Serberine in the *Tragedy*. Charles Crawford exhibited numerous striking resemblances between *Arden* and *Soliman and Perseda*, Boas agreed that in the cadence and diction of many passages, and in the combination of lyrically elaborate verse-structure with colloquial directness of dialogue, *Arden* recalls "'the manner of Kyd."[39] Yet Marlowe was the author of *Arden*, in the judgment of Boas. Kyd, he argued, "so far as we can judge, was not given to repetition. Marlowe, on the other hand, was a frequent borrower, and he might readily have adapted Kyd's lines to his own use, especially at a time when they were in close contact."[40] Substituting Watson for Kyd in this sentence, I support Boas's argument. Of course the most plausible reason for crediting Marlowe with the tragedy of bourgeois marriage is the evidence of the writer's familiarity with Kentish landscapes.

The author of *Arden of Feversham* took remarkable liberties with his material, the chronicle of Holinshed. Perhaps he did this following the instruction of a patron to renovate the old play *Murderous Michael*, acted at court by the Earl of Sussex's men on 3 March 1579; that lost tragedy is commonly considered the source of *Arden*, Holinshed depicted Black Will, the partner of the murderess Alice Arden, as a grim fearless killer. In the play he turns out a ludicrous braggart, shaped in the image of Basilisco of *Soliman and Perseda*. Incidentally, the description of Dick Reed in *Arden* as "the raylingest knaue in christendome" (IV, iv) echoes an allusion to Basilisco—"the braginest knaue in Christendom" (*Soliman and Perseda*, I, iii).

Black Will and George Shakebag are presented as denizens of Marlowe's shire. "Two Ruffer Ruffins neuer liued in Kent." But they are heartily at home in London's wickedest streets. They strongly resemble two men who played evil roles in the life of Marlowe and Watson, also named Will and George. We have already met the murderous Will Bradley. This Will had a comrade, wrynecked George Orrell, a professional soldier, mentioned in a state record of the Earl of Essex's last demonstration as "a most desperate rakehell as lives."[41] He seems to have been more courageous brute than braggart, and could have said with Shakebag: "I cannot paint my valour out with words" (II, ii), or sneered like him at warnings of ghosts and hell, "Nay then lets go sleepe, when buges and feares / Shall kill our courages with their fancies worke."

In the summer of 1589 Watson's brother-in-law, Hugh Swift, requested protection of the law against George Orrell, who had menaced him with death. The Court of the Queen's Bench overlooked the relation of that appeal with Will Bradley's petition against Swift and Watson *ob metum mortis*. He was probably the Bradley who assaulted one Robert Wood with a cudgel in the autumn of 1588, so that Wood's friends despaired of his life. The victim had denounced Bradley on the day of the attack as a worthless fellow, a bully.[42] The likeness between this Will and his cudgel and Black Will in *Arden*, with his boasts of assault and battery, is manifest: "In Temes streete a brewers carte was lyke to haue runne ouer me: I made no more ado, but went to the clark and cult all the natches of his tales and beat them about his head ... I haue broken a Sariants head with his own mace" (V, i). The spitting image of the bully whose doleful days Tom Watson abridged! One of the minor characters in *Arden*, by the way, is named Bradshaw, a petty accomplice in the main crime. The playwright changed the name of another shady person of the story from William Blackburn to Clarke: we cannot tell why. Perhaps he viewed the suggestion of William Bradley's name so close to the names of Bradshaw and Black Will as excessive cruelty to the dead? The rakehell Orrell, we ought to note, lived to win honour for gallantry during the Irish wars.

Among the minor figures of *Arden of Feversham* I detect another contemporary portrait, a caricature of Robert Greene. A poor gentleman named Greene joined the plotters against the actual Master Arden. The poet went to peculiar lengths to make his name infamous. The original Greene was christened John; the playwright changed it to Richard. Robert Green was well known in London as a companion of criminals, in particular one Cutting Ball. Richard Greene makes his first appearance in the play after Alice Arden has declared,

> In London many alehouse Ruffins keepe,
> Which, as I heare, will murther men for gould.

Richard Greene promises to free her from husbanage, to "hyre some Cutter to cut (Arden) short." This Greene is supposed to be a citizen of Faversham; but the play reports that he has known Black Will in London for twelve years (V, i). Despite his pleasure in consorting with cut-throats, Richard, like the literary Robert, is "religious", a man of "great douation" (I, 589). Thus Marlowe might have avenged himself for Robin Greene's reference to "that Atheist *Tamburlan*." Also noteworthy is the fondness of the two Greenes for the fables of Aesop. In *Never Too Late*, and the imitation of Greene called *Groats-worth of Wit*, probably perpetrated by Henry Chettle, actors are taunted with odious comparisons of their profession with the pride of Aesop's crow. In *Arden* the cutters Will and Shakebag are lessoned by Richard Greene with one of Aesop's tales (III, vi). The Greene of the drama is a coward; he does not participate in the final stabbing scene; and the last we see of him is when he trembles in fear of arrest and pleads with the stronger spirited Alice, "But cleaue to vs as we will stick to you." If the author of *Arden* had made him a man of letters, the etching from life would have been unmistakable.

The Epilogue describes the play as bare of ornament: "no filed points are foisted in / To make it gratious to the eare or eye." Yet the speeding pen of the playwright found occasion to "foist" in references to Tisiphone, Hydra, Endymion, and "raving Hercules". Moreover, he set the absurd servant Michael to making love with the elegant phrase from Watson's sonnets in *The Teares of Fancy*: "Let my passions penetrate."[43]

Tom Nashe preserved a memory of Watson jesting about Gabriel Harvey at a supper in the Nag's Head Inn. We wonder if this inn was the same as "the Nages head, the 18 pence ordinarye," at which Arden of Feversham ate supper when he visited London (II, ii). Harvey is said to have provoked Watson's joke by his hexameter lampoon of 1580 on "The Mirror of Tuscanism," the Earl of Oxford. Presumably Watson's irony did not come to the scholar's ears, or we might have been regaled with some heavy darts of wit about him such as Harvey shot at Greene and Nashe. The Earl of Oxford had sold his Bishopsgate mansion, Fisher's Folly, to William Cornwallis, who hired Watson to teach his children Latin. That may have been the way in which Anne Cornwallis began her beautiful collection of courtiers' poetry, including some of Oxford's finest. One of his extant poems, his solitary Sonnet, appears to have been mixed with Watson's work, and came to be published as the last lyric in his posthumous *Tears*.

On 26 September 1592, "Thomas Watson, gent. was buried" at the church of St Bartholomew the Less. A few months before, Edward White obtained licence to print *Arden of Feversham*, which he sold in his shop at "the little north door" in Paul's Churchyard. A month later Abel Jeffes and White wrangled for ownership of *The Spanish Tragedy*. In November White arranged to publish *Soliman and Perseda*. He and Jeffes were called to the court of the Stationers' Company, which resolved, on 18 December, 1592, that "Edward White and Abel Ieffes haue eche of them offended. Viz Edw White in hauinge printed the spanish tragedie belonging to Abell Ieffes / and Abell Ieffes in hauing printed the tragedie of Arden of kent belonginge to Edw White." The two editions were ordered confiscated and forfeited to "thuse of the poore of the companye."[44]

I have tried to prove that the two or three plays on which the artistic reputation of Thomas Kyd is said to rest, together with *The First Part of Ieronimo* and *The Rare Triumphs of Love and Fortune*, were essentially the compositions of a man of superior learning, a poet skilled in classical and Romance literatures, a spirit of quiet and sequestered life, writing plays for pelf but an earnest workman, capable of violence only in self-defence, a fellow of robust humour without malice, having indeed a genius for long friendship, an artist and a lover of the arts. Who else but the poet extolled by Thomas Heywood in these words:

> "Tom Watson ... wrote
> Able to make Apollo's self to dote
> Upon his Muse."?[45]

POSTSCRIPT:
Most of this article I made while enjoying a Harrison Fellowship in Tudor

and Stuart stage productions at the University of Pennsylvania in 1951. Since then I have heard of a doctoral dissertation on Thomas Watson as Latinist, done at the University of California, but could not even get a glimpse of it. And Arthur Freeman's *Thomas Kyd: Facts and Problems* has been issued by the Oxford Clarendon Press in 1967. I have refrained from reading his book, in the hope that my article would be printed, and provide students with the opportunity of comparison of our two arguments which is bound to be educational and entertaining.

Known, or possible, works by Thomas Watson

1573: "A Loving Lady being wounded in the spring time".

A Hundred Sundrie Flowres, published in 1573, was the work of several hands, including those of Edward de Vere who was probably its editor and publisher.

In an introduction to Ruth Loyd Miller (Ed) and Bernard M Ward's modern edition (1975), Miller cites Eva Turner Clark to compare two sonnets in Watson's *Tears of Fancy* (1593) with four stanzas of a poem in *Flowres* called *A Loving Lady being wounded in the spring time*, by "*Spraeta tamen vivunt*". She shows them to be almost identical. Miller believed Watson was too young in 1573 to have composed *A Loving Lady* (Miller and Ward, 90-103), but it is not impossible. Watson may have been studying at Padua in 1573.

Before 1582: "... CERTAIN LATIN VERSES OF HIS OWNE, MADE LONG AGO UPON THE ABUSES OF *IUPPITE*, IN A CERTAIN PIECE OF WORKE WRITTEN IN THE COMMENDATION OF WOMEN KINDE".

Lost. Referred to in the headnote to *Hekatompathia*, Passion LXXV.

Before 1582: TRANSLATIONS INTO LATIN FROM PETRARCH'S *CANZONIERE*.

Referred to in the headnote to *Hekatompathia*, Passion VI. The work is lost, apart from four examples reprinted as Passions VI, LXVI, XC and the Epitaph.

Before 1582: *DE REMEDIA AMORIS*.

Mentioned in the headnote to *Hekatompathia,* Passion I: "which he wrote long since" and "hath lately perfected".

1581: *Sophoclis Antigone.*

Printed by John Wolfe. Dedicated to Philip Howard, Earl of Arundel.

1582: *"Even as the fruitful bee".*

By T.W. A commendatory poem fronting George Whetstone's *Heptameron of Civil Discourses*. Some scholars reject this as a work by Thomas Watson.

1582: *The hekatompathia or Passionate Century of Love.*

Printed by John Wolfe for Gabriel Cawood. Dedicated to 17th Earl of Oxford (Edward de Vere). 94 love sonnets, or "Passions", in English and five in Latin (four translated from Petrarch). Each poem preceded by an explanatory headnote acknowledging the writer's debt to 32 classical writers and 25 Renaissance authors.

A Looking Glasse for Lovers. This undated MS in the British Library contains 78 of Watson's passions together with their headnotes, the dedication to the Earl of Oxford and the concluding Epilogue. Some authorities believe it to be an earlier manuscript presented by Watson to the Earl of Oxford, others a much later copy of the printed work.

1582: *"Ad Oclandum, de Eulogiis serenissimae nostrae Elizabetha post Anglorum praelia cantatis".*

A short commendatory poem fronting *Eirēnarchia, sive, Elizabetha* (1582), the second edition of Christopher Ocland's *Anglorum Praelia* (1580).

1583: *Artificiosae Memoriae Libellus.*

Dedicated to Adelbert (or Albert) Laski, Count Paletine of Siradia, a Polish prince (?1527-1605). Unpublished MS in the British Library. Watson had intended to present it during a banquet in the Middle Temple Hall, but Laski failed to appear. It was subsequently printed as *Compendium Memoriae Localis* in 1585 and dedicated it to the courtier Henry Noell.

Before 1585: PSALMS.

A lost work. Mentioned by Watson in his *Amyntas*, 1585.

1585: AMYNTAS.

Printed by Henry Marsh. Dedicated to Henry Noell.

In 1587 Abraham Fraunce translated this Latin original into English, without acknowledgement. As *The Lamentations of Amyntas for the Death of Phillis, paraphrastically translated out of Latin into English Hexameters* it became very popular and was reprinted in 1588, 1589, and 1596. Fraunce dedicated it to the Countess of Pembroke (Mary Sidney). He admitted his plagiarism in a later work, *The Countess of Pembrokes Yvychurch*, which comprised a reprint of his translation from Watson's work, together with a translation of Tasso's *Aminta*.

1585: COMPENDIUM MEMORIAE LOCALIS.

Printed by John Wolfe. Dedicated to Henry Noell. The published version of *Artificiosae Memoriae Libelluis* of 1583, noted above.

1586: COLUTHI: THEBANI LYCOPOLITANI POETAE: HELENAE RAPTUS.

Printed by John Wolfe. Dedicated to 9th Earl of Northumberland (Henry Percy). Watson's translation into Latin verse of Coluthus' *The Rape of Helen*.

c1588: A LEARNED DIALOGUE OF BERNARD PALESSY CONCERNING WATERS

AND FOUNTAINS BOTH NATURAL AND ARTIFICIAL: TRANSLATED OUT OF FRENCH INTO ENGLISH.

Dedicated to 9th Earl of Northumberland (Henry Percy). Unpublished vellum bound MS in the Houghton Library, Harvard.

1589: "AD LECTOREM HEXASTICON: TULLIES LOVE"

A short poem fronting Robert Greene's *Ciceronis Amor*, praising the author for restoring the honour due to Cicero.

1589: LET OTHERS PRAISE. A GRATIFICATION UNTO MASTER JOHN CASE, FOR HIS LEARNED BOOK, LATELY MADE IN PRAISE OF MUSIC.

A broadsheet printed by Thomas East under license from William Byrd. Four verses of six lines each set to music by Byrd for six voices. The work lauded John Case for defending church music with his *In Praise of Music* (1586) and *Apologia Musices* (1588).

1590: [SUPERIUS] THE FIRST SET OF ITALIAN MADRIGALS ENGLISHED, NOT TO THE SENSE OF THE ORIGINAL DITTY, BUT AFTER THE AFFECTION OF THE NOTE.

Printed by Thomas East. Dedicated to 2nd Earl of Essex (Robert Devereux). An anthology of 26 Italian madrigals for four, five, and six voices, mainly by Marenzio, together with two madrigals by William Byrd. Rather than translating directly from the Italian, Watson wrote mostly new lyrics. There is also an original poem in Latin addressed to Marenzio.

1590: MELIBOEUS THOMAE WATSONI SIVÈ ECLOGA IN OBITUM HONORATISSIMI VIRI, DOMINI FRANCISCI WALSINGHAMI, EQUITIS AURATI. DIVAE ELIZABETHAE A SECRETIS, ET SANCTIORIBUS CONSILIIS.

Printed by Robert Robinson. Dedicated to Thomas Walsingham. A pastoral dialogue between Watson (as Corydon) and Thomas Walsingham (as Tityrus).

1590: *MELIBOEUS, AN ECLOGUE UPON THE DEATH OF THE RIGHT HONOURABLE SIR FRANCIS WALSINGHAM, LATE PRINCIPAL SECRETARY TO HER MAJESTY, AND OF HER MOST HONOURABLE PRIVY COUNCIL.*

Printed by Robert Robinson. Dedicated to Lady Frances Sidney. Watson's translation of the above.

1591: *HONOURABLE ENTERTAINEMENT GIVEN TO THE QUEENS MAJESTY, IN PROGRESSE, AT ELVETHAM IN HAMPSHIRE, BY THE RIGHT HONOURABLE THE EARL OF HERTFORD.*

Printed by John Wolfe (3 versions). A description of the Elvetham entertainment given to the Queen by Sir Edward Seymour. No author is named, but Watson is thought to have contributed to its composition (except for the song lyrics).

1592: *AMINTAE GAUDIA.*

Published posthumously. Printed by William Ponsonby. Dedication in Latin to the Countess of Pembroke (Mary Herbert) initialled C M (Christopher Marlowe). Comprising 10 "letters" and 8 eclogues in Latin, together with an epyllon on Sir Philip Sidney.

1593: *THE TEARS OF FANCY OR LOVE DISDAINED. AETNA GRAVIUS AMOR.*

By T.W. Published posthumously. Printed by John Danter for William Ponsonby. Sole extant copy in Huntington Library, Harvard; lacks 4 pages. Comprising 60 "English" sonnets; the last is by the Earl of Oxford, and scholars disagree as to whether the other 59 are by Watson (see APPENDIX D).

Notes to chapters

Preface

1. The notable exceptions include Mark Eccles' *Christopher Marlowe in London* and Charles Nicholl's *The Reckoning*, which deal at length with Thomas Watson.

One: The background—players and patrons

1. An estimated increase of fifty thousand to over two hundred thousand.

2. Johann Sommerville, review of Robert Zaller, 416-8.

3. Morrison Comegys Boyd, *Elizabethan Music and Music Criticism*, 4; David Lindley, *Shakespeare and Music*, 71.

4. Lindley, 60.

5. Boyd, 6.

6. Boyd, 14.

7. In 1561 he became the first headmaster of the Merchant Taylors' School and in 1596 high master at St Paul's School. Notable pupils at the Merchant Taylors' School were Edmund Spenser, Thomas Lodge and Thomas Kyd.

8. John Buxton, *Elizabethan Taste*, 192.

9. Boyd, 18.

10. In 1585. Howard B. Barnett, "John Case—An Elizabethan Music Scholar", 252-6.

11. Full title: *Apologia Musices, tam Vocalis, quam Instrumentalis, et Mixtae*.

12. Barnett, 252-6.

13. John Case, *Apologia Musices, tam Vocalis, quam Instrumentalis, et Mixtae*.

14. Lindley, 63.

15. Lindley, 63.

16. Roy Strong, *Portraits of Queen Elizabeth* (Oxford, 1963). Cited by Lindley, 87-8.

17. Bruce R. Smith, *The Acoustic World of Early Modern England*, 91.

18. All examples in this paragraph from Smith, 91-2.

19. Buxton, 173-4.

20. Lindley, 87.

21. *Peter Holman, Four and Twenty Fiddlers: The Violin at the English Court, 1540-1690* (Oxford, 1993), 114. Cited by Lindley, 60.

22. Jessie Ann Owens, *"Noyses, sounds, and sweet aires"*, 63; Helen Hackett, *Virgin Mother, Maiden Queen*, passim.

23. Ten years later, in 1571, Bartholemew Clerke published a translation from Italian into Latin, with a preface by the Earl of Oxford. Clerke had been one of Oxford's tutors and it has been speculated that Oxford may have defrayed the costs of publication. See: Charles Vere, Earl of Burford, "Edward de Vere and the Psychology of Feudalism", 40.

24. Baldesar Castiglione, *The Book of the Courtier*, trans. Charles S Singleton, 74.

25. Castiglione, 75.

26. Castiglione, 105. David C Price, *Patrons and Musicians of the English Renaissance*, 5-7. Compare Hamlet's dissembling, too.

27. Price 10, citing L Stone, *The Crisis of the Aristocracy, 1559-1641* (Oxford 1965), Chapters III, IV and V.

28. I follow Mary Ellen Lamb who discredits the notion of a *large* literary "circle" at Wilton House. I also acknowledge that the idea of the "Areopagus" circle attributed to Philip Sidney is of dubious credibility, too. See Mary Ellen Lamb, "The Myth of the Countess of Pembroke: The Dramatic Circle" and Mary Ellen Lamb, "The Countess of Pembroke's Patronage".

29. Philip Sidney, *Discourse on Irish Affairs* (1577).

30. H R Woudhuysen, "Sir Philip Sidney" *DNB*.

31. Alan Stewart, *Philip Sidney: A Double Life*, 12.

32. Gary F Waller, *Mary Sidney, Countess of Pembroke*, 29

33. On Sir Henry Sidney's death in 1586 Pembroke succeeded as Lord President of the Council of the Marches.

34. Edmund Spenser, *Astrophel. A pastorall Elegie vpon the death of the most Noble and valorous Knight, Sir Philip Sidney* (London, 1595). Cited Hannay, *Philip's Phoenix*, 48.

35. Hannay, *Philip's Phoenix*, 112.

36. The "Old" *Arcadia* was written by Philip Sidney around 1580. He was intent on revising this version, but it was unfinished at the time of his death and he requested its destruction. Nevertheless—tipped off by the publisher John Ponsonby about plans afoot to print an unauthorised edition—Fulke Greville instigated an incomplete, but authorised, "New" *Arcadia*. It was published by Ponsonby in 1590. In its turn, this version was revised and in part re-written by Mary Herbert who also added a completed Book III and Books IV and V which she assembled from parts of the "Old" *Arcadia*.

37. Bruce Pattison, *Music and Poetry of the Elizabethan Renaissance*, 62; Katherine

Duncan-Jones, *Sir Philip Sidney, Courtier Poet*, 61.

38. Probably about the time of the birth of Mary's son. Philip likened the *Arcadia's* birth with Mary's physical birth, as "this child which I am loath to father … if it had not in some way been delivered, [it] would have grown a monster …" Jean Robertson (ed) *The Countess of Pembroke's Arcadia (The Old Arcadia)* (Oxford, 1962), 3. Cited Stewart, 226. Also Matthew Zarnowiecki, "Lyric Surrogacy: Reproducing the 'I' in Sidney's *Arcadia", Sidney Journal* 27:1 (2009), 35-39.

39. Stewart, 226.

40. H R Woodhuysen, *Sir Philip Sidney and the Circulation of Manuscripts*, 219-223.

41. Pattison, 67. As opposed to Pattison, Woodhuysen *DNB* thinks Sidney "kept those works to a very small circle", although his list, which includes additional and alternative titles to Pattison's, seems large enough.

42. Thomas Moffett, *Nobilis or, A View of the life and death of a Sidney, and Lessus lugubris.* Translated, Vergil B. Heltzel and Hoyt H. Hudson (San Marino, California, 1940), 75. Cited Duncan-Jones, 115.

43. C. Gregory Smith, *Elizabethan Critical Essays,* Vol I, 153 (Oxford, 1904). Cited Pattison, 20.

44. Price, 171.

45. C. Gregory Smith, 153. Cited Pattison, 20.

46. Philip Sidney, *The Defence of Poesy* in Katherine Duncan-Jones (ed), *Sir Philip Sidney: The Major Works*, 227.

47. Bruce Pattison, "Sir Philip Sidney and Music", 76.

48. W H Grattan Flood, "New light on Late Tudor Composers — XXV, John Dowland". The Musical Times, 8:6 (1 June 1927), 504.

49. Buxton, 185.

50. Woudhuysen, *DNB*.

51. Pattison, "Sir Philip Sidney and Music", 79-80.

52. Tessier dedicated his 1597 book of ayres to Lady Penelope Rich. See Pattison, *Music and Poetry*, 63 and Pattison "Sir Philip Sidney and Music", 77.

53. Pattison, "Sir Philip Sidney and Music", 79.

54. Gerard Kilroy, *Edmund Campion*, 22-3.

55. Celeste Turner, *Anthony Mundy*, 51-2.

56. Woudhuysen, *DNB*.

57. Stewart, 312.

58. H R Woodhuysen, *Sir Philip Sidney and the Circulation of Manuscripts*, 211.

59. Benjamin Woolley, *The Queen's Conjurer*, 9.

60. Sidney was injured on 22 September 1586, his birthday was on 30 November 1554.

61. It appeared first in Greville's *Dedication to Sir Philip Sidney*, drafted between 1604 and 1616 but not published until 1652, and may owe something to Plutarch's yarn that Alexander the Great shared a helmet of water with his troops and went without himself. See Hannay, 232 en 2 and Michael G Brennan, "'Thy necessity is yet greater than mine'", *Sidney Journal*, 2 fn 2.

62. Fulke Greville, *The Life of Sir Philip Sidney* (1652). Cited Buxton, 184. On the other hand, Buxton also cites the first Earl of Essex, who is reputed to have called on *his* musician to play the virginal to accompany him as he lay dying at Dublin in 1576. It seems a coincidence, although not impossible. (Buxton, 184, citing W B Devereux, *Lives and letters of the Devereux, Earls of Essex.* Vol I [1853], 145).

63. Hannay, 59-60

64. Buxton, 246.

65. Hannay, 124-9.

66. John Strype, *The Life of the Learned Sir Thomas Smith, Kt., Doctor of Civil Law, Principal Secretary of State to King Edward the Sixth and Queen Elizabeth*, revised ed (Oxford, 1820). 18. Cited by Mark Anderson, *Shakespeare by Another Name*, 7.

67. J A van Dorsten, *The Anglo-Dutch Renaissance, Seven Essays* (Leiden, 1988), 61, 64. Cited Anderson, 22.

68. Or, perhaps Sidney had become sexually involved with Anne, his former betrothed, during Oxford's absence abroad. For this new, daring, and entirely circumstantial, theory see the careful argument by M J Everingham in "The Tennis Court Affair: Sidney v de Vere" in *De Vere Society Newsletter* (September 2005), 20-25. Only two records of the spat are extant: Fulke Greville's hagiography of Sidney, published many years later, and a letter to Sidney dated October 1579 from his friend Hubert Languet. Both are written by members of the Sidney circle and therefore favour his point of view. They are reported at length in B M Ward, *The Seventeenth Earl of Oxford*, 164-77.

69. Oxfordians support the case for Edward de Vere, seventeenth of Oxford, as the author of Shakespeare's works.

70. E K Chambers, *The Elizabethan Stage* Vol II, 99-102.

71. Frederick S Boas draws attention to Shakespeare's parody of the style in *I Henry IV* (Act II: Sc. iv) through Falstaff's impersonation of King Henry IV. (Frederick S Boas, *Queen Elizabeth in Drama and Related Studies*, 60).

72. G K Hunter, *John Lyly*, 260.

73. Thomas West, second Baron De La Warr (c.1556–1601) married Anne Knollys in 1571. His mother was a member of the Carey family.

74. Anderson 160 citing Theodore L Steinberg, "The Anatomy of *Euphues*". Studies

in English Literature, 1500-1900, 17:1 (Winter 1977), 29; Hunter *passim*.

75. Richard Helgerson, *The Elizabethan Prodigals*, 59-62.

76. Hunter, 41-2.

77. Hunter, *Passim*. Hunter stresses Lyly's influence on Shakespeare, especially in *A Midsummer Night's Dream* and *Love's Labour's Lost*. He suggests that, in time, Shakespeare "grew beyond" Lyly in the subtlety of his character development.

78. The late W Ron Hess (unknowingly) drew my attention to Henry Lok's contribution to the affairs of Edward de Vere.

79. *Churchyard's Chance* and *Churchyard's Charge* (both 1580). Cited Stephen W May, "The Poems of Edward de Vere", 9 fn; Alan H Nelson, *Monstrous Adversary*, 238.

80. The building was large and had two residences. From 1608 Sir George Buc rented the other residency for the Revels Office.

81. Elizabeth Story Donno, "Abraham Fleming", 203.

82. Sarah C Dodson, "Abraham Fleming", 56.

83. Donno, 203.

84. Patrick Collinson, "Andrew Perne", *DNB*.

85. Although it was published a year before the Queen took the throne. Its proper title is *Songes and Sonettes*.

86. William E Miller, "Abraham Fleming", 89-90.

87. *The Bucoliks of Publius Virgilius Maro, Prince of all Latine Poets … Together with his Georgiks or Ruralls, otherwise called his husbandrie, conteyning foure books*.

88. Donno, 203.

89. Nelson, 239.

90. Anderson, 154-5.

91. Nelson, 89-92.

92. The expression "tigers hearts" recalls Shakespeare's famous "Tiger's heart wrapped in a woman's hide" from *Henry VI Part 3* referring to the malign Queen Margaret, and Robert Greene's deliberate misquotation in *Groats-worth of Wit* (1592), "Tygers hart wrapt in a Players hyde". (https://www.bl.uk/collection-items/greenes-groats-worth-of-wit).

93. Donno, 205-10; Cyndia Susan Clegg, "Abraham Fleming", *DNB*.

94. Chambers, II, 134.

95. John Stow, *The Survey of London*, 233-4.

96. Michael R. G. Spiller, "A Literary 'First': The Sonnet Sequence of Anne Locke (1560)," *Renaissance Studies: Journal of the Society for Renaissance Studies*, 11 (1997), *passim*.

97. Patrick Collinson, "Anne Locke", *DNB*.

98. Anthony [à] Wood, *Athenae Oxoniensis*, Vol 1, Columns 661-3.

99. Michael G Brennan, "Henry Lok", *DNB*; Nelson, 325-8.

100. In *The Book of Ecclesiastes* (1597). See also Ward, 298.

101. Spelled thus by Mundy, although frequently spelled "Munday" by others.

102. Turner, 2 fn 4, quoting from Mundy's dedications to John Stow, *Survey of London*, 1618 edition.

103. Reavley Gair, *The Children of St Paul's*, 70-1. A year after Anthony's baptism a lightning bolt sent St Paul's spire crashing down causing fire and much damage. For a month the cathedral's services were held in St Gregory's. Repairs had still not been completely finished even as late as 1584 (Gair, 16-17).

104. Celeste Turner Wright, "Young Anthony Mundy Again", 151.

105. Alfred W Pollard, "Claudius Hollyband", 79; Wheatley suggests no occupancy at the Golden Ball at this date.

106. Pollard, 82-3.

107. Pollard, 80.

108. George, G. D, "Earning a living as an Author in Early Modern England", 41 fn 78. George draws attention to recent opinion that although bibliographic records attribute this work to Thomas Alfield, it may be mainly the work of Robert Persons with some verses the work of Henry Walpole.

109. Gair, 2-5.

110. Turner Wright, 156.

111. Suggested by the late W Ron Hess in a personal email dated 15 February 2012. Thomas Radclyffe, third Earl of Sussex was Lord Chamberlain from 1572 until his death in 1583.

112. R B McKerrow, "Edward Allde as a Typical Trade Printer", 127.

113. Miriam Miller, "John Windet" (Grove Music Online); Wikipedia, "John Windet"; Blog by W Ron Hess (14 May 2012).

114. Hess, 14 May 2012.

115. Turner Wright, 154.

116. Dedication to Anthony Mundy, *The Mirrour of Mutabilitie* (1579).

117. George, 44, 115, citing Thomas Alfield, *A true reporte of the death & martyrdome of M. Campion, Iesuite and preiste, & M. Sherwin, & M. Bryan preistes, at Tiborne the first of December 1581. Observid and written by a Catholike priest, which was present therat Wheruuto* [sic] *is annexid certayne verses made by sundrie persons* (London, 1582).

118. George, 44.

119. Turner, 201, annotated in pencil in my personal copy which was previously owned (presumably in 1956) by I A Shapiro, lecturer and senior lecturer at the University of Birmingham, 1935-70.

120. Turner, 201.

121. Turner Wright, 151. It is quite possible that Jennings and Mundy's father were acquainted through their professions as drapers.

122. Annotations and corrections by I A Shapiro to page 24 of my personal copy of Turner.

123. *View of Sundry Examples* and *Zelauto, the fountaine of fame*.

124. Charles Boyce, *Shakespeare A-Z*, 19; Joe Peel (with Naomi Magri), "The Merchant of Venice" in Kevin Gilvary, *Dating Shakespeare's Plays*, 126.

125. I A Shapiro, "Shakespeare and Mundy", 25.

126. *A Discoverie of Edmund Campion and his Confederates, their most horrible and traiterous practises, against her Majesties most royall person, and the Realme. Wherein may be seene, how thorowe the whole course of their Araignment, they were notably convicted of every cause. Whereto is added the execution of Edmund Campion, Raphe Sherwin, and Alexander Brian, executed at Tiborne the 1 of December. Published by A.M. sometime the Popes Scholler, allowed in the Seminarie at Roome amongst them: a Discourse needefull to be read of every man, to beware how they deale with such secret seducers, Seene, and allowed. Imprinted at London for Edward White, dwelling at the little North doore of Paules, at the signe of the Gunne, the 29 of January 1582.*

127. Turner Wright, 156.

128. Hugh Trevor-Roper, "Nicholas Hill", *DNB*.

129. Cited by Trevor-Roper, quoting Anthony [à] Wood, *Athenae Oxoniensis*, cited in O L Dick, *Aubrey's Brief Lives* (London, 1949), 256.

130. Later, two more companions joined the travellers.

131. Hugh Trevor-Roper, *DNB*. Earlier, Christopher Hill had doubted Nicholas Hill's conversion in his *Intellectual Origins of the English Revolution Revisited* (Oxford, 1997), 130.

132. Trevor-Roper, *DNB*.

133. Trevor-Roper, *DNB*.

134. Trevor-Roper, *DNB*.

135. Ben Jonson, *Poems*. Edited by Ian Donaldson. Epigram 133: *On the Famous Voyage/The Voyage Itself*, 82.

136. *The Merchant of Venice*: 5.1.60-5; *As You Like It*: 3.2.226; *Romeo and Juliet*: 1.4.54-8; *Hamlet* 3.4.70-1.

137. http://oxford-shakespeare.com/Nashe/Anatomy_Absurdity.pdf

138. Ruth Lloyd Miller, *"Shakespeare" Identified* Vol II, 340-55; A J Pointon, *The Man Who Was Never Shakespeare*, 233-7. The full title of the disputed work as printed is *Greenes, Groats-worth of witte, bought with a million of Repentance*.

139. Full title: *Strange Newes of the intercepting certaine letters and a convoy of verses, as they were going privilie to victual the Low Countries.* It was dedicated to "Mr William Apis Lapis", probably the Earl of Oxford.

140. Printed by Harvey's friend John Wolfe. The full title is *Foure Letters, and certaine Sonnets: especially touching Robert Greene, and other Parties, by him abused: but incidently of divers excellent Persons, and some Matters of Note.*

141. W. Ron Hess, *The Dark Side of Shakespeare* Vol II, 442; W Schrickx, *Shakespeare's Contemporaries*, 156.

142. The full title bursts with pizazz: *Have with you to Saffron-Walden. Or, Gabriel Harveys Hunt is up. Containing a full Answere to the eldest Sonne of the Halter-Maker. Or, Nashe his Confutation of the Sinfull Doctor. The Mott or Posie, in Stead of Omne Tulit Punctum: Pacis Fiducia Nunquam. As much to say, as I sayd I would Speake with him.* Details of the dispute are easily accessed online in Rita Lamb's readable "The Harvey-Nashe Quarrel".

143. C S Lewis, *The Allegory of Love* (Oxford 1936).

144. Thomas Nashe, *Pierce Penilesse*, 43.

145. Francis Meres, *Palladis Tamia*. Quoted Chambers, *The Elizabethan Stage*, Vol III, 453.

146. The true reason for the uproar may have been that the play drew attention to some tricky discussions at that time between the Polish Ambassador and Queen Elizabeth. Chambers, *The Elizabethan Stage*, Vol III, 455.

147. Donna N Murphy, *The Mysterious Connection between Thomas Nashe, Thomas Dekker, and T M: An English Renaissance Deception?* (Newcastle-upon-Tyne, 2013) suggests Nashe circumvented the ban by reincarnating himself under a new name, Thomas Dekker.

148. Harvey, Gabriel. *Foure Letters and Certaine Sonnets* (1592).

149. Harvey.

Two: Far from my native land

1. This acrostic has been picked up by several writers, but I believe it was first noted by John Bakeless.

2. A close analysis of *The Hierarchy*, together with reproductions of the title page and page 206 referring to the Elizabethan and Jacobean poet-playwrights, is in W Ron Hess, "Did Thomas Heywood List 'Will Shakespeare' as an Imitator or Front". Shakespeare Matters 6:2 (Winter 2007), 21-31.

3. Chapman, Angel Day, Lucas de Heere, Lok, John Lyly, Nashe and Soothern (Alexander Waugh in *My Shakespeare* [Ed William Leahy, Brighton, 2018], reprinted in The De Vere Society Newsletter April 2018, 17). Ronsard may also have compared Oxford/Shakespeare with Apollo (Malim, 20-1). Gabriel Harvey, in his Latin oration at Audley End in 1578 alluded to "Phoebus Apollo" who "has cultivated" Oxford's "mind in the arts".

4. Eccles, "Marlowe and Watson" (Diss. Harvard, Cambridge Mass, 1932), cited by Ibrahim Alhiyari, *Thomas Watson: New Biographical Evidence*, Chapter 1 (unpaginated), and Alhiyari, "Thomas Watson: New Birth Year and Privileged Ancestry."

5. Alhiyari, *Thomas Watson: New Biographical Evidence*, unpaginated; Alhiyari, "Thomas Watson: New Birth Year and Privileged Ancestry". All previous research is outdated. Alhiyari calculated Watson's birth date from the wills of Thomas's parents (Chapter 1, unpaginated),

6. Arber, 4.

7. Travel on the continent was expensive. In the 1570s, Lord Roger North estimated that to keep a gentleman abroad cost £160 a year . (Lisa Jardine and Alan Stewart, *Hostage to Fortune*, 40).

8. Ibrahim Alhiyari, "Thomas Watson's Father, William: A Renowned, Self-Made, London Draper". The document's most probable date is 1549, although 1554 is a possibility. (Alhiyari's dating of 1449 is obviously an oversight).

9. Alhiyari, "Thomas Watson: New Birth Year and Privileged Ancestry" states in error that Blanche was William Watson's sister. For the correct relationship see Nina Green, "Modern Spelling Transcript of National Archives Probate 11/43, ff.26-7, Will of William Watson". William Watson had a daughter by his second wife Jane Stanney also named Blanche, no doubt after the girl's aunt.

10. Alhiyari, *New Biographical Evidence*, passim; Nina Green, "Modern Spelling Transcript of National Archives Probate 11/47, ff.31-4, Will of Dame Blanche Forman" including, especially, Green's Summary.

11. Green, "Modern spelling transcript of National Archives Probate 11/38/89, Will of Elizabeth (nee Rolleston) Whitlock Lee Wade Onley", 1

12. Elizabeth was born into the Rolleston family, and in succession married William Whitlock (died 1520), Lee (probably died 1522), Robert Wade (died 1529) and, finally, John Onley (died 1538). (Alhiyari, "Thomas Watson: New Birth Year and Privileged Ancestry".) Alhiyari is in error when he states that one of these, John Onley, also became Lord Mayor of London. Perhaps there is confusion with the John Olney [*sic*], who was mayor in 1446.

13. Alhiyari, *Thomas Watson: New Biographical Evidence*, is also in error in stating

that Elizabeth had children only by her second husband (she also had children by her first marriage to William Whitlock), and that all that is known of Lee is his surname. See: Green, "Modern Spelling Transcript of National Archives Probate11/38/89"; Green, "Modern Spelling Transcript of National Archives Probate 11/22/381, Will of Thomas Lee"; Green, "Modern Spelling Transcript of National Archives Probate 11/54, 292, Will of Thomas Lee of Clattercote in Oxfordshire".

14. Alhiyari, "Thomas Watson: New Birth Year and Privileged Ancestry"; Probate 11/43, ff 26-7.

15. Green, "National Archives Probate 11/54, 292".

16. John Danvers inherited on George's death at a date prior to 1575.

17. "Danvers and his household at Christmas time came not to church, but indulged in dancing and some other like pastime. Also the Danvers family assaulted Thomas Brasbridge, their minister. Anne Haile held the said minister by the gown, while Anne Danvers did buffet him very sore about the face and head". *Calendar of Domestic State Papers, 1581-90*. Cited by Francis Nottidge MacNamara, *Memorials of the Danvers Family (of Dauntsey and Culworth)*, 521-2.

18. MacNamara, 521.

19. Alan Haynes, *The Elizabethan Secret Services*, 111 (*Invisible Power*, 94).

20. Arthur F Leach, *A History of Winchester College* (London 1899), 323. Leach "hoped" (*sic*) that from the headmaster's series of Latin couplets in judgment of his predecessors could be discerned a "man of mildness" (289). The couplets ended, "I am the last here, whether good or ill / I will not say, others must find the bill" (Leach's translation, 290).

21. Philip Caraman, *Henry Garnet 1555-1606*, 4.

22. Caraman 4; D K Money, "Christopher Johnson", *DNB*.

23. The Elizabethan world was comparatively small. Before he left for Rome to join the Jesuits in 1575, Garnet worked for at least three years with the printer Richard Tottel as a "corrector for the press" (Caraman, 7-10). Abraham Fleming whom we met in CHAPTER ONE found a similar role for the same employer.

24. Caraman, 6.

25. Leach, 90-1.

26. A widespread opinion of Watson. See especially, Dana F Sutton, *Thomas Watson, the Complete Works*, General Introduction, Section 2 (unpaginated).

27. Anthony [à] Wood, *Athenae Oxoniensis*, I, 601. Wood is frequently cited, but he was writing almost a century after Watson's death and is untrustworthy. Albert Chatterley, in his *Thomas Watson: Italian Madrigals Englished*, xxviii, simply notes that Wood's judgement "may well be correct in essence, though the location seems unlikely".

28. Sutton, General Introduction, Section 3.

29. Anthony [à] Wood, II. Cited Caraman, 6.

30. As a whole, Oxford lost over a hundred during this period. (John Bossy, *The English Catholic Community, 1570-1850*, 12).

31. Caraman, 7.

32. Charles Nicholl, *The Reckoning*, 212-214, seems to think so, and traces Watson's earlier career in this light.

33. Preface to Watson's *Antigone*. Watson wrote in Latin. Conveniently, the Preface is translated by Mark Eccles, *Christopher Marlowe in London*, 130.

34. Alhiyari, *Thomas Watson: New Biographical Evidence*, Section 1:3 (unpaginated); Alhiyari, "Thomas Watson: New Birth Year and Privileged Ancestry."

35. The major bequest to Thomas Watson was "all my said manors, lands, tenements, meadows, pastures, waters, woods, underwoods, rents, reversions & services and my other hereditaments whatsoever with their appurtenances in the said several towns or villages of Nethercote, Sawbridge, Flecknoe and Rugby in the said county of Warwickshire." After Thomas's death these were to be willed to Richard Lee and his descendents. Potential future descendents of Thomas Watson were, it seems, to go wanting. (Green, "Modern Spelling Transcript of National Archives Probate 11/54 292").

36. Alhiyari, *Thomas Watson: New Biographical Evidence*, Section 1:2 (unpaginated); Green, "Modern Spelling Transcript of National Archives Probate 11/54 292".

37. Green, "Modern Spelling Transcript of National Archives Probate 11/54 292".

38. To introduce more threads to our literary web, it should be noted that, after Lee's death, Thomas's elder brother William may have turned to business, perhaps moving back to the family house left to him in his mother's will. The house was situated in Mark Lane in the parish of St Olave near the Tower of London.

Thomas Lee's widow Mary was the daughter of Morgan Wolfe of Meridan, Warwickshire, apparently no relation to John Wolfe, Watson's later printer.

After Lee's death Mary married into another extremely wealthy family, taking as husband Sir Richard Corbet (born 1544) the second son of Sir Andrew Corbet, and nephew of her late husband's father. After her death, William Watson inherited Thomas Lee's estate of Cropredy (near Banbury in Oxfordshire), but there was a legal wrangle and although William won a judgement against Corbet in 1579, Sir Richard was nevertheless seised of the manor when he died in 1606. (Alhiyari, *Thomas Watson: New Biographical Evidence*; National Archives Probate 11/54 292"; http://www.british-history.ac.uk/vch/oxon/vol10/pp157-175; A E C, *The Family of Corbet*, passim). The Corbet family's name is spelled variously as either

"Corbet" or "Corbett". The date of Mary's death is unknown.

The relationships between the families of Corbet, Newport, the Windsors —another important family—and de Vere, were close. (1) Roger Corbet (died 1538/9), the elder brother of Richard Corbet the second husband of Thomas Lee's widow, had been a ward of John de Vere, thirteenth Earl of Oxford. After the thirteenth Earl's death (1513) the wardship of Corbet was sold to Andrew Windsor, first Lord Windsor, who married off his daughter Anne to Corbet. (2) Ursula, the sister of John de Vere, fourteenth Earl of Oxford was the wife of Andrew Windsor's Son, George. (3) Katherine de Vere (died 1575), the seventeenth Earl of Oxford's half-sister, was the wife of Anne Corbet's nephew, Edward Windsor, third Lord Windsor (died 1575). The relationships are described in the Summaries to Green, "Modern Spelling Transcript of National Archives Probate 11/17/471" and especially to "Probate 11/46/40".

Thomas Watson's aunt Mary Lee's marriage into the Corbet family may be important to our knowledge of Watson's career, as it just might have served an entry into his acquaintance with Edward de Vere, seventeenth Earl of Oxford.

Also of interest are two of Watson's more distant connections to the literary world. First, Sir Andrew Corbet, Mary Lee's second father-in-law, was a cousin to Sir Richard Newport (his mother was Anne Corbet) owner of a copy of Hall's *Chronicle* with annotations thought by some to be by Shakespeare (first suggested by Allan Keen and Roger Lubbock, *The Annotator*). Second, Newport was related by marriage to Humphrey Martyn, the addressee of the *Langham Letter* which describes Leicester's Kenilworth entertainment of 1575. (See Nina Green's notes to "Modern Spelling Transcript of National Archives Probate 11/54, 292".)

39. Robert Hutchinson, *Elizabeth's Spy Master*, 46.

40. Several historians have compared Walsingham to a spider at the centre of a web of espionage, a cliché too irresistible not to repeat.

41. By Haynes, *The Elizabethan Secret Services*, 111 (*Invisible Power*, 94) who gives no source for the assertion. Roy Kendall, *Christopher Marlowe and Richard Baines*, 129, while acknowledging that although Watson "was not (or cannot be shown to have been) in Paris in 1572", fairly confidently speculates that, nevertheless, he was an English agent.

42. It was the year of the St Bartholomew's Day Massacre, an event which deeply affected protestant attitudes in this period (Walsingham's Paris house became a safe haven for Huguenot refugees).

43. The suggestion that Watson was an agent for Walsingham from the start is partially bolstered by his need for a government passport. He could hardly have

presented himself to Walsingham in Paris if, like the Catholic seminarians, he had surreptitiously slipped off to the continent from some quiet English harbour.

44. Referred to in his *Eglogue upon the Death of the Right Honourable Sir Francis Walsingham* (1590).

45. Professor Dana Sutton draws attention to another indication of an association between Walsingham and Watson. The British Library copy of Watson's *Amyntas* (1585) was owned by Sir William Waad, Walsingham's private secretary. (Sutton, *Thomas Watson*, Notes to the Introduction).

46. For Morley see CHAPTER FOUR, page 83, and Endnotes 23 and 24, page 276, quoting from *State Papers Domestic*, vol.240, no 119. For Paget see Peter Holmes, "Charles Paget", *DNB*.

47. *Meliboeus Thomae Watsoni sivè Ecloga in Obitum Honoratissimi Viri, Domini Francisci Walsinghami, Equitis aurati. Divae Elizabethae a secretis, et sanctioribus Consiliis.*

48. *Meliboeus, An Eclogue upon the death of the Right Honourable Sir Francis Walsingham, Late principall Secretarie to Her Majestie, and of her moste Honourable Privie Councell.*

49. Eccles' translation, *Christopher Marlowe in London*, 130.

50. Eccles, *Christopher Marlowe in London*, 133.

51. Apart from a break of just a few weeks in 1509.

52. Eccles, *Christopher Marlowe in London*, 135; Hilda Amphlett, "The Golden Age of Padua", Shakespeare Authorship Review, 11 (Spring 1964), 16, a review of a lecture by G Cimino, London, January 1964. (Edited reprint in Paul Altrocchi and Hank Whittemore, *Building a Case for Edward de Vere as Shakespeare*, Vol 5, "So Richly Spun", 144.)

53. *The Taming of the Shrew*, I.i.

54. Anderson, 98; Ian W Archer, "Sir Thomas Smith", *DNB*.

55. Derek Wilson, *Sir Francis Walsingham*, 31.

56. See endnote 37, above.

57. Both Alan Haynes, *Walsingham*, 79-80, and Park Honan, *Christopher Marlowe*, 134, take it as read that Watson studied in Padua, but there is no absolute certainty.

58. Described by Portia in *The Merchant of Venice*, 3:4.82-4,24-32; Anderson, 99; Richard Paul Roe, *The Shakespeare Guide to Italy*, 145-152. For part of the journey, Roe provides illustrations in colour.

59. Although there was no major outbreak of the plague in France at this time, nowhere was altogether safe. Vanessa Harding, *The Dead and the Living in Paris and London*, 25, suggests that in the sixteenth and seventeenth centuries Paris had an outbreak of the plague in almost one year in every three.

60. Fathers of the Congregation of the London Oratory, *The First and Second*

Diaries of the English College, Douay, 112. Oddly, Kendall, *Christopher Marlowe and Richard Baines*, 119, gets this wrong, stating that Watson *arrived* on 15 October 1576. The diary entry clearly states that Watson left for Paris on this date, so he was staying at the seminary until then.

61. The concept suggested by https://en.wikipedia.org/wiki/English College_Douai
62. Eamon Duffy, "William Allen", *DNB*.
63. J W Binns, "Richard White", *DNB*.
64. Sutton. General Introduction, Section 4 (unpaginated).
65. Jardine and Stewart, Chapter 2.
66. Eccles, *Christopher Marlowe in London*, 135-6.
67. *Encyclopédie des gens du monde répertoire universel des sciences, des lettres et des arts avec des notices sur les principales familles historiques et sur les personnages célèbres, morts et vivants; par une société de savants de littérateurs et d'artistes Françaises et étrangers. Tome septième.* Paris, Libraire de Treuttel et Würtz, 1836.
68. Fathers of the Congregation of the London Oratory, 121.
69. Fathers of the Congregation of the London Oratory, 125.
70. Honan, 136-7.
71. Fathers of the Congregation of the London Oratory, 127.
72. Translation by Bronson Feldman (*The Bard*, 1.4., 130, and APPENDIX F, 221) from Watson's Dedicatory Epistle to his translation into Latin of Sophocles' *Antigone* (Arber, 6).
73. They returned to Douai in 1593 under Allen's successor Richard Barrett.

Three: "A very learned man"

1. Charles Nicholl, *The Reckoning*, 213.
2. Amy may have been an illegitimate daughter of Sir Richard Morison of Hertfordshire by his mistress Lucy Peckham. Morison, a humanist and diplomatist, was active under Henry VIII and Edward VI. His wife, the Lady Bridget, later married twice more. Her second marriage was to Sir Edward Manners, the fourth Earl of Rutland.
3. Dana F Sutton, *Thomas Watson, The Complete Works*. General Introduction. Section 9 (unpaginated).
4. The story is related in detail by Mark Eccles, *Christopher Marlowe in London*, 145ff and followed by Nicholl, 219-22. Eccles acknowledged research by Leslie Hotson. It is these documents which bring to light Watson's residence

with William Beale. The assumption, based on good reasoning, is that the Thomas Watson involved is "our" Thomas Watson, and not another of the same name. That has not always been the belief; as recently as 1967, Arthur Freeman, *Thomas Kyd*, 19fn, thought "the identification of the charlatan Thomas Watson with the poet Watson is somewhat tenuous".

5. Her husband said he "fell a laughing & she asked him why he laughed & he said because she was branded on the back as one of the Queen's great horses was on the buttock". Quoted Eccles, *Christopher Marlowe in London*, 150.

6. British Library, Lansdowne MS 53/79, 162-3 (quoted Chatterley, *DNB*). Watson had moved into, or perhaps nearer to, Oxford's house at Fisher's Folly by the time of the trial. St Helen, St Botolph (its church faced Fisher's Folly), and St Ethelburg parishes comprised the Bishopsgate ward.

7. Nicholl, 222. Nicholl is followed by Sutton, General Introduction. Sections 18 and 19 (unpaginated).

8. Nicholl, 220-1.

9. He had a successful career. In 1594 Burghley appointed him Under-Sheriff of London, and in time he rose to the post of Treasurer of the Inn.

10. Eccles, *Christopher Marlowe in London*, 154; Nicholl, 374.n to page 219.

11. There is more: the famous writer Gervase Markham was also related to the Burnells. As the son by Robert's first marriage (to Maria Leeke) Gervase was the stepson of this same Jane Markham, Robert's second wife. Gervase's major literary works were published after Watson's death.

12. The family name is often spelled Goche, Gooche or Gooch, but Barnabe always published it as Googe. See William E Sheidley, *Barnabe Googe*, 122 n23.

13. This point is also made by Eccles, *Christopher Marlowe in London*, 148

14. Sheidley, 19.

15. Possibly through Herefordshire connections. Raphael Lyne, "Barnabe Googe", *DNB*.

16. Darrell's son, another Thomas, oversaw the construction of priest holes there. Between 1591 and 1598 the authorities raided Scotney twice owing to the activities of the Jesuit priest Richard Blount.

17. Sheidley, 124 n48.

18. *A Newe Booke called the Shippe of Safegard*.

19. Lyne.

20. In Thomas Gressop's translation of Nicholas Cabasilas's *A briefe treatise, conteynynge a playne and fruitfull declaration of the popes usurped primacye*. Cited by Lyne.

21. Marcellus Palingenius Stellatus was a pen name, an anagram of Pier Angelo

Mazola from La Stellata, a Village near Ferrara. (Sheidley, 29).

22. Sir Thomas Smith also translated three volumes, acknowledged by Googe in his 1565 edition, but, he said, not known to him until it was too late to abandon his own translation. (Sheidley, 29).

23. The date according to Stow. (*The Annales*, 1605. Cited by Eccles *Christopher Marlowe in London*, 157).

24. Henry B Wheatley, "Signs of Booksellers in St Paul's Churchyard", 74, 93.

25. E K Chambers, *The Elizabethan Stage* III, 395.

26. He also published the second and third Quartos of *Titus* in 1600 and 1611.

27. Alastair Everitt, "The Tragedie of King Lear" in Kevin Gilvary (Ed), *Dating Shakespeare's Plays*, 399-400. The former apprentice was John Wright, who had served under White between June 1594 and June 1604 (Ramon Jiménez, "The Two Lear Plays: How Shakespeare Transformed his first Romance into his Last Tragedy", *The Oxfordian* 15:28 [2013]).

28. Alluded to in his dedication to the sixth Earl in his *A Fig for Momus* (1595).

29. Green, "Modern spelling transcript of National Archives Probate 11/44, f 132, Will of Anne Watson".

30. Charles J Sisson, "Thomas Lodge and His Family", in Sisson (Ed), *Thomas Lodge and Other Elizabethans*, 149. (Also, reprinted in Charles C Whitney [Ed], *Thomas Lodge*).

31. John Dover Wilson thought it may have been called *Honest Excuses* because Gosson referred in a later work to "certain honest excuses" that had been commissioned in reply to his *School of Abuse*. Charles Whitworth, "Thomas Lodge (1558-September 1625)", in David A Richardson, *Dictionary of Literary Biography* (Detroit, 1966), 139. Reprinted, Whitney, 26.

32. Arthur F Kinney, "Stephen Gosson", *DNB*.

33. Alexandra Halasz, "Thomas Lodge" *DNB*.

34. *Wits Misery*, IV. 23. Quoted by Élaine Cuvelier, "Renaissance Catholicism in the Work of Thomas Lodge", in Whitney, 513. (Translated by Philip John Usher from *Thomas Lodge, Témoin de son Temps* [Paris, 1984]).

35. Cuvelier, 511-17 *passim*.

36. Thomas Lodge's *Sonnets to Phillis* (1593) were published in the year after Watson's registered death. In the same year, Watson's own tribute to Phillis, *Amintas for his Phillis* was published posthumously in *The Phoenix Nest* (1593), signed T.W. Gent. It was reprinted in *England's Helicon* (1600), signed Tho. Watson.

Lodge's sonnets surely owe something to his acquaintance with Watson; see especially Sonnet 22 with its echo of *Hekatompathia* VII, as well as Shakespeare's

Sonnet 130 (see CHAPTER FIVE).

>Two lines in Lodge's "The Induction", verse 3, are also worth quoting:
>>And though the fore-bred brothers they have had,
>>(Who in their Swan-like songs Amintus wept) ...
>
>The sentiment resonates with Watson's *Moelibus* in which he remembers the time
>>When milk-white swans did flock to hear thee sing.

Edmond Malone identified "the fore-bred brothers" as Watson and Fraunce, although Watson and Thomas Walsingham is a strong alternative theory; "The Induction" and the Malone reference are quoted at http://spenseraians.cath.vt.edu/TextRecord.php?&textsid=32786

37. Thomas Watson, *Poems*, 157. Watson's translation from his own Latin. The passage recalls a similar sentiment in Ronsard's *Bocage Royale*, where the imagery is related to the Thames. This poem was first published in 1565 and again in 1584. Before his death in 1585 Ronsard revised the verses, which were published in 1587. The 1587 version commences:

>*Bien tost verra la Tamise superbe*
>*Maint Cygne blanc les hostes do son herbe,*
>*Chantant en l'air d'un son melodieux*
>*Tourner ses bords & rejouyr les cieux ...*

Which Richard Malim, *The Earl of Oxford and the Making of "Shakespeare"*, 20, translates:

>Soon the proud Thames will see
>Many a white Swan guests on his grass
>Sing in the air with their melodious sound
>Go by her banks, rejoice the skies ...

38. Nicholl, *The Reckoning*, 216-7; William Honey, *The Life, Loves and Achievements of Christopher Marlowe*, 56-7 and *passim*.

39. Nicholl, 217.

40. Nicholl, 216-7.

41. Park Honan, *Christopher Marlowe*, 120; David Riggs, *The World of Christopher Marlowe*, 140; Nicholl, 143.

42. See APPENDIX A, 197.

43. Constance Brown Kuriyama, *Christopher Marlowe*, 85-6; Riggs, 140.

44. Honey, 58-9. At the least, however, Honey makes a plausible case by aligning three coincidences. A deponent named William Smith living in St Paul's Churchyard around 1 June 1582 knew Sir Thomas Walsingham well; Thomas Kyd

declared later that Marlowe was well known to "some stationers" in the churchyard; Gabriel Harvey in 1593 stated that Marlowe was "the highest mind that ever haunted St Paul's ..."

45. Honan, 51-2.

46. Riggs, 273-9, gives a particularly lucid account of the subversive "Stanley Plot".

47. Park Honan, *Christopher Marlowe: Poet and Spy*.

48. British Museum, Harleian MS 6848 f.190. Photographically reproduced in A D Wraight and Virginia F Stern, *In Search of Christopher Marlowe*, 354-5.

49. Riggs, 319-25; Honan, 336-43; Nicholl, 52.

50. Nicholl, 24-6; 411-12.

51. J Leslie Hotson, *The Death of Christopher Marlowe*.

52. Roy Kendall, *Christopher Marlowe and Richard Baines*, 120-1.

53. Margaret Waugh, *Blessed Philip Howard*, 9.

54. Nevertheless the dedication is a long one, and a curious one, offering more advice than is usual. It is certainly ambiguous, and seems to urge that Philip should be his own man, rather than follow the call of power, government and influence—especially the abuse of illegal power. The final part reads:

> *Haec et plura tuis plane praefiget ocellis*
> *Antigone, studio docta docere meo.*
> *Vive, vale, generose comes. Quot saecula cervus*
> *Vivit, tot foelix saecula vive, vale.*

The Philological Museum translates this as follows:

> These things and more Antigone will set before your eyes, taught to teach by my effort. Love and prosper, noble Earl. Live for as many years as does the stag, and farewell."

What a strange final farewell: "Live as many years as does the stag ..." The Philological Museum explains in a note that, "The stag was supposed to be a very long-lived animal: cf. Juvenal, *Satire* xvi.251, *iam torquet iuvenem longa et cervina senectus* with the Scholiast *ad loc*". Long life, however, was but one of many symbolic meanings ascribed to the stag. Others were as a symbol of lust, and conversely, also of purity, of peace in Christ. Perhaps in drawing attention to the stag, Watson may also have implied some of these other qualities.

Bronson Feldman noted that the main ethical motive of *Antigone* was obedience to the sovereign ("Thomas Watson", 138), a suggestion also pursued by Donna B Hamilton (*Anthony Munday and the Catholics, 1560-1633*, 34-5) who finds evidence in *Antigone*'s dedication that "Watson suggests the futility in pursuing a religious life (a love or passion) that the central government opposes", an argument which seems not to be born out by the quotation above. Hamilton's thesis is perhaps stronger, although strained even here when she suggests that the title "MY LOVE IS PAST" which heads the final 21 Passions of *Hekatompathia* (1582) represents the relinquishment of Catholicism to the secular, a choice made by the dedicatee of the work, the Earl of Oxford, as well as (perhaps) by its author Thomas Watson.

55. Kendall, 129, for example. But examples are legion.
56. William Paget, a patron of William Byrd, is a good example.
57. Kendall, 128-9.
58. Kendall, 129.

Four: Unsavoury colleagues?

1. Charles Nicholl, *The Reckoning*, 218.
2. Nicholl, 158 and 493n. Anne Poley was baptised on 22 August 1583.
3. R E G Kirk and Ernest F Kirk (Eds), *Returns of Aliens Dwelling in the City and Suburbs of London from the Reign of Henry VIII to that of James I* (Aberdeen, 1902). Reprinted by The Publications of the Huguenot Society of London. Vol X Part ii, 1907. Vol ii. 22.
4. Kirk and Kirk, Vol ii. 433.
5. Nicholl, 158.
6. Riggs, David, *The World of Christopher Marlowe* (2005), 144.
7. Quoted: Riggs, 144. There is a (no more than remote) chance that "Elizabeth Yeomans" is the "Elizabeth Broylman" tentatively connected by Bronson Feldman with Stephen Broelmann of Cologne who wrote to Watson when he was in Paris (Arber, 5). See APPENDIX F, 233.
8. The figure is quoted from Nicholl, 159. Alan Haynes, *Walsingham*, 156, states that at any one time the prison held twenty-five to thirty priests.
9. Christopher Devlin, *The Life of Robert Southwell*, 110-12.
10. Nicholl, 195.
11. Nicholl, 161-2.
12. Nicholl, 37.
13. Nicholl, 35-6.
14. Eugénie de Kalb, "Robert Poley's Movements".
15. Roy Kendall, *Christopher Marlowe and Richard Baines*, 375 n15.
16. Park Honan, *Christopher Marlowe*, 345.

17. Kalb.
18. Fully detailed in Nicholl, 147-155.
19. Kendall, 127.
20. Nicholl, 155.
21. Confusion arises from the existence of two records naming a "Richard Baines". Kendall, 309-31, discusses the matter thoroughly and favours the "Tyburn" theory, but does not altogether rule out the "rector" theory of Constance Brown Kuriyama. The theory is offered in "Marlowe's Nemesis, The Identity of Richard Baines" (in Kenneth Friedenreich, Roma Gill, and Constance B Kuriyama, *"A poet and a filthy Play-Maker"*, *New Essays on Christopher Marlowe* [New York, 1988]). Kuriyama's theory was accepted by Nicholl, 153, 421.
22. Kendall, 326-8.
23. *CSP dom., vol. 240, no. 19*. The "Mr Nowell", author of the letters, was possibly the Dean of St Paul's, of that name, but more likely to have been Henry Noell, a courtier friend of the Earl of Oxford who may have joined Morley and others after supper at the tilts of 1595 (E K Chambers, *The Elizabethan Stage*, iii.212).
24. Phelippes' draft reply confirms Morley's activity *(CSP dom., vol. 240, no. 53)*. This correspondence has prompted the view that Morley's sympathies were Roman Catholic despite his appointments in the established church. His inner faith can, of course, never be known for certain, but the texts of some of his Latin motets endorse this view.

The Paget correspondence is also evidence that Morley was a spy; it was not uncommon for musicians to be employed as agents in Elizabethan England.

Five: Poetry, science, wit and wisdom

1. Albert Chatterley, "Thomas Watson: Works, Contemporary References and Reprints", 240. References to most of these pieces are in headings to verses in *Hekatompathia*, which also reprints four examples from *Canzoniere*.
2. http://www.philological.bham.ac.uk/Watson/antigone/intro.html
3. Chatterley, "Thomas Watson: Works, Contemporary References and Reprints", 240.
4. Much was distributed in manuscript, including *Quid Amor* which Watson reprints as Sonnet XCVIII in his *Hekatompathia* (Edward Arber, *Thomas Watson, Poems*, 5).
5. Walter F Staton, "Thomas Watson and Ovidian Poetry".
6. Arber, 36; Sutton, Dana F. *Thomas Watson, The Complete Works*. Arber has "fraight"

in the second line.

7. Eric Lewin Altschuler and William Jansen, "Was Thomas Watson Shakespeare's Precursor?"

8. Giovanni Battista Giraldi (aka Cinthio) published his *Hecatommithi (One Hundred and Ten Stories)* in 1565. It was translated into French by Gabriel Chappuys in 1584, two years after Watson published his work. It was not published in English until 1753. *Hecatommithi* was a major source for Shakespeare's *Othello*. Could it, perhaps, also have inspired the title of Watson's book of sonnets?

9. John Cawood died in 1572, aged fifty-eight.

10. I Gadd, "John Wolfe", *DNB*.

11. *Una essortatione al timor di Dio.*

12. Harry R Hoppe, "John Wolfe", 244-5; W Schrickx, *Shakespeare's Early Contemporaries*, 146.

13. From 1582 until 1588, his London premises were in Distaff Lane "over against the sign of the Castle", until he moved to the Stationers' Hall in 1587.

14. A possible double meaning, referring also to the printer's devices which Wolfe used to print several titles by Machiavelli under false imprints. (Joseph L Black, *The Martin Marprelate Tracts*). Marprelate also made the same accusation. See also endnote 36 below.

15. Gadd, "John Wolfe".

16. The double "Machiavellian" meaning again proving irresistible, as noted in endnote 14 above. (Black, 223).

17. Black, 23. Waldegrave took refuge in Edinburgh from about the end of 1589, and the following year he was appointed Queen's printer. Until 1603 he printed at least a hundred works in Scotland. He returned to London in 1603 on the accession of James to the English throne. (R B McKerrow [Ed], *A Dictionary of Printers*, 279).

18. Schrickx, 184-5.

19. Schrickx, 145-6.

20. Schrickx, 87-9 deduces this from the dedication and a conversation in Florio's *Second Fruits* (1591).

21. Leland H Carlson, *Martin Marprelate, Gentleman*, 24, 68-9.

22. Black, lxxi.

23. Black, lxxii.

24. In association, it seems, with the printers John Danter (an associate of John Chettle) and Cuthbert Burby. The matter is complicated. See Robert Detobel, *Shakespeare*, 70-3.

25. Arber, 9.

26. A E B Coldiron, "Sidney, Watson, and the 'Wrong Ways' to Renaissance Lyric Poetics", 50.

27. Edward Arber, *A Transcript of the Registers*,127.

28. S K Heninger Jr (Ed), *The Hekatompathia; or Passionate Centurie of Love*. (Gainesville,1964).

29. Sutton.

30. A E B Coldiron, "Watson's *Hekatompathia* and the Renaissance Lyric Translation", 9.

31. Although Sidney's sonnets, *Astrophel and Stella*, were not printed until 1591 they were written earlier and probably circulated at around the same time as Watson's.

32. Oxford's confession is usually taken at its face value, but in the shady world of Elizabethan politics the situation may have been more complicated. By making a theatrical public confession before the whole court, in the Presence Chamber, it is possible that Oxford was acting in collusion with the government as *agent provocateur* in order to "out" Howard, Arundell and Southwell. See also W Ron Hess, *The Dark Side of Shakespeare*, Vol I: 279-80, Vol II: 59-63.

33. Mark Anderson, *Shakespeare by Another Name*, 167-8

34. It is in Latin. The translation is Sutton's.

35. Arber, *Thomas Watson*, 31-2; Chatterley, "Thomas Watson (1555/6-1592)"; Alan Stewart, *Philip Sidney*, 148.

36. The tilt was a highly theatrical entertainment. Oxford's "Tree of the Sun" represented Elizabeth. See Alan R Young, "'In Gallant Course before Ten Thousand Eyes'".

37. Katherine Duncan-Jones, *Sir Philip Sidney: Courtier Poet*, 237-8, disparages Watson's achievement and without any evidence whatsoever suggests Sidney "probably" looked on Watson's *Hekatompathia* with "scorn", and that "Watson's 'passions', full of 'swelling phrases'" "may have given an irritant, grit-in-oyster-like impetus to [Sidney's] own quite different sonnet sequence".

38. B J Sokol, "Matthew Roydon", *DNB*

39. In his *Shadow of the Night* (1594). Referenced by Sokol.

40. M C Bradbrook, *The School of Night*, 11.

41. Sokol; F E Halliday, *A Shakespeare Companion*, 426.

42. Campbell, Oscar James. *The Reader's Encyclopedia of Shakespeare*, 727; C S Lewis, *Poetry and Prose in the Sixteenth Century*, 466. However, the general consensus is that *Willobie* is a collaborative effort (see, for example, Bradbrook, 170).

43. Benjamin Woolley, *The Queen's Conjurer*, 280.

44. Arthur Freeman, *Thomas Kyd*, 9-10 thinks not, especially as the same name in the same form appears in Watson's *Antigone*.

45. Coldiron, "Sidney, Watson, and the 'Wrong Ways' to Renaissance Lyric Poetics", 53.

46. Compare G Wilson Knight: "Lyly". *Review of English Studies* 15:58 (April 1939), 146-63. Reprinted in R J Kaufmann (Ed), *Elizabethan Drama*, 41-59.

47. Chatterley, *DNB,* counted the sources; quotation from heading to Passion LXXXV.

48. *Trachiniae* (Poems XXXVIII and XCIII), *Electra* (Poem LXIII), *Ajax Flagellifer* (Poem LXXXII), *Oedipus Rex* (Poem XXXV), *Oedipus Coloneus* (Poem XCIII), and—to make a sixth—perhaps *Philoctetes* (Poem LXVIII). See Feldman, "Thomas Watson, Dramatist", 129-30 or APPENDIX F, 219-20.

49. Feldman, 129-30; APPENDIX F, 219-20.

50. Feldman, 129-30; APPENDIX F, 219-20.

51. Sutton.

52. Arber, *Thomas Watson*, 9; See also F T Palgrave, 98 and fn.

53. British Library. MS Harleian 3277, f.37.

54. Mark Eccles, "*Marlowe and Watson*", Dissertation (Harvard, 1933); and briefly referred to in his *Christopher Marlowe in London,* 161.

55. *Artificiosae memoriae Libellus*, the fore-runner of Watson's *Compendium Memoriae Localis* (1585), and his manuscript translation from the Huguenot *A Learned Dialogue of Bernard Palessy* (c1588).

56. S K Heninger (Ed), *The Hekatompathia; or Passionate Centurie of Love.*

57. Sutton. www.philological.bham.ac.uk

58. Sutton's important Introduction to *Hekatompathia* offers more detail. Moreover, for his setting of the text of the *Hekatompathia,* Sutton has collated the printed version with the manuscript and made various corrections which in general he believes are improvements to the printed version; he expresses his "astonishment" that no previous editor has attempted the same.

59. In his on-line post "Visual Verses" dated 31 August 2016, Christian Algar, Curator of Printed Heritage Collections at the British Library, assumes that *A Looking Glasse for Lovers* was transcribed from the *Hekatompathia* in 1633. However, Sutton agrees with Heninger quoting, "The '1633' in faded ink below the rule of the manuscript's title page is certainly an inscription by a later owner, not the original scribe" (Heninger, xi n2).

60. S K Heninger Jr, quoted by Sutton.

61. J P Brooke-Little, *An Heraldic Alphabet,* 58.

62. Robert Sean Brazil, *The True Story of the Shakespeare Publications*, 113; 89.

63. The first half of Brandes' work was published in 1897 where he clearly attributes this discovery to Hansen (https://archive.org/details/williamshakespeare

01branuoft/page/342-3). In the final three-volume edition published a year later, however, he adds and re-writes several paragraphs to take account of Sidney Lee's *Life of Shakespeare* (1898) which had been published in the meantime. In one of the re-written paragraphs Brandes seems to attribute to Lee the finding previously attributed to Hansen. This may not have been Brandes' intention but the result of imprecise editing of his text. (Georg Brandes, *William Shakespeare*, 287).

64. E Pearlman, "Watson's *Hekatompathia* [1582] in the *Sonnets* and *Romeo and Juliet*".

65. Eric Lewin Altschuler and William Jansen, "Was Thomas Watson Shakespeare's Precursor?".

66. Barboura Flues, "Thomas Watson's *Hekatompathia*: Glossary and Appendices".

67. Noted by J Dover Wilson (and subsequently others) who acknowledges P Cruttwell, *The Shakespeare Moment* (New York, 1954), 18.

68. Christopher Marlowe, *Dr Faustus*, 1604 text. 5:1: 106-112.

69. Occasionally spelled Altschulyer.

70. Eric Lewin Altschuler, "Searching for Shakespeare in the Stars"; Altschuler and Jansen,"Was Thomas Watson Shakespeare's Precursor?"; "Poet described stars in Milky Way before Galileo"; "A poetic challenge?"; "First description of Discrete Stars Composing Milky Way in Thomas Watson's *Hekatompathia* (1582)".

71. Altschuler and Jansen, "Was Thomas Watson Shakespeare's Precursor?", 13-14; "Poet described stars in Milky Way before Galileo"; "A poetic challenge?".

72. It was also discovered independently by the great Danish astronomer Tycho Brahe, an admirer of Dee.

73. Woolley, 133-139; Dan Falk, *The Science of Shakespeare*, 64-9.

74. In his *A Perfit Description of the Caelestiall Orbes according to the most aunciente doctrine of the Pythagoreans, latelye revived by Copernicus and by Geometricall Demonstrations approved*.

75. Hiram Haydn (Ed), *The Portable Elizabethan Reader*, 11.

76. Haydn, 10-11; Falk, 40-42.

77. Peter Usher, "Shakespeare's support of the New Astronomy; Woolley, 133.

78. Woolley,133-4; Falk, 68 and *passim*. Such a device was also reported in 1578 by William Bourne in *Inventions and devices*.

79. Altschuler and Jansen, "Was Thomas Watson Shakespeare's Precursor?", 14.

80. Even allowing for Watson's circulation of the *Hekatompathia* in manuscript before 1582, Digges was probably first.

81. Altschuler and Jansen's translation, "Poet described stars in Milky Way before Galileo".

82. Peter Usher, "An Answer to 'A poetic challenge?'", who supplies the quotation.

Elsewhere, Professor Usher draws attention to Shakespeare's astronomical references, especially to those in *Hamlet* ("Shakespeare's support for the New Astronomy").

83. Watson's suggested stay at Padua may have been too early for Digges' theory to be widely propagated there. The views of Democritus would have been known, however.

84. Altschuler and Jansen, "Was Thomas Watson Shakespeare's Precursor?", 14; "A poetic challenge?".

85. In Dekker's pamphlet *A Knights Conjuring*. See below.

86. Derran Charlton, "Giordano Bruno"; John Bossy, *Under the Molehill*, 1fn, was uncertain about Fagot's identity; Alan Haynes, *The Elizabethan Secret Services*, 36, 110, was certain, but changed his mind by the time of the publication of his *Walsingham, Elizabethan Spymaster and Statesman*, 40.

87. Charles Nicholl, *The Reckoning*, 146; Schrickx, 107.

88. John Bossy, *Giordano Bruno and the Embassy Affair*, 24; Francis A Yates, *The Art of Memory*, 272; Charlton suggests *De la causa* and other of Bruno's works may have influenced Shakespeare's *Hamlet*.

89. Thomas P Roche, Jr., *Petrarch and the English Sonnet Sequences* (New York, 1989), 138-9. (Noted in a review by Jeffrey L Jones, *Sidney Newsletter* 10:2 [1990], 46).

90. The manuscript *Artificiosae memoriae libellus* is dated 1583. The published version entitled *Compendium memoriae localis* is thought to be dated 1585.

91. Yates, 274. Alan H Nelson, *Monstrous Adversity*, 61, considers Watson a "lowbrow" conjuror in comparison with Bruno, a suspect opinion undermined further by Nelson's misnaming of Anne Burnell in the same paragraph.

92. Watson of course relied on the received knowledge of his time, which we now know to be mistaken. (Dana F Sutton, *Introduction* to *Compendium memoriae localis*).

93. Sloane MS3731.

94. In England they called him Albert Alasco. (Dana F Sutton, *Introduction* to *Compendium memoriae localis*).

95. Bossy, *Giordano Bruno*, 23.

96. Chatterley, *DNB*.

97. *Love's Labour's Lost*, IV:3:250-1. Most editors believe the play was written around 1595 or 1596 with allusions to members of the Southampton circle at Essex House in the Strand (summarised by A W L Saunders, *The Master of Shakespeare*, 47). However, Derran Charlton and Kevin Gilvary consider 1578 a more appropriate date, with a revision in 1593 (Kevin Gilvary [Ed], *Dating Shakespeare's Plays*, 110); while M C Bradbrook, basing his evidence on the *New Shakespeare* (Cambridge, 1923), 126-7, considers the play was first performed in the winter of 1593-4

(Bradbrook, *The School of Night*, 127-8). Compare, too, Chapman's *The Shadow of Night* and its shades of the School of Night, entered for publication on 31 December 1593 and published early in 1594. The poem would have been circulated earlier in manuscript.

98. M E Lamb, "The Myth of the Countess of Pembroke", 194 fn 2. Lamb offers a history of the rise of the "school of night" theory, which was formulated as recently as 1903.

99. Peter J French, *John Dee*, 172.

100. Explored in more detail in Nicholl, 245-57 and Charlton. The antipope in *Dr Faustus* is named Bruno.

101. Charlton; Hugh Ross Williamson, *Sir Walter Raleigh*, 70. Another candidate is the earlier astrologer Eliseus Bomelius, whose reputation in London was at one time very high. He suffered a dreadful death in Ivan the Terrible's Russia in 1579.

102. Harvey was yet another Matthew Parker scholarship holder. He too completed his education at Padua.

103. Nicholl, 232-3 and 309-10. On his arrest Kyd named Hariot, Warner and Matthew Roydon as Marlowe's friends.

104. Nicholl, 232.

105. Woolley, 279.

106. It was a shortened version of his book published on the continent, *Elizabethae ... saevissimum edictum ... cum responsione ad singula capita*.

107. Woolley, 279; Paul Hyland, *Ralegh's Last Journey*, 68.

108. In October 1594 Thomas Nashe published a pamphlet *The Terrors of the Night* dedicated to Carey's daughter Elizabeth.

109. When Giordano Bruno arrived in London in 1584, Greville invite him to his Whitehall lodgings to discuss heliocentricity (Saunders, 59).

110. By Anthony [à] Wood in *Athenae Oxoniensis*. Cited by French, 171.

111. French, 217.

112. *Nobilis or a View of the Life and Death of Sidney and Lessus Legubris* (c1593) tr and ed by Vergil B Heltzel and Hoyt H Hudson (San Marino, California, 1940), 75-6. Cited by Duncan-Jones, *Sir Philip Sidney: Courtier Poet*, 115; Roger Howell, *Sir Philip Sidney*, 137; Stewart, 169.

113. Katherine Duncan-Jones, *Sir Philip Sidney: Courtier Poet*, 115-6.

114. French, 129.

115. Woolley, 203-5.

116. French, 126-159 (Chapter 6).

117. James McDermott, *Martin Frobisher*, 132.

118. Dyer in particular was fascinated by the idea of the exploration of unknown lands. John Frampton dedicated three works of discovery to Dyer including, in 1579, his translation of Marco Polo's account of his *Travels* to discover the elusive Cathay.

119. Alden Brooks, *Will Shakspere and the Dyer's Hand*, 474-7.

120. Woolley, 188-200.

121. B M Ward, *The Seventeenth Earl of Oxford 1550-1604*, 50. Henry Howard and Charles Arundell charged Oxford in 1581 with indulgence in necromancy, conjuring and prophesy at or near the Greenwich house of the Master of the Armoury, Sir George Howard. Their accusations need to be treated with caution; both Howard and Arundel were fighting for their lives.

122. Raleigh had also acted as the courier between Oxford and Sidney during the tennis court spat. The favours were no doubt returned when Raleigh laid before the House of Lords his application to explore the New World—de Vere was a member of the board.

123. George Saintsbury, *A History of Elizabethan Literature*, 60-81.

124. G K Hunter, *John Lyly*, 10-11.

125. Charles Nicholl, *A Cup of News*, 54-61, tells a different story. The original Oxford group, he claims, were friendly from around 1581 and comprised Lyly, Watson, Peele, Lodge, and Roydon, as well as Achelley and Buc for whom there are no records of their having studied at either Oxford or Cambridge. (Apart from Lodge, each contributed a dedication to Watson's *Hekatompathia*.) Later, they were joined by a "Cambridge axis" of Greene, Nashe and Marlowe. At first, says Nicholl, the clique was known as the "Holborn Set" because Lyly rented chambers at the old Savoy hospital near the Strand, and Lodge and Roydon studied at the Inns of Court.

126. James P Bednarz includes Watson in the group. (Patrick Cheney [ed], *The Cambridge Companion to Christopher Marlowe*, 90).

127. Saintsbury, 64.

128. Richard Helgerson, *The Elizabethan Prodigals*, 67-8.

129. For example, Judith Cook, *Roaring Boys*, 22, fantasises that they "… sprawled around a table swapping jokes and anecdotes and making sure everyone present knew who they were". Cook, never a trustworthy writer, also describes the earliest wits as "Oxford men" but includes Greene without acknowledging that he was Cambridge educated.

130. Assembling names from various secondary sources we find: Beale, Beaumont, Camden, Chapman, Chettle, Daniel, Davies, Dekker, Drayton, Drummond, Fletcher, Florio, Greene, Harvey, Heywood, Jonson, Kyd, Lodge, Marlowe, Marston,

Massinger, Middleton, Milton, Mundy, Nashe, Peele, Roydon, Spenser, Watson, Webster, and even more—in short, the list inflates to include practically every notable writer from a wide period of some twenty or thirty years.

131. Quoted by Allardyce Nicoll, *Shakespeare in his own Age*, 129.

132. Helgerson, 105.

133. It is generally acknowledged that Queen Elizabeth's counsellor Burghley was the prototype for Queen Gertrude's counsellor Polonius (in *Hamlet*).

134. See Albert Chatterley, *Amyntas and Phyllis* for an "interpretation" in English.

135. In his *Polyhymnia*, an account in verse of the 1590 tilt. See David Greer, "… Thou Court's Delight", 50.

136. Stephen W May, "Henry Noel", *DNB*; Stephen W May, *The Elizabethan Courtier Poets*, 358.

137. For a discussion see Walter F Staton Jr and Harry Morris, "Thomas Watson and Abraham Fraunce", 150-3.

138. John Buxton, *Sir Philip Sidney*, 194; Arber, *Thomas Watson*, 147. Harry Morris considers that, on the contrary, there may have been a "warm friendship" between the two poets (Harry Morris, "'Amyntas' and the Sidney Circle" fn 6) and that Watson's address has been misconstrued: "surely Watson was setting straight the public record" (Staton Jr and Morris, 152). Nashe, he reminds us, said as much in his preface to Greene's *Menaphon* (1589) in writing of Fraunce's "excellent translation of Master Thomas Watson's sugared Amyntas" (Morris, 318).

139. 1587, 1588 and 1589.

140. Ivychurch, on the Avon and just southeast of Wilton, was another of Mary Sidney's seats.

141. Other writers were inspired to tackle the same subject. Between Watson' death in 1592, and 1595, four English works included the name of Amyntas: Spenser's *Colin Clouts come home again* (1595); Nashe's *Pierce Penniless his Supplication to the Devil* (1592); Barnfield's *The Affectionate Shepherd* (1594), and the rare *Greene's Funerals* (1593). (Source: Morris, 318.)

142. Full title, *Coluthi: Thebai Lycopolitani poetae: Helenae Raptus*.

143. Thomas Coxeter, who died in 1747 and was described by W C Hazlitt as "a remorseless forger of titles and facts". (Eccles, *Christopher Marlowe in London*, 160.)

144. In the University Library at Cambridge.

145. Eccles, *Christopher Marlowe in London*, 161.

146. Palissy's work was published in Paris in 1580 as *Discours admirables, de la nature des eaux et fontaines, tant naturelles qu'artificielles, des métaux, des sels et salines, des pierres, des terres, du feu et des maux.*

147. Chatterley, *DNB*; "Thomas Watson: Works, Contemporary References and Reprints", 241.

148. Bradshaw's identification of Watson at the Anne Burnell enquiry at around this time.

149. Sutton (C4) notes that it is possible that Watson had attended Palissy's public lectures in Paris in 1575.

Six: William Byrd, "our Phoenix"

1. Translation by Dana F Sutton, *Thomas Watson: The Complete Works*.
2. Alan Stewart, *Philip Sidney*, 55; Wyman H Herendeen, "William Camden", *DNB*.
3. Perhaps he had known Sidney previously. Thomas Thornton was possibly the "Mr Thornton" who tutored Sidney and his three siblings in his household in 1573 and 1574 (Stewart, 41). Alan Stewart, however, despite the testimony of the monument reading, states that there is no independent authority to affirm that Thornton was Sidney's tutor at Christ Church, only that he was (in Sidney's own words) his "reader" (Stewart, 54 and 331 n67). Dr Thornton was later appointed to the cannonry on Sidney's recommendation—his first venture into public affairs. Thornton became twice vice-chancellor at Oxford and master of Ledbury Hospital in Hertfordshire.
4. John Harley, *William Byrd*, 366; J A Westrup, "William Byrd", 125. In Elizabethan days the term "Phoenix" meant a paragon.
5. Watson's friendship with Camden helped him make another important connection. Camden had a close friend named William Heyther, a lay clerk at Westminster between 1586 and 1615. Heyther was destined for higher things—later he became a gentleman of the Chapel Royal and gave his name to the Oxford chair of music. Camden and Heyther had a mutual friend in William Byrd. (Harley, 27).
6. "*Cantica et servita divina bene modulate*". (Harley, 44).
7. Jeremy L Smith, *Thomas East and Music Publishing*, 29-31.
8. Smith, *Thomas East and Music Publishing*, 29-33.
9. Laurence Dreyfus, "Consort Songs by William Byrd", 19.
10. Harley, 27.
11. William Byrd: *Psalmes, Sonets and Songs*, 1588.
12. Jeremy L Smith, "William Byrd's Fall from Grace".
13. Byrd, William. *Psalmes, Sonets and Songs*, 1588, 155-70.
14. John Milsom, "Byrd, Sidney, and the Art of Melting"; Denise Pelusch, "William

Byrd's Codes"; Harley, 232-3.

15. In 1580, wranglings over the Battyshall lease became particularly irksome for Byrd until Oxford finally sold the lease to Byrd's brother John.

16. For example, Byrd, 63-72.

17. Harley, 232-3.

18. Sybil M Jack, "William Paget", *DNB*.

19. Christopher Harrison, "William Byrd and the Pagets of Beaudesert", 53.

20. Jack.

21. His connections are another revelation of the close interrelationships between the wealthy families of the Tudor period, and the importance of the East Anglian dynasties. He was married in 1562 to Catherine Knyvett of Buckenham, Norfolk, whose niece was Anne Vavasour: her sister Margaret was Anne's mother. On Henry's death Catherine married Sir Edward Carey (after the death of his first wife Catherine, daughter of Henry Walsingham), cousin of Lord Hunsden and father of Henry Carey, First Viscount Falkland, Lord Deputy of Ireland.

22. S A J McVeigh, "The Decline of Recusancy in North-West Middlesex", 57.

23. Harrison, 51.

24. Harrison, 53.

25. Harrison, 53.

26. Harrison, 55.

27. Harley, 50.

28. Harley, 40.

29. Harley, 59.

30. Harrison, 57-61.

31. Parry himself would be less fortunate. Later hanged, drawn and quartered, his case is narrated in Francis Edwards S J, *Plots and Plotters in the Reign of Elizabeth I*, 100-124.

32. John Bossy, "William Byrd Investigated, 1583-84"; Jeremy L Smith, "William Byrd's Fall from Grace".

33. Bossy.

34. Harrison, 54; Harley, 49.

35. Peter Holmes, "Thomas Paget", *DNB*.

36. CHAPTER FOUR, 83 (and 276, en 23 and 24).

37. Noted Harley, 359-61.

38. Harley, 103, fn 194.

39. Harley, 293; Kerry McCarthy, "Byrd's Patrons at Prayer", 504-8.

40. Harley, 101; 103.

41. According to the French ambassador, Mauvissière. (Cited, Mark Eccles, *Christopher Marlowe in London*, 133).

42. McCarthy, 504.

43. Harley, 116; McCarthy, 500.

44. McCarthy, 504.

45. Byrd: *Gradualia I (1605): The Marian Masses,* ed Philip Brett, *The Byrd Edition,* 5 (London 1989), xiii-xiv. Cited, McCarthy, 499.

46. F G Emmison, *Tudor Secretary*, 8-21; David Mateer, "William Byrd, John Petre and Oxford, Bodleian MS Mus. Sch. E.423".

47. Emmison, 32; 123; 210-16; 288.

48. A C Edwards, *John Petre*, 31.

49. Emmison, 215-6.

50. Emmison, 212.

51. Harley, 92-3 fn 143.

52. Emmison, 212.

53. David C Price, *Patrons and Musicians of the English Renaissance*, 87.

54. A C Edwards, 16.

55. Emmison, 213; A C Edwards, 15; Price, 28.

56. A C Edwards, 15-17.

57. A C Edwards, 17.

58. Susan Kybett: "A Malnourished King?" *History Today*, 38:9 (September 1989).

59. Emmison, 268.

60. A C Edwards, 26.

61. Edmund H Fellowes, *The English Madrigal*, 99.

62. A C Edwards, 27.

63. A C Edwards, 85.

64. A C Edwards, 85.

65. Harley, 94.

66. Harley, 40.

67. Harley, 40.

68. Harley, 94.

69. A C Edwards, 73.

70. Emmison, 213.

71. Price, 87.

72. Godfrey Anstruther, *Vaux of Harrowden*, 168; A C Edwards, 30; Emmison, 213. John Bolt has sometimes been confused with Richard Bold, another Catholic convert and a former chamberlain to the Earl of Leicester whose home became a refuge

for some of the Babington plotters.

73. Harley, 251 fn 23.

74. Harley, 251 fn 23; Hilda Andrews (Ed), *My Ladye Nevells Booke*, xlii.

75. Andrews, xlii.

76. Another Norfolk born figure.

77. J H Pollen SJ, "Official Lists of Catholic Prisoners during the Reign of Queen Elizabeth. Part II: 1581-1602". Catholic Record Society, 2 (1906), 226-30, 284, 288. Cited by David Mateer, "William Byrd's Middlesex Recusancy", 5.

78. Harley, 68.

79. William Weston, *The Autobiography of an Elizabethan*, 71.

80. Mateer, 9.

81. Thomas Alfield, *A true reporte of the death and martyrdome of M. Campion Jesuite and preiste, & M Sherwin, & M Bryan preistes, at Tiborne the first of December 1581*, London, Vallenger, 1582 (STC 4537, sig. B3^v.) Cited Gerard Kilroy, *Edmund Campion*, 38.

82. *A discoverie of Edmund Campion* (1581).

83. George Eliot, *A very true report of the apprehension and taking of that arche papist Edmond Campion the pope his right hand* (1581). Cited by Alice Hogge, *God's Secret Agents*, 91 fn; Donna B Hamilton, *Anthony Munday and the Catholics*, 38.

84. In J H Pollen, *A Briefe Historie of the Glorious Martyrdom of Twelve Reverend Priests Father Edmund Campion and His Companions* (London, 1908).

85. Robert Dow the younger, *The Dow Partbooks*. Cited in Rebecca Redmann, "William Byrd, the Catholics and the Consort Song".

86. Weston, 70-71.

87. Philip Caraman S J, *Henry Garnet*, 34.

88. A third sister, Elizabeth, had joined a French convent in 1582.

89. Smith, Jeremy L. "William Byrd's Fall from Grace"; Above, CHAPTER ONE.

90. Dreyfus, 21.

Seven: A brawl in Hog Lane

1. These expressions of personal loss in the *Hekatompathia* are drawn to our attention by Albert Chatterley, "Thomas Watson: Poet—and Musician?", 86.

2. J L Chester, Sir G J Armitage, *The Parish Registers of St Antholin, Budge Lane, London. Containing the Marriages, Baptisms and Burials from 1538-1754.* Harleian Society, London. Registers Vol VIII. 1883, 31; Budge Row was a short road which linked with others to trace the course of Watling Street across the city.

3. Richard died a pauper in 1578, his wife five years later. See Chatterley's painstaking research in "Two Sixteenth-Century East Anglian Families".

4. Joseph Kerman thinks they include three "Areopagite" poems: "Constant Penelope" (no. 23) translated from Ovid, and two unrhymed "Funeral Songs" (nos. 34 and 35) for Sidney. (Joseph Kerman, *The Elizabethan Madrigal*, 10 fn 1). John Harley gives no attribution to "Constant Penelope", and suggests that perhaps either Watson or Edward Dyer wrote nos. 34 and 35. (John Harley, *William Byrd*, 410).

5. Jeremy L Smith, *Thomas East and Music Publishing*, 191 n1.

6. Until 1608. (Smith, 55).

7. Smith gives the fullest information on Thomas East and his background.

8. Chatterley suggests Watson may have met Case during Lasko's visit to England in 1583. (Albert Chatterley, Thomas Watson, Italian Madrigals Englished, xxiv fn2).

9. They are somewhat scattered. The "cantus secundus" is shelved in the Cambridge University Library and the "bassus" in the Bodleian Library. A *copy* of the "medius" part is in the Royal College of Music.

10. Joseph Kerman, *The Elizabethan Madrigal*, 9.

11. Albert Chatterley adopted the same technique in his modern translation, *Amyntas and Phyllis: The Pastorals of Thomas Watson (c1555-1592) interpreted in English Verse*.

12. Chatterley, "Thomas Watson: Poet—and Musician?", 79.

13. Many pieces in Byrd's *Psalms, Sonnets, & Songs of Sadness and Piety*, published a few months earlier, were akin to madrigals, but not described as such. (See, David Brown, "William Byrd's 1588 Volume").

14. Kerman, 57 fn 2.

15. Much of the information in this paragraph is to be found in Mark Eccles, *Christopher Marlowe in London*, passim.

16. His father was a victualler on the eastern corner of Gray's Inn Lane. In 1592 Orrell and a companion broke into the neighbouring house of Aaron Holland, the owner of the Red Bull playhouse, and nearly killed both Holland and his wife. Orrell later became famous as a captain under Lord Monteagle in the Irish campaigns, and was prominent in Essex's rebellion, afterwards described in a state record as "a most desperate rakehell as lives". (Eccles, 61-2).

17. In the first edition of his *Survey of London* dated 1598 Stow dated this change as "these forty-four years last" and in his second edition of 1603 "within these forty years" (John Stow, *The Survey of London*, 116). The earlier view is depicted in the "Agas" map of 1561 and the "Copperplate" map of 1553-9. (Prockter and Taylor [Compilers], *The A to Z of Elizabethan London*); https://mapoflondon.uvic.ca/agas.htm;

https://www.british-history.ac.uk/no-series/london-map-agas/1561

18. There have been several flights of fancy in the narrations of this famous fight. Some have taken to the sky in minor details, such as the one stating that Bradley forced Watson against a ditch on the northern side of Hog Lane. There is no evidence to say whether it was the northern or the southern side. A spiced-up example inspired by Shakespeare's *Romeo and Juliet* I:i depicts Bradley inciting the fight by taunting Marlowe on his fine actor's clothes and insulting him by biting his thumb at him (William Honey, *The Life, Loves and Achievements of Christopher Marlowe Alias Shakespeare*, 200). None of these fictional narrations derive from the primary source, namely the Middlesex Sessions Roll 284, no. 12. I have quoted from Charles Norman's translation of the Latin (Charles Norman, *The Muses' Darling*, 93-4).

19. Not Newgate, as generally narrated. (Clifford Dobb, "London's Prisons", 88 and 253 fn2)

20. Ion Chalkhill (died 1615) I assume to be the father of the minor poet John Chalkhill (c1595-1642).

21. In his accusation of Marlowe in 1592 Richard Baines alleged that Marlowe was involved with Poole in the counterfeiting of coins at Flushing while they were together in the Netherlands. Counterfeiting was a capital offence (the penalty: boiling in oil). Charles Nicholl, *The Reckoning, passim*, gives a good account of the affair.

22. Later indicted for knifing a neighbour named Finch. (Leslie Hotson, "Marlowe Among the Churchwardens", 37-44).

23. Hotson, 37-44.

24. Four years later, in 1593, Thomas Kyd suffered horrific torture when "vile heretical conceits" were discovered amongst papers in a room he shared with Marlowe in Shoreditch or Norton Feldgate. Marlowe's release on bail contrasts with the treatment meted out to Kyd.

25. Thomas Watson, *Poems*, 172-5.

26. Watson, 142; Park Honan, *Christopher Marlowe: Poet and Spy*.

27. Honan, 226-7.

Eight: The Elvetham entertainment

1. Compare with *Amintae Gaudia*, Eclogue VI.38ff. (Dana F Sutton, *Thomas Watson, The Complete Works*).

2. Katherine Chiljan, *Shakespeare Suppressed.*

3. *Honourable Entertainement gieven to the Quenes Majestie, in Progresse, at Elvetham in Hampshire, by the Right Honourable the Earle of Hertford"*, 9. The Latin text is followed by an English translation "Because all our Countrymen are not Latinists, I think it not amiss to set this down in English, that all may be indifferently partakers of the Poet's meaning." (*Ibid,* 8-9).

4. *Honourable Entertainement,* 9.

5. *Honourable Entertainement,* 11.

6. *Honourable Entertainement,*13.

7. Harry H Boyle, "Elizabeth's entertainment at Elvetham", 145-66.

8. Boyle, 149.

9. Boyle, 256, quoting J L Motley: *History of the United Netherlands,* Vol II, 91.

10. Boyle,157, summarising the text of *Honourable Entertainement,* 21-2.

11. *Honourable Entertainement,* 29.

12. *Honourable Entertainement,* 30.

13. Boyle bases much of his material on R Warwick Bond, *The Complete Works of John Lyly* (Oxford, 1902), but questions Bond's evidence for Lyly's contribution to the entertainment.

14. As he called himself in his *History of the Life and Reign of Richard the Third.* (Quoted Mark Eccles, "Sir George Buc, Master of the Revels" in Charles Sisson [Ed], *Thomas Lodge and Other Elizabethans,* 475).

15. Boyle,163-5; Arthur Kincaid, "Sir George Buck", *DNB.*

16. Boyle, 164.

17. Eccles, "Sir George Buc" 447-8. Anne was the first wife of Edmund Tilney, Master of the Revels (whose cousin Philip's son was, incidentally, the Babington conspirator Charles Tilney). Edmund Tilney was the cousin of the husband of Buc's aunt by marriage. See the pedigree in Sisson, 507.

18. Hugh Chisholm, *Encyclopaedia Britannica,* Vol 4 (CUP, 1911. 11th Edition). (Cited Wikipedia).

19. Gascoigne's works have been claimed as sources for Shakespeare's *Comedy of Errors, The Taming of the Shrew, Rome and Juliet* and probably *Othello, Hamlet* and *A Midsummer Night's Dream.* His *Jocasta* provided themes for both *The Taming of the Shrew* and Marlowe's *Tamburlaine.* (Gillian Austen, *George Gascoigne,* 7).

20. Austen 8, 24-5.

21. Michael G Brennan, "Nicholas Breton", *DNB.*

22. De Vere and Gascoigne were no friends. Soon after his unofficial appoint-- ment as Poet Laureate in 1576 (gained with the connivance of Christopher Hatton),

Gascoigne published *The Posies of George Gascoigne* in which he claimed sole authorship of all its poems. The volume was a rehash of *A Hundred Sundrie Flowres* of 1573 which was the work of several hands, including those of de Vere who was probably its editor and publisher. (B M Ward, *The Seventeenth Earl of Oxford*, 130-142; Ruth Loyd Miller [Ed] and Bernard M Ward, *A Hundreth Sundrie Flowres*, 110-302).

23. Although, just as likely, one at least of these may have been by John Lyly.

24. Discussed in Margaret P Hannay, *Philip's Phoenix*, 136-9.

25. Hannay, 109; 131.

26. The son of Sir John Yorke, a former Master of the Mint. Edward was a servant of the Earl of Leicester, and later a vice-admiral in the navy. His brother Rowland Yorke volunteered for the Netherlands in 1572 with two companions, one of whom was George Gascoigne. For a few years Rowland Yorke was the steward and close companion of the Earl of Oxford.

27. Alan H Nelson, *Monstrous Adversary*, 109.

28. By eight years; he was born in 1547. Some historians have confused the brothers.

29. Gabriel Harvey, *Three letters* (1580).

30. Nelson, 287.

31. *The Pilgrimage to Paradise* (1592). See Brennan.

32. Mark Anderson, *Shakespeare by Another Name*, 249-50 and 521 (note) citing Richard Jones and Hyder Edward Rollins (Eds), *Brittons Bowre of Delights, 1591* (Cambridge, Mass., 1933).

33. Eccles, "Sir George Buc", 475-6. Quoted from a manuscript damaged by fire in 1731 at Ashburnham House in the Cotton Library and manuscript collection.

34. W Ron Hess, *The Dark Side of Shakespeare*, I:277-80. See CHAPTER NINE.

35. Sutton corroborates his conclusions, General Introduction, Section 25.

36. *Honourable Entertainement*.

37. See CHAPTER FIVE.

38. Introduction to Robert Green's *Menaphon* (London, 1589).

39. *Honourable Entertainement*; Sutton, *Honourable Entertainement*. Albert Chatterley ("Thomas Watson and the 'Elvetham entertainment'") translates the general tenor of these passages,

> "[Our love speaks a word with his mouth, and produces the olive of peace with his eyes]
> His words speak of duty, the olive means peace;
> Through duty he will summon affection in peace he brings tranquillity;
> And he blesses minds with affection, and limbs with rest."

40. Chatterley.

41. Lillian M Ruff and D Arnold Wilson, "The Madrigal, the Lute Song and Elizabethan Politics".

42. Chatterley.

43. *Honourable Entertainement*, 29.

Nine: Scandal in the Cornwallis household

1. James G McManaway, "The Folger Shakespeare Library", 57-78; Stephen H. Grant, *Collecting Shakespeare: The Story of Henry and Emily Folger*, passim.

2. Searchable online. Filed at the Folger library as *Leaves from a poetical miscellany of Anne Campbell,Countess of Argyll [manuscript] ca.1600*. Digital Image File Name 540.50. Call no (Hamnet) V.a.89.

3. Inaccurately. The eleventh Earl was Richard Vere (1385-1417). The John Vere noted on the family tree is the twelfth Earl (1408-61). Anne was, of course, descended from both!

4. Perhaps the Elizabethan leading actor John Bentley, who died in 1585, described as "inimitable" by Thomas Dekker in *A Knight's Conjuring (1607)*, although William H Bond, "The Cornwallis-Lysons Manuscript and the Poems of John Bentley", casts cold water on this attribution.

5. The poem also appears in *England's Helicon (1600)* where it is—probably wrongly—attributed to Dyer.

6. Perhaps Gervase Markam, or more likely George Montemayor (Jorge de Montemayor, 1520?–1561) a well-travelled Portuguese novelist and poet who may have accompanied Philip II to England in 1555. Shakespeare is said to have translated some episodes in *The Two Gentlemen of Verona* from his works.

7. Mistress of the seventeenth Earl of Oxford. Her works were written between 1579 and 1581.

8. In the *Cornwallis-Lysons Manuscript* the line quoted appears as "When that thine eye hath chose the dame". *The Passionate Pilgrim* was published in two editions in 1598 or 1599 by William Jaggard. The text was undoubtedly pirated. Traditional scholars attribute five of its twenty poems as definitely by Shakespeare. Attribution of the others is open to dispute. Jaggard published a third edition in 1612 to which he added poems from a 1609 volume, Thomas Heywood's *Troia Britanica*. Heywood was extremely annoyed. A good introduction to the problem of attribution in *The Passionate Pilgrim* is by an author who thinks all the poems were

by Shakespeare: Katherine Chiljan, *Shakespeare Suppressed*, 89-96 (these pages were also excerpted in *The Oxfordian*, 14 [2012]).

9. The succession of owners is listed in Ruth Loyd Miller (Ed), *Thomas Looney. "Shakespeare" Identified* Vol. II, 385 fn 1.

10. Despite a long acrimonious relationship with his bibliomaniac father-in-law Sir Thomas Phillipps, on Sir Thomas's death in 1872 Halliwell adopted his name, to become known henceforth as Halliwell-Phillipps. Much of Halliwell-Phillipps' Shakespearian collection ended up in the hands of Henry Clay Folger in 1908. A brief and entertaining biography of Halliwell-Phillipps is narrated in Arthur Freeman and Janet Ing Freeman, "James Orchard Halliwell-Phillipps (1820-1889)."

11. James Orchard Halliwell: *Catalogue of Shakespeare Reliques in the Possession of James Orchard Halliwell, Esq., FRS*.

12. That is, by the time Halliwell's edition of the works of Shakespeare was published in 1853-65, when, because this single attribution did not fit the accepted Shakespearean chronology, he re-dated the manuscript to 1595. (Bond, 685).

13. Bond, 685-6.

14. Bond, 685-6; Curt F Bühler, "Four Elizabethan Poems", 695-706.

15. Bond, 686.

16. Alison Plowden, *Danger to Elizabeth*, 109.

17. P B Whitt, "New Light on Sir William Cornwallis, the Essayist", *passim*.

18. Whitt, 156, quoting from John Gage, *The History and Antiquities of Hengrave in Suffolk* (1822).

19. By his first wife, Mary Cheke.

20. Alan H Nelson, *Monstrous Adversary*, 320, quoting from *A Calendar of the Manuscripts of the most Honourable the Marquis of Salisbury ... at Hatfield House (Cecil Papers)* (1883-1976), iii, 378 (17/60).

21. It lay just north of the junction with Hounsditch, the London Wall and Bishops Gate itself, and nearly opposite St Botolph's Church and the Bethlehem Hospital for the Insane (Bedlam). (Mark Anderson, *Shakespeare by Another Name*, 156, 487n; Adrian Prockter and Robert Taylor, [Compilers], *The A to Z of Elizabethan London*, 12, 30).

22. John Stow: *A Survey of London*, 149.

23. Nelson, 319, quoting *Cecil Papers*, iii, 377.

24. They were first published in 1842. A Modern edition with a good introduction is Joanna Moody (ed), *The Private Correspondence of Jane Lady Cornwallis Bacon, 1613-44* (Rosemont, USA, 2003).

25. *Ruth Loyd Miller (Ed)*, 391-4; Charles Wisner Barrell, "Earliest Authenticated

'Shakespeare' Transcript".

26. Whitt, 157.

27. It is worth reflecting on another curiosity regarding Buc. A copy of the play *George-a-Greene, the Pinner of Wakefield,* printed in 1599 though written before 1593 (H Dugdale Sykes, "Robert Greene and *George a Greene, the Pinner of Wakefield*". The Review of English Studies, 7:26, April 1931, 120) bears an inscription, apparently in Buc's handwriting, "Written by … A minister, who ac[ted] the piners part in it himself. Teste W Shakespea[re]." Because the attention of the literary world was drawn to this material during the period when the notorious forger John Collier was about his dubious work, some have doubted its authenticity. Nevertheless, the consensus seems that it really is in Buc's hand and is authentic. (W W Greg, "Three Manuscript Notes by Sir George Buc"; R C Bald, "The *Locrine* and *George-a-Greene* Title-Page Inscriptions"). Buc refers to Shakespeare not as a writer, but simply as a person connected with the theatre. The inscription illustrates Buc's wide connections as Master of the Revels.

28. For example, Rosalind K Marshall, "Anne Cornwallis", *DNB*, and H R Woudhuysen, *Sir Philip Sidney and the Circulation of Manuscripts 1558-1640*, 258.

29. Albert Chatterley, "Two Sixteenth-Century East Anglian Families at the Court of Star Chamber", 122.

30. Charles Nicholl, *A Cup of News*, 204-5.

31. W Ron Hess, *The Dark Side of Shakespeare* Vol I, 280, Vol II, 1-78 and *passim*, and Hess's website, *passim*. Its discussion requires a volume to itself.

32. Chatterley, 122.

33. Thomas (d.1572); John (1573?-1594); Frances (1575-1625); Elizabeth (1578-1658); Cornelia; Anne (d.1635); Thomas (d.1626). Sir William had two later children by his second wife Jane Meautys. (National Archives Probate 11/118/441, Will of Sir William Cornwallis, 22 October 1611).

34. Worse still, the visit was followed by an outbreak of plague, rumoured to have been brought to the city in the Queen's baggage train. The plague raged for nearly two years and resulted in nearly 5,000 deaths. (June Osborne, *Entertaining Elizabeth*, 50-3; Zillah Dovey, *An Elizabethan Progress*, 87).

35. Osborne, 51; Dovey, 71-2.

36. Osborne, 52, quoting from John Nichols, *The Progresses and Public Processions of Queen Elizabeth I* (London, 1788-1823); Dovey, 80-1, quoting from Thomas Churchyard, *A Discovrse of the Queenes Maiesties entertainement in Suffolk and Norfolk 1540-1642.*

37. Hubert Hall, "An Elizabethan Poet and his Relations". Hall quotes in full a letter from Cornwallis to Sir Thomas Heneage on the 15 March 1593. His source is the Tower Miscellaneous Rolls No 458 (in the Darryll Papers), and from the Star

Chamber Proceedings Eliz. Bundle XXXIII, No 38.

38. Chatterley, 121 quoting Bodleian Library, Tanner MS 97, 35.

39. Michael Drayton in his *Poets and Poesies* (1627) thought little of either:
> *Gascoine* and *Churchyard* after them again
> In the beginning of *Eliza's* rein
> Accounted were great Meterers many a day,
> But not inspired with brave fire, had they
> Liv'd but a little longer, they had seen,
> Their works before them to have buried been.
>
> (Cyril Brett, Ed.: *The Minor Poems of Michael Drayton*, Oxford, 1907, 108-113).

40. In 1593, William's sister, Lady Kytson of Hengrave Hall in Suffolk, took a young lutenist under her wing. His name was John Wilby. By and by he matured into the renowned madrigal composer.

41. See CHAPTER ONE.

42. As much of the story as can now be recovered was unravelled by the late Albert Chatterley from Star Chamber documents and papers in the Bodleian Library, Oxford. The summary here is largely based on Chatterley's research ("Two Sixteenth-Century East Anglian Families at the Court of Star Chamber"), and on Hall.

43. Hall.

44. Since January 1589.

45. Chatterley, 125. Goldingham was a singer and writer who had helped with the Kenilworth and Norwich entertainments. Sprignall, it seems, was a musician in Cornwallis's household, perhaps the successor to Swift. "Sprignall" is likely in error for Springall, a fairly common Norfolk name.

46. Chatterley, 125.

47. 29 April 1595 at St Botolph's.

48. Other reports said that he was killed by a fall from his horse.

49. Chatterley, 127, quoting Bodleian Library, Toner MS 97, 31.

50. Mounson was also on the reserve list.

Ten: "Dearly loved and honoured"

1. 1598.
2. John Stow, *The Survey of London*, 148.
3. John Stow, *The Survey of London*, 149.
4. Paul Slack, *The Impact of Plague in Tudor and Stuart England*, 160.

5. Slack, 68.

6. Slack, 62, Table 3.4. Slack also points out that plague was imported from Portugal into Devon, 66.

7. "26 Sept 1592. Thomas Watson, gent, was buried."

8. Albert Chatterley, "Two Sixteenth-Century East Anglian Families", 127. Chatterley was alerted by Mark Eccles, *Christopher Marlowe in London*, 64. The reference to Swift's reappearance is King's Bench 27/1335, m 588.

9. Margrethe Jolly, *The First Two Quartos of* Hamlet, 170, citing G C Moore Smith, *Gabriel Harvey's Margenali* (Stratford-on-Avon, 1913), 464.

10. For example, Thomas Nashe's anecdote in his *Have with You to Saffron Walden* of 1596, quoted below.

11. R B McKerrow (Ed), *A Dictionary of Printers and Booksellers*, 217-8.

12. In all, Ponsonby published ten volumes of Spenser's works.

13. On 18 May 1593 the Privy Council instructed "Henry Maunder, one of the messengers of H. M. chamber to repair to the house of Mr. Thomas Walsingham in Kent, or to any other place where he shall understand Christopher Marlowe to be remaining, and to bring him to the court." (The National Archives, *Acts of the Privy Council, 1592–3*, 244).

14. Bodleian Library. Rawlinson MS 85.f.16.

15. William Minto, *Characteristics of English Poets.*

16. Sutton, Dana F, *Thomas Watson, The Complete Works.* Another interesting resonance is in Sonnet 25, which reads as follows:

> The private place which I did chose to wail,
> And dear lament my love's pride was a grove;
> Plac'd twixt two hills within a lowly dale,
> Which now by fame was called the vale of love.
> Plaints that betrayed my sick heart's bitter wounding:
> Love sick hearts deep wounds with despair me paining
> The bordering hills my sorrow plaints resounding.
> Each tree did bear the figure of her name,
> Which my faint hand upon their backs engraved:
> And every tree did seem her for to blame,
> Calling her proud that me of joys depraved.
> But vain for she had vowed to forsake me.
> And I to endless anguish must betake me.

Lines 8 and 9, "Each tree did bear the figure of her name / Which my faint hand upon their back engraved" has an echo of Shakespeare's Sonnet 76, lines 7 and 8 quoted at the start of CHAPTER TWO, "That every word doth almost tell my name / Showing their birth, and where they did proceed".

17. Its title page reads, "*Axiochus, a most excellent dialogue written in Greek by Plato the philosopher concerning the shortness and uncertainty of this life, with the contrary ends of the good and wicked. Translated out of Greek by Edw.* [sic] *Spenser. Hereto is annexed a sweet speech or oration spoken at the triumph at Whitehall before her Majesty by the page to the right noble Earl of Oxenford.* At London, printed for Cuthbert Burby, and are to be sold at the middle shop in the Poultry under St. Mildred's Church. Anno 1592". The *Short Title Catalogue* notes that, "Burby printed few if any of the books which bear his name on their title-pages, and according to David Kathman, the *Axiochus* was printed by John Danter and John Charlwood." (STC 19974.6).

18. The Second Quarto was printed by James Roberts for Edward White and appeared in 1600.

19. Nancy Peters Maude, "The Extended Collaboration of John Dante and Edward Allde"; McKerrow, 83-4.

20. Nashe, *Have with you to Saffron Walden*. Cited by Thomas Chatterley, "Thomas Watson: Works, Contemporary References and Reprints", 247.

21. Chatterley, "The Tears of Fancie or Love Disdained by T.W. (1593)."

22. Dana F Sutton, *Thomas Watson, The Complete Works*; Chatterley, "The Tears of Fancie"; APPENDIX D.

23. *Polimanteia or the Meanes Lawful and Unlawfull to Judge of the Fall of a Commonwealth*. (https://archive.org/details/polimanteiaormea00cove)

24. "So well graced Anthonie deserveth immortal praise from the hand of that divine Lady who like Corinna contending with Pindarus was oft victorious". Albert Chatterley offers the best explanation of what he describes as this "complex" reference: "Covell seems to be comparing Mary, Countess of Pembroke (and Watson's final dedicatee) to whom Daniel had addressed prefatory verses in his *Cleopatra* of 1594 (there calling her "divine lady"), to Corinna, the Greek poetess and contemporary of Pindar, who was said to have sometime instructed him, and to have gained a victory over him at the Public Games at Thebes." (Chatterley, "Thomas Watson: Works, Contemporary References and Reprints", 242).

25. In the margin of the previous page, adjoining a text praising Spenser (representing Cambridge) and John Daniel (representing Oxford) appear the notes: "All praiseworthy. Lucrecia Sweet Shakspeare. Eloquent Gaveston". There has been some debate about the meaning of this whole group of marginal comments. Interpreters usually join the phrases together, and add the two phrases "Wanton Adonis. Watson's heir" from the top of the following page, R3, making five phrases

in total. However, a wider space after the first two words "All praiseworthy" which refer to the adjoining body text, are clearly unconnected with the expressions which follow. The comment "Lucrecia Sweet Shakspeare" undoubtedly refers to Shakespeare's then popular poems *Venus and Adonis* (1593) and *Lucrece* (1594); "Gaveston" probably refers to Michael Drayton's *The Legend of Piers Gaveston* (1594?), rather than to the character of Gaveston in Marlowe's *Edward II*. (See, K Duncan-Jones and H R Woudhuysen [Eds]: Shakespeare's *Poems*, Arden Shakespeare, 2007).

26. The printer of Harington's work was John Danter, whom we have already met; for the second work Danter collaborated with John Allde. Both books were printed around the time of the destruction of Danter's presses. It would seem sensible to assume that Danter was forced to call on the aid of a fellow printer to finish any work he had in hand, but recent research has suggested that this is not necessarily the case and that the arrangement between Danter and Allde was a normal business one. (Nancy Peters Maude, *passim*). Around this time, Danter and Allde also collaborated on a corrupt Quarto of *Romeo and Juliet* (Q1).

27. Thus the first edition. "John" was corrected to "Tom" in later editions.

28. Richard Bowers and Paul S Smith, "Sir John Harrington, High Plat, and *Ulysses Upon Ajax*".

29. *The jewell house of arte and nature, conteining divers rare and profitable inventions, together with sundry new experiments in the art of husbandry, distillation and moulding, faithfully and familiarly set downe according to the authors own experience*. Down

30. As briefly noted in CHAPTER FOUR, Heneage was the temporary custodian of Walsingham's spy network after 1590. Some historians suggest (quoting unlikely anecdotal evidence) that Shakespeare's *A Midsummer Night's Dream* might have been written for wedding celebrations held at Copped Hall in 1594 for the elderly Heneage and his young bride (by nineteen years) the Dowager Countess of Southampton. Heneage died the following year.

31. Peters Maude, *passim*.

32. Edward Arber, (Ed). *Thomas Watson: Poems*, 17. Professor Arber edited Watson's English poems, excluding the madrigals, in his series of English reprints in 1870 and another issue in 1895.

33. Walter F Staton Jr, "Thomas Watson and Ovidian Poetry", *passim*.

34. Edmund Spenser's high regard for Watson has sometimes been cited. However, Chatterley discounts the citations of Spenser's reference (in *Colin Clout's come home again* [1595]) to Amyntas as a patron of the poets as well as a poet himself. This, says Chatterley, is "clearly" a reference to Ferdinando Stanley, fifth Earl of Derby

(Chatterley, "Thomas Watson: Works, Contemporary References and Reprints", 248). Spenser also draws Amyntas into his work in Book III of *The Faerie Queene* (1590). Here he describes the Garden of Adonis where in an arbour "grew every sort of flower" including

> Sad Amaranthus, made a flower but late,
> Sad Amaranthus in whose purple gore
> Me seems I see Amintas wretched fate,
> To whom sweet Poets verse hath given endless date.

Again, this "Amintas" is not Watson as he still had two years of life left to him when these lines were published in 1590. One interpretation is that Spenser's "Amaranthus" and "Amintas" refer to the "*verse*" of two "Poets", rather than to the poets themselves, and that the "Poets" are either Watson or Fraunce, or quite probably both. (Harry Morris, "'Amyntas' and the Sidney Circle", who credits William Ringler and C Elliot Browne with this theory). Watson has also been identified, dubiously, with the 'happy Menalcas,' addressed in a laudatory poem by Thomas Lodge in *A Fig for Momus* (1595). See also CHAPTER THREE, note 36.

35. *The Affectionate Shepherd*, Part 2 (1594).
36. *Four Letters* (1592).
37. Chatterley, "Thomas Watson: Works, Contemporary References and Reprints", 247.
38. Chatterley, "Thomas Watson: Works, Contemporary References and Reprints", 246.

Notes to Appendices A-E

1. Constance Brown Kuriyama, *Christopher Marlowe: A Renaissance Life*, 6. Cited by J A Downie, "Marlow, May 1593, and the 'Must-Have' Theory of Biography", 3.
2. William Honey, *The Life, Loves and Achievements of Christopher Marlowe Alias Shakespeare*.
3. Honey, 48.
4. Honey, 51-55.
5. Honey, 48-49; 55.
6. Honey, 55.
7. Kuriyama, 2-3. Cited by Downie, 8.
8. Honey, 59-65.
9. All references to the Dedication are from Edward Arber (Ed), *Thomas Watson: Poems*, 25-6.

10. One of Apelles' most outstanding paintings depicted Alexander the Great holding a thunderbolt. This image reminds one of Gabriel Harvey's Latin oration at Audley End in 1578 which concluded with a comparison of the Earl of Oxford to Pallas Athena, the Goddess of Truth: "Thine eyes flash fire, Thy countenance shakes a speare". To the best of my knowledge, Watson's comparison of Oxford with Apelles has not been taken up by Oxfordians. A hereditary title of de Vere before he succeeded as Earl of Oxford was Lord Bulbec; the Bulbec crest shows a lion brandishing a broken spear.

11. For example, by B M Ward, *The Seventeenth Earl of Oxford 1550-1604*, 196.

12. Arber, 103.

13. Ward, 196.

14. CHAPTER FIVE; Arber, 9.

15. *The Decameron*, X, 8.

16. Eva Lee Turner Clark, *Hidden Allusions in Shakespeare's Plays*, 47-59, argues, surely erroneously, that the court play *The historye of Titus and Gisippus* performed by the "Children of Pawles" on Shrove Tuesday in 1576 was *Titus Andronicus*.

17. Kevin Gilvary (ed), *Dating Shakespeare's Plays*, 57.

18. Arber, 107.

19. Franklin M Dickey, "The Old Man at Work: Forgeries in the Stationers' Registers". *Shakespeare Quarterly*, 11 (1960), 39-47.

20. Dana F Sutton, *Thomas Watson: The Complete Works*.

21. Albert Chatterley, "The Tears of Fancie or Love Disdained by T.W. (1593)".

22. Quite recently Michael J Hirrel, "Thomas Watson, Playwright: Origins of Modern English Drama", has been another voice to put forward the case for Watson as playwright using much the same evidence as offered here. Hirrel boldly commences his essay, "Thomas Watson surely was the most important playwright in English none of whose plays survive."

23. "These are our best for Tragedy, the Lord Buckhurst, Doctor Leg of Cambridge, Doctor Edes of Oxford, master Edward Ferris, the Author of the *Mirrour for Magistrates*, Marlowe, Peele, Watson, Kyd, Shakespeare, Drayton, Chapman, Decker, and Benjamin Johnson ...". (Francis Meres, *Palladis Tamia. Wits Treasury. Being the second part of wits Commonwealth.* [London, 1598]).

24. Lillian M Ruff and D Arnold Wilson, "The Madrigal, the Lute Song and Elizabethan Politics", 13, also believe that by employing the expression "knaveries" Cornwallis affirmed that Watson had expressed political or "topical allusion".

25. Only a few plays were published during the 1580s. See John H Astington,

"The London Stage in the 1580s", 1-18.

26. CHAPTER FIVE.
27. CHAPTER FIVE.
28. Arthur Freeman, *Thomas Kyd*, 17-18, 21.
29. CHAPTER NINE.
30. E K Chambers, *The Elizabethan Stage* II, 105-7; Freeman, 22-4.
31. *Gratiae Theatrales, or a Choice Ternary of English Plays Composed upon especial occasions by several ingenious persons* (1662).
32. J O Halliwell-Phillips, FRS, *Cursory Memoranda on Shakespeare's Tragedy of Macbeth. With Early Notices of the Moving Wood Stratagem*. Brighton: Printed by John King Bishop, 1880 (Presscom.co.uk/Macbeth.html).
33. E K Chambers, *The Elizabethan Stage* Vol III, 506.
34. E H C Oliphant, "Problems of Authorship in Elizabethan Dramatic Literature". Modern Philology 19 (1910-11), 437-9.
35. Samuel Schoenbaum, *Internal Evidence and Elizabethan Dramatic Authorship*, (Evanston, 1966), 177; William M Baillie (ed), *A Choice Ternary of English Plays: Gratiae theatrales (1662)* (Binghampton NY, 1984), 25-42, 263-75; Freeman, 20; Sutton, "Notes to Minor Works of Thomas Watson: *Thorny-Abbey or the London Maid"*, unpaginated, from which some of these references are drawn.
36. Abraham Bronson Feldman (1914-1982) sometimes omitted his first name or signed himself A Bronson Feldman.
37. Bronson Feldman, "Thomas Watson, Dramatist". *The Bard*. 1:4 (1977), 129-152; APPENDIX F; *Shakespeare, Marlowe, and Other Elizabethans* (Buchholz, Germany, 2021/22), provisional title of a new collection of Feldman articles pending publication.
38. A Bronson Feldman, *The Unconscious in History*. (New York, 1959).
39. A Bronson Feldman, *Stalin: Red Lord of Russia*. (Philadelphia, 1962).
40. Bronson Feldman, *Hamlet Himself*. (Philadelphia, 1977).
41. Biographical details: A H, "Abraham Bronson Feldman (1914-82)". Shakespeare Oxford Society Newsletter. 18:2 (Spring 1982), 1-3. (https://shakespeareoxfordfellowship,org/wp-content/uploads/SOSNL-1982.compressed.pdf).
42. Feldman, 132-3; APPENDIX F, 224.
43. Feldman, 133. He quotes Alexander Witherspoon, *The Influences of Robert Garnier on Elizabethan Drama* (New York,1924) to support his claim; APPENDIX F, 225.
44. For example: Philip Edwards (ed), *Thomas Kyd, The Spanish Tragedy*, xxiii and 139-40.
45. Freeman, 49.

46. Edwards, xvii.

47. Feldman, 149; APPENDIX F, 251.

48. Freeman, 3.

49. Freeman, 8.

50. Robert Garnier, *Cornélie* (1574).

51. Lukas Erne, *Beyond the Spanish Tragedy*, 203-16.

52. Josephine A Roberts and James F G Gaines, "Kyd and Garnier: The Art of Amendment". *Comparative Literature*, 31 (1979), 124-33.

53. Erne, 209-210. Frank Ardolino has disputed Erne's assertion that Garnier's *Cornélie* "is, in fact, the only contemporary play of which definite traces can be found in *The Spanish Tragedy*, and its influence on Kyd may have been of greater importance than that of any other play of his century" (Erne, 215). Ardolino sees Garnier's *Les Juifves* as a more significant influence (*Notes & Queries*, 62:1 [2015], 64-6).

54. Feldman, 133; APPENDIX F, 225; Note by Edward White, *The Spanish Tragedy*, IV.iv.

55. Feldman, 129-30; APPENDIX F, 220.

56. *The Tragedye of Solyman and Perseda. Wherein is laide open, Loues constancy, Fortunes inconstancy, and Deaths triumphs* (1592). Downloadable from https://sourcetext.files.wordpress.com/2018/01/1599_kyd_soliman.pdf

57. At one time thought to be lost. Only a single 1599 edition is extant, also printed by Allde for White.

58. See CHAPTER THREE.

59. There seems to have been an earlier edition, now lost.

60. The process was deemed illegal by the Stationers' Company which fined both Jeffes and White 10s each for having works printed which belonged to the other. It was reprinted in 1594 by "Abel Jeffes to be sold by Edward White" (Q2), and in the same year White produced yet a third edition.

61. Dating *The Spanish Tragedy* is difficult and complicated. For a good summary of the problems see Laurence Manley and Sally-Beth MacLean, *Lord Strange's Men and Their Plays*, 78-85.

62. Edwards, xxx-xl.

63. "Kyd's handwriting, as it survives in two letters of 1593-4 to Sir John Puckering, is remarkably clear and formal: it is perhaps the finest secretary hand among all those represented in Greg's *English Literary Autographs*, and Greg himself thinks it shows the training of a scrivener" (Feldman, 12; APPENDIX F).

64. Feldman, 131; APPENDIX F, 222.

65. *A Courtlie Controversie of Cupids Cautels containing five Tragicall Historyes*

by three Gentlemen and two Gentlewomen.

66. J R Mulryne in Thomas Kyd, *The Spanish Tragedy*, xvii.67. APPENDIX F, 222-3; Manley and MacLean, 79, maintain that "claims that the play must have been written before the Armada on the grounds that it does not celebrate the English victory are largely subjective".

68. Feldman, 132; APPENDIX F, 210.
69. Feldman, 132; APPENDIX F, 212.
70. Feldman, 132-3; APPENDIX F, 224.
71. Erne, 50.
72. Edwards, xxiv-xxvii.
73. See also Erne, 51-4.
74. Edwards xxv.
75. Feldman, 134; APPENDIX F, 227.
76. Feldman, 134-5; APPENDIX F, 227.
77. Freeman, 17.
78. Feldman 134; APPENDIX F, 213.
79. Feldman 134 APPENDIX F, 227
80. *Soliman and Perseda*, IV:i. 68-90.
81. Edwards, Appendix D, 142.
82. *The Spanish Tragedy*, I.iv. 27-8.
83. Edwards, 143.
84. Freeman, 73.
85. *The Spanish Tragedy*, II.i: 3-10.
86. William Shakespeare, *Much Ado About Nothing*, First Folio I.i: p103 lines 7-21 (modernised here).

87. Because its first publication was in 1600, some academics have dated it to the late-1590s. Gilvary, 98, is more logical: "Three factors, (a) the availability of the major sources and their literary currency between the late 1570s and 1590, (b) the striking linguistic links with texts current in the 1580s, especially with Lyly's *Endimion*, and (c) the contemporary references, strongly support a date of composition in the mid 1580s. There is no reason why a play with such dated roots would be *newly* written in 1598-1600 but it could easily have been *revived* then (as now) due to its enduring qualities."

88 However, Kyd, an acquaintance of Watson, might have read the work in manuscript before its publication.

89. Erne, 55-9, considers 1587 the most likely date.

90. L L Schücking: "Zur Verfasserschaft der 'Spanish Tragedy'" (Munich, 1963).

91. S Schoenbaum, *Internal Evidence and Elizabethan Dramatic Authorship: An Essay in Literary History and Method*. (Evanston, 1966), 177 fn 52.

92. Philip Edwards, *Thomas Kyd and Early Elizabethan Tragedy*, 25-7.

93. Edwards, 25-7.

94. Erne, 48.

Bronson Feldman's notes to
Appendix F: "Thomas Watson, Dramatist"

1. Arber, ed. *Thomas Watson: Poems* (English Reprints, 1870) 17.

2. Nashe, *Haue with you to Saffron-Walden*, in *Works*, ed. McKerrow (London 1910) III, 126.

3. Wood, *Athenae Oxonienses*, ed. Bliss (London 1813) 1, 601.

4. Quoted by E, K. Chambers, *The Elizabethan Stage* (1913) III, 506.

5. *Ibid*.

6. Meres, *Palladis Tamia: Wits Treasury* (1598) fol. 283A.

7. *Malone Society Collections* (4923) II, ii,167.

8. John Strype, *Annals of the Reformation* (1731) Ill, 345.

9. Watson, *Meliboeus*, in Arber, *op. cit.*, 155.

10. Arber, *op. cit.* 6.

11. *Relations Politiques des Pays Bas et l'Angleterre, sous le Regne de Philippe II*, ed. Lettenhove (1900) IX, 62, 252, 328.

12. Arber, *op. cit. Supra*.

13. Harvey, *Gratulationes Valdinenses* (1578) in *Works*, ed. Grosart, I, xxxix.

14. *Soliman and Perseda* (I, ii), in *The Works of Thomas Kyd*, ed. Boas (Clarendon Press, 1901).

15. Cf. Marlowe, *Doctor Faustus*, I, i.

16. J L Motley, *The Rise of the Dutch Republic* (New York 1880) III, 384, 389.

17. Chambers, *op. cit.*, IV, 157. See Arthur Acheson, *Shakespeare, Chapman, & Sir Thomas More* (London: Bernard Quaritch 1931) 195.

18. Alexander Witherspoon, *The Influence of Robert Garnier on Elizabethan Drama* (1924). Cf. Boas, *op. cit.*, xviii-xix,

19. Boas, *op. cit.*, lvi.

20. Mark Eccles, *Christopher Marlowe in London* (1934) 146.

21. *Ibid*, 151.

22. B M Ward, *The Seventeenth Earl of Oxford* (1928) 99.

23. Calendar of State Papers, Domestic Series, cxl, 665.

24. Arber, *op. cit.*, 77.

25. *Ibid*, 15.

26. Claudian, *De Tertio Consulatu Honorii*, 96-98.

27. Ambassador Castelnau, quoted in *Philip Howard, First Earl of Arundel*, ed. Pollen and MacMahon (Catholic Record Society 1919) 29.

29. Chambers, *op. cit.*, 1V, 157.

29. *Henslowe's Diary*, ed, Greg (A. H. Bullen, 1904) 150, 154. *Jeronimo* was published by Thomas Pavier in 1605, anonymously.

30. *Philip Howard*, 31.

31. Boas, *op. cit.*, xvii ff.

32. *Returns of Aliens Dwelling in the City and Suburbs of London from the Reign of Henry VIII to that of James I*, ed. Kirk (1900) II, 220.

II

1. Pollen and McMahon, *op. cit.*, 29.

2. *Ibid.*, 30.

3. Fulke Greville, *The Life of the Renowned Sir Philip Sidney*, ed. Nowell-Smith (1907) 63.

4. Watson, *Poems*, ed. Arber, 7.

5. *Returns of Aliens ...* III, 397.

6. Arber, *op. cit.*, 36.

7. *Ibid.*, 157.

8. "The Journey of Sir Francis Walsingham," ed. Martin, in *Camden Miscellany* (1870) VI, 29.

9. Arber, *op. cit.*, 25.

10. *The Elizabethan Stage*, IV, 28. .

11. Quatorzain xxxv; *Love and Fortune*, in Dodsley's *Old English Plays*, ed. Carew Hazlitt, VI, 166.

12. Dodsley, *op. cit.*, 219. The idea of Bomelio doubtless came from the astrologer and magician Dr Elis Bomelius who was imprisoned early in 1570 for practising medicine without a licence and other perilous labours (Thomas Wright, *Queen Elizabeth and Her Times*, 1838, I, 361). He published an *Almanac and Prognostications* in 1567 and 1568, and arranged to leave England in April 1570.

13. Calendar of State Papers, Foreign Series, xx, 25.

14. Sidney Lee, (ed.) *Dictionary of National Biography* xvii, *s.v.*, "Elizabeth."

15. Boas, (ed.) *Works of Thomas Kyd* 340-1.

16. British Museum: Rawlinson MS. Poet. 148; Arber, *op. cit.*, 11. John Case's *Apologia Musices* is known only in the 1588 edition.

17. *Acts of the Privy Council*, ed. Dasent, xv, 141. On 16 April, 1595, Richard Jones registered *Raptus Helenae*, "Helen's Rape by the Athenian Duke Theseus."

18. *The Lyfe and Death of Heliogabilus* was registered in June 1594. Greene, *Complete Works*, ed. Grosart (1886) VII, 7, 8.

19. Boas made an error in transcribing Kyd's letter: he read the number of Kyd's years in the service of his Lord as iij instead of vj.: T W Baldwin, "On the Chronology of Thomas Kyd's Plays," *Modern Language Notes*, XL, 1925, 343f. Tucker Brooke upheld Baldwin's correction in his edition of the *Works of Christopher Marlowe*, Dial Press, 1930.

20. Boas, *op. cit.*, cviii-cix.

21. G F Warner, *Catalogue of the Manuscripts & Muniments of Alleyn's College of God's Gift at Dulwich* (1881) 251, 252. See Eccles, *op. cit.*, 65, and Gwynneth Bowen, *The Shakespearean Authorship Review*, no. 29, Summer 1974, 4-8.

22. Ward, *op. cit.*, 257.

23. British Museum: Lansdowne MS. 103:38.

24. Colonel Bernard Rowland Ward, "Shakespeare and Elizabethan War Propaganda," *Royal Engineers Journal*, Dec, 1928, reprinted in Looney, *"Shakespeare" Identified*, ed. Ruth Loyd Miller, 1975, II, 469-482.

25. Calendar of State Papers: Venetian, viii. 182 (1581-91).

26. Robert S. Rait & Annie Cameron, (eds.) *King James's Secret: Negotiations between Elizabeth and James VI relating to the Execution of Mary Queen of Scots, from the Warrender Papers* (London 1927) 171.

27. John Tucker Murray, *English Dramatic Companies* (1910) II, 80.

28. *Acts of the Privy Council*, xv. 141. See John Bakeless, *The Tragical History of Christopher Marlowe* (1942) I, 77.

29. Calendar of State Papers: Domestic Series, Eliz. Add. 1580-1625, 217.

30. Boas, *op. cit.*, xx. We may suspect that it was this translation from the Italian that prompted Francis Meres to put Kyd on a plane with Tasso in his *Wits Treasury*. Absurd as that piece of pedantry may seem, we must admit there is method in Meres' madness when he ranks Watson ahead of Kyd and Shakespeare among Britain's chief dramatists.

31. Calendar of State Papers: Domestic Series (1587) cciii. 50.

32. British Museum: Lansdowne MS. 103:38.

33. Letter to Walsingham, 5 May, in *Calendar of State Papers: Domestic Series* (1587) cci.3.

34. Gwynneth Bowen, *The Shakespearean Authorship Review*, no, 28, Summer 1973, 3, 6, where she corrects a mistake of Rowland Ward concerning Oxford's Covent Garden in *The Mystery of "Mr. W. H."* (1923) 29.

35. Eccles, *op. cit.*, 8ff.

36. Yelverton MS. clxii, quoted by Conyers Read, *Mr Secretary Walsingham* (1925, I) 431.

37. E Tenison, *Elizabethan England* (1930-39) VIII, 299. Watson's transmutations of the Italian to English have been reprinted in A Obertello's *Madrigali italiani in Inghilterra* (1949) 259ff. Arber repeats the Latin of the poem to Luca Marenzio (*Watson: Poems*, 12), which may be Englished for the sake of these lines: "The sweet power of your music stabs me; so may I often die, for in your song is life. When you sing, I dream it is the music of the spheres, the harmony of the Muses.

38. Quoted in *Athenaeum*, 23 August 1890, 256.

39. C F Tucker Brooke, *The Life of Marlowe* (1930) xiii. Frederick Gard Fleay, *Biographical Chronicle of the English Drama* (1891) II, 28. Charles Crawford, *Collect Collectanea* (1906) 101-130. Boas, *op. cit.*, xc.

40. Boas, *Christopher Marlowe* (1940) 199.

41. Eccles, *op. cit.*, 61.

42. *Ibid.*, 49, 57.

43. *Watson, Poems*, 200. Cf. *Arden of Feversham*, II, ii.

44. *Records of the Court of the Stationers' Company*, ed. Greg and Boswell (1930) 44.

45. Thomas Heywood, *Hierarchy of the Blessed Angels* (1635).

Bibliography

ALGAR, Christian, "Visual Verses: Thomas Watson's Hekatompathia, or Passionate Century of Love, 1582". https://britishlibrary.typad.co.uk/english-and-drama/-poetry/page/4/ (2016).

ALHIYARI, Ibrahim, "Thomas Watson: New Biographical Evidence and his Translation of Antigone" (Diss. Texas Tech University, 2006).

ALHIYARI, Ibrahim, "Thomas Watson: New Birth Year and Privileged Ancestry", *Notes and Queries* 53:1 (2006).

ALHIYARI, Ibrahim, "Thomas Watson's Father, William: A Renowned, Self-Made, London Draper", *ANQ: A Quarterly Journal of Short Articles, Notes and Reviews* (19 Feb 2019), https//doi.org/10.1080/0895769X.2019.1576494

ALTSCHULER, Eric Lewin, "An astronomical whodunnit", *Astronomy and Geophysics* 40:5 (1999).

ALTSCHULER, Eric Lewin, "Searching for Shakespeare in the Stars". https://archive.org/details.arxiv-physics9810042 (1998).

ALTSCHULER, Eric Lewin and JANSEN, William, "First description of Discrete Stars Composing Milky Way in Thomas Watson's *Hekatompathia* (1582)", http://arxiv.org/html/physics/0305010 (2003).

ALTSCHULER, Eric Lewin and JANSEN, William, "A poetic challenge?", *Astronomy and Geophysics* 45:1 (2004).

ALTSCHULER, Eric Lewin and JANSEN, William, "Poet described stars in Milky Way before Galileo", *Nature* 428 (8 April 2004).

ALTSCHULER, Eric Lewin and JANSEN, William, "Was Thomas Watson Shakespeare's Precursor?", *Shakespeare Oxford Society Newsletter* 40:4 (Fall 2004).

ANDERSON, Mark, *Shakespeare by Another Name* (New York, 2005).

ANDREWS, Hilda (ed.), *My Ladye Nevells Booke of Virginal Music by William Byrd* (New York, 1969).

anonymous (attributed to Thomas Kyd), *The Tragedye of Solyman and Perseda. Wherein is laide open, Loues constancy, Fortunes inconstancy, and Deaths Triumphs* (London, 1592). Modern edition, *Soliman and Perseda* (Oxford, 2008).

ANSTRUTHER, Godfrey, *Vaux of Harrowden: a Recusant Family* (Newport, Mon. 1953).

ARBER, Edward (ed.), *Thomas Watson: Poems* (London, 1870). https://goo.gl/rmj6xF

ARBER, Edward (ed.), *A Transcript of the Registers of the Company of Stationers of London, 1555-1640 AD. Vol 5. Index.*(London 1894). Columbia Digital Collections, cu/lweb/digital/collections/cul/texts/ldpd_6177 070_005/pages/ldpd_6177070_00 5 _ 0 0000001.html? toggle=image&menhttp://www.columbia.edu/

ARCHER, Ian W, "Sir Thomas Smith (1513-1577)", *Oxford Dictionary of National Biography* (2004).

ASTINGTON, John H, "The London Stage in the 1580s", in Magnusson, A L and McGee, C E (eds.), *The Elizabethan Theatre XI* (Ontario, 1990).

AUSTEN, Gillian, *George Gascoigne* (Cambridge, 2008).

BALD, R C, "The *Locrine* and *George-a-Greene* Title-Page Inscriptions", *The Library* 4th Series, 15 (1934).

BARNETT, Howard B, "John Case—An Elizabethan Music Scholar", *Music and Letters* 50:2 (April 1969).

BARRELL, Charles Wisner. "Earliest Authenticated 'Shakespeare' Transcript Found with Oxford's Personal Poems: A Solution of the Significant Proximity of Certain Verses in a Unique Elizabethan Manuscript Anthology", *The Shakespeare Fellowship Quarterly* April 1945. (https://sourcetext.com/the-writings-of-charles-wisner-barrell-17/)

BINNS, J W, "Richard White (1539-1611)", *Oxford Dictionary of National Biography* (2004).

BLACK, Joseph L, *The Martin Marprelate Tracts: A Modernized and Annotated Edition* (Cambridge, 2008).

BOAS, Frederick S, *Queen Elizabeth in Drama, and Related Studies* (London, 1950).

BOAS, Frederick S, *Sir Philip Sidney: Representative Elizabethan, His Life and Writings.* (London, 1955).

BOND, William H, "The Cornwallis-Lysons Manuscript and the Poems of John Bentley" in James G McManaway, Giles E Dawson, Edwin E Willoughby (eds.), *Joseph Quincy Adams: Memorial Studies* (Washington, 1948).

BOSSY, John, *The English Catholic Community, 1570-1850* (London, 1976 pbk.).

BOSSY, John, *Giordano Bruno and the Embassy Affair* (New Haven and London, 2002 pbk.).

BOSSY, John, *Under the Molehill: An Elizabethan Spy Story* (New Haven and London, 2002 pbk.).

BOSSY, John, "William Byrd Investigated, 1583-84", *Early Music Review* 81 (June 2002).

BOWERS, Richard and SMITH, Paul S, "Sir John Harrington, High Plat, and *Ulysses Upon Ajax*". *Notes and Queries* 54:3 (September 2003).

BOYCE, Charles, *Encyclopedia of Shakespeare: The Essential Reference to his Plays, his Poems, his Life and Times, and More (New York; Oxford, 1990).*

Boyd, Morrison Comegys, *Elizabethan Music and Music Criticism* (Pennsylvania, revised 1967).

Boyle, Harry H, "Elizabeth's entertainment at Elvetham: War Policy in Pageantry", *Studies in Philology* 68:2 (April 1971).

Bradbrook, M C, *The School of Night: A Study in the Literary Relationships of Sir Walter Ralegh* (Cambridge, 1936, 2011 pbk.).

Brazil, Robert Sean, *The True Story of the Shakespeare Publications* Vol 1 (New York, 2000).

Brennan, Michael G, "Henry Lok (d. in or after 1608)", *Oxford Dictionary of National Biography* (2004).

Brennan, Michael G, "Nicholas Breton (1554/5-1626)", *Oxford Dictionary of National Biography* (2004).

Brennan, Michael G, "'Thy necessity is yet greater than mine': The Re-mythologizing in the Literary and Visual Arts of Fulke Greville's Water-bottle Anecdote (1750-1930)", *Sidney Journal* 28:2 (2010).

Brooke-Little, J P, *An Heraldic Alphabet* (London, 1996).

Brooks, Alden, *Will Shakspere and the Dyer's Hand* (New York, 1953).

Brown, David, "William Byrd's 1588 Volume", *Music And Letters* 38:4 (October 1957).

Bühler, Curt C, "Four Elizabethan Poems" in James G McManaway, Giles E Dawson, Edwin E Willoughby (eds.), *Joseph Quincy Adams: Memorial Studies* (Washington, 1948).

Buxton, John, *Elizabethan Taste* (New Jersey; Sussex, 1963).

Buxton, John, *Sir Philip Sidney and the English Renaissance* (London and New York, 1964 2nd ed.).

Byrd, William, *My Ladye Nevells Booke of Virginal Music* (ed. Hilda Andrews [New York, 1969]).

Byrd, William, *Psalmes, Sonets and Songs*, 1588 (ed. Jeremy Smith), *The Byrd Edition* 13 (ed. Philip Brett [London, 2004]).

C , A E, *The Family of Corbet: Its Life and Times. Vol II.* (London, 1915). https://archive.org/stream/familyofcorbetit02corb#

Campbell, Anne, Countess of Argyll, *Leaves from a poetical miscellany of Anne Campbell, Countess of Argyll [manuscript] ca.1600.* [aka *Cornwallis-Lysons Manuscript*] (Washington, Folger Library website). Digital Image File Name 540.50. Call no (Hamnet) V.a.89.

Campbell, Oscar James, *The Reader's Encyclopedia of Shakespeare* (New York, 1966).

Caraman S J, Philip, *Henry Garnet 1555-1606* (London, 1964).

Caraman S J. Philip (trans.), *William Weston: The Autobiography of an Elizabethan* (London, 1955).

CARLSON, Leland H, *Martin Marprelate, Gentleman: Master Job Throkmorton Laid Open in His Colors* (San Marino, 1981).

CASE, John, *Apologia Musices tam Vocalis quam Instrumentalis et Mixtae* (1588). A hypertext critical edition trans. by Dana F. Sutton (California). http://www.philological.bham.ac.uk/music/text.html.

CASTIGLIONE, Baldesar, *The Book of the Courtier*, trans. Charles S. Singleton (New York, 1959).

CHAMBERS, E K, *The Elizabethan Stage* Vols I-IV (Oxford, 1923).

CHARLTON, Derran, "Giordano Bruno: Mad, Bad and Dangerous to Know", *The Oxfordian* 14 (2012). https/shakespeareoxfordfellowship.org wp-content/uploads/Oxfordian2012_Charlton_Giordano_Bruno.pdf

CHATTERLEY, Albert, *Amyntas and Phyllis: The Pastorals of Thomas Watson (c1555-1592) interpreted in English Verse* (Norwich, 2012).

CHATTERLEY, Albert, "The Tears of Fancie or Love Disdained by T.W. (1593)", *Notes and Queries* 59:1 (March 2012).

CHATTERLEY, Albert, "Thomas Watson (1555/6-1592)", *Oxford Dictionary of National Biography* (2004).

CHATTERLEY, Albert, "Thomas Watson and the 'Elvetham entertainment', *Notes and Queries* 47:1 (March 2000).

CHATTERLEY, Albert (ed.), *Thomas Watson: Italian Madrigals Englished (1590)*, Musica Britannica, 74 (London, 1999).

CHATTERLEY, Albert, "Thomas Watson: Poet (c1556-1592)", *The Marlowe Society Newsletter* 23 (Autumn 2004).

CHATTERLEY, Albert, "Thomas Watson: Poet—and Musician?", *Musical Times* 148:1900 (Autumn 2007).

CHATTERLEY, Albert, "Thomas Watson: Works, Contemporary References and Reprints", *Notes and Queries* 48:3 (September 2001).

CHATTERLEY, Albert,"Two Sixteenth-Century East Anglian Families at the Court of Star Chamber", *Norfolk Archaeology* 44: Part 1 (2003).

CHENEY, Patrick, *The Cambridge Companion to Christopher Marlowe* (Cambridge, 2004).

CHILJAN, Katherine, *Shakespeare Suppressed. The Uncensored Truth About Shakespeare and His works: A Book of Evidence and Explanation* (San Francisco, 2011).

CLARK, Eva Lee Turner Clark, *Hidden Allusions in Shakespeare's Plays: A Study of the Early Court Revels and Personalities of the Times* (Port Washington, New York, 1974 revised).

CLEGG, Cyndia Susan, "Abraham Fleming (c1552-1607)", *Oxford Dictionary of National Biography (2004)*.

COLDIRON, A E B, "Sidney, Watson, and the 'Wrong Ways' to Renaissance Lyric Poetics", *Renaissance Papers* (ed. T H Howard-Hill and Philip Rollinson) (Woodbridge, 1997).

COLDIRON, A E B, "Watson's *Hekatompathia* and the Renaissance Lyric Translation", *Translation and Literature* 5:1 (1996).

COLLINSON, Patrick, "Andrew Perne (1519-1589)", *Oxford Dictionary of National Biography* (2004).

COLLINSON, Patrick, "Anne Locke (1530-1607)", *Oxford Dictionary of National Biography* (2004).

COOK, Judith, *Roaring Boys: Playwrights and Players in Elizabethan and Jacobean England* (Stroud, 2004).

DETOBEL, Robert, *Shakespeare: the Concealed Poet* (Privately published, Germany, 2010).

DEVLIN, Christopher, *The Life of Robert Southwell: Poet and Martyr* (London, 1956, rpt. 1967).

DOBB, Clifford, "London's Prisons", *Shakespeare Survey* 17 (*Shakespeare in His own Age*) (Cambridge, 1964).

DODSON, Sarah C, "Abraham Fleming, Writer and Editor", *University of Texas Studies in English* Vol. 34 (1955).

DONNO, Elizabeth Story, "Abraham Fleming: A Learned Corrector in 1586-7", *Studies in Bibliography* Vol. 42 (1989).

DOVEY, Zillah, *An Elizabethan Progress: the Queen's Journey to East Anglia 1578* (Stroud, 1996).

DOWNIE, J A, "Marlow, May 1593, and the 'Must-Have' Theory of Biography", *Review of English Studies* 58:235 (June, 2007).

DREYFUS, Laurence, "Consort Songs by William Byrd (1539-1623)", *The Viol* 5 (Winter 2006-7).

DUFFY, Eamon, "William Allen (1532-1594)", *Oxford Dictionary of National Biography* (2004).

DUNCAN-JONES, Katherine, *Sir Philip Sidney: Courtier Poet* (London, 1991).

DUNCAN-JONES, Katherine, *Sir Philip Sidney: The Major Works* (Oxford; New York, 2002 revised).

ECCLES, Mark, *Christopher Marlowe in London* (Cambridge Mass, 1934).

EDWARDS, A C, *John Petre: Essays on the life and background of John, 1st Lord Petre, 1649-1613* (London and New York, 1975).

EDWARDS, Philip, *Thomas Kyd and Early Elizabethan Tragedy* (London, 1966).

EDWARDS S J, Francis, *Plots and Plotters in the Reign of Elizabeth I* (Dublin, 2002).

EMMISON, F G, *Tudor Secretary: Sir William Petre at Court and Home* (London, 1961).

ERNE, Lukas, *Beyond the Spanish Tragedy: A Study of the Works of Thomas Kyd* (Manchester, 2001).

FALK, Dan, *The Science of Shakespeare* (New York, 2014).
FATHERS OF THE CONGREGATION OF THE LONDON ORATORY (eds.), *The First and Second Diaries of the English College, Douay, and an Appendix of Unpublished Documents. With an Historical Introduction by Thomas Francis Knox DD, Priest of the Same Foundation* (London, 1878). https://archive.org/stream/firstsecond diari 00engl#page/n7/mode/2up/
FELDMAN, Bronson, "Thomas Watson, Dramatist", *The Bard* 1:4 (1977); *Shakespeare, Marlowe, and Other Elizabethans* (Buchholz, Germany, 2021/22), provisional title of a new collection of Feldman articles.
FELLOWES, Edmund H, *The English Madrigal* (London, 1925).
FLUES, Barboura, "Thomas Watson's *"Hekatompathia*: Glossary and Appendices". http://www.elizabethanauthors.org/hek06.htm
FREEMAN, Arthur and FREEMAN, Janet Ing, "James Orchard Halliwell-Phillipps (1820-1889)", *Oxford Dictionary of National Biography* (2004).
FREEMAN, Arthur, *Thomas Kyd: Facts and Problems* (Oxford, 1967).
FRENCH, Peter J, *John Dee, the World of an Elizabethan Magus* (London, 1972).
GADD, I, "John Wolfe (1548?-1601)", *Oxford Dictionary of National Biography* (2004).
GAIR, Reavley, *The Children of St Paul's: The Story of a Theatre Company 1553-1608* (Cambridge, 1982).
GEORGE, G. D, "Earning a living as an Author in Early Modern England: The Case of Anthony Munday" (Diss. Graduate College of Bowling Green State University, 2006). http://etd.ohiolink.edu/rws_etd/document/get/bgsu1143500898/nline
GILVARY, Kevin (ed.), *Dating Shakespeare's Plays: A Critical Review of the Evidence* (Tunbridge Wells, 2010).
GRANT, Stephen H, *Collecting Shakespeare: The Story of Henry and Emily Folger,* (Baltimore, 2014).
GREER, David, " '... Thou Court's Delight: Biographical Notes on Henry Noel", *The Lute Society Journal* Vol 17 (1975).
GREG, W W, "Three Manuscript Notes by Sir George Buc", *The Library* 4th Series 12, (1931-2).
HACKETT, Helen, *Virgin Mother, Maiden Queen: Elizabeth I and the Cult of the Virgin Mary,* (New York, 1995).
HALASZ, Alexandra, "Thomas Lodge (1558-1625), *Oxford Dictionary of National Biography* (2004).
HALL, Hubert, "An Elizabethan Poet and his Relations", *The Athenaeum* 3278 (23 August 1890).
HALLIDAY, F E, A Shakespeare Companion, 1564-1964 (London, 1964).

HAMILTON, Donna B, *Anthony Munday and the Catholics, 1560-1633* (Aldershot, 2005).
HANNAY, Margaret P, *Philip's Phoenix* (Oxford, 1990).
HARDING, Vanessa, *The Dead and the Living in Paris and London, 1500-1670* (Cambridge, 2002).
HARLEY, John, *William Byrd: Gentleman of the Royal Chapel* (Aldershot, 1999).
HARRISON, Christopher, "William Byrd and the Pagets of Beaudesert: A Musical Connection, *Staffordshire Studies* 3 (1990-1).
HARVEY, Gabriel, *Foure Letters and Certaine Sonnets* (1592). http://www.oxford-shakespeare.com/ Nashe/Four_Letters.pdf
HAYDN, Hiram (ed.), *The Portable Elizabethan Reader* (Harmondsworth, rpt. 1980).
HAYNES, Alan, *Invisible Power: The Elizabethan Secret Services 1570-1603* (Stroud, 1992).
HAYNES, Alan, *The Elizabethan Secret Services* (Stroud, 2000, pbk. rpt. of *Invisible Power*).
HAYNES, Alan, *Walsingham: Elizabethan Spymaster and Statesman* (Stroud, 2004).
HELGERSON, Richard, *The Elizabethan Prodigals* (California; London, 1976).
HENINGER Jr, S K (ed.), *The Hekatompathia; or Passionate Centurie of Love* (Gainesville, 1964).
HERENDEEN, Wyman H, "William Camden (1551-1623), *Oxford Dictionary of National Biography* (2004).
HESS, W Ron, *The Dark Side of Shakespeare: An Elizabethan Courtier, Diplomat, Spymaster, and Epic Hero,* (Lincoln USA, 2003, 2 vols).
HIRREL, Michael J, "Thomas Watson, Playwright: Origins of Modern English Drama". In David McInnis and Matthew Steggle (eds.), *Lost Plays in Shakespeare's England* (London, 2014).
HOGGE, Alice, *God's Secret Agents: Queen Elizabeth's Forbidden Priests and the Hatching of the Gunpowder Plot* (New York, 2005).
HOLMES, Peter, "Charles Paget (c1546-1612)", *Oxford Dictionary of National Biography* (2004).
HOLMES, Peter, "Thomas Paget (c1544-1590)", *Oxford Dictionary of National Biography* (2004).
HONAN, Park, *Christopher Marlowe: Poet and Spy* (Oxford, 2005).
HONEY, William, *The Life, Loves and Achievements of Christopher Marlowe Alias Shakespeare.* Volume 1 (only volume published) (London, 1982).
Honourable Entertainment gieven to the Quenes Majestie, in Progresse, at Elvetham in Hampshire, by the Right Honourable the Earle of Hertford" (London, 1591). www.royalcollection.org.uk/ collection/1024755).
HOPPE, Harry R, "John Wolfe, Printer and Publisher, 1579-1601", *The Library* 4th Series, 14:3 (December, 1933).
HOTSON, J Leslie, *The Death of Christopher Marlowe* (London, 1925).

HOTSON, Leslie, "Marlowe Among the Churchwardens", *Atlantic Monthly* 138 (July-December 1926).
HOWELL, Roger, *Sir Philip Sidney: The Shepherd Knight* (London, 1968).
HUNTER, G K, *John Lyly, the Humanist as Courtier* (London, 1962).
HUTCHINSON, Robert, *Elizabeth's Spy Master: Francis Walsingham and the Secret War that Saved England* (London, 2007 pbk.).
HYLAND, Paul, *Ralegh's Last Journey.* (London, 2003, 2004 pbk.).
JACK, Sybil M, "William Paget (1505/6-1563)", *Oxford Dictionary of National Biography* (2004).
JARDINE, Lisa and STEWART, Alan, *Hostage to Fortune: The Troubled Life of Francis Bacon* (New York, 1999).
JOLLY, Margrethe, *The First Two Quartos of* Hamlet*: A New View of the Origins and Relationship of the Texts* (Jefferson, 2014).
JONSON, Ben, *Poems* (ed. Ian Donaldson) (London, 1975).
KALB, Eugénie de, "Robert Poley's Movements as a Messenger of the Court, 1588 to 1601", *Review of English Studies* 9:33 (January 1933).
KAUFMANN, R J (ed.), *Elizabethan Drama: Modern Essays in Criticism* (New York, 1961).
KEEN, Allan and LUBBOCK, Roger, *The Annotator* (London, 1954).
KENDALL, Roy, *Christopher Marlowe and Richard Baines: Journeys through the Elizabethan Underground* (Madison; London, 2003).
KERMAN, Joseph, *The Elizabethan Madrigal: A Comparative Study* (New York, 1962).
KILROY, Gerard, *Edmund Campion: Memory and Transcription* (Aldershot, 2005).
KINCAID, Arthur, "Sir George Buck (Buc) (bap 1560-1622)", *Oxford Dictionary of National Biography* (2004).
KINNEY, Arthur F, "Stephen Gosson (bap 1554-1625)", *Oxford Dictionary of National Biography* (2004).
KURIYAMA, Constance Brown, *Christopher Marlowe: A Renaissance Life* (New York, 2010).
KYD, Thomas, *Soliman and Perseda* (Oxford, 2008).
KYD, Thomas, *The Spanish Tragedy* (ed Philip Edwards) (London, 1959).
KYD, Thomas., *The Spanish Tragedy* (ed J R Mulryne) (London, 1970).
LAMB, Mary Ellen, "The Countess of Pembroke's Patronage", *English Literary Renaissance* 12:2 (Spring 1982).
LAMB, Mary Ellen, "The Myth of the Countess of Pembroke: The Dramatic Circle", *Yearbook of English Studies* 11 (1981).
LAMB, Rita, "The Harvey-Nashe Quarrel". http://sicttasd.tripod.com/quarshort.html (nd).
LEACH, Arthur F, *A History of Winchester College* (London, 1899). http://archive.org/details/historyofwinches00leacuoft.

LEWIS, C S, *Poetry and Prose in the Sixteenth Century* (Oxford 1954, reprint 1990).
LINDLEY, David, *Shakespeare and Music* (London, 2006).
LODGE, Thomas, *Phyllis: Honoured with Pastorall Sonnets, Elegies and Amourous Delights* (1593).
LOONEY, John Thomas, *"Shakespeare" Identified in Edward de Vere, Seventeenth Earl of Oxford* (London, 1920). *See*, MILLER, Ruth Loyd.
LYNE, Raphael, "Barnabe Googe (1540-1594)", *Oxford Dictionary of National Biography* (2004).
MACNAMARA, Francis Nottidge, *Memorials of the Danvers Family (of Dauntsey and Culworth): their ancestors and descendants from the conquest till the termination of the eighteenth century, with some Account of the Alliances of the Family and of the Places where they were Seated* (London, 1895). (https://archive.org/details/memorialsofdanve00macn).
MALIM, Richard, *The Earl of Oxford and the Making of "Shakespeare"* (Jefferson, 2012).
MANLEY, Lawrence and MACLEAN, Sally-Beth, *Lord Strange's Men and Their Plays* (New Haven & London, 2014).
MARLOWE, Christopher and NASHE, Thomas, *Dido, Queen of Carthage.* (London, 1594). https://classic-literature.co.uk/christopher-marlowe-the-tragedy-of-dido-queen-of-carthage/
MARSHALL, Rosalind K, "Anne Cornwallis (1590-1635)", *Oxford Dictionary of National Biography* (2004).
MATEER, David, "William Byrd, John Petre and Oxford, Bodleian MS Mus Sch E 423", *Royal Musical Association Research Journal* 29 (1996).
MATEER, David,"William Byrd's Middlesex Recusancy", *Music and Letters* 78:1 (February 1997).
MAY, Steven W, *The Elizabethan Courtier Poets: the Poems and their Contexts* (Missouri, 1991).
MAY, Steven W, "Henry Noel (d.1597)", *Oxford Dictionary of National Biography* (2004).
MAY, Stephen W, "The Poems of Edward de Vere, Seventeenth Earl of Oxford, and of Robert Devereux, Second Earl of Essex", *Studies in Philology* 78:5 (Early Winter 1980).
MCCARTHY, Kerry, "Byrd's Patrons at Prayer", *Music and Letters* 89:4 (November 2008).
MCDERMOTT, James, *Martin Frobisher: Elizabethan Privateer* (New Haven and London, 2001).
MCKERROW, R B (ed.), *A Dictionary of Printers and Booksellers in England, Scotland and Ireland, and of Foreign Printers of English Books 1557-1640* (Connecticut, 2005).
MCKERROW, R B, "Edward Allde as a Typical Trade Printer", *The Library* 4th Series, 10:2 (September 1925).

McMANAWAY, James G, "The Folger Shakespeare Library", *Shakespeare Survey* 1 (Cambridge, 1948).

McVEIGH, S A J, "The Decline of Recusancy in North-West Middlesex", *The London Recusant* 4:2 (1974).

MILLER, Ruth Loyd (ed.) and WARD, Bernard M, *A Hundreth Sundrie Flowres: From the Original Edition of 1573* (New York, 2nd ed. 1975). Incorporates Bernard M Ward's 1926 edition.

MILLER, Ruth Loyd (ed.), *Thomas Looney, "Shakespeare" Identified in Edward de Vere, Seventeenth Earl of Oxford and The Poems of Edward De Vere.* Volume I: *Looney, "Shakespeare" Identified* (London, 1920, rpt. New York, 1948); *The Poems;* Volume II: *Oxfordian Vistas.* (New York, 1975).

MILLER, William E, "Abraham Fleming: Editor of Shakespeare's Holinshed", *Texas Studies in Literature and Language* 1 (1959-60).

MILSOM, John, "Byrd, Sidney, and the Art of Melting", *Early Music* 31:3 (August 2003).

MINTO, William, *Characteristics of English Poets* (Edinburgh and London, 2nd ed. 1885). http://www.sonnets.org/minto5.htm

MONEY, D K, "Christopher Johnson (?1536-1597)", *Oxford Dictionary of National Biography (2004).*

MORRIS, Harry, "'Amyntas' and the Sidney Circle", *Publications of the Modern Language Association of America* (PMLA) 74:4 (September 1959).

NASHE, Thomas, *The Anatomie of Absurditie* (London, 1588). http://oxford-shake speare.com/Nashe/Anatomy_Absurdity.pdf

NASHE, Thomas, *Pierce Penilesse, His Supplication to the Divell.* http://www.oxford-shakespeare.com/Nashe/Pierce_Penilesse.pdf

NASHE, Thomas, *Strange Newes of the intercepting certaine letters, and a Convuoy of Verses, as they were going Privilie to victuall the Low Countries* (London, 1592). http://www.oxford-shakespeare.com/Nashe/Pierce_Penilesse.pdf

NASHE, Thomas, *Christ's Tears Over Jerusalem* (London, 1593). http://www.oxford-shakespeare.com/Nashe/Christs_Tears_1.pdf).

NASHE, Thomas, *Nashe's Lenten Stuff.* (London, 1599). http://oxford-shakespeare. com /Nashe/ Nashes_Lenten_Stuff.pdf

NASHE, Thomas, *Summer's Last Will and Testament* (London, 1600). http://www.ox ford- shakespeare.com/Nashe/Summers_Last_Will_Testament.pdf

NASHE, Thomas, *The Terrors of the Night* (London, 1594). http://222.oxford-shake speare.com/Nashe/Terrors_Night.pdf

NASHE, Thomas, *The Unfortunate Traveller, or the Life of Jack Wilton* (London, 1594). http://oxford-shakespeare.com/Nashe/Unfortunate_Traveller.pdf

Bibliography 319

National Archives Probate 11/17/471, Will of Sir Robert Corbet, dated 23 April 1509. (Modern spelling transcript by Nina Green, 2007). http://www.oxford-shakespeare.com/

National Archives Probate 11/22/381, Will of Thomas Lee, dated 24 August 1527. (Modern spelling transcript by Nina Green, 2009). http://www.oxford-shakespeare. com/

National Archives Probate 11/38/89, Will of Elizabeth (nee Rolleston) Whitlock Lee Wade Onley, dated 28 June and 18 July 1554. (Modern spelling transcript by Nina Green, 2010) http://www.oxford-shakespeare.com/

National Archives Probate 11/43, ff.26-7, Will of William Watson, dated 10 November 1559. (Modern spelling transcript by Nina Green, 2009). http://www.oxford-shakespeare. com/

National Archives Probate 11/44, ff.31-4, Will of Anne Watson, dated 8 May 1561. (Modern spelling transcript by Nina Green, 2010). http://www.oxford-shakespeare. com/

National Archives Probate 11/47, ff.31-4, Will of Dame Blanche Forman, dated 29 March 1563.(Modern spelling transcript by Nina Green, 2010). http://www.oxford-shakespeare. com/

National Archives Probate 11/54,292, Will of Thomas Lee of Clattercote in Oxfordshire, dated April 1572. (Modern spelling transcript by Nina Green, 2009). http://www.oxford-shakespeare.com

National Archives Probate 11/118/441, Will of Sir William Cornwallis, dated 22 October 1611. (Modern spelling transcript by Nina Green, 2010) http://www.oxford-shakespeare.com/

NELSON, Alan H, *Monstrous Adversary: The Life of Edward de Vere, 17th Earl of Oxford* (Liverpool, 2003).

NICOLL, Allardyce (ed.), *Shakespeare in his own Age, Shakespeare Survey* 17 (Cambridge, 1964).

NICHOLL, Charles, *A Cup of News: The Life of Thomas Nashe* (London, 1984).

NICHOLL, Charles, *The Reckoning: The Murder of Christopher Marlowe* (London, 1992, revised 2002).

NICHOLS, John, *The Progresses and Public Processions of Queen Elizabeth* (London, 1823).

NORMAN, Charles, *The Muses' Darling: Christopher Marlowe.* (New York, 1946, 1950, pbk., 1960).

OSBORNE, June, *Entertaining Elizabeth: The Progresses and Great Houses of her Time* (London, 1989).

OWENS, Jessie Ann, *"Noyses, sounds, and sweet aires": Music in Early Modern England* (Washington, 2006).

PALGRAVE, F T, "Thomas Watson the Poet", *The North American Review* 0114:234 (January 1872).

PATTISON, Bruce, *Music and Poetry of the Elizabethan Renaissance* (London, 2nd ed. 1970).

PATTISON, Bruce, "Sir Philip Sidney and Music", *Music and Letters* 15:1 (January 1934).

PEARLMAN, E, "Watson's *Hekatompathia* [1582] in the *Sonnets* and *Romeo and Juliet*", *English Studies* 74 (1993).

PELUSCH, Denise, "William Byrd's Codes in his Eulogies and Lament Songs". https://antigo.anppoom.com.br/anais/anaiscongresso_anppom_2006/CDROM/COM/04_Com_Musicologia/sessao02/04COM_MusHist_0201-238.pdf

PETERS MAUDE, Nancy, "The Extended Collaboration of John Dante and Edward Allde". *The Library* 16:3 (September 2015).

PLOWDEN, Alison, *Danger to Elizabeth* (London, 1973).

POINTON, A J, *The Man who was Never Shakespeare: The Theft of William Shakespeare's Identity* (Tunbridge Wells, 2011).

POLLARD, Alfred W, "Claudius Hollyband and his French Schoolmaster and French Littleton", *The Library* 13:1 (1 January 1913).

POLLARD, A W and REDGRAVE, G R (eds.), *A Short-Title Catalogue of Books Printed in England, Scotland and Ireland, and of English Books Printed Abroad 1475–1640*. Second ed revised by W A Jackson, F S Ferguson, K F Pantzer (London, 1976, 1991).

PRICE, David C, *Patrons and Musicians of the English Renaissance* (Cambridge, 1981).

PROCKTER, Adrian and TAYLOR, Robert (compilers), *The A to Z of Elizabethan London* (London, 1979).

REDMANN, Rebecca, "William Byrd, the Catholics and the Consort Song: The Hearing Continued", *The Viol* 5 (Winter 2006-7).

RIGGS, David, *The World of Christopher Marlowe* (London, 2004, 2005 pbk.).

ROE, Richard Paul, *The Shakespeare Guide to Italy: Retracing the Bard's Unknown Travels* (New York, 2011).

RUFF, Lillian M and WILSON, D Arnold, "The Madrigal, the Lute Song and Elizabethan Politics", *Past and Present* 44 (1969).

SAINTSBURY, George, *A History of Elizabethan Literature* (London, 1887, 2nd ed. 1890).

SAUNDERS, A W L, *The Master of Shakespeare. Volume I: The Sonnets* (BVI, 2007).

SCHRICKX W, *Shakespeare's Early Contemporaries: The Background of the Harvey-Nashe Polemic and* Love's Labour's Lost (Antwerp, 1956; New York, 1972).

SHAPIRO, I A. "Shakespeare and Mundy", *Shakespeare Survey* 14 (1961).

SHEIDLEY, William E, *Barnabe Googe* (Boston, 1981).

SIDNEY, Philip, *Discourse on Irish Affairs* (1577) http://www.ebooks downloads.xyz/search/delphi-complete-works-of-sir-philip-sidney-illustrated

Sisson, Charles J (ed.), *Thomas Lodge and Other Elizabethans* (Cambridge MA, 1933).
Slack, Paul, *The Impact of Plague in Tudor and Stuart England* (London, 1985).
Smith, Bruce R, *The Acoustic World of Early Modern England* (Chicago; London, 1999).
Smith, Jeremy L, *Thomas East and Music Publishing in Renaissance England* (Oxford, 2003).
Smith, Jeremy L, "William Byrd's Fall from Grace and his First Solo Publication of 1588: A Shostakovian 'Response to Just Criticism'?" *Music and Politics* 1:1 (Winter 2007) http://uod.lib.umich.edu/m/mp/9460447.0001.104/-william-byrds-fall-from-grace_-and-his-first-solo-publication?rgn=main;view=fulltext.
Sokol, B J, "Matthew Roydon (ff1583-1622)", *Oxford Dictionary of National Biography* (2004).
Sommerville, Johann, Review of Robert Zaller "The Discourse of Legitimacy in Early Modern England", *English Historical Review* 124:507 (April 2009).
Staton Jr, Walter F, "Thomas Watson and Ovidian Poetry", *Studies in the Renaissance* 6 (1959).
Staton Jr, Walter F and Morris, Harry, "Thomas Watson and Abraham Fraunce". *Publications of the Modern Language Association of America* (PMLA) 76:1 (March, 1961).
Stewart, Alan, *Philip Sidney: A Double Life* (London, 2000).
Stow, John. *The Survey of London.* (London, 1912, reprint of 1603 2nd ed.); British History Online (https://www.british-history.ac.uk/no-series/survey-of-london-stow/1603).
Sutton, Dana F, *Thomas Watson: The Complete Works* (Irvine, 2010). (http://www.Philological.bham.ac.uk/watson).
Trevor-Roper, Hugh, "Nicholas Hill (1570-c1610)". *Oxford Dictionary of National Biography* (2004).
Turner, Celeste, *Anthony Mundy: An Elizabethan Man of Letters* (Berkeley; Cambridge, 1928).
Turner Wright, Celeste, "Young Anthony Mundy Again", *Studies in Philology* 56:2 (April 1959).
Usher, Peter, "An Answer to 'A poetic challenge'", *Astronomy and Geophysics* 45:3 (June 2004).
Usher, Peter. "Shakespeare's support for the New Astronomy", *The Oxfordian* 5 (2002).
Vere, Charles, Earl of Burford, "Edward de Vere and the Psychology of Feudalism", *Elizabethan Review* 3:2 (1995).
Waller, Gary F, *Mary Sidney, Countess of Pembroke: A Critical Study of her Writings and Literary Milieu* (Salzburg, 1979).
Ward, B M, *The Seventeenth Earl of Oxford 1550-1604: from Contemporary Documents* (London, 1928).

WATSON, Thomas, *Italian Madrigals Englished*. Transcribed and ed. by Albert Chatterley. *Musica Britannica* 74 (London, 1999).

WATSON, Thomas, *Poems*, ed. Edward Arber (London, 1870).

WAUGH, Margaret, *Blessed Philip Howard, Earl of Arundel and Surrey, Courtier and Martyr* (London, 1961).

WESTON, William, *William Weston: The Autobiography of an Elizabethan*, trans. Philip Caraman S J (London, 1955).

WESTRUP, J A, "William Byrd", *Music and Letters* 24:3 (July 1943).

WHEATLEY, Henry B, "Signs of Booksellers in St Paul's Churchyard", *The Library* Volume TBS-9:1 (January 1906).

WHITNEY, Charles C (ed.), *Thomas Lodge* (Burlington, 2011).

WHITT, P B, "New Light on Sir William Cornwallis, the Essayist". *Review of English Studies* 8 (1932).

WILLIAMSON, Hugh Ross, *Sir Walter Raleigh* (London, 1951).

WILSON, Derek, *Sir Francis Walsingham: A Courtier in the Age of Terror* (New York, 2007).

WOOD, Anthony à, *Athenae Oxoniensis, an Exact History of all the Writers and Bishops who have had their Education in the University of Oxford from 1500 to 1690* Vols I-IV (Oxford, 1691-2; 3rd ed. London, 1813). https://archive.org/details/athensaexoniensw01wooduoft

WOOLLEY, Benjamin, *The Queen's Conjurer: The Science and Magic of Dr John Dee, Adviser to Queen Elizabeth I* (New York, 2001).

WOUDHUYSEN, H R, "Sir Philip Sidney (1554-1586)", *Oxford Dictionary of National Biography* (2004).

WOUDHUYSEN, H R, *Sir Philip Sidney and the Circulation of Manuscripts 1558-1640* (Oxford, 1996).

WRAIGHT, A D and STERN, Virginia F, *In Search of Christopher Marlowe: A Pictorial Biography* (Chichester, 1993).

YATES, Frances A, *The Art of Memory* (Harmondsworth, 1969).

YOUNG, Alan R, "'In Gallant Course before Ten Thousand Eyes': The Tournament in the 1580s", *The Elizabethan Theatre* 11 (1990).

ZARNOWIECKI, Matthew, "Lyric Surrogacy: Reproducing the 'I' in Sidney's *Arcadia*", *Sidney Journal* 27:1 (2009).

Index

Accadamei della Nuova Poesia 22
Achelley, Thomas 96, 118, 205, 208, 213
Acheron 243
Act of Uniformity 12, 16, 123
"*Ad lectorem Hexasticon*: Tullies Love" 245, 255
Admiral's Men 150, 236, 239
"*Ad Oclandum* …" 119, 244, 253
Advertisement written to a Secretary of my L. Treasurer's … 114
Aeneas 97
Aeropagus Movement 95, 115
Aesop 242, 249
Africa 12
Agas Map x,
Ajax Flagellifer 219
Alcântara, Portugal 226
Aldersgate Street, 34, 136, 137, 146
"Alecto" 235
"Alexander, King" 211, 223, 234
Alexander the Great (Alexander III of Macedon) 199
Alfield, Thomas 39, 40-41, 142
Algonquian language 113
Alhiyari, Ibrahim x, 49, 50, 54, 86
Allde, Edward 39
Allde, John 39, 40, 41, 42, 189, 210
Allde, Margaret 40
Allen, William 58, 61
Alleyn, Edward 35, 150, 236, 239, 240
Alleyn, John 150, 239, 245
Alphonsus, King of Aragon 237
Altschuler, Lewin and Jansen, William 85-6, 106, 108, 109, 110
Alva, Duke of 40, 55, 226
Amaryllis 187
"Ambassador of Portugal" 228
"Ambrose the smith" 137

America 12
Amiens 83
Aminta (Tasso) 120, 254
Amintae Gaudia x, 110, 164, 188, 166, 194, 245, 256
"Amintas" 194, 195, 300
Amores 73
Amyntas x, 119-20, 145, 148, 164, 244-5, 254
Amyntas and Phyllis (Chatterley) x
Anatomy of Absurdity, An 44
"Andrea" 226
Andrewes, Lancelot 210
Anglicanism 12, 14, 17, 25, 52, 76, 129, 141
Anglican Settlement , see Act of Uniformity
Anglorum Praelia 119, 244, 253
Angus, 10th Earl of (William Douglas) 23
Anjou and Alençon, Duke of (Francis) 21, 28, 55, 70, 197, 229, 232
"Anne Cornwallis her Booke". *See* Cornwallis-Lysons Manuscript
Antigone 54, 57, 76, 85, 97, 122, 164, 205, 219, 220, 222, 233, 245, 253
"Antigone" 219
Antonie 209
Antonio, Prior of Crato (claimant to the throne of Portugal) 226
Antwerp, Netherlands 60, 147, 221
Apelles of Kos 199
"Apis Lapis" 188
"Apollo". *See* "Phoebus Apollo"
Apologia Musices 15, 148, 255
Apology for Actors, An 207, 224
Arber, Edward x, 50, 98, 100, 194, 200, 204, 218, 219
Arcadia (See also *Countess of Pembroke's Arcadia, The*) 22, 23, 24, 25, 38, 187
"Arden, Alice" 247, 248, 249

"Arden, Master" 248, 249
Arden of Faversham 217, 246, 247, 248-9, 250
Aretino, Pietro 45-6
Argyll, Countess of (Anne Campbell, née Cornwallis) 168-70, 173, 174, 175-6, 177, 250
Argyll, 7th Earl of (Archibald Campbell) 175-6
Ariosto, Ludovico 147, 239
Aristotle, Aristotelians 18, 111
Armagh, Archbishop of (Richard Creagh) 80
Arnhem, Netherlands 26
Artificiosae memoriae libellus 112, 253, 254
Art of English Poesy, The 23, 127
Art of Rhetorique, The 221
Arundel Castle 76
Arundel, Countess of (Anne Howard) 76
Arundel family 229, 230
Arundel, 12th Earl of (Henry Fitzalan) 40, 74, 232-3
Arundel, 13th Earl of, Earl of Surrey (Philip Howard) 38, 57, 76, 95, 131, 132, 220, 221, 225, 226, 230, 231, 232, 233, 253
Arundell, Charles 94, 133, 184, 226, 232, 233
Ashridge, Hertfordshire 171
Asia 12
Astrophel and Stella 22, 23, 89, 127
As You Like It 67
Athens 219
Aubrey, John 43
Audley End, Essex 133
Augustine of Hippo 176
Axiochus 188, 189
Aylmer, John. *See* London, Bishop of
Azores 158, 160

Babington, Anthony 38, 64, 80-1, 82, 143, 147
Babington Plot 35, 62, 79, 80-1, 83, 111, 131, 132, 143, 147, 196, 235
Babylon 144
Bacheler, Daniel 25
Bacon, Anthony 71
Bacon, Francis 12, 36, 60, 70
Bacon, Nathaniel 174

Bacon, Nicholas 14
Baines, Richard 76, 82-3, 152
Bakeless, John 197
Baker, George 41, 221
Baldwin, John 123
Ball, "Cutting" 45, 248
Ballard, John 80
Balliol College, Oxford 54
"Balthazar" 215
Banbury, Oxfordshire 52
Bannister, Edward 25
"Barabas" 82
Bard, The 207, 218
Barker, Christopher 87, 126
Barking Abbey, Essex 134
Barley, William 188
Barn Elms, Richmond 80, 115
Barnes, Barnabe 203
Barnfield, Richard 194, 195
Barningham, Suffolk 174
Barrow, Thomas 174
Bartholomew Fair 226, 230
"Basilisco" 223, 247
Basing, Hampshire 154
Bassano circle 17
Bassett, Laurence 44
Bassett, Robert 43-4
Bastille, Paris 83
Bath, Countess of (Bourchier, née Cornwallis) 172
Bath, 3rd Earl of (William Bourchier) 172
Bath, Somerset 32
Battlehall, Worcestershire 193
Battyshall Manor, Ongar, Essex 127, 139, 176
Baxter, Nathaniel 43
Baynard's Castle, 21
BBC x
Beale, Amy 62
Beale, Robert Sr 62
Beale, Robert Jr 62, 202, 246
Beale, William 62, 63, 225
Beaudesert House, Staffordshire 128, 129

Index

Beaumont, Francis 202, 203
Bedingfield, Thomas 162
Bedlam. *See* Bethlehem Hospital
"Belimperia" 230
Bell, The, Gracechurch Street 206
Bellay, Joaquim du 22
Bel Sauvage, The, Ludgate 206
"Benedick" 215
Bentley, John 118, 169, 205, 208
Berkeley, Lady (Elizabeth Carey) 188-9
Berkshire 142
"Berowne" 112
Bethlehem Hospital 29, 146, 185
Birmingham, University of x
Bishop, George 33
Bishopsgate 29, 78, 80, 143, 145, 149, 151, 172-3, 177, 185, 206, 219, 221, 231, 239, 249
Bishop, The, Gray's Inn Road 150
"Blackburn, William" 248
Blackfriars, Norwich 178
Blackfriars Theatre, London 39, 124
Black Horse Alley, Aldersgate Street 146
"Black Will" 246, 247, 248, 249
Blount, Christopher 80
Blount, Edward 103
Blount, Penelope. *See* Devonshire, Countess of
Blundeville, Constance. *See* Googe, Constance
Boar's Head Inn, Whitechapel 29
Boas, F S 197, 225, 242-3, 247
Boccaccio, Giovanni 200
Bohemia 25, 96, 116
Boke named the Governour, The 200
Bold, Richard 143
Bologna 56, 57
Boleyn, Anne, Queen of England 134
Boleyn, George. *See* Rochford, 2nd Viscount
Boleyn, Thomas. *See* Wiltshire, 1st Earl of
Bolt, John 139-40
"Bomelio" 235
Bonaventure, The 158
Bond, William H 170

Book of Common Prayer, The 12
Book of the Governor, The ...
    See *Boke named the Governor, The*
Bottesford, Leicestershire 35, 36
Bourchier (née Cornwallis).
    See Bath, Countess of
Bourchier, William. *See* Bath, 3rd Earl of
Bourges, France 60
Bourne, John 193-4
Bowers, Richard and Smith, Paul S 193
Bow Lane, Bishopsgate 78
Boyle, Harry H 158, 159-60
Boyes, Edward 161
Bradley, William 150-3, 180, 245, 247-8
"Bradshaw" 248
Bradshaw, Elizabeth 63, 110
Braithwait, Richard 203
Brandes, Georg 104
Brandon, Katherine. *See* Suffolk, Duchess of
Brenta river, Northern Italy 58
Brentwood, Essex 138
Breton, Anne 160
Breton, Elizabeth 160-1
Breton, Nicholas 158, 159, 160-2
Breton, William 160
Britannia 122
British Library 98, 99, 112, 132, 211, 253, 254
Britton's Bowre of Delights 163
Broadgates Hall 122
Broelmann, Stephen 233
Brome Hall, Suffolk 170, 171, 183
Brooke, First Baron (Fulke Greville) 20, 22, 25, 111
Brooke, Tucker 246
Brooke-Little, J P 101
Brooksby, Eleanor (née Vaux) 143
Brough, Robert 139
Brouncker, Henry 23
Browne, Peter 145
Broylman, Elizabeth 233
Bruno, Giordano 43, 110-12, 113, 202 245
Brussels, Netherlands 60, 162

Buc (Bucke), George 95, 159-63, 174-5, 205, 234
Buckhurst, Baron (Thomas Sackville. After Calvin, John 29, 36 1604, 1st Earl of Dorset) 38-9
Buckhurst Place, Sussex 38
Bucoliks (Eclogues) 34
Budge Row, City of London 145
Bull, Eleanor 74
Bull, The, Bishopsgate 206
Burbage, James 221
Burbage, Richard 237, 246
Burghley, First Baron (William Cecil) 13, 27, 28, 29, 31, 32, 34, 36, 37, 38, 51, 55, 56, 57, 58, 64, 65, 66, 69, 70, 72, 74, 75, 80, 81, 89, 96, 119, 126, 152, 153, 162, 172, 173, 182, 221, 223, 239, 240, 241, 243-4
Burghley, Thomas 172
Burn, Mr 60
Burnell, Anne 62-4, 66, 68, 110, 180, 186
Burnell, Edward 63-4, 65
Burnell Family 64
Burnell, Jane 64
Burnell, William 63
Burton House, Staffordshire 128, 129-31
Burton-on-Trent, Staffordshire 128, 129
Bury St Edmunds, Suffolk 160
Byrd, Christopher 124, 133
Byrd, Ellen 127
Byrd, John 123
Byrd, Julian 124, 140, 141, 143
Byrd, Katherine (née More) 133
Byrd, Margery 123
Byrd, Symond 123
Byrd, Thomas 53, 123. 126
Byrd, William ix, 16, 25, 43, 53, 84, 122-44, 146-9, 165-6, 176-7, 246, 255
"Byrd's boy" 139

"Caesar" 234, 243
Caius College, Cambridge 82, 181
Calais, France 171
California, University of 204, 251

Calpurnius, Titus 69
Calthorpe, Oxfordshire 52
Calvinism 25, 60
Cambridgeshire 146
Cambridge, University of 14, 23, 27, 32, 36, 44, 64, 68, 71, 72, 74, 78, 82, 96, 111, 118, 120, 128, 130, 133, 146, 153, 172, 176, 192, 193, 196, 197, 218, 220, 239, 241
Camden, William ix, 23, 122-3, 127, 202
Camp, John 180-1
Campaspe 211, 223
Campbell, Archibald. *See* Argyll, 7th Earl of
Campion, Edmund 20, 25, 39, 42, 86, 129, 141-3
Canada 116
Candlewick Street, Candlewick Ward 239, 244
Canossa, Count Ludovico da 18
Canterbury 68, 71, 72, 125
Canterbury, Archbishop of (John Whitgift) 45, 47, 183
Canterbury, Archbishop of (Matthew Parker) 65, 68. *See also* Matthew Parker Scholarship
Canterbury Cathedral 125
Cantiones quae ab argumento sacrae vocantur 16, 126, 146
Cantiones sacrae 143
Canzoniere 86, 252
Capitol Hill, Washington 167
Cardanus's Comfort 162
Carey, Elizabeth. *See* Berkeley, Lady
Carey, George. *See* Hunsdon, 2nd Baron
Carey, Henry. *See* Hunsdon, 1st Baron
Carl H Pforzheimer Library, University of Texas, USA 189
Carlos, Prince of Asturias (Don Carlos) 228
Case, John 15, 148, 236, 255
Casimir, John (Johann [Hans]) of the Palatine-Simmer 223, 231
"Cassimero" 231
Castelnau, Catherine de (daughter of Michel de Castelnau) 111
Castelnau, Michel de, Sieur de la Mauvissière, French Ambassador 111-2, 226, 232

Index

Castiglione, Baldesar 18-19, 30, 39, 161-2, 234
Castile 227, 228, 229
"Castile, King of" 228
Cathay Company 37, 115-6
Catharos 119
Cawood, Gabriel 86-7, 90, 100, 102, 103, 146, 234, 253
Cawood, John 86
Caxton, William 13
Cecil family 34, 36, 51, 65, 84
Cecil House 28
Cecil, Anne. *See* Oxford, Countess of
Cecil, Elizabeth (later Wentworth) 38
Cecil, Robert 38, 82, 89, 184
Cecil, Thomas. *See* Exeter, 1st Earl of
Cecil, William. *See* Burghley, First Baron
Cena de la ceneri, La 111
"Certain Latin verses of his owne …" 252
Chalkhill, Ion 152
Challoner, Thomas 64
Chambers, E K 206, 234
Chapel Royal 14, 16, 17, 84, 124, 125, 136, 139, 141
Chaplin, Charles 207
Chapman, George 96, 98, 100, 113, 187, 202, 203
Charles I, King of England 176
Charles IX, King of France 55
Charlwood, John 240
Charterhouse 130
Children of St Paul's 14, 16, 39, 84, 123, 124
Children of the Chapel Royal 71, 136, 142
Christ Church, Dublin, 24
Christ Church College, Oxford 14, 122
Christopher Marlowe and Richard Baines 76
Christopher Marlowe in London 219
Christopher Marlowe: Poet and Spy 153
Christ's College, Cambridge 64
Christ's Tears over Jerusalem 46
Chronicles of England 43
Chronicles of England, Scotland, and Ireland, The (Holinshed's Chronicles) 33, 34-35, 43, 247
Church of England. See Anglican church

Churchyard's Chips 31
Churchyard's Choice 32
Churchyard, Thomas 31-32, 89, 178-9, 202
Cicero, Marcus Tullius 59, 112, 245, 254, 255
Ciceronis Amor 245, 255
Clare College, Cambridge 78
Clarenceaux King of Arms 101
"Clarke" 248
Clattercote, Oxfordshire 51
Claudian (Claudius Claudianus) 227
Clerke, Bartholemew 39
Clerkenwell, London 131
Clerk of the Revels 212, 224
Clifford's Inn 152
Chaste, Aymar de, French Ambassador 16
Chatterley, Albert x, 148, 163, 164-6, 177, 183, 186, 192, 204
Chaucer, Geoffrey 118, 187
Cheapside, London 36, 183, 192
Chelmsford, Essex 138
Cheney, Jane 138
Cheshire 55
Chettle, Henry 45, 118, 188, 202, 249
Chichester, Sussex 154Chislehurst, Kent 80
Cholmeley, Richard 73
Clink Prison, Southwark 140, 172
Cob, Mr 36
Coke, Edward (Solicitor General) 183
Colchester, Essex 160
Coldiron, A E B 94
College of Physicians 39
Collier, J Payne 204
Cologne 233
Coluthi … Helenae Raptus. See *Helena Raptus*
Coluthus 120, 236, 254
"Come to me grief for ever" 127
Commedia dell'arte 210
Community College of Philadelphia, USA 207
Company of Scriveners 208-9
Compendium Memoriae Localis 110, 112, 119, 244, 254

Compendius Rehearsal, A 116
Complaints 187
Congress of the United States 167
Constable, Henry 23, 187
"Constant Penelope" 127
Contworthe, Edward 50
Copernicus, Nicholas, and his theory 108-9
Corbet family 58
Corbet, Mary. *See* Lee, Mary
Cornelia 207-9, 224, 225, 238
Cornwallis, Anne (née Barrow) 174
Cornwallis, Anne (née Fincham) 174
Cornwallis, Anne (married William Halse) 175
Cornwallis, Anne (née Jerningham) 170-1, 175
Cornwallis, Anne. *See* Argyll, Countess of
Cornwallis, Charles 172, 174-5, 180
Cornwallis, Cornelia 175
Cornwallis, Elizabeth 175
Cornwallis family x, 23, 76, 167-74, 176, 177, 179, 181
Cornwallis, Frances 177, 178, 179-183
Cornwallis, Frederick 174, 184
Cornwallis, John 76, 149, 170, 175, 176, 177, 180, 183
Cornwallis, Lucy (née Neville) 172-3, 175, 177, 184
Cornwallis-Lysons Manuscript 167-76, 178
Cornwallis, Mary. *See* Bath, Countess of
Cornwallis, Thomas 149, 170-2, 173, 177, 181, 184, 194
Cornwallis, Thomas (son of William and Lucy) 177
Cornwallis, William 149, 172-5, 176, 177, 178-84, 185, 193-4, 205, 218, 246, 249
Cornwallis, William (essayist) 174
Cornwallis, William (priest) 172
Corpus Christi College, Cambridge 36, 72, 196
Cortegiano, Il Libro dl (*The Book of the Courtier*), 18, 22, 39, 161, 234
"Corydon" (Thomas Watson/Calpurnius) 68, 187, 201, 255
Countess of Pembroke's Ivychurch, The 120, 254

Courtlie Controversie of Cupids Cautels, A 211, 222
Court of Chancery 14, 161
Court of Common Pleas 150
Court of the Queen's Bench 186, 248
Covell, William 190-1, 192
Coxeter, Thomas 120
Cranmer, Thomas, Archbishop of Canterbury, 125, 128
Crapper, Thomas 218
Crawford, Charles 247
Creagh, Richard. *See* Armagh, Archbishop of
Cromwell, Thomas 128, 134
"Crowned with flowers and lilies" 144
"Cruse" 162
Cuisse Rompue, La 26
Cujas, Jacques de 60
Cup Field, Lincoln's Inn 81
Currance (school of dancing) 137
Curtain Road, Shoreditch 151
Curtain Theatre, Shoreditch 150, 151, 206, 221, 245
Cymbeline 35
Cynthia 187
"Cynthia" 235
"Cyprian, Duke of Castile" 227

Dale, Valentine 59
Dalton, James 62, 193
Danby, William, Coroner of the Queen's Household 74-5
Daniel, Samuel 23, 47, 187, 188, 195, 202
Danter, John 188-9, 256
Danvers, George 51-2, 54
Danvers, John 51
Daphnaïda 187
Darcy, Thomas 138
Dark Horse, The, Aldersgate 146
Darloe, Robert 246
Darrell, Frances 65
Darrell, George 65
Darrell, Mary, 64-5

Darrell, Philippa 65
Darrell, Thomas 64-5
Dartmoor, Devonshire 134
Davies, John 202
Davies of Hereford, John 203
Davis, Captain John 116, 117
Day, John (printer) 36, 87, 88, 126, 188
Day, John (dramatist) 202
Day, Richard 88
Day, William. *See* Windsor, Dean of
Dead Man's Fortune, The 246
Decameron, The 200
De Circulo Artium et Philosophiae 59
Dedication to Sir Philip Sidney, 22
Dee, John 23, 26, 39, 108-9, 113-7, 202
De Eloquentia et Cicerone 59
Defence of Poetry, A 68
Defence of Poesy, The 22, 68, 85
Dekker, Thomas 110, 118, 121, 202, 205, 208
De la causa, principio e uno 111
De Laude Pisonis 69
De La Warr, 2nd Baron (Thomas West) 30
Delights for Ladies 193
Democritus 44, 110
Denham, Henry 33
Denmark 44, 81, 104
Denny, Edward 25
Deptford, Kent 35, 74, 81, 83
Derby, Countess of (Elizabeth de Vere) 117
Derby circle 117, 238
Derby, 4th Earl of (Henry Stanley) 67, 224, 226, 229, 234, 238
Derby, 5th Earl of (Ferdinando Stanley, Lord Strange) 114, 229, 238, 246
Derby, 6th Earl of (William Stanley) 117
Derbyshire 36
De Remedia Amoris 252
De Revolutionibus 108
Desiderata curiosa 34
Deus venerunt gentes" 142-3
Devereux, Penelope.
    See Devonshire, Countess of

Devereux, Robert. *See* Essex, 2nd Earl of
Devonshire 37, 134
Devonshire, Countess of (Penelope Rich) 23, 127
"Dick the horse-keeper" 83
Dido, Queen of Carthage, The Tragedy of 46, 47, 189
Digges, Leonard 109
Digges, Thomas 108-10
Dillenburg, Netherlands 32
Discourse of a Discovery for a New Passage to Cataia, A 117
Discourse on Irish Affairs 22
Discourse on the Late Earthquakes 41
Discoverie of Edmund Campion and his Confederates, A ... 42
Diss, Suffolk 170
Doctor Faustus 73, 83, 113, 235, 237
Don Carlos 228
Don John. *See* John of Austria
Donno, Elizabeth Story 33
"Don Pedro" 215
Dorset, 1st Earl of (Thomas Sackville).
    See Buckhurst, Baron
Dorset, 2nd Earl of (Robert Sackville) 38-9
Douai, Netherlands 60, 220-1
Douai, University of.
    See English College, Douai
Douglas, William. *See* Angus, 10th Earl of
Dover, Kent 65
Dover Priory, Kent 125
Dow, Robert 25
Dowland, John 24, 25
Dowland, Robert 24
Downhall (?Downham), Gregory 96, 205
"Downhalus, C" 96, 205
Downie, J A 197
Drake, Sir Francis 230
Drapers' Company 38, 50
Drayton, Michael 114, 194, 202
Drummond, William 202
Drury Lane, London 176

Drury, Sir William 232
Dublin, Ireland 24
Duchy of Lancaster 135
Dudley, Ambrose. *See* Warwick, Third Earl of
Dudley group 42
Dudley, Lord Guildford 20
Dudley, Jane. *See* Grey, Jane
Dudley, John. *See* Warwick, 1st Duke of, 1st Duke of Northumberland
Dudley, Lord Guildford 20
Dudley, Katherine. *See* Huntingdon, Countess of
Dudley, Mary. *See* Sidney, Mary
Dudley, Robert. *See* Leicester, 1st Earl of
Dudley, Robert (illegitimate son of 1st Earl of Leicester) 42
Durham House 112, 113
Dutch immigrants 73, 231
Dutch Church, Broad Street 73, 74, 231
Dutch Revolt 12, 55, 60-61, 176, 211, 220-1, 222, 223, 231
Dyer, blacksmith 139
Dyer's Cape, Canada 116
Dyer, Edward 20, 95, 115-6, 127, 169, 187, 202
Dymocke, Edward 23
Dyson, Henry 43

Earl of Derby's Men 114, 212, 224, 229, 234
Earl of Leicester's Boys 39, 42
Earl of Oxford's Men 29, 138
Earl of Pembroke's Men 46
Earl of Sussex's Men 39, 247
Earl of Warwick's Men 29, 41
Earl of Worcester's Men 239
East Anglia 33, 44, 62, 160, 178, 179, 186.
    See also Essex, Norfolk, Suffolk
East Bilney, Norfolk 33
East Cheap 62
East Horndon, Essex 135
East, Thomas 42, 44, 87, 146, 147, 187, 246, 255
Eccles, Mark 57, 60, 63, 98, 219
Ecclesiastes 37
Eclogues, Epitaphs, and Sonnets 66

Ede, Richard 79
Edinburgh, Scotland 32, 37
Edward Bonaventure 243
Edwards, Philip 208, 211, 212-13, 214, 216, 217
Edyall, Henry 131
Effingham, 2nd Baron Howard of (Charles Howard) 35, 160, 163
Edward VI, King of England 12, 27, 125, 128, 135
Eirēnarchia sive Elizabetha 119, 244, 253
"E K" 97, 222
Electra 219
Elegie, or, Friends Passion for his Astrophill 96
Eliot, George 142
Elizabeth I, Queen of England 12-13, 14, 15-16, 17, 18, 20-21, 22, 23, 26, 27-9, 32, 34, 36, 37, 38, 42, 43, 53, 55, 56, 70, 72, 73, 81, 83, 88, 94-5, 111, 114, 116, 119, 123, 125, 126, 128, 132, 133, 135, 138, 139-40, 141, 144, 147, 149, 153, 154, 155, 156-9, 162, 165, 166, 171, 173, 177-9, 184, 187, 188, 197, 205-6, 221, 226, 229, 231, 232, 233, 235, 239, 240, 241, 245, 253, 256
and *passim*
Elizabethan Stage, The 206
Ellison, Matthew 243
Ellyson, Cuthbert 50
Elyot, Thomas 200
Elysium 208, 195, 214, 242, 243
Elvetham 155-66, 174, 206, 256
Endymion 112
"Endymion" 249
England's Helicon 161, 213, 227
English Channel 27, 162
English College, Douai 58-9, 60, 75-6, 141, 220-1, 225, 236
English College, Rheims.
    See English College, Douai
English College (Venerable English College), Rome 40
English College, Valladolid 53
Epistle of St Paul to the Ephesians 34

Epitaph to Anne Lodge, An 68
Epping Forest, Essex 20
"Erastus" 212, 224
Erne, Lucas 209, 212, 217
Essex 125, 127, 133, 134, 135, 138, 160, 173, 176, 182, 193
Essex House, The Strand 46
Essex, 2nd Earl of (Robert Devereux) 36, 43, 46, 81, 84, 90, 114, 134, 174, 181, 203, 246, 247, 255
Este (Est), Thomas. *See* East, Thomas
Eton College 52
"Euphues" 30, 45
Euphues and his England 30, 87
Euphues, the Anatomy of Wit 30, 87, 117, 118, 146
Euphuism, school of 30, 41, 45, 97, 234
Europe 13, 17, 20, 22, 27, 28, 50, 53, 56, 57, 59, 77, 85, 87, 97, 100, 108, 123, 176, 185, 220 and *passim*
Evans, Henry 124
"Even as the fruitful bee" 85, 253
Exequiae Illustratissimi Equitis D Philippi Sidnaei … 22
Exeter, Devon 37
Exeter, 1st Earl of (Thomas Cecil) 172, 240
Eye, Suffolk 170

Faerie Queene, The 187, 238
"Fagot, Henri" 111
"Falstaff, Sir John" 45
Farnham, Surrey 154
Faunt, Nicholas 71
"Faustus, Dr" 113
Feldman, Abraham Bronson 97, 206-51
Felix and Philiomena 206
Ferrabosco, Alfonso 17, 124, 147, 149
Ferrara, Italy 57
Ferryman, Peter 96
Ficino, Marsilio 111
"Fidelia" 234
Field, John 108
Field, Richard 37, 114

Fincham, Norfolk 174
Fincham, Thomas 174
Finsbury Fields, Islington 151
Finsbury Prison 15
Firenzuola 97
First Book of Madrigals 138
First Folio 101, 103, 167, 215
First Set of Italian Madrigals Englished, The x, 23, 53, 148-150, 165, 180, 246, 255
Fisher, Jasper 29, 172
Fisher's Folly 29, 31, 119, 149, 150, 172-3, 174, 175, 176, 177, 221, 239, 244, 249
Fishmongers' Company 87
Fitzalan, Henry. *See* Arundel, 12th Earl of
Five Hundred Points of Good Husbandry 130
Five Plays in One 206
Fleay, Frederick Gard 246
Fleet Prison 133, 183, 192
Fleet Street 39, 44
Fleetwood, William (Recorder of London) 153
Fleming, Abraham 31, 32-6, 37, 43, 202
Fleming, Samuel 35
Fletcher, John 49, 202
Floraes Paradise Beautified 193
Florence, Italy 43, 87
Flores, Battle of 158
Florio, John 89, 111, 202, 203
Flourish upon Fancy, A 161
Flues, Barboura 106
Flushing, Netherlands 25, 72
Folger, Emily 167
Folger, Henry Clay 167
Folger Shakespeare Library, Washington, USA 167, 169, 189
Ford, John 202
Fore Street, Cripplegate 40, 51
"Fortuna" 234
Forman, Blanche 51
Forman, Simon 114
Forman, William
Fotheringay Castle, Northamptonshire 81, 143
Four Letters and Certain Sonnets 45, 47

France 17, 22, 23, 30, 31, 40, 41, 46, 55, 56, 57, 64, 80, 82, 83, 96, 112, 133, 158, 170, 197, 198, 211, 219, 220, 221, 222, 226. 229, 233 and *passim*
Franchiotto, Tomaso 55
Francis, Duke of Anjou and Alençon. *See* Anjou and Alençon, Duke of
Frankfurt Book Fair 88
Fraunce, Abraham 47, 120, 148, 187, 194-5, 202, 254
Freeman, Arthur 205, 208-9, 214, 251
French Littelton 38
French, Peter J 115
French Schoolmaster 38, 39
Friar Bacon and Bungay 45, 237
Frizer, Ingram 74-5
Frobisher, Martin 32, 37, 41, 115, 117

Gadbury, Ellen. *See* Googe, Ellen
Gager, William 22
Galileo Galilei 108
"Gardens, The", Bishopsgate 80
Garnet, Henry 52-3, 54, 133, 143
Garnet, Richard 54
Garnier, Robert 208, 209
"Garter, Bernard". *See* Googe, Barnabe
Gascoigne, George 87, 117, 161, 179, 202, 233
Gate House, The, St Botolph's without Aldgate 244
"Gaunt, John of" 228
Geneva, Swiss Confederacy 36, 37, 71
George, G D 40
Germany 56, 71, 218, 223, 233 and *passim*. *See also* separate states
Ghent, Netherlands 60
Gifford, Gilbert 82
Gilbert, Adrian 115, 117, 202
Gilbert, Gifford 82, 83
Gilbert, Humphrey 116-7, 202
Gilded Cup, Fore Street, Cripplegate 40
Gilder the tumbler 135
Globe, The 189

"G M" (Gervase Markham or George Montemayor?) 169
Goes, Netherlands. *See* Tergoes
Golden Ball, The, St Paul's Churchyard 38
Golding, Arthur 29, 34
Goldingham, Henry 182
Gonzaga, Elizabetta. *See* Urbino, Duchess of
Googe, Barnabe 34, 64-6
Googe, Constance 64
Googe, Ellen 64
Googe, Margaret 64
Googe, Robert 64
Googe, William 64
Gorbuduc 38
Gosson, Stephen 31, 68-9
Governor of Portsmouth. *See* Sussex, 5th Earl of
Gradualia 128, 134
Gradualia II 134
Gratiae Theatrales 206
Gratification unto Master John Case ... 148, 150, 236, 255
Graves, Siege of 158
Gray's Inn Road, Holborn 150
Great Yarmouth, Suffolk 46-7
"Greene, Richard" 248-9
Greene, Robert 31, 44-6, 49, 89-90, 117-9, 173, 202, 207, 225, 237, 239, 241, 245, 248-9, 255
Greensleeves 25, 66
Greenwich, Kent 16, 34, 74, 197, 244
Grenville, Sir Richard 158
Gregory XIII, Pope 70, 226
Gresshop, John 72, 73
Greville, Fulke. *See* Brooke, First Baron
Grey, Henry 156
Grey, Jane 20, 128, 135, 154, 171
Griffith, Mr 61
Groats-worth of Wit, A 45, 90, 118, 249
Grocers' Company 67
Gruithuissens, Mrs 26
Guise, Henry I, Duke of 61, 229
Gun, The, St Paul's Churchyard 66

Index

Gunpowder Plot 52, 134
"Gylham" 136
Gynge Abbess, Essex 134

Hacket, Thomas 44
Hackney, Middlesex 29, 143
"Haemon" 97, 219
Hakluyt, Richard 23
Hales, Robert 180-1, 182, 183
Hall, William 39-40
Halliwell, James Orchard 169-70, 206
Hamlet 44, 207, 241, 242
Hamlet Himself 207
Hampton Court, Richmond, Surrey 16, 135
Handel, George 207
Hansen, Adolf 104
Harington, John 23, 25, 35, 119, 192-3, 218
Hariot, Thomas 113-4, 202
"Harley" 60
Harley, John 127, 140, 141
Harlington, Middlesex 131, 140, 143, 147
Harrison Fellowship 250-1
Harrison, John 33
Harrow-on-the-Hill 81
Harsnett, Samuel 90
Harte, John, Lord Mayor of London 152
Hart Street, St Olave's Parish 50
Harvard University 170, 189, 254, 256
Harvey, Gabriel 30, 45, 46, 47, 48, 76, 89, 90, 162, 187, 192, 194-5, 202, 218, 221-2, 249
Harvey, John 76
Harvey, Mercy 76
Harvey, Richard 45, 76
Harvey, William 113
Hathaway, Anne 169
Hatton, Christopher 17, 32, 147, 153
Have with you to Saffron-Walden ... 45, 189
"Have with yow to Walsingame".
    See "Walsingham"
Hayward, John 90
Hedingham Upland 243
Hekatompathia or Passionate Century of Love,
    The 86, 87, 90-119, 145, 148, 162, 163, 199-201, 204, 205, 210, 212, 213, 214-16, 219, 221, 224, 227, 233, 234, 236, 243, 252, 253
"Helen of Troy" 107, 120
Helenae Raptus 120, 194, 236, 254
Hemmingsen, Niels 34
Heneage, Thomas 81, 82, 193-4, 205
Hengrave Hall, Suffolk 159
Heninger Jr, S K 93, 98, 100
Henri III, King of France 111
Henry I, Prince of Joinville, Duke of Guise, Count of Eu. *See* Guise, Duke of
Henry VII, King of England 14,
Henry VIII, King of England 14, 15, 17, 31, 47, 125, 128, 134, 135
Henry the Fourth Part Two 101
Henslowe, Philip 240
Hentzner, 16
Heptameron of Civil Discourses, An 85, 204, 244, 253
Herbert circle. *See* Sidney circle
Herbert, Henry. *See* Pembroke, 2nd Earl of
Herbert, Katherine 27
Herbert, Mary. *See* Pembroke, Countess of
Herbert, Philip. *See* Montgomery, 1st Earl of
Herbert, William. *See* Pembroke, 3rd Earl of
"Hercules" 249
Herefordshire 23, 44
"Hermione" 234, 235
Hero and Leander 73
"Hero and Leander" 235
Heron Hall, East Horndon, Essex 135
Hertford, 1st Earl of (Edward Seymour) 128, 154-66, 256
Hertford, Countess of (Frances Howard) 31, 154, 157, 158, 160
Hertford, Countess of (Katherine Grey) 154
Hertfordshire, 171
Hess, W Ron 177
Heywood, Thomas 48-9, 202, 207, 208, 216, 224, 250

"Hieronimo" ("Ieronimo") 213, 225, 227, 228, 229, 230, 231, 237, 243.
　See also *Ieronimo, The First Part of*
Highgate, Hornsey/St Pancras 184
High Holborn 150
Hill, Goodwife 137
Hill, Nicholas 31, 43-4, 202
Hinton, Mistress 180
Hippolytus 97, 219
History of English Literature, A 117
History of Galien of France 41
History of Love and Fortune.
　See *Rare Triumphs of Love and Fortune, The*
History of Richard III 160
History of the Soldan and the Duke of—, The 212, 224
Hoby, Thomas 18, 39
Hog Lane, Bishopsgate 151
Holborn 32, 150, 161, 188
Holinshed, Raphael 34, 43, 247
Holinshed's Chronicles. See *Chronicles of England, Scotland, and Ireland, The*
Hollyband, Claudius 38, 39
Holt, Worcestershire 193
Holy Cross Abbey, Waltham, Essex 125
Holy Ghost, The, St Paul's Churchyard 86
Holy League 229
Homer 41, 97
Honan, (Leonard Hobart) Park 72, 73, 153
Honey, William 71, 196-8
Honourable entertainment given to the Queen's Majesty in Progress ... 163-6, 256
Hopton, Owen, Lieutenant of the Tower of London 152, 245
Horace 97, 237
Horne, Robert. *See* Winchester, Bishop of
Hoskins, William 188
Hotson, Leslie 74, 75
Houghton Library, Harvard University 170, 255
Householder's Philosophy, The.
　See *Padre di Famiglia, Il*
Howard, Anne. *See* Arundel, Countess of

Howard, Charles.
　See Effingham, 2nd Baron Howard of
Howard family 229, 230, 232
Howard, Frances. *See* Hertford, Countess of
Howard, Henry. *See* Northampton, 1st Earl of
Howard, Henry. *See* Southampton, Earl of
Howard, Philip.
　See Arundel, 13th Earl of, Earl of Surrey
Howard, Thomas (Admiral).
　See Suffolk, 1st Earl of
Howard, Thomas. *See* Norfolk, 4th Duke of
Howell, James 202
Hues, Robert 114, 202
Huguenots 38, 77, 111, 121, 126
Humanism ix, 29
Hundreth Good Points of Husbandrie, A 130
Hungerford of Farleigh, Walter 156
Hunsdon, 1st Baron (Henry Carey) 16
Hunsdon, 2nd Baron (George Carey) 114, 156, 189, 202
Huntingdon, Countess of (Katherine Dudley) 21
Huntington Library, Harvard 189, 256
Hurleyford, Middlesex 143
Hyde, Thomas 52
"Hydra" 249

"Ieronimo, Marshal" 230, 231
Ieronimo, The First Part of 230, 231, 243, 250
"In angel's weed" 143
Index Librorum Prohibitorum 66
Ingatestone, Essex 127, 134-37
Ingatestone Hall, Essex 134-9, 182
Inns of Court 62, 65, 85, 95, 112, 137, 152, 192, 254
In Praise of Music 15, 148, 255
Ipswich, Suffolk 171
Ireland 17, 20, 22, 24, 31, 32, 65, 122, 141, 174
Isle of Dogs, The 46
Italian Madrigals Englished. See *First Set of...*
Italy ix, 18, 30, 40, 56, 57, 58, 59, 85, 162, 219, 220, 221

Ivychurch, Wiltshire 21

Jaggard, Isaac 103
James IV 45
James VI of Scotland and I of England 31, 37, 133, 134, 160, 175, 240
Jeffe, Thomas 136
Jeffes, Abel 210, 250
Jennings, Miles 41
Jerningham, John 170
Jeronimo. *See* Ieronimo
Jerusalem 46, 125, 142, 143
Jesus Christ 46
Jesus, Society of 13, 20, 25, 39, 40, 42, 52, 53, 81, 86, 114, 129, 133, 141-3, 176, 232
Jewell House of Art and Nature, The 193
Jew of Malta, The 73, 82
Jews (in Babylon) 144
John (Juan) of Austria, Don 20, 60, 221
"John the Frenchman" 136
Johnson, Christopher 52-53, 54, 59
Johnson, Edward 159
Jonson, Ben 44, 46, 49, 96, 202, 226, 230
Joyce, James 207
Justinian I 57

Kendall, Roy 76, 77, 82
Kendall, Timothy 34
Kenilworth, Warwickshire 20, 179
Kent 20, 64, 65, 74, 80, 124, 125, 161, 188, 245, 247, 128, 250
Kerman, Joseph 149
Ket, Robert 171
Keymis, Laurence 114
King Lear 35, 38, 67
"King of Spain" (*Ieronimo*) 231
"King of Spain" (*The Spanish Tragedy*) 226, 228
King's College Chapel, Cambridge 14
King's Council (Henry VIII) 134
King's (Queen's) School, Canterbury 68, 72, 73
Kirkeby, Joan. *See* Laxton, Joan
Kitchen, Richard 152

Kitson, Thomas. *See* Kytson, Thomas
Knight, (E K?) 222
Knights Conjuring, A 118, 205
Knox, John 36, 37
Knyvett, Thomas 28
Kuriyama, Constance Brown 197
Kurosawa, Akira 118, 205
Kyd, Francis 241
Kyd, Thomas ix, 45, 49, 67, 73, 74, 82, 117, 118, 119, 202, 205, 206, 207-11, 212, 214, 216, 219, 224-5, 230, 231, 234, 235, 237-8, 241, 243, 246-7, 250, 251
Kytson, Thomas 159, 171, 172

Lady of May, The 20, 22
"Laertes" 246
Lamb, Mary Ellen 113
Lamberhurst, Kent 65
Lamentations of Amyntas for the Death of Phillis, The 120, 254
Lamentations of Jeremiah 125
"Lane, John" (Marlowe alias?) 197-8
Lane, William 68
Lanier family 17
Laski, Adalbert 112, 116, 254
Lasso, Orlando di 123
Latymer, 4th Baron (John Neville) 172-3
Laugwitz Verlag 218
Laxton, Joan 68
Laxton, William 68
Learned Dialogue of Bernard Palessy ..., A 121, 254
Leaves from a poetical miscellany of Anne Campbell, Countess of Argyll. See *Cornwallis-Lysons Manuscript*
Lee, Anne. *See* Watson, Anne
Lee family 51-2
Lee, Henry 23
Lee, Mary (remarries as Mary Corbet) 55, 56, 58
Lee, Richard 55
Lee, Robert 246
Lee, Thomas 51, 52, 53, 54, 55, 56
Leez (Leighs) Priory, Essex (Lord Rich) 138

Leicester, 1st Earl of (Robert Dudley) 17, 20-1, 22, 28, 32, 39, 42, 55, 56, 79, 80, 81, 83, 112, 114, 115, 116, 141, 158, 235, 236
Leicester's Commonwealth 83
Leicestershire 35, 52, 143
Leire King of England and his Three Daughters. See *King Lear*
Lennard, Sampson 65
"Lentulo" 235
Lethe 236
Let Others Praise ... See *Gratification unto Master John Case, A*
Letter to Queen Elizabeth, A 21
Leucippus 44
Lewes Priory, Sussex 39, 132
Lewis, C S 45
Lewisham, Kent 38
Liber primus sacrarum cantionum quinque vocum 132
Liber secundus sacrarum cantionum 133
Lichfield, Henry 137, 138
Lichfield, Staffordshire 20, 130
Life and Death of Heliogabilus, The 237
Life and Reign of King Henry IV, The First Part of the 90
Life, Loves and Achievements of Christopher Marlowe ..., The 196
Lincoln 63, 124, 130, 131, 139, 149
Lincoln, Bishop of (John Aylmer). See London, Bishop of
Lincoln Cathedral 124
Lincolnshire 64, 65, 83, 160
Lincoln's Inn 67
Lincoln's Inn Fields 81
Lippomano, Hieronimo 240
Lodge, Anne 68
Lodge, Sara 67, 68
Lodge, Sir Thomas 68
Lodge, Thomas ix, 31, 67-8, 69, 117, 119, 194, 202, 210
Lok, Anne 36-37
Lok, Henry 31, 36, 37, 202, 203

Lok, Henry (the elder) 36, 37
Lok, Michael 37, 115-6
London, Bishop of (John Aylmer, former Bishop of Lincoln) 140
London, City of x, 17, 19, 21, 27, 29, 32, 33, 35, 37, 38, 39, 40, 43, 44, 45, 46, 49, 50, 51, 54, 59, 62, 63, 64, 66, 67, 68, 70, 71, 73, 77, 78, 79, 80, 84, 85, 87, 88, 89, 109, 111, 112, 114, 118, 119, 124, 125, 128, 129, 130, 131, 132, 135, 138, 139, 140, 141, 142, 143, 145, 146, 151, 152, 153, 154, 160, 161, 169, 171, 172, 173, 175, 176, 185, 186, 188, 204, 206, 211, 219, 222, 231, 235, 236, 237, 239, 240, 241, 243, 244, 245, 247, 248, 249 and *passim*
London Stone 239
Looking Glasse for Lovers, A 98-100, 109-10, 211, 253
Lopez, Roderigo 114
Lord Admiral's Men 35, 236, 239
Lord Chamberlain. See Hunsden, 2nd Baron
Lord Chamberlain. See Sussex, 3rd Earl of
Lord Chamberlain's Men 189
Lord High Steward. See Arundel, 12th Earl of
Lord Howard's Men. See Lord Admiral's Men
Lord Mayor of London. See Forman, William
Lord Mayor of London. See Harte, John
Lord Mayor of London. See Lodge, Sir Thomas
"Lorenzo" 215, 243
Louvain, France 59
Love and Fortune. See *Rare Triumphs of Love and Fortune, The*
Love's Labour's Lost 112
Low Countries. See Netherlands, The
Lowestoft, Suffolk 44
Lucan (Marcus Annaeus Lucanus) 49, 73, 97
"Lucentio" 57, 176
Lucrece, Sign of, St Paul's Churchyard 38
Luddington family 68, 69
Luddington, Henry 68
Luddington, Joan. See Laxton, Joan
Ludgate, London 206

Ludlow, Shropshire 21, 31
Lumley, 1st Baron (John Lumley) 132-3, 220
Lumley family 132
Lumley, John. *See* Lumley, 1st Baron
Lundy Island 44
Luther, Martin 88
Luton, Bedfordshire 138
Lyly, John 30, 31, 41, 44, 45, 68, 87, 89, 95, 97, 98, 100, 112, 117, 118, 119, 124, 146, 173, 189, 202, 205, 211-2, 223-4, 228, 234, 239
Lysons, Samuel 167-9, 173, 175

Macander, Thomas 35
Macbeth 35, 206
Machiavelli 87
Madrid, Spain 227, 228, 230, 240
Magdalen College, Oxford 122
Manchester, Lancashire 117
Manners, Edward. *See* Rutland, 3rd Earl of
Manners, Elizabeth. *See* Ros, 15th Baroness of
Manners, Elizabeth. *See* Rutland, Countess of
Manners, John. *See* Rutland, 4th Earl of
Manners, Roger. *See* Rutland, 5th Earl of
Mantell, Margaret. *See* Googe, Margaret
Mantuanus, Baptisa 97, 195
Manucci, Jacomo 55
Manwood, Roger 152, 245
Map of Modern London x
Marenzio, Luca 147, 149, 236, 246, 255
Margaretting, Essex 136
Markham, Catherine 64
Markham family 36
Markham, Gervase 203
Markham, Robert 64
Marlowe, Christopher ix, 35, 46, 49, 68, 71-5, 76, 77, 81, 82-3, 95, 96, 107, 110, 113, 117, 118, 119, 120, 150, 151, 152-3, 186, 187-8, 189, 196-8, 202, 218, 219, 223, 231, 235, 236, 237, 238, 239, 241, 245, 247, 249, 256
Marlowe, John 71
Marlowe, Katherine 71
"Marprelate, Martin" 33, 42, 45, 88, 89, 90, 161

Mars 57, 246
Marsh, Henry 187, 254
Marshalsea Prison, Southwark 46, 79, 132, 182, 192
Marston, John 202
Martial 97
"Martin, Giles" 84, 132
Martin, Gregory 76
Mary I, Queen of England (Mary Tudor) 36, 40, 62, 86, 123, 125, 128, 135, 144, 149, 171
Mary, Queen of Scots (Mary Stuart) 12, 13, 16, 25, 26, 38, 80, 81, 83, 84, 111, 131, 132, 133, 143, 171, 232, 240
Massacre at Paris, The 73, 77
Massinger, Philip 202
Master of the Revels. *See* Buc, George
Master of the Wards. *See* Burghley, 1st Baron
Matthew Parker Scholarship 71, 72, 197
Mawde, Bernard 81
Mawdeley, Elizabeth (sister of William Watson Sr) 51
Mayor of Newcastle. *See* Ellison, Cuthbert
Measure for Measure 244
Meautys, Hercules 173
Meautys, Jane 173, 184
Medici, Catherine de' 226, 229
Meditation of a Penitent Sinner, A 36
"Meliboeus" (Francis Walsingham) 69
Meliboeus Thomae Watsoni, sivè Ecloga ... 56, 69, 120, 148, 153, 187-8, 194, 201, 214, 243, 245, 255
Melville, James 16
Menaphon 44, 207, 208, 225, 241, 243, 245
Mendoza, Bernardino de 89, 211, 222, 230, 232
Merchant of Venice, The 41
Merchant Taylors' School 14, 67, 119, 209-10, 225
Meres, Francis 30, 46, 194, 205, 210, 219
"Michael, a servant" 249
Mervyn, Sir James 156
Messenger of the Chamber 42, 74, 241

Metamorphoses 29
Midas 228
Middlesex 29, 112, 129, 131, 132, 140, 143, 147, 152, 245
Middlesex County Coroner 152
Middlesex Sessions 143, 245
Middle Temple, Inns of Court 112, 137, 139, 254
Middleton, Thomas 202, 284
Milan, Italy 58
Milky Way (Galaxia) 108-10
Millington, Thomas 67, 189
Milton, John 202, 209
"Minola" household 176
Minster-in-Thanet, Kent 125
Mirror for Man, A 31
Mirror of Mutability, The 38, 40, 41, 221-2
"Misodiaboles" 193-4
Moffet, Thomas 115
Molyneux, Edmund 22
Molyneux, Emery 115, 202
Monmouthshire 83
Montacute, Somerset 137
Montemayor, George 169
Montgomery, 1st Earl of (Philip Herbert) 27, 101
Montgomery, Countess of (Susan de Vere) 101, 244
Moore Smith, G C 197
Moorning Dittie 40
More, Katherine. *See* Katherine Byrd
More, Thomas 133
Morgan, Thomas 80, 83-4
Morley, Thomas 43, 56, 84, 123, 130, 132, 157
Morrison, Bridget. *See* Sussex, Countess of
Mortlake, Surrey 115, 116
Mounson, Thomas 182
Mount Fisher. *See* Fisher's Folly
Much Ado About Nothing 215
Mulcaster, Richard 14, 67, 119, 126, 175, 209-10, 225
Mundy (Munday), Anthony 31, 37-43, 89, 124, 142, 173, 202, 221-2, 239, 241

Mundy, Jane 38
Mundy, Christopher 38
Mundy, William 124
Murderous Michael 247
Muses, The 56
Musical Banquet, A 24
Musica Britannica x
Musica Transalpina 147, 148
My Ladye Nevells Booke of Virginal Music 139, 140

Nag's Head, Cheapside, London 192, 218, 249
Namur, Netherlands 60, 221
Nashe, Thomas ix, 31, 44-7, 89, 95, 117, 118, 119, 164, 173, 188, 189-92, 195, 202, 203, 207, 208, 224-5, 241-2, 243, 245, 249
Nashe's Lenten Stuff 47
Needlers Lane, St Pancras 35
Nelson, Alan H 163
Netherlands, The 12, 25, 26, 29, 31-32, 37, 38, 40, 55, 56, 58, 59, 60, 72, 73, 74, 80, 81, 83, 84, 87, 132, 147, 158, 176, 186, 220-1, 223, 226, 227, 231, 235, 236
Never Too Late 249
Neville, Charles. *See* Westmorland, 6th Earl of
Neville, Dorothy 172
Neville, John. *See* Latymer, 4th Baron
Neville, Lucy. *See* Cornwallis, Lucy
Newberie, Ralph 33
Newcastle-upon-Tyne, 50
New College, Oxford 15, 53, 54, 59, 64, 122
New College School, Oxford 15
New Discourse of a Stale Subject ... 25, 192-3
Newgate Prison 150, 152, 180, 245
New Year's Gift, A 66
Nicholl, Charles 63, 70, 78, 82, 176
Nichols, John 155
Noell, Henry 112, 119, 244-5, 254
Nonsuch Palace, Surrey 16, 132
Norfolk 25, 33, 127, 129, 133, 135, 145, 170, 171, 174 and *passim*
Norfolk, 4th Duke of (Thomas Howard) 40, 76, 133, 171

Norreys, 1st Baron (Henry Norris) 129, 142
Norris, Henry. *See* Norreys, 1st Baron
Norris, Sir John ("Black Jack") 158
Northampton, 1st Earl of (Henry Howard) 94, 111, 128, 133-4, 226, 232
Northampton, Marquess of (William Parr) 171
Northern Rising 28, 53, 76, 171
Northumberland, 7th Earl of (Thomas Percy) 53
Northumberland, 9th Earl of (Henry Percy) 43, 112, 113, 119, 120, 121, 202, 236, 254, 255
Northwest Passage 32, 115
Norton Folgate, London 146, 149, 151, 152, 185, 239, 245
Norton, Thomas 25
Norwich, Norfolk 145, 171, 178, 179, 186, 240
Norwich Castle 171
Nottingham, 1st Earl of.
  See Effingham, 2nd Baron of
Nottinghamshire 36, 62, 63
"Nowell, Mr" 84. *See also* Noell, Henry
Nowell, Thomas 40
Nuremberg 126

Ocland, Christopher 119, 244, 253
Odiham, Hampshire 154, 156
Oedipus 97, 219
"Oedipus" 234
Oedipus Coloneus 219
Oedipus Rex 219
Of the Markes of the Children of God 37
Old Bailey (sessions house of the City of London) 152, 245
Old Testament 107
Oliphant, E H C 206
"Olympians" 234
Ongar, Essex 127
Onley, Elizabeth. *See* Rolleston, Elizabeth
Oriel College, Oxford 161
Orrell, George 150, 247-8
"O that most rare breast" 127
Ovid 29, 30, 49, 72, 85, 97
Oxford, Oxfordshire 14, 15

Oxford, 11th Earl of (Richard de Vere) 167, 169
Oxford, 12th Earl of (John de Vere) 167, 169, 173
Oxford, 13th Earl of (John de Vere) 101, 173
Oxford, 14th Earl of ("Little" John de Vere) 101, 173
Oxford, 15th Earl of (John de Vere) 101
Oxford, 16th Earl of (John de Vere) 29, 101, 173
Oxford, 17th Earl of (Edward de Vere) x, 13, 27-47, 48, 49, 58, 62, 65, 66, 67, 76, 85-6, 87, 94-5, 96, 98, 100, 101, 116, 117, 119, 124, 127-8, 133, 134, 138, 149, 161-3, 169, 170, 173, 174, 176-7, 179, 188, 189, 199-200, 202, 206, 207, 221, 226, 229, 232, 233-4, 238, 239-40, 241, 243, 244, 246, 249-50, 251, 252, 253, 256. *See also* Oxford, 17th Earl of, circle
Oxford, 17th Earl of, circle 30, 31-47, 49, 119, 163, 171, 173, 174, 206-7, 221-2, 238-9
Oxford, 18th Earl of (Henry de Vere) 29
Oxford, Countess of (Anne Cecil) 28, 34, 173, 221, 244
Oxford, Countess of (Elizabeth Trentham) 29
Oxford Dictionary of National Biography x
Oxford, Earls of, family and estate 28
Oxford House 239, 244
Oxfordian views 29, 34, 48, 49, 85, 206-7
Oxfordshire 51, 52
Oxford, University of 14, 20, 23, 25, 43, 44, 53, 54, 56, 58-9, 62, 64, 67, 111, 112, 118, 122, 134, 141, 161, 193, 220, 225, 239
Oxford University Press 15, 251

Pacification of Ghent 60
Padre di Famiglia, Il 241
Padua, University of 56, 57-8, 59, 71, 110, 123, 176, 252
Paget, 1st Baron of Beaudesert (William Paget) 55, 128, 135
Paget, 2nd Baron (Henry Paget) 129
Paget, 3rd Baron (Thomas Paget) 128, 129, 130, 131-2, 142

Paget, Anne (née Preston) 129
Paget family 129, 131, 132
Paget, Charles 56, 83-4, 129, 130, 131, 132
Paget, Henry. *See* Paget, 2nd Baron
Paget, John (Sheriff of London) 128
Paget, Nazareth (née Southwell) 129
Paget, Thomas. *See* Paget, 3rd Baron
Paget, William. *See* Paget, 1st Baron.
Pain of Pleasure, The 42
Palladis Tamia 30, 195, 205
Pallas Athena 57, 301
Palissy, Bernard 121, 254
Pandora 116
Pantometria 109
"Panza, Sancho" 37
Papacy 13, 53, 54, 70, 71, 89, 219, 226
Parabosco, Girolamo 97
Paradise of Dainty Devices, The 67
"Paris" 120
Paris, France 22, 41, 55, 56, 58, 59, 60, 69, 70, 71, 73, 76, 77, 78, 80, 82, 83, 112, 123, 131, 193, 194, 196, 198, 211, 218, 220, 232, 233, 241 and *passim*
Parker, Matthew. *See* Canterbury, Archbishop of
Parliament (English) 12, 160, 184, 235
Parr, William. *See* Northampton, Marquess of
Parry, Blanche 74
Parry, William 131
"Pasquill". *See* Breton, Nicholas
Passionate Pilgrim, The 169, 170
Passionate Shepherd, The 161
Passionate Shepherd to His Love, The 73
Paston, Edward 25, 127
Paulet, Amias 60
Pavia, Italy 57
Payne, John 138
Peacham, Henry 123, 202
Pearlman, E 106
Peck, Francis 34, 36
"Pedringano" 243, 246-7
Peele, George 85, 87, 96, 113, 117, 118, 119, 195, 202, 205, 219, 233, 234

Pelham, William 25
Pembroke, 2nd Earl of (Henry Herbert) 21, 31, 47, 119
Pembroke, 3rd Earl of (William Herbert) 101
Pembroke, 4th Earl of (Philip Herbert) *See* Montgomery, 1st Earl of
Pembroke, Countess of (Mary Herbert, née Sidney) 21-7, 94, 115, 119, 120, 161, 187, 202, 209, 211, 254, 256
Pembroke circle and estates. *See* Sidney circle
Pembroke College, Oxford 122
Pennsylvania, University of 251
Penshurst Place, Kent 20
Percy, Henry. *See* Northumberland, 9th Earl of
Percy, Mary (housekeeper and music teacher to the Petre family) 136
Percy, Thomas. *See* Northumberland, 7th Earl of
Perimedes the Blacksmith 237
Perne, Andrew 32-3
Persons, Robert 114, 129
Perugia, Italy 57
Peterhouse, Cambridge 32, 33
Petrarch 66, 85, 90, 97, 145, 162, 194, 195, 204, 218, 252, 253
Petre, Anne (née Tyrell) 135
Petre, Dorothy 136
Petre family 19, 127, 132, 134, 136, 138, 139, 146
Petre, Gertrude (née Tyrell) 135
Petre, John. *See* Petre of Writtle, 1st Baron
Petre, John 139
Petre, Katherine 136
Petre, Mary (née Waldegrave) 137, 138, 139, 142
Petre of Writtle, 1st Baron (John Petre) 132, 134, 135-40, 182
Petre of Writtle, 2nd Baron (William Petre) 139
Petre, Robert 138
Petre, Thomas 139
Petre, Thomasine 137-8
Petre, William. *See* Petre of Writtle, 2nd Baron

Petre, William, Sir (Secretary of State) 134-6, 137-8
Petreius, John 126
"Petrus beautus" 139
Petty France, London 185
Petworth House, Sussex 113, 121, 154
Phalèse, Pierre 147
Pharsalia 73
Phelippes, Thomas 83, 84
Philadelphia, USA 207
Philip II of Spain 27, 55, 62, 63, 76, 128, 135, 220, 226, 228, 229, 231, 232, 240
"Philippo" 231
"Phillida and Coridon" 158, 162
Phillips, David Graham 207
Philoctetes 219
Philological Museum x
Philosophia epicurea 44
"Phoebus Apollo" 49, 61, 106, 108, 214, 221, 250
Phoenix and the Turtle, The 96
Phoenix Nest, The 213, 227
Phyllyda and Corin 206
Pléiade, La 22, 30
Physicorum Libri X 109
Pierce Penniless, his Supplication to the Devil 44, 45
Pietro, Mr 137, 138
Pilgrimage to Paradise, Joined with the Countess of Pembroke's Love, The 161-2
Pisa, Italy 71
"Piston" 223
Pius V, Pope 53
Placenta, Palace of, Greenwich 16, 74, 197, 244
Plague, The 35, 53, 58, 73, 113, 154, 183, 185, 186, 187
Plat, Hugh 193-4
Plato 18
Plattner, Thomas 16
Pliny the Elder 97
Plough, The, Temple Bar 80
Poems (Watson, ed. Arber). *See* Arber, Edward
Poetical Exercises at Vacant Hours 37
Poland 112, 116, 254

Poley, Anne 78, 79
Poley, Robert 74-5, 78-82, 83, 196
Polimanteia 189-92
Poliziano, (Agnolo Ambrogini) 97
"Polonius" 119
"Pompae" 233
"Pompey the Great" 234
Ponsonby, William 187, 188, 256
Pontano, Giovanni 97
Poole, John 152
Pope. *See* Gregory XIII *and* Pius V
Pope's bull in Dutch with the answer thereto ..., The 89
Popish Kingdom, or the Reign of Anti-Christ, The 66
"Portia" 41
Portsmouth, Hampshire 52, 154, 238
Portugal 209, 226-8, 229, 230, 231
Positions Concerning the Training Up of Children 175
Poultry, City of London 39
Prague, Bohemia 25, 96
Presbyterianism 88, 176
Preston, Anne. *See* Paget, Anne
Price, David C 19
Printemps d'Yver 211, 222
Printer to the City of London 39
Privy Council 34, 46, 56, 63, 72, 73, 74, 80, 88, 90, 110, 114, 129, 131, 135, 142, 153, 171, 180, 193, 196, 236, 241, 256
Proctor, John 41
Prognostication Everlasting, A 109
Progresses and Public Processions of Queen Elizabeth, The 155
Propertius, Sextus 97
"Proserpina" 243
Protestantism, protestants 14, 15, 18, 20, 26, 20, 31, 35, 36, 37, 55, 60, 65, 66, 73, 86, 88, 108, 126, 129, 141, 144, 172, 176, 220, 221
"Psalm 51" 36
"Psalm 79" 143
Psalms 14, 88, 146

Psalms (Mary Sidney) 94
Psalms, Sonnets & Songs of Sadness and Piety 146, 147
Psalms (Watson) 254
Ptolemists 111
Public Record Office 74
Puckering, John 237, 238
Purfoot, Thomas 38,
Puritans and Puritanism 13, 15, 21, 45, 52, 71, 124, 140, 148, 240
Puttenham, George 23, 127, 173
Pymmes Park, Midddlesex 244

Quartos (Shakespeare) 40, 67, 101, 189
Queen's College, Cambridge 192
Queen's Company (Queen's Men) 205-6
Queen's Coroner (Coroner of the Queen's Household). *See* Danby, William
Queen's Musick 17
Queen's Palace, Greenwich.
    See Placenta, Palace of
Queen's Printer 86, 87, 126
Queen's School, Canterbury.
    See King's School, Canterbury
"Quixote, Don" 37

Radclyffe, Robert. *See* Sussex, 5th Earl of
Radclyffe, Thomas. *See* Sussex, 3rd Earl of
Raleigh, Walter 23, 81, 112, 113, 114, 115, 116, 117, 119, 187, 202
Ramsbury, Wiltshire 21
Ramus, Peter 111, 112
Rare Triumphs of Love and Fortune, The 39, 234, 236, 250
Rathgeb, Jacob 16
"Reede, Richard" ("Dick") 247
Reformation 12, 13, 140
Regnans in Excelsis (Papal bull) 13, 53, 69
Renaissance ix, 13. 22, 86, 120, 253
Reading, Berkshire 53
Reason, John 140, 143
Reckoning, The 63

Recorder of London. *See* Fleetwood, William
Recusancy 25, 32, 42, 52, 65, 69, 125, 129, 131, 132, 133, 138, 140, 141, 143, 147, 150, 172, 194
Red Cross Street, St Giles 160
Revels, Office of the 95, 159, 163, 174, 212, 224, 229, 234
Revenge, The 158, 160
Revenger's Tragedy, The 206
"Rhadamanth" 235
Rheims, France 40, 61, 72, 76, 82, 176, 236
Rheims New Testament 76
Rhodes 212, 222, 224
"Rhodes, Lord of" 212, 224
Rich, Barnabe 31
Rich, 3rd Baron (Robert Rich) 138
Rich, Penelope. *See* Devonshire, Countess of
"Richard" (government spy) 73
Richard II, King of England 90
Richardson, Ferdinando 126
Richmond upon Thames, Surrey 16, 80, 135
Ridolfi Plot 38, 132
Roberts, Josephine A and
    Gaines, James F G 209
Robinson, Mr 60
Robinson, Robert 187, 188, 255, 256
Rochford, 2nd Viscount (George Boleyn) 134
Rockefeller, John D 167
Rolleston, Elizabeth (later Onley) 50
Roman Catholicism, Roman Catholics ix, 12, 13, 14, 18, 20, 21, 23, 25, 26-7, 32, 33, 36, 39, 40, 42, 43, 51-2, 53-4, 56, 58-9, 60, 63, 64, 65, 66, 67, 69, 70, 72, 73, 75-7, 78, 79, 80, 81, 82, 83, 84, 86, 94, 108, 123, 124, 125, 127, 129, 131, 132, 133-4, 135, 138, 140, 141, 142, 143, 144, 146, 147, 152, 154, 171, 172, 176, 177, 189, 195, 220, 221, 229, 231, 232, 242, 245 and *passim*
Romanesque literature 236
Rome 12, 40, 53, 57, 66, 72, 112, 141, 219, 232, 237, 242 and *passim*
Romeo and Juliet 189

Ronsard, Pierre de 22, 30, 96, 97
Ros, 15th Baroness (Elizabeth Manners) 130
Rose Theatre, Rose Alley, Bankside 210, 240
Rotterdam, Netherlands 44
Rouen, France 131
Rowland, Humphrey 152
Royal Bedchamber 64, 233
Royal Exchange, City of London 12
Roydon, Matthew 95-6, 113, 202, 205, 234
Ruff, Lillian M and Wilson, D Arnold 166
Rutland, 3rd Earl of (Edward Manners) 35-6, 130
Rutland, 4th Earl of (John Manners) 35, 130
Rutland, 5th Earl of (Roger Manners) 36
Rutland, Countess of
 (Elizabeth Manners, née Sidney) 36
Rutland Estates 36

Sackville House, Fleet Street 39
Sackville, Robert. *See* Dorset, 2nd Earl of
Sackville, Thomas. *See* Buckhurst, Baron
Sainliens, Claude de. *See* Hollyband, Claudius
St Andrews, Norwich 178
St Antholin's, Budge Row 145, 236
St Barbe, Edith 62
St Bartholemew's Day Massacre 20, 55, 56, 77, 111
St Bartholemew's, Smithfield 152, 181, 186, 250
St Botolph's without Aldgate 152, 185, 244, 246
St George's Chapel, Windsor 16, 182
St George's Fields, Windsor 182
St Giles without Cripplegate 139, 160
St Gregory's by St Paul's 37-38
St Helen's Church, Bishopsgate 221
St Helen's Parish, Bishopsgate 63, 65, 77, 110, 121, 146, 219, 221, 231
St John's College, Cambridge 44, 193
St John's College, Oxford 43
St Mary-at-Hill, Billingsgate 125
St Michael's Parish, Cornhill 147
St Mildred's Church, Poultry 39
St Nicholas' Church, Deptford 35, 75
St Olave Parish, Tower Street Ward 50
St Pancras Church, Cheap Ward 35,
St Paul's Cathedral 13, 16, 26, 32, 37, 38, 66, 71, 84, 86, 123, 147, 157, 189, 250
St Paul's Hill 32, 123
St Paul's School. *See* Children of St Paul's
Saintsbury, George 117-8, 119
Salisbury, 1st of *See* Cecil, Robert
Salisbury Court, Southwark 111
Salisbury, Wiltshire 19
Saltonstall, Richard (Sheriff of Middlesex) 245
Savoy, The Strand 28, 29, 46, 132
Saxe-Weimar, Duke of 16
Scadbury, Kent 74, 80, 188
Schick, J 226
Schiller, Friedrich 228
Schoenbaum, Samuel 216-7
School of Abuse.... 68
"School of Night, The" 43, 109, 112-7, 202
Schücking, Levin Ludwig 216-7
Scotland 27, 31, 32, 34, 37, 81, 176-7, 240 and *passim*
Scot, Reginald 34
Scotney, Kent 64-5
Scrope family 133
Seething Lane, St Olaves Parish 245
Seine, Paris 69, 70, 148, 233
Seneca, Lucius Annaeus 49, 97, 210, 216, 219-20, 234, 242, 243
Serafino dell'Aquila 97
"Serberine" 247
Seymour, Edward. *See* Hertford, 1st Earl of
Seymour, Lord Edward 162
Seymour, Edward (Lord Protector). *See* Somerset, 1st Duke of
Seymour, Katherine. *See* Hertford, Countess of
"Shakebag(ge)" 246, 249
Shakespeare Institute, University of Birmingham x
Shakespeare, William 31, 34, 35, 38, 39, 40, 41, 43, 44, 45, 46, 48, 49, 66, 67, 85, 86, 96, 101-7, 112, 114, 119, 167, 169-70, 176, 187, 196, 200, 213, 215, 218, 219, 244

Sheffield, Baroness (Lady Douglas Sheffield) 42
Sheffield, Lady Douglas. *See* Sheffield, Baroness
Shelley, Richard 25
Shelton, Ralph (Sherriff of Norfolk
 and Suffolk) 171, 174
Shepheardes Calender, The 97, 222
Sheppard, John 124
Sheriff of London. *See* Paget, John
Sheriff of Middlesex. *See* Saltonstall, Richard
Sheriff of Norfolk and Suffolk.
 See Shelton, Ralph
Shoby, Leicestershire 143
Shooters Hill, Greenwich 34
Shoreditch 151, 185, 239
Shrewsbury, 6th Earl of (George Talbot) 83
Shrewsbury, Shropshire 31
Shropshire 21, 23, 31, 50, 67, 68
"Shylock" 41
Sidney circle x, 21, 22, 27, 30, 31, 39, 41, 42,
 44, 46, 53, 58, 95, 112, 114, 116, 122, 123,
 127, 140, 170, 187, 188, 194
Sidney, Elizabeth. *See* Rutland, Countess of
Sidney, Frances (née Frances Walsingham)
 23, 46, 57, 80, 115, 118, 246, 256
Sidney, Mary (Mary Herbert).
 See Pembroke, Countess of
Sidney, Henry 19-20, 21, 24, 27,31, 32, 41, 115, 141
Sidney, Mary (née Dudley) 20, 115
Sidney, Philip 19-27, 28, 30, 31, 36, 38, 39, 46,
 53, 56, 57, 58, 65, 66, 68, 69, 80, 82, 85, 87,
 88, 89, 94, 95, 96, 98, 111, 112, 114, 115,
 116, 119, 120, 122, 123, 127, 141, 143, 169,
 187, 188, 202, 229, 232-3, 246, 256
Sidney, Robert 14, 23, 24, 82
Siena, Italy 57
Sigillis Hermetis, De 245
Sign of Lucrece, St Paul's Churchyard 38
Sign of the Bell, Gracechurch Street 206
Sign of the Bel Sauvage, Ludgate 206
Sign of the Bishop, Gray's Inn Road 150
Sign of the Boar's Head, Whitechapel 29
Sign of the Bull, Bishopsgate 206

Sign of the Dark Horse, Aldersgate 146
Sign of the Golden Ball,
 St Paul's Churchyard 38
Sign of the Gun, St Paul's Churchyard 66
Sign of the Holy Ghost,
 St Paul's Churchyard 86
Sign of the Plough, Temple Bar 80
Sign of the Star, Aldersgate 34
Sign of the White Hart, Bishopsgate 145-6
Sign of the (White) Swan, Bankside 46
Silvius 97
Skeres, Nicholas 74-5
Slack, Paul 186
Smithfield, London 90, 129, 142, 152, 181,
 186, 188, 142
Smith, Thomas 27, 28, 29, 57, 62, 128, 135
"Soliman" 211, 213-4, 223, 224
"Soliman and Perseda" (play within
 The Spanish Tragedy) 210, 211, 225
Soliman and Perseda, The Tragedy of 210, 211, 212,
 213, 222-4, 225, 226, 234, 235, 243, 247, 250
Somerleyton, Suffolk 170-1
Somerset, Edward, Lord Herbert.
 See Worcester, 4th Earl of
Somerset, 1st Duke of (Edward Seymour,
 Lord Protector) 128, 135
Song of Songs, The 107
Sonnets (Shakespeare) 40, 48, 86, 104-7, 114, 213
Soothern, John 116
Soper Lane, St Pancras 35
Sophocles 54, 57, 76, 85, 97, 122, 164, 205, 210,
 219-20, 222, 227, 233, 245, 253
Sophoclis Antigone. See *Antigone*
Sorbonne 110
Sotheby's 169, 189
Southampton, Hampshire 154
Southampton, 3rd Earl of
 (Henry Wriothesley) 46, 114, 128, 203
Southwark 46, 79, 111, 132, 140, 172, 182, 192
Southwell, Francis 94, 133, 232
Southwell, Robert 81, 86, 89, 143
Southwell, Nazareth. *See* Paget, Nazareth

Spa, The Netherlands 176
Spain 12, 13, 25, 27, 29, 56, 60, 61, 62, 64, 89, 113, 158, 160, 176, 211, 213, 216, 219, 220, 221, 222, 223, 225, 226-7, 228, 229, 230, 231, 232, 235, 239, 240, 243, 244 and *passim*
Spanish Armada 113, 158, 160, 172, 216, 243
Spanish Tragedy, The 67, 97, 206-51
Speght, Thomas 187
Spenser, Edmund 21, 47, 89, 97, 114, 118, 119, 187, 188, 194, 202, 210, 222, 238, 239
Spitalfields, London 172
Sprignall (?Springall), Robert 182
Stafford, Edward 42
Staffordshire 129, 130
Staines, Middlesex 131
Stalin: Red Lord of Russia 207
Standard Oil Company 167
Stanley, Ferdinando, Lord Strange. *See* Derby, 5th Earl of
Stanley, Henry. *See* Derby, 4th Earl of
Stanley, William. *See* Derby, 6th Earl of
Stanney, Blanche. *See* Forman, Blanche
Stanney, Fr Thomas 53
Stanyhurst, Richard 47, 194
Staple Inn 64
Star, The, Aldersgate 34
Star Chamber 38, 88, 179, 183, 239
Stationers' Company 33, 38, 39, 44, 86-7, 88, 89, 146, 188, 189, 204, 210, 216, 240, 241, 244, 250
Stationers' Hall. *See* Stationers' Company
Stationers' Register. *See* Stationers' Company
Stellatus, Marcellus Palingenius 66
Stempe, Thomas 52-3, 54
Stondon Massey, Essex 127, 176
Story of—, The 229
Story of Hieronimo, The 229, 231, 243
Stow, John 34, 35, 37, 43, 151, 173, 186
Strand, The, Westminster 28, 29, 46, 132
Strange News of the intercepting certain letters ... 45, 188
Strasbourg 58

Stratford-upon-Avon, Warwickshire 169, 170
Strode, Somerset 137
Strozza, Hercules 97
Strype, John 27, 86
Stubbs (Stubbe), John 21, 229
Suffolk 44, 62, 130, 170-1, 172, 174
Suffolk, 1st Earl of (Admiral Thomas Howard) 158, 160
Suffolk, Duchess of (Katherine Brandon) 36
Summer, Will 4
Summer's Last Will and Testament 47
Sundry Christian Passions 37
Superius. See First Set of Italian Madrigals Englished, The
Surrey, Countess of (Frances de Vere) 31
Surrey, Earl of (Henry Howard) 31, 46
Survey of London, A 35, 173
Sussex 38, 39, 64, 113, 121, 132, 154
Sussex, 3rd Earl of (Thomas Radclyffe) 39, 247
Sussex, 5th Earl of (Robert Radclyffe) 238
Sussex, Countess of (Bridget Morrison) 238
Sutton, Dana F x, 53, 62, 85, 93, 98, 100, 192, 204
Swan, The (*aka* The White Swan), Bankside 46
Swift, Anne. *See* Watson, Anne
Swift, Elizabeth 146
Swift, Hugh 150, 180, 181, 185, 186, 245, 248
Swift, Richard 145-6, 178-9
Swift, Thomas 177-84, 185, 186, 192
Sylvester, Josuah 187, 203
Syon House, Middlesex 112, 113

Tabitha the Temptress 46
Talbot, George. *See* Shrewsbury, 6th Earl of
Talbot, John 136
Tallis, Thomas 16, 124-7, 130, 144, 146
"Tamburlaine" 73, 249
Tamburlaine the Great 73, 153, 217, 236-7
Taming of the Shrew, The 57, 176
Tasso, Torquato 120, 145, 209, 241, 243, 254
Tears of Fancy, The 104, 188, 189, 192, 204, 218, 249, 250, 252, 256

Teares of the Muses 187
Temple Bar, The Temple 80
Temple, The, London 137.
   See also Middle Temple
Temple University, Philadelphia, USA 207
Tergoes, Siege of 32
Terrors of the Night, The 46, 188
"Te spectant Reginalde Pole" 123
Tessier, Charles 25
Texas Tech University 49
Texas, University of 189
Thames, River 120, 145
Thames Street, City of London 248
Thavies Inn 95
Theatre, The, Shoreditch 151, 189, 206 221
Theocritus 97, 195
Thomas Kyd: Facts and Problems 251
Thomas Watson: Poems. See Arber, Edward
Thorndon, Essex 138, 139
Thornton, Thomas 122-3
Thorny Abbey or the London Maid 206
Throckmorton, Francis 111
Throckmorton Plot 131, 133, 140, 211
Tibillus, Albius 97
"Tisiphone" 234, 235, 249
Titchfield, Hampshire 154
Titus Andronicus 67, 189, 200-1
"Titus mine" 98, 200-1
"Tityrus" (Thomas Walsingham/Virgil) 69, 187, 221, 256
T.K. 237
Toddington, Bedfordshire 138
Toledo, Spain 225
Tolleshunt Darcy, Essex
   (estate of Lord Darcy) 138
Topcliffe, Richard 73
Torporly, Nathaniel 114
Tottel's Miscellany 31, 33, 93
Tottel, Richard 33
Tower of London 28, 36, 63, 64, 76, 81, 95, 128, 132, 152, 171, 233, 245
Trachiniae 219

"Translations into Latin from Petrarch's
   Canzoniere" 85, 225
Trentham, Elizabeth. *See* Oxford, Countess of
Trinity College, Cambridge 14, 172
Trinity College, Oxford 67
Troilus and Cressida 45
"Troilus and Cressida" 234
Troy 165-6
True Report of the Death and Martyrdom of M Campion Jesuit and Priest ... , A 39, 42, 142
Turin, Italy 57
Turkey 56
Tusser, Thomas 130
T.W. 85, 188, 204, 206, 244, 253, 256
Twelfth Night 34
Two Gentlemen of Verona 200
Two godly and learned sermons ... 42
Twyne, Thomas 39
Tyburn 13, 45, 83, 142
Tyrell, Anne. *See* Petre, Anne
Tyrell, Gertrude. *See* Petre, Gertrude
Tyrell, John 135

Ulysses upon Ajax 70, 192-3, 218, 231, 235
Unconscious in History, The 207
Unfortunate Traveller, or the Life of Jack Wilton, The 46
United Provinces of the Netherlands
   (Dutch Republic). *See* Netherlands, The
"University Wits" 117-9, 189, 202
Urbino, Italy 18, 161
Urbino, Duchess of (Elizabetta Gonzaga) 161
Utrecht 241

Vallenger, Stephen 142
Valois, Francis. *See* Francis, Duke of Anjou
   and Alençon
Vautrollier, Thomas 38, 126, 146
Vaux, Anne 143
Vaux, Eleanor. *See* Brooksby, Eleanor
Vaux family 132
Vaux, Henry 143

Vavasour, Anne 28, 95, 169, 233
Vavasour family 28
Velikovsky, Emmanuel 207
Venice, Italy 24, 25, 46, 57, 58, 65, 71, 116, 240
"Venus" 234
Vere, Lady Frances de 244
Vere, Elizabeth de. *See* Derby, Countess of
Vere, Frances de. *See* Surrey, Countess of
Vere, Dorothy de 173
Vere, Edward de. *See* Oxford, 17th Earl of
Vere, George de 173
Vere, Henry de. *See* Oxford, 18th Earl of
Vere, John de. *See* Oxford, 12th Earl of
Vere, John de. *See* Oxford, 14th Earl of
Vere, John de. *See* Oxford, 15th Earl of
Vere, John de. *See* Oxford, 16th Earl of
Vere, Richard de. *See* Oxford, 11th Earl of
Vere, Susan de. *See* Montgomery, Countess of
Vergil, Polydore 57
"Verginella, La" 147
Verro, Sebastian 109-10
Verses of Praise and Joy, The 237
Viceroy of Portugal 217, 227
Virgil (Publius Virgilius Maro) 33-4, 49, 69, 195, 243
Virginian Expedition 113
Virgin Mary 18, 154
"Vitus". *See* White, Richard

Waldegrave, Edward 137
Waldegrave Mary. *See* Petre, Mary
Waldegrave, Robert 88-9, 187
Wales 20, 31, 35
Waller 62
Walpole, Henry 142
Walsingham circle x, 95, 153, 177, 206
Walsingham, Frances. *See* Sidney, Frances
Walsingham, Francis 13, 23, 27, 55-7, 58, 59-60, 62, 65, 69, 69, 70, 71, 76, 77, 79-80, 81, 82, 83, 84, 96, 111, 115, 116, 120, 123, 131, 132, 140, 143, 153, 187, 188, 197, 201, 205, 231, 233, 240, 245, 255, 256

"Walsingham" ("Have with yow to Walsingame") 140
Walsingham, Norfolk 140
Walsingham, Thomas 56, 69-70, 71-4, 75, 80, 81, 123, 148, 153, 187, 188, 194, 196, 197, 201, 230-1, 233, 241, 245, 255-6
Waltham, Essex 125
Waltham, Lincolnshire 83
Wanstead, Essex 20, 22, 42
Ward, B M 200
Ward, B R 239
Warner, Walter 113, 187, 202
Warwick, 1st Duke of, 1st Duke of Northumberland (John Dudley) 171
Warwick, 1st Earl of. *See* Rich, 3rd Baron
Warwick, 3rd Earl of (Ambrose Dudley) 20,
Warwickshire 20, 169, 170, 171
Washington, USA 167, 189
Waters, William 41
Watson, Anne (née Lee) 50, 51, 66-7, 183, 192
Watson, Anne (née Swift) 145, 146, 151, 177, 183, 185, 186, 211, 236, 245
Watson, Captain Thomas 235
Watson, Elizabeth 67
Watson, Elizabeth, the elder.
    See Mawdeley, Elizabeth
Watson, Elizabeth ("wife of John Watson") 221
Watson, John 221
"Watson, John" 221
Watson, Margaret 78
Watson, Maudlin 67, 119, 189, 210
"Watson's daughter" 77

WATSON, THOMAS
ARUNDEL, 13th Earl of, and advice to 56, 75 76, 119, 244-5, 253, 254;
ASSOCIATES, known companions and possible or presumed acquaintances. *See also* Elizabethan schools of literature and science 202-3; and *passim*; Achelley, Thomas 96, 118, 205, 208, 213; Alleyn, John 150, 239; Baines, Richard 82;

Beale, William 62, 63, 225; Bentley, John 118, 205, 208; Breton, Nicholas 159, 160-2; Buc (Bucke), George 95, 159-63, 174, 205, 234; Byrd family *qv*; Camden, William ix, 122-3; Case, John 148, 236, 255; Cornwallis family *qv*; Dekker, Thomas 110, 118, 121, 202, 205, 208; "Downhalus, C" 96, 205; Faunt, Nicholas 71; Fraunce, Abraham 23, 47, 120, 148, 187, 194, 195, 202, 254; Garnet, Henry 52-3, 54, 143; Gascoigne, George 87, 161, 202, 233; Googe, Barnabe 64, 65-6; Greene, Robert 49, 117-9, 173, 202, 245, 255; Harvey, Gabriel 47, 187, 192, 194-5, 218, 249; Johnson, Christopher 52-53, 54, 59; Kyd, Thomas ix, 117, 118, 119, 202, 205, 206, 210, 214, 216, 219, 230, 231, 250; Lodge, Thomas and family ix, 67-8, 69, 117, 119, 194, 202; Lyly, John 87, 95, 97, 98, 100, 117, 119, 173, 189, 202, 205, 212, 224, 234, 239; Marlowe, Christopher *qv*; "Misodiaboles" 193-4; Northumberland, 9th Earl of (Henry Percy) 113, 120, 121, 202, 236, 254, 255; Oxford, 17th Earl of *qv*; Peele, George 85, 87, 96, 113, 117, 118, 119, 195, 202, 205, 219, 233, 234; Poley, Robert 78, 79, 82; Raleigh, Walter 113, 187, 202; Ronsard, Pierre de 96, 97; Roydon, Matthew 95, 96, 113, 206, 234; Sidney circle *qv*; Swift family *qv*; Walsingham, Francis *qv*; Walsingham, Thomas *qv*; White, Edward 67-8, 189, 210; Wolfe, John 85, 86, 87, 90, 98-100, 103, 110, 163-4, 187, 233, 253, 254, 256

BIRTH and family background, 50-2, 85
BRADLEY affair 150-3, 180, 245, 247-8
BRUNO Giordano 110, 112, 245
BURNELL affair 62-4, 66, 68, 110, 180, 186
BYRD, William ix, 123, 127, 140, 144, 146, 147-9, 165-7, 246, 255
CAWOOD, Gabriel, Watson's principal publisher 86-7, 90, 100, 102, 103, 234, 253, 277
CLASSICS and mythology 97; Ovid, 86, 97; Seneca, 97, 210, 216, 219, 220; Sophocles 86, 97, 206, 210, 219, 220, 233, 253; Theocritus 97, 195; Virgil 69, 97, 195

CONTEMPORARY opinions of Watson Barnfield 194, 195; Bradshaw ("wise man") 110, 121, 219; Dekker 110, 118, 121, 205; Harvey 47, 187, 194-5; Heywood 49-9, 250; "Learned" ix, 62, 63, 110, 118, 121, 195; Meres 30, 195, 205, 210, 219; "Misodiaboles" 70, 192-3, 218, 235; Nashe 164, 189-92, 195, 245, 249; Peele 86, 96, 113, 195, 219

CORNWALLIS household 76; "Anne Cornwallis her Booke" 170 (*See also* Cornwallis-Lyson Manuscript in general index); Tutor to John Cornwallis 76, 149, 170, 176, 177, 179, 246; William Cornwallis 149, 180, 185, 193, 205, 218, 249-50.

"CORYDON" appellation 69, 187, 201, 256
COSMOLOGY and science 108-10, 121
DEATH 77, 182, 185-7, 210, 250
DEDICATIONS 54, 56-7, 76, 77, 86, 94, 95, 98, 112, 113, 119, 120, 187-8, 199, 200, 220, 221, 233, 236, 244-5, 245-6, 253-6
DEGREE/LAW 53-4, 56, 57, 59, 60, 220
DRAMATIST ix, 85, 120, 180, 193, 205-251 159, 161-6, 174, 206, 256
ELVETHAM entertainment 154, 156-7, 159-66
ENGLISH COLLEGE, Douai 58-61, 75-6, 220-1, 225, 236
FAMILY relationships 51-6; 119; 67-9; 145-248
FINANCES 31, 53, 54-5, 180, 206, 246
FISHER'S FOLLY 31, 76, 119, 149, 170, 173, 176, 177, 249
FRANCE 55-6, 57, 82, 96, 211, 220, 222, 233
GAOLED in Newgate Prison 74, 150, 152, 153, 180, 245, 150, 151, 152, 180
GENTLEMAN x, 50, 78-9, 90, 152, 195, 231, 233, 237, 245, 246
GOVERNMENT service 55-6, 63, 69, 75-6, 77, 78-9
HEYWOOD, Thomas 48-9, 202, 216, 250

ITALY 57-8, 59, 86, 219, 220
LONDON x, 49-50, 54, 63, 68, 70, 71, 77, 78, 85, 87, 145-6, 151-3, 154, 161, 187, 219, 222 and *passim*;
LOST works ix, 85, 117, 120, 205, 206, 236, 252, 254
MARLOWE, Christopher ix, 71, 74, 75, 76, 77, 81, 82, 95, 96, 107, 110, 113, 117, 118, 119, 120, 150, 151-3, 186, 187-8, 189, 202, 219, 223, 230-1, 235, 236, 245, 247, 256
MARRIAGE 145-6, 177
MEMORY 100, 110, 112, 119, 244-5, 254
MUSIC ix, x, 23, 49, 52-3, 56, 69, 71, 106-7, 122, 148-9, 165-6, 173, 180, 236, 246, 255. Singer 69, 70
NASHE, Thomas ix, 31, 47, 119, 164, 173, 189-92, 195, 245, 249
OCLAND, Christopher 119, 244, 253
OXFORD, 17th Earl of x, 31, 47, 48-9, 58, 62, 65, 76, 85-6, 87, 94, 95, 96, 98, 100-1, 116, 119, 127-8, 161, 162-3, 170, 173, 176-7, 179, 188, 189, 199-201, 202, 221, 233-4, 236, 246, 249-50, 252, 253, 256. *See also* Oxford circle
OXFORD Circle, 17th Earl of 31, 85-86, 119, 175-7, 199-201, 202. *See also* Oxford, 17th Earl of
OXFORD, University of 53-4, 56, 58-9, 62, 64, 117-8, 122, 193, 220, 225
PADUA 56-9, 110, 123, 176, 252
PARIS 55, 56, 58, 59-60, 69, 70, 71, 76, 77, 193-4, 218, 220, 233, 241
PERCY, Henry 113, 120-1, 236, 254, 255
PETWORTH House, Sussex 113, 121
PLAGUE 53, 58, 185-7
PLAT, Hugh 193-4
POLEY, Robert 78-9, 81;
POLIMANTEIA 190-1, 192;
PRINTERS and publishers ix, 66-8, 86-90, 98, 100, 163, 164, 187, 188, 189, 192, 211, 225, 237 145, 162, 194, 195, 218, 252, 253. *See also* Cawood, Gabriel
PRIVY COUNCIL 63, 110, 153, 180, 256
QUEEN'S COMPANY 206
RALEIGH, Walter 113, 187
RENAISSANCE influence ix, 86, 97, 120, 253;

Mantuanus 97, 195; Petrarch 85, 90, 97, 145, 162, 194, 195, 218
RESIDENCES: Norton Folgate 146, 149, 151, 185; St Helen's Parish 63, 65, 77, 78, 110, 121, 146, 221, 231; Westminster 62, 122, 225-6, 233. *See also* Fisher's Folly
ROMAN CATHOLICISM ix, 51-2, 53, 54, 56, 69, 75-7, 78, 146, 176, 177, 195, 220, 245
RONSARD, Pierre de 96, 97
"SCHOOL OF NIGHT" 113, 119
SHAKESPEARE 48, 85, 86, 101-7, 170, 176, 200, 213-5, 219
SIDNEY circle x, 23, 56, 58, 85, 94, 95, 98, 112, 116, 119, 120, 122, 123, 170, 187-8, 194, 245-6, 254, 256
SOLIMAN AND PERSEDA 210, 213, 222, 224, 250
SPANISH TRAGEDY, The 205, 206-50
SPEGHT, Thomas 187
STEMPE, Thomas 52-3
SWIFT, Hugh 150, 180, 181, 185, 186, 245
SWIFT, Thomas 177, 179-80, 182, 185
SYON House 113
TRAVELS 54-61, 206. *See also* named countries and towns
ULYSSES upon Ajax 70, 192-3, 218, 235
"UNIVERSITY WITS" 117-9, 202
VERRO, Sebastian 110
WALSINGHAM, Frances 56-7, 246, 255
WALSINGHAM, Francis x, 55-6, 58, 59, 60, 69, 70, 71, 76, 77, 79, 95, 120, 123, 153, 177, 187-8, 201, 205-6, 231, 245-6
WALSINGHAM, Thomas 55, 56, 69, 70, 71, 80, 81, 95, 123, 148, 153, 177, 187-8, 194, 201, 230-1, 233, 241, 245-6, 255-6
WHETSTONE, George 85, 204, 244, 253
WHITE, Richard, 58
WINCHESTER COLLEGE 52-4, 56, 59, 69
WOLFE, John 85, 86, 87, 90, 98-100, 103, 110, 163-4, 187, 233, 253, 254, 256
WORKS. *See* general index and 252-6

Index

Watson, Thomas, "yeoman" 77, 78-9
Watson, William, Sr 50
Watson, William, Jr 51, 55
Webster, John, 202
Wedel, Lupold de 16
Welsh Marches 20
Wentworth, 2nd Baron (Thomas Wentworth) 171
Wentworth, Thomas. *See* Wentworth, 2nd Baron
West Drayton, Middlesex 128, 129, 131
West Ham, Essex 173
West Harling, Suffolk 44
West, Thomas. *See* De La Warr, 2nd Baron
Westcote, Sebastian 123-4
Westminster 49, 62, 183, 225, 233, 245
    and passim
Westminster Abbey 16, 122, 244
Westminster Hall 150, 245
Westminster School 122
Westmorland, 6th Earl of (Charles Neville) 53
Weston, William 79, 141, 143
Whall, Thomas 145
"When as thine eye hath chose the dame" 169
Whetstone, George 34, 85, 204, 244, 253
White, Edward 66-7, 68, 189, 210, 222, 225, 226, 234, 250
Whitehall Palace 16, 17, 28, 111, 119, 171
White Hart, Bishopsgate 145-6
White, Richard ("Vitus") 59
Whitgift, John. *See* Canterbury, Archbishop of
"Why do I use my paper, ink and pen?" 142
William I, Prince of Orange ("the Silent") 20, 31, 32, 60, 221, 223, 231, 235
William of Wykeham 52
Willobie his Avisa 96
Wilson, Thomas 221
Wilton House, Wiltshire 19, 21, 24, 115, 120, 202
Wiltshire 19, 21, 24, 115, 120, 162
Wiltshire, 1st Earl of (Thomas Boleyn) 134
Winchester, Bishop of (Robert Horne) 53
Winchester College 52-3, 54, 56, 59, 69
Windet, John 39, 42, 89
Windsor 16, 182

Windsor, Dean of (William Day) 129, 130
Windsor, Edward (son of 3rd Baron) 81
Windsor, Edward. *See* Windsor, 3rd Baron
Windsor, 3rd Baron (Edward Windsor) 25
Winkburn, Nottinghamshire 62
Winter's Tale, The 45
Wither, George 203
Withipole, Edmond 183
Wit's Trenchmour 161
Wolfe, John 39, 42, 85, 86, 87-90, 98-100, 103, 110, 163-4, 187, 233, 253, 254, 256
Wolsey, Cardinal. *See* York, Archbishop of
"Wood" (Catholic tailor) 78
Wood, Anthony (à) 37, 53, 218, 220
Woodbridge, Suffolk 62
Woodcocke, Thomas 33
Woodhuysen, H R 21, 22, 26
Woodleff, Drew 74
Wood, Robert 248
Wood Street Counter 40
Worcester, 4th Earl of (Edward Somerset, until 1588, Lord Herbert) 130, 132
Worcestershire 193
Works of Chaucer 118, 187
Worship Street, London EC2A 151
Worthiness of Wales, The 31
Wotton, Henry 211, 222
Wriothesley, Henry.
    See Southampton, 3rd Earl of
Wybunbury, Cheshire 55
Wyld, Stephen 152, 245

Xenephon 97

Yaxley, Francis 194
Yeomans, Joan 79
Yeomans, William 79
"Ye Sacred Muses" 127
Yonge, Nicholas 147, 148
York, Archbishop of (Cardinal Wolsey) 17
York, Archbishop of (Thomas Young) 83
Yorke, Edward 162

Young, Justice Richard 25
Young, Thomas. *See* York, Archbishop of
Yver, Jacques 211, 222

Zelauto, the Fountain of 41
Zodiacus vitae 66
Zodiake of Life 66
Zutphen, Netherlands, Battle of 25, 80

CPSIA information can be obtained
at www.ICGtesting.com
Printed in the USA
BVHW042354270422
635486BV00005B/525